# FRENCH FILM: TEXTS AND CONTEXTS

This innovative textbook provides detailed analyses of twenty-two key films with the canon of French cinema, from the 1930s to the 1990s. Films discussed include masterpieces such as Renoir's *Le Crime de Monsieur Lange* and *La Bête humaine*, and Carné's *Les Enfants du paradis;* popular classics such as *Les Vacances de Monsieur Hulot* and *Coup de foudre;* landmarks of the New Wave such as *Les 400 coups* and *A bout de souffle*, and important contemporary films such as *Cyrano de Bergerac, Nikita* and *La Haine.*

*French Film: Texts and Contexts* brings together leading scholars to discuss these films in relation to such issues as the history of French cinema, the social and cultural contexts of the films' production and reception, the relationship with Hollywood cinema, gender politics, authorship, and genre.

This revised and updated second edition includes:

- Coverage of the major periods, film-makers and genres in French sound cinema;

- New chapters on key films of the 1990s;

- A guide to further reading and a filmography of the director accompanying each analysis;

- A fully revised Introduction and Bibliography on French cinema.

Contributors: Dudley Andrew, Jacques Aumont, Richard Dyer, Christopher Faulkner, Jill Forbes, Anne Gillain, Susan Hayward, Jean-Pierre Jeancolas, H. R. Kedward, Norman King, Michèle Lagny, Colin McArthur, Michel Marie, Julianne Pidduck, Keith Reader, Bérénice Reynaud, Pierre Sorlin, Carrie Tarr, Maureen Turim, Ginette Vincendeau.

**Susan Hayward** is Professor of French Studies at the University of Exeter. She is the author of *French National Cinema* (1993) and *Key Concepts in Cinema Studies* (1996). **Ginette Vincendeau** is Professor of Film Studies at the University of Warwick. She is the author of *Jean Gabin: anatomie d'un mythe* (1993), *The Companion to French Cinema* (1996) and *Pépé le Moko* (1998).

# FRENCH FILM: TEXTS AND CONTEXTS

## Second edition

*Edited by Susan Hayward and Ginette Vincendeau*

London and New York

First published 2000
by Routledge
11 New Fetter Lane, London EC4P 4EE

Simultaneously published in the USA and Canada
by Routledge
29 West 35th Street, New York, NY 10001

Reprinted 2002

*Routledge is an imprint of the Taylor & Francis Group*

© 2000 Susan Hayward and Ginette Vincendeau for selection and
editorial matter. Individual chapters © 2000 contributors

Typeset in Garamond by RefineCatch Limited, Bungay, Suffolk
Printed and bound in Great Britain by
Biddles Ltd, Guildford and King's Lynn

*British Library Cataloguing in Publication Data*
A catalogue record for this book is available from the British Library

*Library of Congress Cataloging in Publication Data*
A catalogue record for this book has been requested

ISBN 0–415–16117–7 (hbk)
ISBN 0–415–16118–5 (pbk)

# CONTENTS

*List of plates*      ix
*Notes on contributors*      xi
*Preface*      xv
*Acknowledgements*      xvii

Introduction      1
SUSAN HAYWARD AND GINETTE VINCENDEAU

1 In the name of the father: Marcel Pagnol's 'trilogy' *Marius*
(1931), *Fanny* (1932), *César* (1936)      9
GINETTE VINCENDEAU

2 Paris, Arizona; or the redemption of difference: Jean
Renoir's *Le Crime de Monsieur Lange* (1935)      27
CHRISTOPHER FAULKNER

3 The fleeing gaze: Jean Renoir's *La Bête humaine* (1938)      42
MICHELE LAGNY

4 Poetic realism as psychoanalytical and ideological operation:
Marcel Carné's *Le Jour se lève* (1939)      63
MAUREEN TURIM

5 Beneath the despair, the show goes on: Marcel Carné's *Les
Enfants du paradis* (1943–5)      78
JEAN-PIERRE JEANCOLAS

CONTENTS

6 The sacrament of writing: Robert Bresson's *Le Journal d'un curé de campagne* (1951)    89
KEITH A. READER

7 A breath of sea air: Jacques Tati's *Les Vacances de Monsieur Hulot* (1952)    100
PIERRE SORLIN

8 *Casque d'or, casquettes*, a cask of ageing wine: Jacques Becker's *Casque d'or* (1952)    112
DUDLEY ANDREW

9 No place for homosexuality: Marcel Carné's *L'Air de Paris* (1954)    127
RICHARD DYER

10 The script of delinquency: François Truffaut's *Les 400 coups* (1959)    142
ANNE GILLAIN

11 'It really makes you sick!': Jean-Luc Godard's *A bout de souffle* (1959)    158
MICHEL MARIE

12 The fall of the gods: Jean-Luc Godard's *Le Mépris* (1963)    174
JACQUES AUMONT

13 Mise-en-scène degree zero: Jean-Pierre Melville's *Le Samouraï* (1967)    189
COLIN McARTHUR

14 Eye for irony: Eric Rohmer's *Ma nuit chez Maud* (1969)    202
NORMAN KING

15 Sex, politics and popular culture: Bertrand Blier's *Les Valseuses* (1973)    213
JILL FORBES

16 The anti-carnival of collaboration: Louis Malle's *Lacombe Lucien* (1974)    227
H. R. KEDWARD

# CONTENTS

17 Maternal legacies: Diane Kurys' *Coup de foudre* (1983)                240
   CARRIE TARR

18 Representing the sexual impasse: Eric Rohmer's *Les Nuits de
   la pleine lune* (1984)                                                253
   BERENICE REYNAUD

19 Beyond the gaze and into femme-filmécriture: Agnès Varda's
   *Sans toit ni loi* (1985)                                            269
   SUSAN HAYWARD

20 Versions, verse and verve: Jean-Paul Rappeneau's *Cyrano de
   Bergerac* (1990)                                                     281
   JULIANNE PIDDUCK

21 Recycled woman and the postmodern aesthetic: Luc Besson's
   *Nikita* (1990)                                                      297
   SUSAN HAYWARD

22 Designs on the *banlieue*: Mathieu Kassovitz's *La Haine* (1995)      310
   GINETTE VINCENDEAU

   *Selected bibliography on French cinema*                             328
   *Index*                                                              337

# LIST OF PLATES

Plates are courtesy of The National Film Archive, London, BFI Stills, Posters and Designs and BIFI, Paris.

| | |
|---|---:|
| *Marius* | 16 |
| *Fanny* | 17 |
| *César* | 19 |
| *Le Crime de Monsieur Lange* | 33, 35 |
| *La Bête humaine* | 48 |
| *Le Jour se lève* | 70, 71 |
| *Les Enfants du paradis* | 83, 85 |
| *Le Journal d'un curé de campagne* | 93 |
| *Les Vacances de Monsieur Hulot* | 105 |
| *Casque d'or* | 119 |
| *L'Air de Paris* | 135 |
| *Les 400 coups* | 150, 151 |
| *A bout de souffle* | 165 |
| *Le Mépris* | 181, 183 |
| *Le Samouraï* | 195 |
| *Ma nuit chez Maud* | 208, 209 |
| *Les Valseuses* | 221 |
| *Lacombe Lucien* | 233 |
| *Coup de foudre* | 247 |
| *Les Nuits de la pleine lune* | 261 |
| *Sans toit ni loi* | 275 |
| *Cyrano de Bergerac* | 287, 289 |
| *Nikita* | 302, 303 |
| *La Haine* | 317, 319 |

# NOTES ON CONTRIBUTORS

**Dudley Andrew** directs the Institute for Cinema and Culture at the University of Iowa where he is the Angelo Bertocci Professor of Critical Studies. He has written widely on film theory and film criticism, and is the author of *The Major Film Theories* (1984), *Film in the Aura of Art* (1984) and *André Bazin* (1978). His book on Poetic Realism, *Mists of Regret, Culture and Sensibility in Classic French Film*, was published in 1995.

**Jaques Aumont** worked as a critic for *Cahiers du cinéma* for several years. He now a teaches film aesthetics in the Film Department of the University of Paris III at Censier. He edited the French version of the works of Sergei M. Eisenstein and is the author of a book on the Soviet director (*Montage Eisenstein*). Among his publications are *L'Oeil interminable* (1989), a book on the relationship between painting and cinema, and *L'Image* (1990).

**Richard Dyer** is Professor of Film Studies at the University of Warwick. He has published widely on issues of stardom, popular cinema and lesbian and gay cinema; in particular he is the author of *Stars* (1979), *Heavenly Bodies* (1987) and *Now You See It: Studies on Lesbian and Gay Film* (1989). His 1997 book *White* was nominated an Outstanding Academic Book of the Year by *Choice* magazine. He is currently working on a book on the composer Nino Rota.

**Christopher Faulkner** is Professor of Film Studies at Carleton University, Ottawa, Canada. In addition to various articles on French cinema and the work of Jean Renoir, he is the author of *Jean Renoir: A Guide to References and Resources* (1979) and *The Social Cinema of Jean Renoir* (1986). Current research includes the completion of a book on the construction of difference in French cinema of the 1930s, the editing of a collection of essays on Jean Renoir and, with Olivier Curchod, an annotated critical edition of the original shooting script of *La Règle du jeu*.

**Jill Forbes** is Professor of French at Queen Mary and Westfield, University of London and author of numerous books and articles on cinema including

*The Cinema in France: After the New Wave* (1992), *Les Enfants du paradis* (1997) and, with Sarah Street, the forthcoming *European Cinema.*

**Anne Gillain** teaches film and literature in the French Department at Wellesley College, Massachusetts. She is the author of a critical study of François Truffaut's films *François Truffaut: le secret perdu* (1991) and a collection of his interviews in France and North America, *Le Cinéma selon François Truffaut* (1988).

**Susan Hayward** is Professor of French Studies at the University of Exeter. She has published widely on French cinema and is the author of *French National Cinema* (1993), *Key Concepts in Cinema Studies* (1996), *Luc Besson* (1998). She is currently working on a book on Simone Signoret.

**Jean-Pierre Jeancolas** teaches film history and is a film critic for *Positif.* He is the author of numerous books on cinema including *15 ans d'années trente: Le Cinéma des Français 1929–1944* (1983), *Le Cinéma des Français: La V$^e$ République* (1979). He is the vice-president of the French Association for Research in Film History.

**H. R. Kedward** is Professor of History at the University of Sussex. He is currently researching a third volume of his trilogy on Resistance in southern France. The two published volumes are *Resistance in Vichy France* (1978) and *In Search of the Maquis* (1993), which was awarded the 'Prix Philippe Viannay-Défense de la France'. His work features oral histories of French men and women at the grassroots of Resistance as well as national and local archives.

**Norman King** is the author of a book on Abel Gance, *Abel Gance, a Politics of Spectacle* (1984), and has written extensively on early Romantic French literature.

**Michèle Lagny** is Professor of Film and History at the University of Paris III at Censier. She is the co-author with Marie-Claire Ropars and Pierre Sorlin, of *Générique des années 30* (1986). She is the author of *De l'histoire du cinéma: Méthode historique et histoire du cinéma* (1992) and *Senso* (1990). She is currently researching on cinema and popular culture.

**Colin McArthur** was Head of the Distribution Division of the British Film Institute. He is now a freelance writer, teacher and graphic artist. He has written extensively on Hollywood cinema, British television and Scottish culture and has exhibited at galleries in English and Scotland. Among his publications are *Underworld USA* (1972), *Scotch Reels: Scotland in Cinema and Television* (1982) and *The Big Heat* (1992).

**Michel Marie** is Professor of Film History and Aesthetics in the Film Department of the University of Paris III at Censier. His numerous publications include contributions to *Muriel, Histoire d'une recherche* (1975),

*Lectures du film* (1980), *L'Esthtéthique du film* (1983) and *L'Analyse des films* (1988). His book *La Nouvelle vague* was published in 1998.

**Julianne Pidduck** lectures in the Department of Theatre, Film and Television Studies at the University of Glasgow. Specializing in feminist approaches to popular culture, she has contributed to the journals *Screen* and *Cineaction!*, *Problématique*, and to the anthology *semiotext(e) canadas*. She is currently writing a book entitled *Still Longings: Femininity, Space and Movement in 1990s Costume Drama*. In addition to her academic work, she has written widely for the Canadian popular press as a feminist political columnist and freelance arts journalist.

**Keith Reader** is Professor of French Studies at the University of Newcastle-upon-Tyne. He is the author of numerous articles and reviews on French cinema. He is the author of *Cultures on Celluloid* (1981), *Intellectuals and the Left in France since 1968* (1987) and co-editor with Ginette Vincendeau of *La Vie est à nous: French Cinema of the Popular Front 1935–1938* (1986). He is currently working on a book on Robert Bresson.

**Bérénice Reynaud** is an independent film scholar, critic and curator whose work has been published in many journals, including *Afterimage, American Film, October, Screen, Cahiers du cinéma, CinémAction*, and *Libération*. A regular correspondent for international women's film and video festivals in Créteil (Paris) and Montreal, she has also curated film and video series for the Festival d'Automne in Paris, the Jerusalem Cinémathèque, The Collective for Living Cinema, and Artists Space in New York. Among her publications are *Front Line*, a series of essays on independent cinema and *20 ans de théories féministes* (1993), a co-edited collection of essays on feminist film theory. She teaches film theory at the California Institute of the Arts in Los Angeles.

**Pierre Sorlin** has written extensively on French and European cinema. He is the author of, among other books, *European Cinemas, European Societies 1939–1990* (1991) and *Italian National Cinema* (1996).

**Carrie Tarr** is Senior Research Fellow at Thames Valley University. Her articles on gender and ethnicity in French cinema have been published in journals such as *Screen, Iris, SubStance, Contemporary French Civilisation* and *Modern & Contemporary France*. She has recently published a book on Diane Kurys (*Diane Kurys*, 1999) and is currently working on a book on twenty years of women's film-making in France, co-authored with Brigitte Rollet.

**Maureen Turim** teaches Film Studies in the Department of English at the University of Florida, Gainsville. She is the author of *Abstraction in Avant-Garde Cinema* (1985) and *Flashbacks in Films: Memory and History* (1989). Her work on a number of topics has appeared in *Enclitic, Semiotica*, the AFI monograph *Cinema Histories, Cinema Practices,* and the anthology *New German Film Makers: From Oberhausen through the Seventies.*

**Ginette Vincendeau** is Professor of Film Studies at the University of Warwick. She has published widely on popular French cinema, French stars and women's cinema. She is co-author of *Anatomie d'un mythe: Jean Gabin* (1993) and co-editor of *20 ans de théories féministes du cinéma* (1993). She is the editor of *The Encyclopedia of European Cinema* and the author of *The Companion to French Cinema* (1996), *Pépé le Moko* (1998) and *Stars and Stardom in French Cinema* (2000).

# PREFACE

This volume is a revised edition of our book published under the same title, *French Film: Texts and Contexts*, in 1990. The present edition contains a large selection of chapters from the first book, and nine new chapters. We would have liked to reprint the original book together with a second volume containing analyses of a whole new set of films. Unfortunately this was not possible, and we agreed to Routledge's suggestion of deleting some chapters and replacing them with new ones in order to bring the book up to date. We are very sorry to lose the excellent pieces that had to be cut out (on *La Souriante Mme Beudet/La Coquille et le clergyman*, *Napoléon vu par Abel Gance*, L'Herbier's *L'Argent*, *Sous les toits de Paris*, *La Belle et la bête*, *Hiroshima mon amour*, *Sauve qui peut (la vie)* and *A nos amours*), although they remain, of course, available in the first edition. At the same time, we are delighted to include the new essays on *Le Crime de Monsieur Lange*, *L'Air de Paris*, *Le Samouraï*, *Lacombe Lucien*, *Les Valseuses*, *Coup de foudre*, *Cyrano de Bergerac*, *Nikita* and *La Haine*. After much soul-searching, our decisions as to what to include and what to exclude were chiefly pedagogic, given that the book is aimed at students and scholars of French cinema. We also wished to expand the book's coverage in three directions: the 1970s (absent from the first book), more emphasis on popular cinema and some coverage of the 1990s. In this difficult set of choices, we were guided by colleagues, readers and reviewers of the initial volume, whom we thank for their incisive and helpful comments.

SH
GV

# ACKNOWLEDGEMENTS

First of all, we are grateful to our contributors for their excellent work, their willingness to engage with the ethos of the book and their good grace in responding to our editorial comments. For their remarks, suggestions and/or practical help in the writing of individual chapters as well as in the editing of this volume, we wish to thank the following: José Arroyo, Simon Caulkin, Jim Cook, Ed Gallafent, Peter Graham, Laurent Marie, Valerie Orpen, Ulrike Sieglohr, Carrie Tarr. We are also grateful to Rebecca Barden at Routledge for her support and patience.

SH
GV

# INTRODUCTION

*Susan Hayward and Ginette Vincendeau*

In the introduction to the 1990 first edition of *French Film: Texts and Contexts*, we wrote that 'The study of French cinema in English-speaking countries presents something of a paradox. Whereas, undoubtedly, "the landscape of film studies in Britain and the United States has been transformed by post-1968 developments in French film theory" (Harvey 1978, 1), the study of the cinema of France has in the main seemed to be by-passed by these developments and remained the province of rather conventional approaches: the study of film as "reflection" of society on the one hand, and traditional auteurism on the other.' We then went on to argue that, as the study of French cinema was often situated in Modern Language departments, 'with the primary aim of giving students an increased access to French *culture* filtered through the work of individual artists on a literary analogy, as a result French film *as film* and French cinema as an institution tend[ed] to be neglected'. However, we also noted that, when studied within Film Studies, French cinema was frequently reduced to the work of a few exceptional 'masters' or subsumed under the category of European art cinema, with the effect of losing its national specificity.

Ten years later, this description is both true and untrue. Some of the peculiarities of French cinema studies have endured. Many Modern Language courses still teach film as a 'window' on French culture rather than in terms of the specificity of the medium. There are now, however, some welcome exceptions where French cinema is analysed within its socio-political and historical contexts as well as industrial and national ones. In Film Studies, there has been, throughout the 1990s, a rising interest in issues of national cinema, although the emphasis on the film text and the overriding distinction between Hollywood and 'national cinemas' still tends to erase national specificities. This edition, like the preceding one, thus attempts to bridge the two disciplines by turning some of the concerns and methods of Film Studies towards French cinema, while remaining attentive to the films' cultural inscription, a dual objective reflected in our title *French Film: Texts and Contexts*.

The period elapsed since the first edition has also seen a remarkable expansion in French cinema studies in the English-speaking world. This has been linked to factors such as the creation of professorships in French and European film within Modern Languages, the development of film courses, the growth of the subtitled video market and a boom in new publications on French cinema throughout the 1990s, in French and in English (including: Forbes 1992, Williams 1992, Crisp 1993, Hayward 1993, Abel 1994, Andrew 1995, Billard 1995, Frodon 1995, Austin 1996, Burch and Sellier 1996, Vincendeau 1996, Powrie 1997, Marie 1998, Tremois 1998. These and other publications have been added to the bibliography at the end of the book, while the bibliographies at the end of chapters have been updated where necessary.) These developments have increased the exposure of scholars and students to French film, and somewhat blurred the boundaries between disciplines. We hope that, in the same way that our first edition made a useful intervention in this area, the present one will contribute to this welcome phenomenon.

Several sets of choices and constraints determined the format of this book and the corpus of films examined within it. The decision to concentrate on single-film essays, in the first as in the present edition, was methodological and practical: to provide a forum for detailed analyses, and to offer a useful format for lecturers, scholars and students. More than any other discipline, film studies is materially bound to the availability of single texts. Thus our list of films reflects a desire to concentrate on works that are easily available on film hire or on video, or that are frequently found on repertory cinema programmes. This is the case, as we write these lines, with all the films examined in this volume. It is also one reason why we, sadly, deleted the section on silent cinema.

This book does not claim to offer a comprehensive portrait or history of French cinema. We would be the first to agree that many other titles – e.g. *L'Atalante, Pépé le Moko, Le Roman d'un tricheur, Touchez pas au grisbi, La Grande Vadrouille, Céline et Julie vont en bateau, Le Dernier métro, Passion, Les Visiteurs* and many others – are as central to French cinema as the films represented here. But the titles that *are* contained in this book are, as the chapters make clear, key French films. Together, they do not construct a homogeneous canon but they illustrate, we think, the wealth of French cinema. Our selection includes critically revered films (e.g. *Le Crime de Monsieur Lange, Le Jour se lève, A bout de souffle, Le Mépris, Ma nuit chez Maud, Sans toit ni loi*), popular classics (e.g. *Marius, Fanny* and *César, Les Enfants du paradis, Les Vacances de Monsieur Hulot, Cyrano de Bergerac*), films that might be called 'popular *auteur* films', such as *Les Valseuses, Coup de foudre* and *Lacombe Lucien*, and cult movies like *Le Samouraï, Nikita* and *La Haine*.

Film *texts* emerge from a complex network of *contexts*, or determinants, which include the aesthetic project of their author(s), industrial and financial constraints, historical circumstances and discourses about history, the presence (or absence) of stars, generic patterns and critical discourses. To investigate the various ways in which individual films textually inscribe and rework these contexts as other 'texts', the way they can be seen as 'tissue[s] of quotations drawn from the innumerable centers of culture' (Barthes 1977, 146), is the project of this book. Within this overall framework, different emphases and points of entry are possible, determined by the texts themselves, as well as by the methodologies adopted by each writer. The diversity of disciplines – history, literary studies, semiotics, psychoanalysis, film studies, cultural studies – which form the background of our contributors' work (a complexity itself representative of the way the study of film has developed in the last twenty years) produces a variety of approaches.

It is our hope therefore that this book will offer its readers both in-depth analyses of single films and an illustration of how different methodologies may be applied to them. For instance, the chapters by Maureen Turim, Jean-Pierre Jeancolas and Richard Dyer employ diverse methods to analyse three films directed by Marcel Carné: Turim draws on textual analysis, psycho-analysis and semiotics for her reading of *Le Jour se lève,* Jeancolas offers an empirical study of the circumstances in which *Les Enfants du paradis* was made, while Dyer meshes textual analysis with cultural studies for his reading of the 'place' of homosexuality in *L'Air de Paris*. On the other hand, for their essays on *Les Valseuses* and *Lacombe Lucien*, Jill Forbes and Rod Kedward both draw on the notion of the carnivalesque, pointing to the fact that *Les Valseuses* (an anarchic contemporary comedy) and *Lacombe Lucien* (a revisiting of the German occupation) are both readable against the context of the immediate post-May-1968 era.

If the definition of the film 'text' is relatively unambiguous, that of 'context' is more problematic. Each individual chapter alludes to more than one type of 'context' and all the essays in this book address the question of intertextuality in a number of different ways. Given the wealth and variety of French cinema, it is hard to generalize. Some patterns however do emerge, which we will briefly point out here, before leaving the reader to discover them in greater detail and make their own connections between the films.

## Cultural references: 'high' and 'low'

Literature and the theatre have been the most immediate intertexts of French cinema since the early days, and several films examined in this book are based on novels or plays. But reading across the chapters reveals a huge variety of relationships between film and writing as well as a wide range of sources, drawn from different corners of the culture. *Marius* and *Fanny* were 'straight' adaptations of plays by Marcel Pagnol, already a 'popular classic' *auteur* at the time. By the time of the third film in the trilogy, *César,* the relationship was inverted and the play was published after the film. More recently, directors of successful movies based on original scripts have followed in Pagnol's foot-steps: for instance Mathieu Kassovitz published a book of the screenplay of *La Haine*. Robert Bresson's *Le Journal d'un curé de campagne* is as much about the process of writing as it is an adaptation of Georges Bernanos' novel. In *Le Mépris*, Jean-Luc Godard turns Alberto Moravia's novel of 1950s Italy into a quintessential Godardian reflection on film-making, yet he remains quite faithful to the book. Jean-Paul Rappeneau's version of the much-adapted (and much-performed) play *Cyrano de Bergerac* adds another layer to the *mise-en-abyme* of nostalgia present in the original text by Edmond Rostand, yet at the same time he makes a film very much of the 1990s. The two Jean Renoir films in this book draw on two very different sources and show two very different treatments of literature by the same director: in *Le Crime de Monsieur Lange* Renoir and his scriptwriter Jacques Prévert play on the relationship of film to popular literature (such as crime magazines), filtered through Surrealism, while in *La Bête humaine* Renoir updates Zola's classic naturalist novel for the post-Popular-Front period; both offer interesting reflections on the process whereby a film-maker such as Renoir reworks texts from different ends of the 'popular literature' spectrum. At the same time, reputedly the most 'literary' film-maker, Eric Rohmer, works from original scripts (see chapters on *Ma nuit chez Maud* and *Les Nuits de la pleine lune*), as did Carné and Prévert for their depiction of the theatre world in *Les Enfants du paradis*.

Thus, if French cinema corresponds to its reputation as a 'literary cinema' (if one makes a stereotypical comparison to Hollywood action movies), this literariness is multi-faceted and it draws equally on the classic literary canon and on popular artefacts, including Hollywood cinema. The hero of *Lange* invents his version of 'Arizona' from Western films. The humour of Tati in *Les Vacances de Monsieur Hulot* owes much to early cinema comics. Godard reworks American B movies and other cinematic sources in *A bout de souffle* and *Le Mépris*, while Truffaut pays tribute to, among others, Bergman in *Les 400 coups*. More recently *Nikita* and *La Haine* display cinematic allegiances firmly placed in Hollywood. At the same time, these films, and others in the book, like the majority of French cinema, work mostly within a 'realist' framework: often shot on location, they offer overt and latent portraits of French life and society. The attraction of French cinema, for home and inter-national audiences alike, is that combination of cinematic talent and social relevance.

## History and society

Earlier in this introduction, we mentioned the shortcomings of seeing films as mere reflections of society. It is however the case that all films deal with aspects of the society that produced them and which they address, more or less directly. This is true whether we are talking about history in the sense of momentous events (*histoire événementielle*) or history 'from below'. Whereas some of the films in this book deal with extraordinary creatures (Brigitte Bardot in *Le Mépris*, the hero of *Le Samouraï*, Cyrano and Nikita), many focus on the depiction of quotidian lives, an aspect of French cinema traditionally praised. Writing in the 1930s, Graham Greene contrasted British film, which he said often focused on 'the leisured class', with American and especially French films which looked at more ordinary situations: 'Even in the worst of French films one is not conscious of [the British] class division, the cafés and dance-halls are of the kind familiar to the majority of the audience' (Greene 1980, 39). As an illustration of this point, we can look at the people in the courtyard of *Lange* or the harbour in Pagnol's trilogy, the engine driver and his mates in *La Bête humaine*, the holidaymakers of *Hulot*, Antoine Doinel's family and friends in *Les 400 coups*, the *banlieue* dwellers of *Les Nuits de la pleine lune* and (in a different social register) *Les Valseuses* and *La Haine*, the young peasant of *Lacombe Lucien*. Lucien, who unwittingly (at first) falls in with the occupying forces in his small town in the south west of France, also draws our attention to a topic which reverberates through French post-war cinema, that of the defeat of the French army in 1940 and the German occupation.

Since our first edition was published, the traumatic impact of the Second World War on French culture and society has emerged as a key topic, addressed in several important books (Rousso 1991, Burch and Sellier 1996, Lindeperg 1997). Kedward's analysis of *Lacombe Lucien* and McArthur's study of *Le Samouraï* offer two contrasting readings of the ways French films have been shaped by the war, in terms of the film-makers' experience of it (respectively Louis Malle and Jean-Pierre Melville) and in relation to discourses in French culture and society at large. Other events, such as those of May 1968, find an echo in *Les Valseuses* and *Sans toit ni loi*, which both testify to the momentous changes triggered off by May 1968. In a more wide-ranging sense, we might say that all the post-May-1968 films in the book engage with the issue of national identity, as French society in the 1970s, 1980s and 1990s has seen its social cohesion very much contested. This contestation has taken place under a variety of circumstances: increasingly uncertain economic climate as the *Trente glorieuses* come to an end, the transformation of gender, sexual and family relations, the impact of a multi-ethnic and multi-cultural society and the struggle over cultural specificity, especially under the onslaught of global (American-dominated) culture. It is clear that such different 1990s films as *Cyrano de Bergerac*, *Nikita* and *La Haine* address the issue of national identity. For example, from *Le Crime de Monsieur Lange* to *La Haine*, one can measure the sea-change in French society, both in quite direct terms – for instance the representation of the community – and more obliquely in relationship to American popular culture: the idyllic vision of Arizona in *Lange*, drawn from the Western, has become the hell of the US ghetto in *La Haine*.

5

The chapters in this edition, as in the preceding one, consider gender and sexuality as a fundamental part of social and historical change and we invite the readers to chart the changing gender and family roles across the various films. The films examined here are very diverse, and they represent only a tiny selection of the whole French production. Therefore we would not draw any absolute patterns from the films in this book. But we would point to the following lines of development: the threat to the father figure, from his towering presence in *Marius* in 1931 to his complete absence in *La Haine* in 1995, and generally the sense of a crisis in masculinity (discussed for instance by Forbes in *Les Valseuses* and Pidduck in *Cyrano*). Like any selection of French films, ours highlights the dominance of male directors (all but two: Agnès Varda and Diane Kurys) and male stars to French cinema: Jean Gabin and Gérard Depardieu notably. At the same time, some films reveal the cracks in this patriarchal culture and promote women, as film-makers and representations, and different sexualities, in however problematic terms: see for instance Dyer on *L'Air de Paris*, Andrew on *Casque d'or*, Reynaud on *Les Nuits de la pleine lune*, Hayward on *Nikita*. Though they are in the minority, a few films challenge the reign of the father by focusing on the mother figure, whether it is from the point of view of the young male hero (*Les 400 coups*), or, even more unusually, from a female point of view, as discussed by Carrie Tarr in Kurys' *Coup de foudre*.

## Authorship and the popular

One interesting shift in the way French cinema is perceived by the general public and especially in academic studies, has been the move from a pre-dominantly *auteur* cinema towards more popular texts. This is true especially of postwar films. Before the war, this critical division was not operative: the films of Renoir and Carné were addressed to a wide audience. The success of the *politique des auteurs*, developed by *Cahiers du cinéma* critics, especially Truffaut (see Hillier 1985, Truffaut 1976) and of the films of the New Wave, drove a wedge between 'auteur' and 'popular' cinema from the late 1950s onwards, arguing for films above all based on personal vision, to distinguish them from the mainstream cinema based on genre and popular modes of address. Though there are some figures in the postwar period who straddle the two (for instance Jacques Tati and Bertrand Blier), the division has remained. Our selection of films in the earlier edition was very much slanted towards *auteur* cinema, and we have now incorporated popular genre films like *Les Valseuses*, *Cyrano de Bergerac*, *Nikita* and *La Haine*. Our decision to include *L'Air de Paris* was also similarly motivated. As Dyer puts it, this film 'is an example of high-quality popular French studio production of the postwar years, simply an instance of that wealth of mainstream production that it has taken film (especially European film) history so long to pay attention to'.

The present volume as a result contains a variety of types of film. The list of films still speaks of *auteur* cinema, as we recognize the centrality, in France, of *cinéma d'auteur* as a mode of production and a stylistic approach. Our aim, however, is to approach the films from perspectives that do not equate authorship with the personal in a narrow sense. This is the case even in instances which exemplify an individualist approach to film-making, to the point of autobiography. As Anne Gillain puts it in her chapter on *Les 400 coups*, 'autobiographies, even the least sophisticated, involve elements of stylization. By turning experience into language, autobiographical narration injects it with meaning.' Similarly, the chapter on *L'Air de Paris* factors in the director's sexuality in a complex way, and the essays on the films of Carné and Prévert – *Le Jour se lève* and *Les Enfants du paradis* – are not concerned with unravelling the relative parenthood of the films in any anecdotal sense.

Finally, we would point to two important shifts in recent French cinema with regard to authorship and the popular. First, a new type of *auteur* has appeared, epitomized by Luc Besson and Kassovitz. Both developed an *auteur* persona but one based less on personal vision and more on high media profile, technical prowess and an address to a youth audience. The second point, which we also wanted reflected in the book, is the growth of 'heritage cinema', represented here by perhaps its best exponent, *Cyrano de Bergerac*. Much has been written on heritage film, especially from a British perspective (Higson 1989). In the French context, as Pidduck discusses, the genre has a special, historic, relationship both to French history and to French cinema, especially the 1940s and 1950s Tradition of Quality of which Jacques Becker's *Casque d'or* can be seen as a representative (though, atypically, a critically revered) one. The distance that separates the 'innocent' craftsman-like *Casque d'or* from the self-conscious super-production *Cyrano* is aesthetic (the New Wave happened in between) and it reflects changes in the French film industry. But Andrew's comment on *Casque d'or* could equally be said of Cyrano: 'an exquisite period piece'.

A few words remain to be said about the practical organization of this book. All twenty-two chapters in this book are original contributions. They are arranged in chronological order. Each focuses on one film, followed by a selected bibliography of works in French and in English, a filmography of the director and other films cited in the text (the national origin of films is indicated only when not French). A general bibliography of works on French cinema (also in French and in English) is at the end of the book. Titles of French films are given in French only within the text, while the filmographies at the end of each chapter indicate English/American release titles (if different). American spelling has been retained in contributions from American writers. Throughout the book the Harvard system of references has been used: a short mention of author, publication date and page number is indicated in brackets within the text, with a fuller citation in the bibliography at the end of each chapter.

## Selected bibliography

Abel, Richard (1994) *The Ciné Goes to Town: French Cinema 1896–1914*, Berkeley and Los Angeles, University of California Press.

Andrew, Dudley (1995) *Mists of Regret: Culture and Sensibility in Classic French Film*, Princeton, Princeton University Press.

Austin, Guy (1996) *Contemporary French Cinema: An Introduction*, Manchester, Manchester University Press.

Barthes, Roland (1977) *Image, Music, Text*, London, Fontana/Collins.

Billard, Pierre (1995) *L'Age classique du cinéma français*, Paris, Flammarion.

Burch, Noël and Sellier, Geneviève (1996) *La Drôle de guerre des sexes du cinéma français, 1930–1956*, Paris, Nathan.

Crisp, Colin (1993) *The Classic French Cinema: 1930–1960*, Bloomington, Indiana University Press.

Forbes, Jill (1992) *The Cinema in France After the New Wave*, London, British Film Institute.

Frodon, Jean-Michel (1995) *L'Age moderne du cinéma français, de la Nouvelle Vague à nos jours*, Paris, Flammarion.

Greene, Graham (1980) *The Pleasure Dome, The Collected Film Criticism 1935–40*, edited by John Russell Taylor, Oxford, Oxford University Press.

Harvey, Sylvia (1978) *May '68 and Film Culture*, London, British Film Institute.

Hayward, Susan (1993) *French National Cinema*, London, Routledge.

Higson, Andrew (1989) 'Re-presenting the National Past: Nostalgia and Pastiche in the Heritage Film', in Lester D. Friedman (ed.), *British Cinema and Thatcherism*, London, University College London Press.

Hillier, Jim (ed.) (1985) *Cahiers du cinéma, the 1950s: Neo Realism, Hollywood, New Wave*, London, Routledge & Kegan Paul, British Film Institute.

Lindeperg, Sylvie (1997) *Les Ecrans de l'ombre: La seconde guerre mondiale dans le cinéma français (1944–1969)*, Paris, CNRS Editions.

Marie, Michel (ed.) (1998) *Le Jeune cinéma français*, Paris, Nathan, Collection 128.

Powrie, Phil (1997) *French Cinema in the 1980s: Nostalgia and the Crisis of Masculinity*, Oxford, Clarendon Press.

Prédal, René (1991) *Le Cinéma français depuis 1945*, Paris, Nathan.

Rousso, Henry (1991) *The Vichy Syndrome: History and Memory in France since 1944*, trans. Arthur Goldhammer, London, Harvard University Press.

Trémois, Claude-Marie (1997) *Les Enfants de la liberté: le jeune cinéma français des années 90*, Paris, Seuil.

Truffaut, François (1976) 'A Certain Tendency of the French Cinema', in Bill Nichols (ed.), *Movies and Methods*, vol. I, Berkeley, University of California Press.

Vincendeau, Ginette (1996) *The Companion to French Cinema*, London, BFI/Cassell.

Williams, Alan (1992) *Republic of Images: A History of French Filmmaking*, Cambridge, Mass., Harvard University Press.

1

# IN THE NAME OF THE FATHER

## Marcel Pagnol's 'trilogy': *Marius* (1931), *Fanny* (1932), *César* (1936)

*Ginette Vincendeau*

Marcel Pagnol's series of three films, *Marius, Fanny* and *César*, usually referred to as 'the trilogy', has conformed to the fate of many truly popular classics: adored by the public – they were all box-office hits – the films were put down by contemporary critics as bad boulevard theatre or Marseillais melodramas (Bardèche and Brasillach 1948, 411). Pagnol did not seem to care and would blithely declare 'I only write about clichés' (Leprohon 1976, 388). Such professed candour, however, was underpinned by considerable intellectual and economic assets.

Pagnol was a forceful participant in the debates surrounding the coming of sound cinema in France, and particularly the question of 'filmed theatre'. He launched his own (short-lived) film magazine *Les Cahiers du film* in 1933 partly to publicize his provocative views on the primacy of dialogue over image, such as 'any sound film that can be projected silently and still remain comprehensible is a very bad film' (Pagnol 1933, 293). But Pagnol's contribution to the filming of theatrical texts was far more sophisticated than such bravado remarks would credit. If Pagnol the intellectual could give as good as he got, Pagnol the businessman could afford to brush off criticism. Between the release of *Marius* in 1931 and that of *César* in 1936, Pagnol, already the latest prodigy among France's playwrights and an experienced literary editor, made his name also as a film-maker, a novelist and a journalist. In addition, he became a producer, first with Rocher Richebé in 1932, then with his own company in 1933, Les Auteurs associés (changed in 1934 to Les Films Marcel Pagnol), and the owner of a studio in Marseilles – almost his home town as he came from nearby Aubagne – complete with labs, editing rooms, viewing theatres and a regular staff. In 1935, he was the first to publish the full dialogue of one of his films (*Merlusse*) and two years later he started his own publishing company, Les Editions Marcel Pagnol.

Pagnol had complete control over the technical side of his productions and his collaborators have testified that his equipment was, in many ways, the most advanced in France. This technological state of the art, as well as exceptional financial freedom – unheard of in 1930s French cinema – allowed him, for example, to experiment with direct sound and multiple re-takes, going as far as shooting both *Merlusse* and *Cigalon* twice over in 1935. Unlike Sacha Guitry, the other 'theatrical' director with whom he is often compared, and who would shoot a film like *Le Mot de Cambronne* in an afternoon, Pagnol always showed a keen interest in the cinematic process – thus belying his (part self-fostered) image as a despiser of film as a 'minor art'. The completion of Pagnol's vertically integrated film 'empire' came with the opening of his own cinema in Marseilles, the Noailles, for the release of *César* in 1936, used as a 'sneak preview' theatre for his productions until 1938. Pagnol went on to make films until 1954 and subsequently published autobiographical works, among which *La Gloire de mon père* and *Le Château de ma mère* now figure on many schoolchildren's set book lists both in France and abroad.

Though it has had passionate defenders (Bazin, the *Cahiers du cinéma* editors in the late 1960s), Pagnol's work has generally suffered from critical discredit, with the exception of the Giono-inspired trio of *Jofroi, Angèle*, and *Regain*, which have been hailed, by Rossellini for instance, as precursors of Neo-Realism. Together with *La Femme du boulanger* (also based on Giono), it is the trilogy, however, which has remained the most popular part of Pagnol's oeuvre, regularly repeated on French television as well as in film clubs, its outrageously 'melodramatic' plot still bringing tears to the most cynical eyes, despite a cast of comic actors. Yet it is also the trilogy which has contributed most to the derogatory label of 'Pagnolade' given to anything set in Marseilles – a tribute, if anything, to its iconic power. Outside France, the trilogy has suffered from its association with a certain notion of quaint populist French film, evoking dusty film clubs, or, worse, holidays in the south of France and French cuisine (publicity material for one of the trilogy's American remakes advised local exhibitors to 'link the film with all local off-licences, wine importers, and hotels'); more recently, an expensive gourmet restaurant near San Francisco, 'Chez Panisse', has taken the name of one of the trilogy's key characters, a *panisse* in Marseillais patois being also a type of bread loaf. Thus Pagnol's films have acquired, in film studies, a somewhat debased cultural image. Their enduring popularity, however, remains, and we only need to look at the international success of Claude Berri's *Jean de Florette* and *Manon des sources*, both based on Pagnol's scripts, to perceive the centrality and actuality of Pagnol's work to a definition of French film.

The plot of the trilogy is disarmingly simple. In Marseilles' Vieux Port, Fanny (a shellfish seller) and Marius (who works in his father's bar) love each other, but Marius longs for the sea. After he sails away Fanny, now pregnant, has to marry the older and wealthier Panisse to save the family's honour.

Marius later comes back to claim his 'wife' and son Césariot, but his father, César, sends him away. When Panisse dies twenty years later, Césariot learns the truth about his paternity and seeks out his real father. Fanny and Marius are finally reunited.

Equally disarming is the explicitness of these three films. The mechanics of desire, repression, and economics that propel the narrative along are practically spelt out by the dialogue. Furthermore, the *mise-en-scène* of the trilogy is what might be called 'exoteric'. Camera set-ups, predominantly static, are unashamedly put to the service of the dialogue, and the editing – bar a couple of montage scenes – simply juxtaposes one episode after another, and this whether the films were technically directed by Alexandre Korda (*Marius*), Marc Allégret (*Fanny*), or Pagnol himself (*César*). Does this mean, as some would claim, that the trilogy is 'the end of cinema' and, pushing the image further, the end of analysis? Perhaps not quite. While Pagnol's cinema is far from experimental, it is nonsense to describe it as 'utterly anti-cinematic' (IDHEC 1958, 31). For one thing, as Claude Beylie points out (1986, 56), the trilogy makes imaginative use of *sounds*, not just dialogue. And if it is not quite a documentary on Marseilles, the iconography of the city is present in all three films, and most effectively in Fanny's long walk to Notre-Dame de la Garde in *Fanny*. Pagnol's views on the grounding of authorship in the written word have been publicized well enough, and the debates on 'filmed theatre' sufficiently aired[1] for me not to have to rehearse them here. More importantly, Pagnol's works owe their genesis and appeal to a variety of intertexts that go beyond their dramatic basis: cast, performances, and iconography create a strong identity, in excess of a simple illustration of the written texts. The trilogy, however, because of its close relationship to a set of plays, is also a good test-case for a study of the interaction of the theatrical and the filmic.

Though conceived with a perfect ending for sequels (Marius sailing away), *Marius* was written as a single play for the stage, first performed in March 1929. Its filming in 1931, however, belongs to the early history of sound cinema in France, during which playwrights – including the most prestigious – turned out play adaptations and 'original' material, notably for the infamous Parisian branch of Paramount.[2] It is in this context that, in harmonious collaboration with Alexander Korda who was drawn in by Bob Kane (the head of Paramount in Paris) to palliate Pagnol's lack of experience in filmmaking, Pagnol adapted his stage hit for the screen, with almost the same cast: Raimu as César, Pierre Fresnay as Marius, Orane Demazis as Fanny, Charpin as Panisse. In line with the contemporary practice of making multiple-language films, German and Swedish versions were shot at the same time, with, according to Pagnol, much tinkering with the narrative compared with the French original (Pagnol 1981, 242).

The triumph of *Marius* prompted Pagnol to write a follow-up, *Fanny*, also for the theatre but clearly with a film in mind. Though Harry Baur (a considerable name and talent then) took the part of César on stage, a questionnaire among audiences showed overwhelming demand for the return of the same cast for *Fanny* (the film) as in *Marius*, the intertext already sliding from a theatrical to a filmic one. As André Bazin remarked, 'even though Marius triumphed at the Théâtre de Paris, its essential form is now and forever cinematic. Any new production of it on stage can only be a theatrical adaptation of the film' (Bazin 1975, 181). As would be expected, *Fanny* (the film) shows far fewer changes compared to the play than *Marius* does. As for *César*, it was written directly as a screenplay and performed on stage only after the release of the film. The fact that *César* took a directly cinematic form is, paradoxically, a function of the success of *Marius* and *Fanny*: the cast, and in particular Raimu and Pierre Fresnay, had become far too expensive as film stars for them to be immobilized for months in a theatre. The published text of *César* does away with the traditional theatrical divisions into acts and tableaux present in the first two works. The gradual evolution away from the stage play is echoed in the increasing amount of outdoor shooting. Pagnol moves from the earlier, studio-bound *Marius* to *César*, where almost a quarter of the film is shot on location, and which, significantly, ends on a long open-air scene. These technical distinctions between 'play' and 'screenplay', between stage and cinema, are not, however, the only way the trilogy articulates the theatrical with the filmic.

Though the importance of performance is a feature of French 1930s cinema as a whole, the primacy of the cast in the trilogy is unique and works on several levels: as a marketing strategy (Raimu and Pierre Fresnay were stars of the Parisian stage before *Marius* was shot), as a way of consolidating the coherence of the narrative across three films, and as a way of successfully blending different generic codes. Alongside its obvious references to classical tragedy (the trilogy structure, the unity of space and action and, for the most part, time, and the 'chorus' formed by M. Brun, Panisse, Escartefigue and friends), Pagnol's trilogy has recourse to thematic and structural patterns that belong to melodrama, such a conjunction – of tragedy and melodrama – connecting it to the tradition of specifically *French* stage melodrama (Turim 1987). The cast of characters includes a suffering mother, an illegitimate child, a wealthy tutor and an overbearing father. Marius' sudden return in the middle of the night at the end of *Fanny*, to reclaim woman and child from the clutches of the older man, bears the hallmark of stage melodrama (as well as modern soap opera), as does his alleged involvement with smugglers in *César*. Something else links the trilogy to specifically French melodrama: that is the constant juxtaposition of comic and tragic modes. Structurally, this informs the trilogy throughout, where a comic episode almost invariably follows, or is interspersed with, a 'tragic' one, as in the burlesque orange episode after the writing of the letter to Marius in *Fanny*, or the comical arguments in the kitchen while Panisse is dying at the beginning of *César*. The same principle works at the level of practically each scene and rests not just on dialogue and situation but on performance.

The cast of the trilogy is largely composed of actors whose range included music-hall revue and boulevard plays (Raimu), and classical tragedy (Charpin), and it mixes specific comic types (Dullac, Maupi) with an archetypal Comédie Française actor and later matinée idol like Pierre Fresnay. They were thus well equipped for the shifts in mood demanded by the text. But it is Raimu who most spectacularly achieves this duality through his constant recourse to a double register of acting. Like the others, Raimu's performance is pivotal in moving constantly between 'drama' and comedy, but, uniquely, his also shifts from the register of – comic as well as melodramatic – excess, to that of total sobriety. This he achieves through a body language which veers within instants from the exaggeration typical of the burlesque tradition he came from, and the emphatic gestures of the Marseillais (at least according to their accepted representation, a question I will come to later), to the restraint characteristic of modern sound cinema acting – and which is why Raimu was later much admired by Orson Welles. In other words, his two registers correspond to the enunciatory marks of the two forms of the trilogy: theatre and cinema. This capacity to shift instantaneously between the two is particularly effective in such set pieces as the breakfast scene in *Marius*, the reading of Marius' letter in *Fanny*, the conversation with Césariot after he has learnt his true paternity in *César*. Not surprisingly the theatrical mode corresponds to moments when as a character César is in situations of intense representation, usually on a comic register (demonstrating how to make a 'Picon-grenadine' apéritif in *Marius*, his rendering of the supposed effects of the plague or whooping cough in *Fanny*), and the cinematic mode often to 'serious' moments of intimacy or solitude. In these passages, the gestures acquire a precise and moving sociological weight: sweeping the café, setting the breakfast table, etc. Through the dialectical relation between the two modes, an effect of realism emerges. The naturalistic gestures, the spectacle of realism, are embedded in moments of flaunted theatricality reinforced by the fact that all key locations in the trilogy are themselves public representational spaces: César's Bar de la Marine, Panisse's sailing equipment shop, and Fanny's shellfish stall (it is in the logic of gendered representation that the woman's stall – in the open, in full view of the bar – is itself a spectacle within the spectacle). Finally, the enclosed, U-shaped, Vieux Port is not unlike a stage, while being itself turned towards the spectacle offered by the sea and the ships.

In the same way as the trilogy combines different registers of theatre and cinema, it reconciles opposed ideological positions throughout. This mythic structure can be seen, to start with, in the contradictory discourse on Marseilles and the Marseillais proposed by the three films. Legend has it that Pagnol was initially opposed to the filming of *Marius* on the grounds that 'they would not understand it in Lille'. As it turned out, the regional aspect of the trilogy greatly helped its universal success. But Marseilles in the trilogy means more than local colour.

Although in other works, such as *Le Schpountz*, Pagnol shows the dichotomy Provence/France (or to be more precise, Paris) as a basically rural/urban divide, here we are talking of two rival urban cultures. The only French city capable of offering an alternative popular entertainment culture to the Parisian monopoly, Marseilles in the 1930s was a city thriving on the colonial trade and one which had been, since the nineteenth century, characterized by its own rich theatrical and music-hall traditions within which forms such as cabaret and operetta were particularly popular. Concurrently, the early 1930s saw one of the peaks of a fashion for Marseillais – and southern – lore in the rest of France. Clearly linked to the arrival of sound cinema which showcased the southern accent (in addition to the locations already well documented by silent films), this trend was noticeable in other mechanically reproduced artefacts such as records, printed music sheets, postcards, etc. (see Peyrusse 1986 for a detailed study of Marseillais culture). It is in the midst of this fashion for 'Le midi' that film stars such as Fernandel and singers like Tino Rossi shot to national fame. Most of the trilogy performers – Raimu, Alida Rouffe, Charpin, Orane Demazis, Maupi – hailed from this milieu. But whereas the Marseillais live entertainment was aimed at an indigenous population, in Pagnol's trilogy, as in a spate of other films of the period, the effect is to represent Marseilles to outsiders, and notably Parisian audiences. Though he later claimed it had been originally designed for the Alcazar in Marseilles, Pagnol wrote *Marius* while 'in exile' in Paris, where his career had taken off, and he worked very hard at having it performed on a Parisian stage. Thus Marseilles was already the object of nostalgic longing: 'I did not know I loved Marseilles . . . I discovered this after four years of Parisian life' (Pagnol 1981, 145). Some of the best-known Marseillais actors were also well integrated in Parisian society; for instance Raimu who started his career as a *comique troupier* (military comic) in Toulon at the turn of the century, but had by the late 1920s become an established pillar of the smart Champs-Elysées bars, while continuing to base his screen persona on his 'southernness'.

The objectification of Marseilles in the trilogy takes specific linguistic and performance channels: the exaggerated gestures and accent traits, such as Raimu's excessive opening of the vowel 'o' as in 'pôvre' for 'pauvre', become the ostentatious signs of 'Marseillais-ity', though outside France (where the cliché representation of the French is as excitable and gesticulating anyway), they tend to be seen simply as 'French'. Within the French context, this promotion of a regional culture through accent and gestures is a recognition of cultural difference which is not without ideological ambiguities. It is as well to remember that the picturesque southern accent is but a trace of a previous language, *provençal*, obliterated by French hegemonic culture; as Peyrusse (1986) points out, live shows in Marseilles up to the First World

War would have been performed in *provençal*. The coming of sound cinema spread southern entertainment as long as it made itself acceptable to the dominant culture.

Alongside dialogues that remain classically theatrical, with an emphasis on well-turned phrases and clear diction,[3] the inflated rhetoric of speech and gestures in the trilogy is itself explicitly shown up as 'theatrical', with many self-conscious references in the lines, and with a constant shifting of the attributes of 'Marseillais-ity' across characters and situations. For example, M. Brun as a Lyonnais stands for the non-Marseillais in his encounters with other characters, including César; but when César himself is with Escartefigue, it is Escartefigue who becomes the outrageously exaggerated cliché Marseillais, forever boasting and disinclined to work, compared to the then sober César. The Marseillais/rest of the world split covers other divisions too, class in particular. M. Brun as a customs clerk is the most middle-class character – he recites Sully-Prudhomme after Panisse's death, while Panisse himself in *Marius* quotes 'poetry' taken from a tobacconist window. Throughout the trilogy, talking '*pointu*' (with a Parsian/northern accent) equals being educated. But to be an educated Marseillais is to lose one's cultural specificity; to 'make it' as a Marseillais is to leave Marseilles – a paradox evident in the character of Césariot, but equally close to Pagnol's (and Raimu's) own experience. Thus despite the explicit discourse of the film which presents Marseilles as a coherent self-evident norm – against which other cities like Lyons and Paris are comically measured – it is positioned from the start as 'other', as culturally distanced.

While rooted in urban culture, the celebration of Marseilles by the trilogy is also a paean to archaic values. Central to this celebration is the running comparison between two types of knowledge as belonging to different generations. For example, Marius corrects his father's arithmetic in the 'Picon-grenadine' demonstration, and M. Brun corrects several characters' French.[4] Although in each case the correctors are technically right, the Marseillais and the older generation's superiority is constantly re-asserted by the narrative, their knowledge presented as 'natural' as opposed to acquired – folklore rather than culture. César may count four 'thirds' in his Picon-grenadine cocktail, but it is he, not Marius, who runs the bar efficiently. Although signs of modernity are increasingly apparent as the trilogy progresses, the three films cling to these nostalgic values. By the end of the trilogy, twenty years later, Marius himself has graduated to his father's position, and sharply criticizes Cesariot's superior scholarly knowledge.

It is indeed the character of Césariot which most acutely shows this split between two types of knowledge, class and culture. As a gifted student at the *Polytechnique* school, Césariot, who wears the uniform of his difference at Panisse's funeral, has reached one of the heights of the French education system, a fact echoed naturally in his (and his friend Dromar's) lack of Marseillais accent. However, Pagnol makes the divide between him and the

*Marius* – above: César (Raimu, seated centre) and Panisse (Charpin, standing right); below: Marius (Pierre Fresnay).

*Fanny* – above: Fanny (Orane Demazis, centre) with her mother (Alida Rouffe, right) and Aunt Claudine (Milly Mathis, left); below: César (Raimu, left), Marius (centre) and Fanny.

rest of the family and cast even more radical. André Fouché, as Césariot, has no Marseillais accent (unlike Pierre Fresnay, the only other major trilogy actor not from the south, who, as is well-known, took great pains to acquire a convincing one); his speech pattern is also different from the others', and so are his elocution and type of performance; whereas Robert Vattier as M. Brun, though coded as non-Marseillais, blends in his performance with the rest of the group. An elegant young man with a silk polka-dot dressing-gown and brillantined hair, Césariot seems straight out of a Parisian high society boulevard play or a Sacha Guitry film – even the decor of his bed-room, with its modish art deco furniture, seems to belong to another film. This jarring effect is itself of course a function of the iconic coherence of the rest of the trilogy, and of Pagnol's work in general. Although traditional film history has retained the radical works of Vigo, early Clair and Renoir, and the populist works of Duvivier, Chenal and Carné, as the image of French cinema in the 1930s, these film-makers were in fact a minority who defined their work against the bulk of French films which focused on high society and the *demi-monde* (the double legacy of boulevard theatre and of Hollywood). Pagnol's contribution was to give a local inflexion to the populist icono-graphy of working-class and *petit-bourgeois* milieux: cafés and shops, 'ordin-ary' people in everyday clothes: baggy trousers, cloth caps, aprons, rolled-up sleeves; and of course the accent. These attributes were more than merely functional, they established a Pagnol 'genre', metonymically representa-tive of a 'sub'-culture (Marseilles), and metaphorically of a whole (French) culture.

Powerful as performance and iconographical motifs in Pagnol's work are, they cannot alone account for the lasting popularity of the trilogy. We now have to turn to the type of narrative offered by *Marius, Fanny* and *César*, and its symbolic and historical significance.

Pagnol's contention that he wrote only about clichés is a useful starting point. The trilogy deals in an apparently candid way with archetypal family relationships and it comes as no surprise that these accord with the dominant patriarchal ideology of the period, a set of values certainly not challenged by Pagnol. However, in its very 'naïvety' and in its explicitness, the discourse on the family proposed by the trilogy comes close, if not exactly to a critique, at least to a laying bare of its own contradictions – in terms of the conflict between generations, of the place of desire within the patriarchal family, and of the figure of the mother. In doing so it allows, crucially, for a variety of normally irreconcilable spectator positions.

Near the final resolution of the trilogy, in *César*, Fanny delivers an angry speech against César's (and her mother's) life-long interference in her affairs. Her heartfelt tirade against *les vieux* (the old ones) is undercut by the narra-tive, since César at this point is about to reunite her with Marius, but it underlines a basic structure of the three films. In the trilogy, power is still

*César* – above: (from left to right) Césariot (André Fouché), César (Raimu), the mechanic (Maupi) and Escartefigue (Paul Dullac); below: Marius (Pierre Fresnay) and Fanny (Orane Demazis).

firmly in the hands of the older generation. In contrast to the overt justification of building up wealth for the sake of the younger generation, as seen in Panisse's dream of bequeathing his business to his heir, characters who do have children, such as César and Honorine, show absolutely no inclination to relinquish their power to them. There lies one of the crucial narrative determinants of the trilogy – the symbolic Oedipal blockage from César (who, in *Marius*, repeatedly emphasizes his son's infantile status), and on a lesser register Honorine (who, as a widow, is endowed with phallic power), parallels an economic blockage, and effectively sends Marius on his journey and Fanny into her marriage to Panisse. The thematic configuration of powerful old men, and their marriage to young women, is a staple of French theatre, both comic (Molière's *vieux barbons*) and melodramatic, and is found in a wide range of 1930s French films, as I have developed elsewhere.[5] Its peculiar French predominance has to be seen against the background of the socio-historical structure of 1930s French society. Marriages between mature men and much younger women were still widespread among the middle classes in 1930s France, within a legal system geared towards keeping wealth and property, and hence authority, in the hands of the older generation. Work on contemporary media aimed at women has shown that in the women's magazines of the period discourses aimed at 'preparing' women for such an eventuality coexisted alongside romantic notions of ideal (young) love. These perfectly contradictory positions are exemplified in the trilogy's treatment of the marriage between Fanny and Panisse. An object of mirth when it is first proposed, it is later commented on in terms of its sexual inadequacy despite its economic necessity, a divide succinctly expressed by Honorine ('nightshirts don't have pockets'). What the narrative subsequently and at great length justifies is the desirability of such a marriage in terms of legitimacy.

In the same way as the trilogy contrasts the 'natural' and 'learned' types of knowledge, it opposes two types of inheritance, attached to the two father figures: César and Panisse. Césariot is heir to a 'natural' legacy from César through Marius, and to property from Panisse. This is logical in class terms: the rise of the *petite bourgeoisie* into the elite depends on the money of commerce. In return, the ambitious provincial shopkeeper is stimulated by Parisian-inspired initiative: Panisse modernizes his business for 'the little one'. Though Césariot is the 'true' son of the Bar de la Marine (César and Marius merge into one another on more than one occasion as César explicitly identifies with Marius as lover of Fanny and father of Césariot in Marius' absence), he needs Panisse's money and, even more, his name. For, above all, the point of the marriage is to give Césariot 'a name' – the name of the father, materialized in the letters '& Fils' kept by Panisse in a drawer and triumphantly added to the shop front.

We can see the trilogy, then, as a long declension on the name and nature of the father, a series of variations with, at their core, the character of César enhanced by the star status of Raimu, who understood the centrality of the part of César and turned down the role of Panisse originally intended for him by Pagnol, thus changing the course of the subsequent two works. With the death of Panisse, Marius can return; but more importantly César can be acknowledged as the true ancestor of the child, having occupied all the positions of fatherhood – father, godfather, and grandfather – as well as that of 'father' of the narrative: sending Marius away symbolically in *Marius*, literally in *Fanny*, and bringing him back in *César*, even though this entails a certain amount of 'cheating'. For the law of the father is also shown to be making its own rules as it goes along – a fact comically echoed by the various card games in which César always cheats in order to win. But if the trilogy repeatedly reasserts the power of the father(s), it also explores contradictory, and potentially threatening, forces against this power: the desire of the 'son' on the one hand, and the place of the mother within a patriarchal, Catholic, culture on the other.

Like most classical narratives, the trilogy is the story of a quest by the male hero, on the Oedipus model. Marius' actual and symbolic voyage condenses classical mythology, French popular myths of the 1930s and Marseillais folklore.[6] Marius and Fanny as Ulysses and Penelope is a clear enough equivalence. Marius' longing for the South Seas, while motivated by the Marseilles location, also corresponds to the obsession with exoticism and sea voyages in 1930s French culture. Clearly, it is traceable, in part, to colonial history, and it is certainly dominant in the cinema of the period in a variety of genres – from Navy melodramas to operettas (including a specifically Marseillais sub-genre) – but best known internationally from 'Poetic-Realist' films. Unlike its expression in Duvivier's *Pépé le Moko* or Carné's *Le Quai des brumes*, where the Gabin hero's voyage is always blocked, the journey in the trilogy does take place. Its object, however, according to the logic of desire, is shown to be an unattainable illusion. In order for Marius' mythic (and Oedipal) journey to be successful, an object approved by the law – marriage – has to be substituted for his own irrepressible desire for 'elsewhere', while the nature of his desire, threatening the cohesion of the family, is dealt with by his virtual exclusion from *Fanny* and *César*.

In keeping with the patriarchal emphasis, gender roles in the trilogy are unsurprisingly ultra-traditional, not to say archaic, and totally grounded in the family and its rituals. However, as is common in the French cinema of the period, gender divisions within male characters are far more complex than the overt definition of gender roles. Panisse for example occupies both masculine and feminine positions – he gives a name and wealth to the child, but he is also caring and protective; this is the object of the long scene towards the end of *Fanny* in which Panisse's tender nurturing of Césariot is given as justification of his superior claim to fatherhood over Marius' recognized status as biological father. This dual nature of the father is even more explicit in the character of César who is both father and mother to Marius, being, for instance, strongly connected with domesticity while at the same time presented as sexually active (his weekly visits to a mysterious mistress). In this configuration the trilogy is typical of a wide range of 1930s French films, as is the fact that the actual mothers, the older women such as the wives of Panisse and César, are eliminated from the narrative before the films begin. It is true that Fanny's mother, Honorine, is present in all three films, but her narrative function is minimal and her sexuality certainly denied. Though she would seem at first to be the female equivalent of César, the real 'couple' is formed by the latter and Panisse, a couple ultimately consecrated by the name of 'their' child: César(iot) Panisse.

If Honorine is marginalized in the trilogy, her daughter Fanny occupies centre stage as 'the mother'. Within the terms of French and especially Catholic culture, the place accorded to her is central (as bearer and educator of the child) but concurrently suppresses her as an individual subject in her own right. A good contemporary parallel can be found in Mauriac's novel *Thérèse Desqueyroux*, published in 1927, in which the pregnant Thérèse is acutely aware that her only value is as a 'container'. Though it is tempting to see the emphasis on motherhood in the trilogy – as in all Pagnol's work – as related to the contemporary concern with low birth rates, it relates more pertinently to generic structures, and in particular those of melodrama in which the classic opposition between the 'good' and the 'bad' woman is really an expression of the conflict between the woman as mother and the woman as individual subject, an antinomy which uncannily evokes Freud's scenario of 'family romances'. Freud's description of the male child's fantasy 'to bring his mother . . . into situations of secret infidelity and into secret love-affairs' (Freud 1977, 223) reads like a blueprint for the scene in *César* where Césariot learns of his true paternity and angrily reproaches Fanny for her love affair with Marius, seeing it as a dereliction of her 'duty', towards her husband Panisse and towards him. Fanny's response is to provoke guilt: she points to the suffering she has endured in order to carry him, give birth to him and bring him up; such is the mother's revenge under patriarchy.

As is also typical of the maternal melodrama, sacrifice is the only option left to Fanny, one which despite its negativity can be seen at least to validate women's experience, but more fundamentally to point to the fact that this sacrifice is itself also a 'problem';[7] she sacrifices her love for Marius to his greater love for 'the sea' in *Marius*, sacrifices all for her child in *Fanny*, and, arguably, sacrifices her newfound freedom after Panisse's death for the (re)formation of her couple with Marius in *César*. However, despite its masculine bias, the trilogy can be seen to appeal directly to women spectators. As *Fanny* is the film which concentrates most on the female heroine, both as mother and as 'fallen woman' (a combination which is a recurrent thematic thread in Pagnol's work – see for instance *Angèle* and *La Fille du puisatier*), one might speculate on its increased appeal to women. It is telling that, of the three films, *Fanny* enjoyed the highest attendance (Pagnol 1981, 203), and unsurprising that it attracted the strongest critical disapproval. In this respect, Beylie's view is typical of the traditional attitude to melodrama, when he describes *Fanny* as the part of the trilogy where 'male rigorousness' gives way to 'a lacrymose excess a little out of place' (Beylie 1986, 59). Simultaneously offering the image of perfect womanhood and the image of its transgression, the trilogy addresses contradictory impulses and ideological positions in its audience, though of course these contradictory positions are themselves defined by patriarchy. The 'good' and especially the 'bad' aspects of the female heroine are shown as inherent to her 'nature': there are hints of Fanny's own illegitimate birth and there is the often evoked spectre of Fanny's aunt Zoé, a prostitute. At the end of the trilogy César, as always, has the last word. As he is reminded by Marius that Césariot does not bear his (their) name, he retorts: 'This one doesn't, but the other ones will.' Cancelling out the past twenty years (and the last two films of the trilogy), César rewrites Fanny's future as a mother and the perpetuator of his own name.

## Notes

1 For an introduction to the contemporary debates on 'filmed theatre' and reactions to the coming of sound in general, see René Clair (1972) *Cinema Today and Yesterday*, trans. Stanley Applebaum, New York, Dover, and various contributions – including by Clair and Pagnol – in Marcel Lapierre (ed.) (1946) *Anthologie du cinéma*, Paris, La Nouvelle Edition. Beylie (1986) also provides a good overview of the reactions to Pagnol's place in the debate.

2 The Parisian branch of the Paramount studios, located in Joinville, was nicknamed 'Babel-on-Seine' on account of its high production of multi-language versions (including the three versions of *Marius*), and provoked much commentary and criticism. See Pagnol (1965) in *Cahiers du cinéma* (1932) 173, Henri Jeanson, 'Cinq semaines à la Paramount, choses vécues', *Le Crapouillot*, special issue, November, and Vincendeau (1988) 'Hollywood-Babel', *Screen*, 29 (2).

3 This is itself a feature of a majority of French films of the 1930s that focused strongly on actors' performances, whether they were based directly on theatrical texts or not. For a close study of dialogue in a Pagnol film, see Marie's contribution (on *Le Schpountz*) to Michel Marie and Francis Vanoye, 'Comment parler la bouche pleine?', *Communications*, 38 (1982), special issue 'Enunciation and Cinema'.

4 In a scene from *Marius* (the play) which was not retained in the film, Fanny also corrects her mother's pronunciation of the word 'inventaire' (stall).

5 'Daddy's Girls, Oedipal Narratives in 1930s French Films', *Iris*, 'Cinema and Narration 2' (2nd semestre, 1988).

6 Within the film's paradigm of sea voyages, the ferry-boat that crosses the Vieux Port functions metonymically, as part of the Marseillais familiar scene. It also works metaphorically, both as sign of a doomed folklore (its existence is threatened by the construction of a new bridge), and as representative of the small-scale, routine existence Marius wants to leave behind by embarking on the glamorous sailing ship.

7 This is a problematic identified notably by Ann Kaplan in relation to Hollywood melodrama. See Kaplan, 'Mothering, Feminism and Representation: The Maternal in Melodrama and the Woman's Film 1910–1987', in Christine Gledhill (ed.) (1987) *Home Is Where the Heart Is*, London, British Film Institute.

## Selected bibliography

Audouard, Yvan (1973) *Yvan Audouard raconte Marcel Pagnol*, Paris, Stock.

Bazin, André (1975) 'Le Cas Pagnol', in *Qu'est-ce que le cinéma?*, Paris, Editions du Cerf. This essay is not included in the English translation of Bazin's book.

Bardèche, Maurice and Brasillach, Robert (1948) *Histoire du cinéma*, Paris, André Martel.

Beylie, Claude and Brancourt, Guy (1969) interview with Marcel Pagnol, *Cinéma 69*, 134.

Beylie, Claude (1986) *Marcel Pagnol ou le cinéma en liberté*, Paris, Editions Atlas, Lherminier – an enlarged, up-to-date, edition of Beylie (1974) *Marcel Pagnol*, Paris, Seghers. The best single book on Pagnol, it contains an excellent bibliography and a very complete filmography.

Biret, Philippe (1995) *A la rencontre de Marcel Pagnol*, Marseille, Editions Jeanne Laffitte.

Caldicott, C. E. J. (1977) *Marcel Pagnol*, Boston, Twayne, G. K. Hall.

Castans, Raymond (1978) *Il était une fois Marcel Pagnol*, Paris, Julliard.

Castans, Raymond and Bernard, André (1982) *Les Films de Marcel Pagnol*, Paris, Julliard.

Daries, Henri (1995) *Un bout de chemin avec Marcel Pagnol*, Aix-en-Provence, Edisud.

Delahaye, Michel (1969) 'La Saga Pagnol', *Cahiers du cinéma*, 213.

Freud, Sigmund (1977) *The Pelican Freud Library,* Vol. 7: *On Sexuality*, Harmondsworth, Penguin Books.

Gauteur, Claude (1970) 'Marcel Pagnol aujourd'hui', *Avant-Scène cinéma*, 105/106 (contains excellent bibliography).

Gauteur, Claude (1973) 'Marcel Pagnol inconnu?', *Image et Son*, 275.

IDHEC students' analysis of the trilogy, *Image et Son*, 114 (July 1958).

Labarthe, André S. (1965) 'Pagnol entre centre et absence', *Cahiers du cinéma*, 173 followed by an interview with Marcel Pagnol.

Lagnan, Pierre (ed.) (1989) *Les Années Pagnol*, Renens, FOMA/5 Continents.

Leprohon, Pierre (1976) *Marcel Pagnol, Avant-Scène cinéma*, supplément d'anthologie, 88.

Pagnol, Marcel (1933) 'Cinématurgie de Paris', *Les Cahiers du film*, reprinted in Marcel Lapierre (ed.) (1946) *Anthologie du cinéma*, Paris, La Nouvelle Edition.

Pagnol, Marcel (1981) *Confidences*, Paris, Julliard.

Peyrusse, Claudette (1986) *Le Cinéma méridional*, Toulouse, Eché.

Roud, Richard (1980) 'Marcel Pagnol', in Richard Roud (ed.), *Cinema, A Critical Dictionary*, London, Secker & Warburg, II.

Sadoul, Georges (1938) article in *Regards*, reprinted (1979) in *Chroniques du cinéma français*, Paris, Union Générale d'Editions.

Turim, Maureen (1987) 'French Melodrama: Theory of a Specific History', *Theater Journal*, fall.

Turk, Edward Baron (1980) 'Pagnol's Marseilles Trilogy', *American Film*, VI (I).

## Scripts

All three parts of the trilogy have been published in book form and reprinted many times (they are all currently available in the *Livre de poche* collection). The original editions are:

Pagnol, Marcel (1931) *Marius*, Fasquelle.
Pagnol, Marcel (1932) *Fanny*, Fasquelle.
Pagnol, Marcel (1937) *César*, Fasquelle.

# Appendix

### Marcel Pagnol (1895–1974): filmography

(Main films directed or supervised by Marcel Pagnol; for a complete filmography, see Beylie 1986.)

1931  *Marius* (technically directed by Alexander Korda)
1932  *Fanny* (technically directed by Marc Allégret)
1933  *Le Gendre de Monsieur Poirier*
1933  *Jofroi*
1934  *L'Article 330*
1934  *Angèle*
1935  *Merlusse*
1935  *Cigalon*
1936  *César*
1936  *Topaze*, second version – a first version of Pagnol's play was directed in 1932 by Louis Gasnier
1937  *Regain*
1937  *Le Schpountz*
1938  *La Femme du boulanger*
1940  *La Fille du puisatier*
1941  *La Prière aux étoiles*
1943  *Arlette et l'amour* (technically directed by Robert Vernay)
1945  *Naïs* (technically directed by Raymond Leboursier)
1948  *La Belle meunière*
1950  *Topaze*, third version
1952  *Manon des sources*
1953–4  *Les Lettres de mon moulin*
1967  *Le Curé de Cucugnan*

### Remakes of the trilogy

(a) simultaneous foreign-language versions

1931  *Zum Goldenen Anker* (Germany), directed by Alexandre Korda

1931  *Längtan till Havet* (Sweden), directed by John W. Brunius

(b) remakes

1933  *Fanny* (Italy), directed by Mario Almirante
1934  *Der Schwarze Walfisch* (Germany), directed by Fritz Wendhausen, with Emil Jannings as César
1938  *Port of Seven Seas* (USA), directed by James Whale, scripted by Preston Sturges, with Wallace Berry as César, Maureen O'Sullivan as Fanny
1961  *Fanny* (USA), musical directed by Joshua Logan, with Maurice Chevalier as César, Charles Boyer as Panisse and Leslie Caron as Fanny

## Other films cited in the text

*Jean de Florette*, Claude Berri (1985)
*Manon des sources*, Claude Berri (1986)
*Le Mot de Cambronne*, Sacha Guitry (1936)
*Pépé le Moko*, Julien Duvivier (1937)
*Le Quai des brumes* (*Port of Shadows*), Marcel Carné (1938)

# 2

# PARIS, ARIZONA; OR THE REDEMPTION OF DIFFERENCE

## Jean Renoir's *Le Crime de Monsieur Lange* (1935)

*Christopher Faulkner*

> The cinema? Three cheers for darkened rooms.
>
> (André Breton)
>
> Be a realist, ask for the impossible.
>
> (May 1968 slogan)

Notwithstanding received opinion, *Le Crime de Monsieur Lange*, which was released in January 1936, has little to do with the ideas and ideology of the Popular Front coalition that came to power in May and June on a vote of confidence in social, cultural and economic change.[1] The film extends no hand to the clergy, takes a position for women and against colonialism and racism, embraces popular culture, has an idea of the nation (or community) that would suit no political party of the time and proposes its own solution to the abuses of capital. In defiance of the stated policies of the Popular Front alliance of Socialist, Radical and Communist Party interests, *Le Crime de Monsieur Lange* imagines, projects and creates its own vision of a society transformed. Since what it favoured was never realized, however, *Le Crime de Monsieur Lange* is one of those films that functions as a future memory. How would we know how to form the content of our political imaginings today without films like *Le Crime de Monsieur Lange* to serve as models for us?

At a café on the Franco-Belgian border, Valentine (Florelle) tells the assembled patrons that she and her lover Amédée Lange (René Lefèvre) are on the run because Lange has committed a murder. In a long flashback, she explains how Batala (Jules Berry), the boss of the local printworks, had ruled over the workers and friends living around their courtyard in a popular area of Paris. Batala is a social and sexual tyrant, who seduces women and rapes the young Estelle (Nadia Sibirskaïa), who later gives birth to a stillborn baby. While Batala's swindles and bankruptcy force him to go on the run,

27

the courtyard community forms a co-operative and produces popular fiction written by Lange. When Batala comes back (disguised as a priest) to reclaim his now thriving company, the outraged Lange kills him. The people in the café declare Lange 'innocent' and help the couple escape across the border.

*Le Crime de Monsieur Lange* is a film that has received extensive critical attention, and is usually analysed in direct relation to its historical and political context in the Popular Front period (the capitalist boss, the workers' co-operative, community solidarity, etc.). However, there is another context for the film that deserves to be examined, namely its relationship to culture and fiction – in particular surrealism and popular literature, precisely because they mediate and shape the film's politics. Furthermore, in view of what I take to be the film's anarchist tendencies rather than its commitment to the platform of the Popular Front, the undervalued role of the Catalan painter, set designer and contributor to the script, Joan Castanyer (known in French as Jean Castanier or sometimes Castaigné), needs to be considered.

The value of fiction is that it enables people to take into themselves, to internalize in an *affective* way, through dream, fantasy or imagination, their required sense of their world. A set of attitudes, values, convictions and beliefs is supported by the projections, displacements, substitutions and investments that the work of fiction – that fiction at work – helps to organize and make manifest. Making sense in this way depends upon a consensus among social subjects that is more often felt than understood. *Le Crime de Monsieur Lange* is not a mirror held up to life, then; it is a mirror held up to a measure of desire circa 1936. That is why it unabashedly uses the narrative methods and materials of dream and fantasy to make the conditions of people's existence intelligible to them.[2]

The story which is embedded in the flashback structure of the film is not literally dreamt by Lange. That it might seem to be so is suggested not only by the (already) classic fictional device of the flashback as a spectatorial cue for dreaming, remembering or imagining, but also because of the obvious replacement of Lange by Valentine who tells his tale on his behalf even while he sleeps in a new bed on clean sheets in the back room of a frontier hotel on the borderlands between France and Belgium. Indeed, frontiers and borders, as between waking and sleeping, conscious and unconscious, reality and fiction, day or night, a priest and a capitalist, the courtyard and greater Paris, Paris and Arizona (or Mexico, or Tonkin), all structure an important thematic field in the film that has to do with the very definition of community that the film articulates. These pairings should not be taken as opposed, contradictory or even dialectical, however. Let us say, for the moment, that the film proves frontiers to be accessible and borders porous.

But this story of crossings, displacements and substitutions belongs to a woman, is told by a woman. In surrealism, men dream of women (a woman), as in the notorious Magritte portrait *Je ne vois pas (la femme) cachée dans la forêt,*

28

surrounded by photographs of the surrealists; but that is only because women dream *for* men (as well as for themselves), as in the 1927 surrealist photograph *L'Ecriture automatique*, which appeared on the cover of *La Révolution Surréaliste*, nos 9/10 (cf. Conley 1996). At the frontier hotel, Lange dreams in his new bed of Valentine dreaming the film of our desires. Woman is the surrealist unconscious, even perhaps, as here, the political unconscious of surrealism. What the woman dreams and/or writes mediates between one's conscious thoughts and unconscious wishes. Subject and object of desire both, she (Valentine) is our medium. She is the agent for the telling of the story; and it is Lange's (un)premeditated action of which she tells.

The casting of the film adds to the disturbance around received ideas of sexual difference created by its narrative mode of address. Florelle's forceful, good-humoured character type was established in the music hall and familiar to movie audiences from roles like her Polly in Pabst's French version of his *Die Dreigroschenoper*, entitled *L'Opéra de quat'sous* (1930). René Lefèvre's persona was already that of the reluctant, red-faced lover in films such as *Jean de la lune* (Jean Choux, 1930) and *Le Million* (René Clair, 1931) before he came to *Le Crime de Monsieur Lange*. Valentine is the practical, active one in their relationship, who urges Lange to confront the immediate world of everyday injustice and whose sexual openness and experience – based on the reputation of laundresses in French cultural mythology, which this film cites to interrogate – initiate their romance.

As the local representatives of the people (and the audience) at the border hotel discuss what the daily newspapers have reported about the murder incident, one man suggests with a joke that Lange may have displaced the physical presence of Batala into the image of a 'nuisible' (like a rat, for example), while another admits that he has readily killed many men in his dreams. Some of Lange's peers are prepared to accept that dream and the unconscious can release us from the moral constraints of public life and enable the hallucinatory desires of the private self. The knowledge gained may lead to the just overthrow of social and economic forces that only a massive internalized repression acting upon every individual member of society helps keep in place. This, in effect, is the conclusion the group at the frontier arrives at based on the story they hear. Their debate at the outset and their judgement at the end are a dramatized instance of the acquisition of political consciousness through the process of 'negotiation' that audiences undertake with their world through the agency of cultural fictions. By making the social relations of the people at the hotel intelligible to them, Valentine's tale must have made sense, even appealed to 'common sense,' a common sense which questions the hegemony of bourgeois capitalism. The exercise of their judgement is what makes the filmic text ideologically effective.[3]

The (Freudian) 'royal road' that has brought the couple to the inn at the frontier and the confrontation with the jury of their peers has been visually superimposed over the prone body of the evil Batala. This is the ground that literally has to be gone over, the story that has to be retold, inasmuch as *Le Crime de Monsieur Lange* has to justify Lange's murder of Batala, filmically as well as politically. Filmically, the murder is justified by the famous 360-degree pan of the courtyard which makes it clear that Lange acts on behalf of the public interest. For us, as for the audience at the frontier, the visual and aural treatment of this moment communicates how a sense of the justice of Lange's action has been internalized in an affective way. Bazin was of course right to insist upon the impression of 'dizziness' and 'madness' conveyed by the 360-degree pan; although such an impression, important as it is, cannot stand by itself, but must be understood as the intentionally powerful subjectivization of a social act (Bazin 1973, 46).

Lange also finds the act 'easy,' perhaps because it is an act that arises from the unrepressed self, an act performed in the hallucinatory atmosphere of a night-time when capitalists can be confused with priests and the effects of drink and celebration overcome one's daytime inhibitions. The noise of the partygoers, the cries of the drunken concierge, heighten the sensation of abandon. Night brings on the delirium of writing, too, when one might assume a persona like Arizona Jim to act out in life the *mise-en-page* of fiction. Perhaps, indeed, Lange has been emboldened by his cowboy hero, Arizona Jim, since he has just left a party to the success of his creation to develop yet another new story idea. Was Surrealism not originally defined by Breton as 'Psychic automatism in its pure state, by which one proposes to express – verbally, by means of the written word, *or in any other manner* – the actual functioning of thought'? (Breton 1972, 26; my emphasis).

From the very beginning of the flashback, Amédée Lange is introduced as a dreamer, and references are made to the fact throughout the film. (People think him mad; Batala taps his head and says, 'What a strange world is there.') We first meet him in his room on the first morning of the film, where he has been writing all night in a reverie, a fantasist who acts out his characters' roles as he writes. So lost is he to a sense of location that his room has become Arizona itself, dominated by a map of the American West and decorated with the props of fiction. Apparently oblivious to the passage of time, and without any apprehension of fatigue, or consciousness of craft, what he spins out of his fertile imagination seems to fall to the page like automatic writing. No surrealist himself, he and the film are nevertheless the creation of surrealists, of the Catalan Joan Castanyer who wrote the first scenario with Renoir, of the dissident surrealist Jacques Prévert and the members of 'Prévert's gang' who formed the agit-prop Groupe Octobre and spent days and nights sending up all manner of intellectual pretention and social and political injustice (for instance in their 1932 film *L'Affaire est dans le sac* and the antiwar satire *La Bataille de Fontenoy*).

Consequently, there is in *Le Crime de Monsieur Lange* a deliberate penchant for incongruity. Arizona has come to Paris; a swindler disguises himself as a priest, and calls for a priest as he dies; the man who kills this priest is an angel; his name is a clever pun in the tradition of surrealist wordplay and language games; Amédée Lange = 'à m'aider, l'ange' (help me, angel); a song about Christmas is sung at the height of summer to celebrate the success of the co-operative; one of Lange's cowboy heroes gulps Ranimax pills and takes Flaconnet powder in the middle of his daring exploits (Robert Desnos had once promoted the idea of the 'automatic' advertisement that would suddenly appear in the midst of unrelated text.[4] Valentine finds this hilarious, while for Meunier *fils* these are his favourite bits); timid M. Lange is referred to as a 'real satyr'; Lange says to Estelle, 'You look Mexican', but 'I'm from Limoges' is the deadpan reply. *Le Crime de Monsieur Lange* is not about slitting the white eyelid of the screen with the shock of *Un chien andalou* (Buñuel and Dalí, 1929), but the subversive potential of its laughter is likely to be far more popular and practical.[5]

As a way of making meaning, the surrealist devotion to incongruity[6] becomes an interesting verbal and visual figure in a film which sets forth the possibilities for community like *Le Crime de Monsieur Lange*. Incongruity depends upon a discontinuity or dissimilarity between two things juxtaposed that borders on the illogical. What the threat of illogicality raises is a question about the decidability of meaning. With incongruity there is no disavowed, repressed or excluded term; there are no 'others'. The two terms are entirely equal in value, and yet utterly different. If neither term takes priority over the other, if neither is the privileged ground for the figure of meaning, then in a way the undecidability of meaning is the point. Furthermore, the absence of privilege means that either or both terms can be substituted to infinity by newly incongruous juxtapositions. Meaning will always be elsewhere, because the potential for the introduction of a new term postpones indefinitely the closure of sense. Incongruity works by a continual relay of difference, and in a system of exchange which does not necessarily have anything to do with oppositional, contradictory or dialectical relationships. Quite simply, it is a both–and rather than an either–or strategy. While there is not space to develop this here, there may be an argument for saying that Renoir's moving camera and shooting in depth have the effect of leaving the visual field continually open to the play of difference. This suggests a new take on Renoir's famous socialization of space. As characters, objects and actions appear and disappear from view with the camera's movement or the shot in depth, the visual field is always potentially available to the unexpected arrival of new meanings through the substitution of new characters, new objects or new actions. Among innumerable examples in this film, one thinks of the shot that includes the bearded man at his courtyard window complaining of the noise, or the shot that inexplicably discovers Valentine playing with a dog. In short, this valuation of difference and process rather than position and sameness is central to the complex idea of community at work in the film.

31

No one who has written about *Le Crime de Monsieur Lange* has failed to remark that it is a film about a community, by a community, for a community. However, communities, as we know, are defined by their exclusions as much as they are by their inclusions. The broad question about how exclusions get justified and differences annihilated is more than ever pertinent today, as old ideas of the nation–state are now in conflict with the real-life practices of new diasporic communities, who may or may not have their avenging angels. This conflict can already be observed in French cinema of the 1930s. There are works that actively dramatize the struggle for the redemption of differ-ence in the 1930s and there are works that do not. In retrospect, a film like *La Marseillaise* (Renoir, 1938), for example, seems increasingly dated and oppressive, because its equation of the nation with a soft, homogeneous idea of the popular actually annihilates most differences. As we shall see, *Le Crime de Monsieur Lange*, on the other hand, was able to negotiate a relationship between some of the practised inclusions and exclusions that prevailed in contemporary French society in order to imagine a community of the future that redeemed difference. Any prospect for social change depends entirely upon negotiating the meaning of difference.

In *Le Crime de Monsieur Lange* community is articulated through the pro-duction and consumption of cultural forms, through the making and sharing of narratives and representations. They are what make social relations intelli-gible. After the departure of the evil Batala, the co-operative gets to make and distribute its own illustrated magazine stories and its own movies. In this regard, the film makes a genuine attempt to draw attention to the necessity of a counter-discourse and the existence of an alternative public sphere. This is as close as Renoir comes to illustrating his own (somewhat doctrinaire) plea at the time that, because cinema is under the control of the bourgeoisie and the profiteers, 'we must restore the French cinema to the people of France' in order that it recover the spirit of 'cooperative endeavour.' (Renoir, in Abel 1988, 211–12).

The fictions that the co-operative and its members create belong to the domain of popular culture, the culture of everyday life. Theirs is the world of the *roman feuilleton*, the cheap pulp fiction serialized throughout the 1920s and 1930s in innumerable weekly magazines in a variety of genres (*le policier*, *le Far-West*, *la presse du coeur*, the colonial adventure, etc.) with huge circula-tions for a variety of popular tastes (boys and girls, midinettes and factory workers, shopkeepers and concierges). This species of popular literature was held beneath contempt by the guardians of high culture and has still been largely ignored as a subject of critical interest. The film's acknowledgement of this literature was not sanctioned by the cultural policy of the 'Popular' Front, whose Bibliobus brought to the factory gates only such fiction as might lead to the 'improvement' of the workers. The surrealists had a selec-tive interest in some of this work, when it played to their anti-conformist tastes or when it provided evidence of everyday surrealist moments (the

*Le Crime de Monsieur Lange* – above: (front row, facing) Valentine (Florelle, left), Charles (Maurice Baquet, centre) and Lange (René Lefèvre, right); below: Workers in the co-operative line up for an *Arizona Jim* picture.

adoration of the *Fantômas* stories in film and print is the most celebrated instance of surrealist approval). Although its title obviously recalls this genre of fiction, *Le Crime de Monsieur Lange* is indebted to no one magazine in particular. Renoir, Castanyer and Prévert were, however, clearly familiar with a wide range of such literature and correctly presumed on their audience's knowledge. There were popular fiction papers like *Vidocq* and *Police-roman* (largely for men), and *Mes romans* and *Le Dimanche de la femme* (for women), children's magazines like *Benjamin* (which reached a circulation of 200,000 in 1935!), *Lisette* and *Guignol*, not to mention the highly imaginative treatment of contemporary *faits divers* in the likes of *Détective*, which had a weekly circulation of over 250,000 and drew on contributors like Georges Simenon, Pierre Mac Orlan, Francis Carco and Paul Morand (Bellanger *et al.* 1972, 597–602). All of this represents a literary culture of the popular that was actually co-extensive with the cinema through correspondences between subject-matters and audiences and forms of presentation. On the one hand, *romans feuilletons* were photo-illustrated, or sometimes offered as *bandes dessinées*. On the other hand, films found their literary equivalent in the widely published *films racontés* of the interwar years. Something of the order of ten thousand titles were turned out in the form of novellas and serialized stories in long running series like *Cinéma Bibliothèque* and *Le Film complet* during this period. A single film might undergo three or four different novelizations. It is safe to say that French cinemagoers of the 1930s formed an enormous popular *readership* whose discursive knowledge of their world was reinforced by this reciprocity and overlay between the two media of film and literature. A great deal has been made of French cinema of the 1930s as an actor's cinema. In light of the evidence of the intricate relations between a certain kind of mass produced literature and the mass circulated film, perhaps we should redress the emphasis and allow that story-types were at least as important as actors and performance to the appeal of cinema for popular audiences. Not that cross-over story material as between popular literature and film was any guarantee of box office returns. Despite Renoir's claim that *Le Crime de Monsieur Lange* was 'a great success' (Renoir 1974, 125), the film was not a great hit and generated little critical excitement at the time.

Perhaps that is because *Le Crime de Monsieur Lange* is entirely self-conscious about its debt to both the *roman feuilleton* and the *ciné-roman*. First of all, it aims at popular tastes, and its casting and its mixture of genres (comedy, *policier*, Western, melodrama, romance) serve that end. Batala's assault on Estelle is presented as high melodrama when the camera tracks quickly in (to the appropriate music) as she cowers in a corner of his office. *Le Crime de Monsieur Lange* also recalls an earlier age and another kind of film-making in the casting of Marcel Levesque as the concierge. Levesque had a major silent film career, largely in comic parts, and achieved lasting fame in *Les Vampires* (Louis Feuillade, 1915) and above all in *Judex* (Feuillade, 1917) where he played the detective Cocantin. *Le Crime de Monsieur Lange* parodies the serial

*Le Crime de Monsieur Lange* – The power of Western iconography: left: the cover of film magazine *Cinèa*; right: the cover of youth magazine *Guignol*.

film or *ciné-roman* in the music that accompanies the flight of the characters, and it mocks the quality of this kind of low-budget film production in Lange's concern about phoney sets when the prospect of making movies is first mentioned. Furthermore, we see assorted characters within the film reading or walking about with various *feuilletons*. Not only does the community get to imagine the world in its own interests, it does so in the forms of popular expression nearest to its own experience. This makes it easy to think of the community's productions as the work of the collective imagination.

When Batala is running his company and exploiting the printwork employees, he publishes titles like *Policeman* and *La Cuisse de Paris* ('The Thigh of Paris', no doubt in pornographic imitation of Zola's *Le Ventre de Paris*) which the printers object to turning out.[7] But Batala's favourite is the eponymous hero of his serial *Javert*, 'hebdomadaire littéraire et policier', who is not on the side of the angels since he is the fearsome detective from *Les Misérables* in relentless pursuit of Jean Valjean. Batala's billboard for the forthcoming *Javert* is used to wall-up Charles (Maurice Baquet) in his room.

Tellingly, Lange looks not to France but to America for his story material, to American popular culture and above all to the Western, the genre that features a hero who undertakes an action that advances the well-being of a group of people on the frontier of change from lawlessness to community. The model for Lange and his cowboy adventures was no doubt William S. Hart, whose persona was known in France as 'Rio-Jim'. Rio-Jim put wrongs to right in dozens of two-reelers and feature films between 1914 and 1925 and had an extraordinary French following. As American society has been synonymous with a popular democracy, so has American culture been synonymous with popular experience, and the Western with social optimism. Lange's longing is for a country and a culture that never was his, that never even existed as he imagines it, and which therefore can function only as a future memory for himself and for the community.

I have so far mentioned the ways in which *Le Crime de Monsieur Lange* looks to redress some of the injuries of patriarchy, class privilege, capital and high art. But it also reworks prevailing discourses about colonialism and ethnicity to remind us of other differences that have been sidelined in French culture and society. Racism is inseparable from colonialism, and Arizona Jim combats them both. Cathala, the name of the publisher in an earlier draft, 'hates Indians', so one magazine cover illustrates Arizona Jim's rescue of an 'Indian' girl (Estelle). If the 'gangsters' (in Arizona!?) can be imagined stealing 'the miners' pay' (six thousand miners, three gangsters), while Arizona Jim spends half his time rescuing 'Negroes' (in Arizona!?) from the slave-driver or from a lynching, that is because these fictions are a reminder that French workers suffer from an internal colonialism that is homologous with France's external colonialism in North and sub-Saharan Africa. This is a discursive reach that is by no means extravagant, inasmuch as the homology is drawn in other films of the period like *Pépé le Moko* (1936) – the Casbah as Montmartre – and *Princesse Tam Tam* (1935) – see for instance the sense of ease at the *bal populaire* experienced by Aouina (Josephine Baker), compared with the stuffiness of the upper crust. Lange's Arizona signifies French workers' displacement from their 'homeland'. The projected community (the 'nation'), with its imaginary geography, that is to be restored to the 'miners' and 'Negroes' and 'Indians' through the exploits of Arizona Jim will clearly not be one with the existing French state of 1936. This is a new meaning for the film's courtyard, for the geography of its social relations, a meaning that does not include the principles of territoriality and sovereignty that define the contemporary nation–state.

Paris *is* in Arizona now, an imagined Paris which redeems all differences. Paris is in Arizona when Lange's fantasy world becomes the model for the conduct of the fantasy world of the film. That in turn becomes a model for the conduct of real life, a *mise-en-abyme* in which the members of the collective find their own identities projected and extended in the fictional roles they assume. Valentine sees herself as the 'Mexican' woman in love with Arizona Jim (Lange), while his sidekick is played by the printwork foreman (Marcel Duhamel), and the enemy is the General played by the old concierge.

Inspector Juliani, Batala's cousin, who was forced to resign from the Sûreté Nationale and became a croupier, is also cast as an enemy of the people. The newsboy Charles is a cowboy and his sweetheart Estelle an 'Indian'. Even the loss of her baby, fathered by her rape by Batala, has been worked into one of Lange's Arizona Jim stories ('She was lucky; the baby died'). Thus the characters in *Le Crime de Monsieur Lange* have parts to play in the movies or stories they make which frequently intersect with the parts they play in the 'real life' community to which they belong. This community even puts itself at risk, by admitting individual racism in the person of the old concierge, who makes no distinction between 'Indians', 'Indo-Chinese' and 'Negroes', and places them all in Tonkin as his representative French colonial outpost. Because the concierge is a veteran and wears a beret, I assume we are to associate him with one of the fascist leagues, perhaps Colonel de la Rocque's Croix de Feu (he is, ironically, associated with waste throughout, since he is shown either hauling the garbage or fussing about the plumbing). *Le Crime de Monsieur Lange* articulates the relationship between personal subjectivity and communal identity. It does this by representing cultural fictions (stories and movies) as the very *mise-en-scène* of people's conflicts. Their very existence is therefore mediated and transformed by their cultural practices. Film, this film, represents a new form of desire for the 1930s. It is in this way that the film makes radical sense of the politics of culture. The imagined has become the imaginary. The community in itself has become the community for itself.

That the community projected by the film was never a lived community, never actualized outside the collective imaginations of film-makers and spectators, is not quite the point. First of all, the aspirations of the film and the conditions of the historical Popular Front alliance were not in fact identical, and one should not confuse the two. As I have argued, *Le Crime de Monsieur Lange* invented a sort of popular front rather different from the actual one that preserved the established community/nation(as)–state. But this is why *Le Crime de Monsieur Lange* also raises the question of who gets to imagine the nation or community and on whose behalf. The film may have fallen short of reality because what it imagined spoke for no strong political movement in French society. The film's recommendation of direct action (through violence), worker control of production and a spontaneous transformation of society through new forms of social organization from below belongs to an anarchist or revolutionary syndicalist model of change. Such a model is in the tradition of a libertarian socialism that was resolutely anti-Bolshevik and would therefore have had no sympathy for the PCF (French Communist Party) and its solidarity with the Comintern. Nor could such a model countenance anything like the sort of Popular Front tactics that made a distinction (and set a priority) as between the defeat of fascism and the movement for worker control. Furthermore, the film's very idea of community involves the rejection of all forms of political authority, including the laws and judicial processes of the nation–state, in favour of the decentralized socialism of the self-regulated group. If France in 1935 could offer no strong political movement that articulated this anarchist model of revolutionary change, Spain did (the long history of the Confederación Nacional de Trabajo), and the Spanish Civil War would soon pit competing left-wing models at one another's throat (the PSUC versus the POUM). One might imagine or project a transformation of society like that dreamt by *Le Crime de Monsieur Lange*, but the political reality in France, even before the elections of 1936, was always much more like *La Marseillaise*.

However, if the Spanish political tradition is kept in mind, then the political origins and the political tenor of *Le Crime de Monsieur Lange* may indeed lie much more with its Spanish contributor, Joan Castanyer, than with either of its principal French voices, Jean Renoir and Jacques Prévert (not to discount the latter's *cultural* anarchism). Castanyer was a minor member of the Groupe Octobre, and a painter and a designer, who did sets for Renoir's *La Nuit du carrefour* (1932), *Boudu sauvé des eaux* (1932) and *Chotard et Cie* (1933) and worked on a short film with Jacques Becker. An anarchist and a Catalan, he had been in Paris since the late 1920s, but when the Spanish Civil War broke out he returned to Barcelona where he set up Laia Films in November 1936 under the Propaganda Commissariat of the Generalitat of Catalonia. From this point until the end of the war Castanyer supervised the production of over 200 newsreels and documentaries and wrote commentaries for all of them in his native Catalan. When the war was lost, he went into exile in Paris.[8] Castanyer's association with dissident causes in art and political life seems difficult to ignore in relation to his probable influence upon *Le Crime de Monsieur Lange*.

In early versions of the screenplay, the frontier at which the opening sequence of the film is set is not with Belgium; it is in the Pyrennées with (Catalonian?) Spain. And one draft of the screenplay includes the instruction to 'give to this first scene the aspect of an idyll'. At least in somebody's mind, Spain (anarchist Spain), and not the Soviet Union, was the promised land in 1935–6. In view of the quick turn taken by events, in France, in Spain, and in the Soviet Union, *Le Crime de Monsieur Lange* continues to live simply as a future memory for another popular front.

## Notes

1 For the rhetoric, speeches, sloganeering and promises of the Popular Front, see Julian Jackson (1988) *The Popular Front in France*, the best book in English on the subject.
2 Here (and later) my use of terms like 'sense', 'common sense' or 'negotiate' should advertise my debt to Gramsci's account of the interactive relationship of the base/superstructure model, his notion of hegemony and the active role he allows for a popular, social consciousness in political, economic and cultural life (see Hoare and

Nowell-Smith 1971, and Forgacs and Nowell-Smith 1984). For example, *Le Crime de Monsieur Lange* makes no direct allusion to the Aéropostale, Marthe Hanau, Albert Oustric or Serge-Alexandre Stavisky affairs, but an audience could not fail to recognize that these and similar scandals lay behind the creation of Batala and his swindles. Batala's fortunes are also explicitly tied to the false witness of the clergy, the influence of the right-wing press, the power of the fascist leagues (the repeated reference to the right-wing terrorist *Cagoulards*: 'Arizona Jim vs cagoulard'). When Batala returns to Paris disguised as a priest, he stops to buy *L'Echo de Paris*, the daily paper of the Catholic right, a paper which, incidentally, hated the Groupe Octobre with an undisguised passion. It is noteworthy that in an early version of the screenplay Batala was called Carbuccha (or Carbuccia), after Horace de Carbuccia, the publisher of *Gringoire*, the largest weekly in the country, and one of the most extreme anti-republican and anti-Semitic newspapers of the 1930s. When the character's name was next changed to Cathala, the allusion now tied the publishing house to the government, because Pierre Cathala was the Minister of Agriculture in the 1935–6 Laval government. Working through all of these names and their associations in this way shows how the creative process produced meanings designed to situate the film within the dynamics of its moment.

3 A hegemonic model of the social formation, and this is the point, understands different levels or forms of consciousness, such that contradiction within as well as between classes and interest groups is not only inevitable but always potentially productive. So the dim-witted son of the innkeeper at the Franco-Belgian frontier is given a voice that contradicts the best interests of his class; Meunier *fils* is a wealthy, upper-class buffoon who indulges the notion of a workers' co-operative. In an early look at the film in *The Social Cinema of Jean Renoir* (Faulkner 1986, 58–71), I drew attention to the film's contradictions, but under the influence of a somewhat straitened Althusserianism saw them as evidence of ideological compromise. The example of Gramsci creates a place for the concept of 'intelligibility' while acknowledging the contradictory social and historical dynamics that lie behind it.

4 Robert Desnos' idea to plant advertising prospectuses in the midst of other texts is mentioned by Dawn Ades (1978, 189).

5 The phrase 'the white eyelid of the screen' ('el párpado blanco de la pantalla') is Buñuel's, from his essay 'Cinema, Instrument of Poetry', in Aranda (1975, 273).

6 My thoughts about incongruity were stimulated by an article on Desnos by David Wills (1996).

7 Early drafts of the screenplay invent other titles from the sensational and the serial press. In the very first synopsis, dated 15 April 1935, the Lange character corrects proofs for *Les Causes célèbres*, a paper that deals with 'des affaires policières'. In a later draft, the publishing house is called 'Société Anonyme de Publications Populaires' and produces *Le Boy-Scout, La Petite Lisette* and *L'Hebdomadaire illustré*. MS drafts of the screenplay are at Bifi, Paris, Fonds Jean Renoir, Boîte 2, Dossier 5. My deep thanks to Caroline Fieschi and the staff of the Archives at Bifi for providing access to this material.

8 Information on Castanyer's career – still rather scanty – comes from Gubern (1979, 169–70). My thanks to José Sanchez Mosquera for help with the translation from Spanish.

## Selected bibliography

Abel, Richard (1988) *French Film Theory and Criticism 1907–1939,* vol. II: *1929–1939,* Princeton, Princeton University Press.
Ades, Dawn (1978) *Dada and Surrealism Reviewed,* London, Arts Council of Great Britain.
Andrew, Dudley (1995) *Mists of Regret, Culture and Sensibility in Classic French Film,* Princeton, Princeton University Press.
Aranda, Francisco (1975) *Luis Buñuel: A Critical Biography,* London, Secker & Warburg.
Bazin, André (1973) *Jean Renoir,* New York, Simon & Schuster.
Bellanger, Claude, Godechot, Jacques, Aviral, Pierre and Terron, Fernand (1972) *Histoire Générale de la Presse Française,* vol. III, Paris, Presses Universitaires de France.
Bernard, Philippe and Dubief, Henri (1985) *The Decline of the Third Republic, 1914–1938,* Cambridge, Cambridge University Press.
Breton, André (1972) *Manifestoes of Surrealism,* Ann Arbor, University of Michigan.
Conley, Katharine (1996) *Automatic Woman,* Lincoln, University of Nebraska.
Faulkner, Christopher (1986) *The Social Cinema of Jean Renoir,* Princeton, Princeton University Press.
Fauré, Michel (1977) *Le Groupe Octobre,* Paris, Christian Bourgois.
Forgacs, David and Nowell-Smith, Geoffrey (eds) (1984) *Antonio Gramsci, Selections from the Cultural Writings,* Cambridge, Cambridge University Press.
Gauteur, Claude (ed.) (1974) *Jean Renoir, Ecrits 1926–1971,* Paris, Belfond.
Gubern, Roman (1979) *Cine Español en el exilio (1936–1939).* Barcelona, Lumen.
Hoare, Quintin and Nowell-Smith, Geoffrey (eds) (1971) *Antonio Gramsci, Selections from the Prison Notebooks,* New York, International Publishers.
Jackson, Julian (1988) *The Popular Front in France,* Cambridge, Cambridge University Press.
Prévert, Jacques (1990) *Le Crime de Monsieur Lange, Les Portes de la nuit* (with an introduction by André Heinrich), Paris, Gallimard.
Renoir, Jean (1974) *My Life and My Films,* New York, Atheneum.
*La Révolution Surréaliste* (1924–8), nos 1–11.
Wills, David (1996) 'Slit Screen', in Rudolf Kuenzli (ed.), *Dada and Surrealist Film,* Cambridge, Mass., MIT Press, 86–98.

## Appendix

### *Jean Renoir (1894–1979): filmography*

See Chapter 3, on *La Bête humaine,* for full filmography.

### *Other films cited in the text*

*L'Affaire est dans le sac,* Pierre Prévert (1932)
*La Bête humaine (The Human Beast* [UK]; *Judas Was a Woman* [USA]), Jean Renoir (1938)

*Boudu sauvé des eaux* (*Boudu Saved from Drowning*), Jean Renoir (1932)
*Un chien andalou*, Luis Buñuel and Salvador Dalí (1929)
*Chotard et Cie*, Jean Renoir (1933)
*Le Crime de Monsieur Lange*, Jean Renoir (1935)
*La Grande illusion* (*Grand Illusion*), Jean Renoir (1937)
*Jean de la lune*, Jean Choux (1930)
*Le Jour se lève* (*Daybreak*), Marcel Carné (1939)
*Judex*, Louis Feuillade (1917)
*La Marseillaise*, Jean Renoir (1938)
*Le Million*, René Clair (1931)
*La Nuit du carrefour* (*Night at the Crossroads*), Jean Renoir (1932)
*L'Opéra de quat'sous*, G. W. Pabst (1930)
*Pépé le Moko*, Julien Duvivier (1937)
*Princesse Tam Tam*, Edmond Gréville (1935)
*Les Vampires*, Louis Feuillade (1915)

# 3

# THE FLEEING GAZE

## Jean Renoir's *La Bête humaine* (1938)

*Michele Lagny*

'*La Bête humaine* is dead': that headline, which appeared in a January 1987 issue of the newspaper *Le Monde*, quoted a remark made by a train driver during one of the most serious strikes in the history of French railways. The report then listed his lengthy complaints about working conditions and, above all, the 'loneliness on the engines; there used to be two of us, and we'd always talk a bit. We've been driving alone for the last three years.'[1] The visual memory of the reader immediately conjures up the opening shot of Renoir's film, where the camera, by tracking back to reveal, behind the gaping mouth of the locomotive, the fireman shovelling in coal and the engine driver at his controls, constructs a centaur with a steel body and a double human bust. At the same time, echoes of old interviews crowd back into the mind – interviews that explicitly recognized the railwaymen's right to dignity in their work which was one of the strikers' demands during the winter of 1986–7: 'The railwayman's job is no joke, it is a grand profession. For some, it's almost a vocation.'[2]

The 'human beast' that persists in our collective memory clearly has nothing to do with Emile Zola's main source of inspiration for his novel: 'the strange case of hereditary criminals who, although not mad, commit murder one day in a morbid fit, driven on by an animal instinct'.[3] That cliché surely harks back to the railway world of the prewar film, rather than the one portrayed in Zola's late nineteenth-century text. The railway setting, although important, is no more than a backdrop in the opening two chapters of the novel, which are devoted to the murderous jealousy of Roubaud, the deceived husband, and the hereditary *fêlure* (flaw in its twin senses of 'defect' and 'crack') caused by Jacques Lantier's alcoholic antecedents. It is only when the murder sets the story going that Zola begins to emphasize the collective nature of the railwaymen's work and their relationship with their engines: 'Usually the two men got on very well in this long intimacy that took them from one end of the line to the other, shaken together side by side, taciturn, united in the same job with the same dangers'; this remark in fact comes as a

secondary one, for it is preceded by a description of the almost sexual relationship Lantier has with his locomotive, which he loves 'with masculine
gratitude' (Zola 1977, 156 and 155).

Renoir, on the other hand, devotes his opening sequence to the activity of
the locomotive, a powerful beast driven by human toil, and turns what was
a sometimes criticized book ('Zola's novel is very bad . . . it is an interminable and insipid serial') into a widely admired film: 'It is true cinema, and
of the best kind. . . . All film-makers have dragged bits of railway engines
into their stories, whether relevant or not. This time, the engine is the
subject of the film, and it is very thoroughly worked . . . with the driver
handling his controls on one side, and the fireman shovelling in his coal on
the other.'[4]

Publicity for the film emphasized the popular imagery of the railwayman
right from the moment it was being prepared up until its release, which was
aided by a massive press campaign. Reactions were unanimous, from the
Communist daily, *Ce Soir*, which ran a whole series of interviews with
Renoir, to right-wing papers and trade journals. Maurice Bessy (*Cinémonde*)
was the most enthusiastic: 'This is the finest film I have seen in ten years'
(Chardère 1962, 265). But even the extreme right-wing critic François
Vinneuil (alias Lucien Rebatet) recognized that 'the film is the least fatuous
of any based on a Zola novel' (Chardère 1962, 268). It did well at the box
office: its first run lasted for four months after a meticulously prepared opening at the cinema La Madeleine just before Christmas 1938; it was later
shown at the Venice Biennale and won the Prix Méliès.[5]

The success of *La Bête humaine* has continued ever since: articles and chapters of books devoted to Renoir all pass favourable judgment on the 'thirty-
year-old masterpiece'.[6] Equally admired are Renoir's faithfulness to the spirit
of Zola and the film's value as a documentary on railwaymen's lives or on the
atmosphere in France at the end of the Popular Front; 'Renoir assimilates
Zola, and surpasses him in analytical insight' (Serceau 1985, 77); 'He is
totally in sympathy with the two engine drivers';[7] 'No one could have failed
to notice the pessimistic content of the film . . . It buried the hopes of the
Popular Front' (Viry-Babel 1986, 109, 111). In the last analysis, the 1987
rail striker was absolutely right: the relevance of *La Bête humaine* remains
undimmed.

## A three-star film

At the end of 1938, the constellation in question – Zola, Renoir and Gabin –
stood out brightly against a rather sombre sky. Both the shooting (in September) and the release (on 23 December) of *La Bête humaine* took place at a
time when the storm clouds were gathering: not only was the Popular Front
in its death throes, but above all there was enormous anxiety about the
international crisis, which had been only temporarily eased by Munich.

The organizers of the advertising campaign for *La Bête humaine* must have asked themselves: what does the film offer by way of reassurance and escape? What they decided to bank on were, in the following order:

1   'The fame of Zola, whom everyone has read'
2   'The reputation of Renoir, the wonderful director of *La Grande illusion*'
3   'Gabin's talent'[8]

It would seem, in fact, that it was Gabin who, whether intentionally or not, was the driving force behind the making of the film. He had prepared to play a railwayman in a film which Jean Grémillon had been asked to make by the Hakim brothers; but Grémillon's screenplay, entitled *Train d'enfer*, was not to the producers' liking, so they turned to the celebrated Renoir, who had the idea of adapting the popular Zola novel (Viry-Babel 1986, 107). Whatever their respective importance, there was a strong link between the three partners: Renoir and Zola were old acquaintances (*Nana*, 1926); the Renoir–Gabin connection was more recent but well-established (*Les Bas-fonds*, 1936, *La Grande illusion*, 1937); and Gabin–Zola was an ideal combination: 'I only regret one thing, and that is that Zola can't see Gabin interpret the character. I think he'd be pleased.'[9]

It would be hard to say which of the three stars had the greatest charisma. Zola, 'whom everyone has read', was a staple of middle-class culture: his success was reflected by the many editions of his works and the large number of copies printed.[10] While school anthologies included extracts from his novels[11] the Société Littéraire des Amis de Zola invited Renoir to lecture on his adaptation at the Sorbonne.[12] Renoir in 1938 was not just 'the wonderful director of *La Grande illusion*' (which topped the box office in 1937): unlike most directors at that time, he enjoyed the status of an *auteur*, like a writer. True, not all his films had been outright successes, but the failure of *Toni* and the cool reception given to *Les Bas-fonds* and *La Marseillaise* were compensated for by the critical acclaim accorded to *Le Crime de Monsieur Lange* and the critical and box office triumph of *La Grande illusion*. As for Gabin, 'the only French star' (Vincendeau 1985a, 243–397), he had built up his brand image in ten or so films which, from *La Bandera* to *Le Quai des brumes*, made him the working-class hero *par excellence* of the French cinema: as late as 1986 a photograph of him wearing a cloth cap in *La Belle équipe* appeared on the cover of Geneviève Guillaume-Grimaud's book on Popular Front cinema. The way Gabin's star image was built up has been so thoroughly analysed elsewhere that there is no point in covering that ground again.[13] As I have already noted, the producers were prompt to seize on that image as the linchpin of the film.

Interestingly, the triple combination of Zola, Renoir and Gabin gives us a clue as to why *La Bête humaine* was such a success: it reflected both the vigour of the French cinema of the 1930s and a society which contemporary nostalgia had transformed into a stable model. 'This most perfect form of Poetic Realism' (Viry-Babel 1986, 108) has been perceived as a model of social documentary, but also as 'a symphony of the railways, of speed, of the engine, of work' (Guillaume-Grimaud 1986, 72), the lyrical expression of a lost world. It was, basically, an excellent 'populist recipe' of the 1930s. The film displayed all the right credentials: it was an adaptation of a text whose literary worth was recognized, and Renoir made it quite clear that he had remained faithful to the spirit of Zola, putting the name of Denise Leblond-Zola on the credit titles, which conclude with Zola's signature and portrait, and announcing that he had used the novelist's own preparatory notes. Let me list its basic ingredients:

*A story of love and fatality:* 'Jean Renoir says: my first love story for a long time.'[14] Its theme echoed that of 'the great Greek tragedies . . . Jacques Lantier, the humble railway mechanic, could belong to the family of the Atridae'.[15]

*Realism, based on documentary value:* the engine driver was based on a possible character in real life who had to be described in as accurate a manner as possible thanks to the research which Renoir says he carried out (along the lines of Zola's own researches)[16] – he insisted on the contribution made by the French railways management and of the railwaymen's trade union, and even more on the efforts made by the actors (Gabin and Carette) to learn the skills of the characters they were playing. This 'document effect' justified the making of certain changes to Zola's original: by setting the film in the 1930s instead of the late nineteenth century and thus rendering an expensive reconstruction unnecessary, Renoir not only made a vital saving but avoided the faintly ridiculous quaintness of 1860–70 rolling stock. The use of modern engines entailed a change in the characters: in the 1930s 'railway workers are an elite; they are well educated and very conscious of their duties'.[17] Better even:

> Transposing the story to a contemporary setting also made me change its ending. First of all because modern railway control methods are such nowadays as to render the story of this runaway train, tearing driverless through the countryside, more than improbable. Secondly, the France of today is not that of Napoleon III and as it stands with its qualities and its faults, I think that it deserves to be defended to the last breath by all its citizens. The author of *J'accuse . . . !* would probably agree with me on that point.[18]

I wonder whether I have quoted Renoir at sufficient length to give the flavour of his hypocrisy – or the illusions of his period(?) Zola's driverless train careering through the countryside with its cargo of cannon fodder would surely not have struck filmgoers in 1938 as an absurd invention.

*A touch of socio-political commitment* added vital zest to the film. It was provided by the model of Zola who, 'in situating his heroes in the working class, in allowing them concerns which, in previous literary works, seemed to be the preserve of bourgeois and aristocratic characters', acted as a 'great revolutionary'.[19] The authors of the film were regarded as left-wing: Zola, author of *J'accuse . . . !*, was the man whose portrait was carried on Popular Front marches alongside those of Léon Blum and Maurice Thorez (and whose defence of the crushing of the Commune was occulted); and Renoir was the leader of Ciné-Liberté, who worked for the Communist Party (*La Vie est à nous*) and with the CGT (*La Marseillaise*), before being accused of betraying the working class – precisely in *La Bête humaine*. Political commitment, which is obvious in Zola's original (though he set his novel twenty years before the time at which he wrote it), is less clear-cut in Renoir, even if he saw his work as a manifesto against 'ordinary fascism' and even a weapon against Hitler (though these statements were made in interviews given thirty years after he made the film[20]). Lastly, a popular actor was needed to play a working-class figure – no one could have suspected that Gabin would turn into the big landowner of 1962 who was sued by evicted farmers (Vincendeau 1985a, 252).

Built on an intertextual grid which takes us constantly from the film to the novel, from contemporary criticism to historicizing analysis, from authorial discourse to hagiographical excess, Renoir's *La Bête humaine* is an unavoidable monument – hence the cultural reference brought out by the *Le Monde* headline in the article quoted at the beginning of this chapter.

## Discordant notes

*La Bête humaine* has, however, come in for occasional criticism. The attacks on the film on grounds of immorality which, when it was re-released in 1945, resulted in its being banned in various parts of France, were no doubt circumstantial epiphenomena. On the other hand, François Poulle (writing not long after May 1968) demanded that the director should stand trial before the Court of History on a charge of betrayal and a 'missed rendez-vous' with the French working class. He criticized Renoir mainly for being unfaithful to Zola, who had 'succeeded in turning the novel into a weapon and a study' for 'a social stocktaking' before a process of reorganization; the director, on the other hand, had not understood a thing about the working class 'whereas *La Bête humaine* could have been the springboard for an authentic French realist school' if only 'Zola's analysis and construction' had been respected 'in the first place' (Poulle 1969, 28, 163).

Most analyses have similarly concentrated on the comparative – in this case social – value of the film and the novel. Apart from one analysis of Renoir's cinematic transposition of the visual qualities displayed by Zola (Gauthier 1968, 29–34), the main subject of debate has been Renoir's departures from the original story line, for example the elision of the socio-political background (resulting from Renoir's drastic slimming down of the role of the investigating magistrate Denizet), the deformation of certain characters (Cabuche in particular, who changes from a quarryman to a kind of drop-out who – as played by Renoir himself – foreshadows Octave in *La Règle du jeu*), the removal of certain spectacular episodes (the snowing up of the locomotive, or the derailment caused by Flore) or the intrusion of new elements such as the 'railwaymen's dance', which is very much in the tradition of the popular merrymaking scenes that run right through the French films of the 1930s.[21]

All these analyses, like the sometimes critical examination of the documentary value of Renoir's reconstitution of the railwaymen's world, regard the film as a vehicle for a series of psycho-sociological representations, but lose sight of its cinematic specificity. This relative indifference to the cinematic text is confirmed by the fact that *La Bête humaine* has been the subject of far fewer articles than *La Grande illusion* or *La Régle du jeu*.[22] It is almost as if critics were content merely to recognize its intrinsic value while at the same time baulking at an ambiguity in it which is difficult to circumscribe – but which one critic sensed as early as 1939: 'This film, like [Renoir's] others, is a remarkable film . . . But there is a certain clumsiness in its construction and in the delineation of its characters. At times it is ponderous and slow. One loses sight of a subject one was just about to get interested in. . . . And overall it is a little disappointing . . . despite some brilliant moments.'[23]

These remarks suggest that it might be worthwhile circumscribing both the way in which an image that is easily identifiable and appropriable by the spectator has been built up, and its possible weaknesses. In order to do so, I shall strive to evaluate structurally the mythical figure of *La Bête humaine* as constructed by intertextual analysis. I shall restrict myself here to two of the factors which encourage spectator involvement: first, the coherence of filmic causality which makes narrative comprehension possible and, secondly, the complex interplay of gazes which facilitates secondary cinematic identification,[24] especially when the spectator is placed in the characters' line of vision. A careful reading of the film from these two angles produces surprising results.

## Dislocation of the narrative thread

In order to test filmic continuity and analyse the relationship it sets up between successive diegetic events, I have used the analytical grid proposed by *Générique des années 30* (Lagny, Ropars and Sorlin 1986), which was established on the basis of a corpus of films dating from 1936 to 1939. It makes it possible to break the film down into twenty-three sequences whose demarcation hinges on punctuations and on the pinpointing of narrative units. To bring out the articulation of those units, I have given priority to the notion

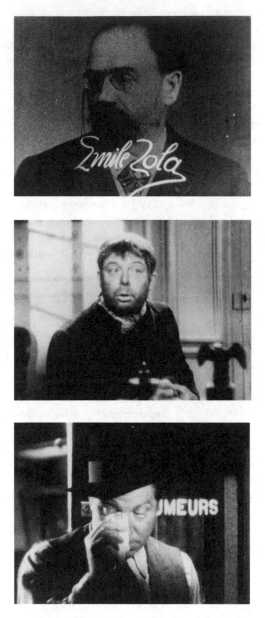

*La Bête humaine* – 'a three-star film': above: Emile Zola;
center: Jean Renoir; below: Jean Gabin.

of 'implication', i.e. to the type of causality that holds the series of sequences together, whether it is logical–diegetic, chronological or indeterminate ('suspended implication').[25]

| SEQUENCE LENGTH AND CONTENT | 'IMPLICATION' | INTERNAL TEMPORALITY | PLACE |
|---|---|---|---|
| Seq. 1 <br> 4'12" <br> Pecqueux (Carette) and Lantier (Gabin) on locomotive | | Continuity | Railway line |
| | Fade-out, chrono. | | |
| Seq. 2 <br> 2'17" <br> Engine arrives at platform; quarrel between Roubaud (Ledoux) and passenger; engine backs out of station | | Continuity | Station |
| | Cut, chrono. | | |
| Seq. 3 <br> 3'1" <br> Roubaud and Séverine (Simone Simon) decide to go to Paris to see her godfather | | Continuity | Flat in Le Havre |
| | Cut, suspension | | |
| Seq. 4 <br> 4' <br> Evening spent together by driver and fireman | | Continuity with ellipses, dissolves | Engine depot |
| | Fade-out, logical–diegetic | | |
| Seq. 5 <br> 2'20" <br> Lantier at his godmother's | | Continuity with ellipses | Gatekeeper's house |
| | Cut, logical–diegetic | | |
| Seq. 6 <br> 5'3" <br> Flore and Lantier; his first fit | | Continuity | Countryside |
| | Fade-out, suspension | | |
| Seq. 7 <br> 5'3" <br> Roubauds in Paris; Séverine beaten up and admits relationship with Grandmorin | | Continuity with beginning of alternation | Station; flat, Paris; Hotel Grandmorin; flat |
| | Fade-out, chrono. | | |

| | | | |
|---|---|---|---|
| Seq. 8<br>5'3"<br>Train journey; murder of<br>Grandmorin; Lantier and<br>Séverine meet | | Alternation | Train<br>platform/<br>carriage/<br>corridor |
| | Fade-out, chrono. | | |
| Seq. 9<br>5'11"<br>Discovery of murder;<br>Roubaud, then Lantier,<br>at home | | Successive<br>continuities | Station;<br>engine;<br>depot; flat |
| | Fade-out,<br>suspension,<br>indeterminate<br>chrono. | | |
| Seq. 10<br>1'55"<br>Séverine and Lantier meet<br>and talk | | Continuity | Public<br>garden |
| | Fade-out<br>suspension,<br>indeterminate<br>chrono. | | |
| Seq. 11<br>4'11"<br>Magistrate's<br>investigations;<br>arrest of Cabuche<br>(Renoir) | | Alternation | Magistrate's<br>office;<br>corridor |
| | Fade-out,<br>suspension,<br>indeterminate<br>chrono. | | |
| Seq. 12<br>6'20"<br>Lantier at Roubaud's flat;<br>replaces him in Séverine's<br>affections | | Continuity,<br>successive<br>scenes | Flat; railway<br>track; flat |
| | Fade-out,<br>suspension | | |
| Autonomous segment<br>34"<br>Driver and fireman on the<br>engine | | Continuity | Engine |
| | Dissolve,<br>suspension | | |
| Seq. 13<br>2'2"<br>First nocturnal meeting<br>between Lantier and<br>Séverine | | Continuity<br>with ellipses | Engine<br>depot, night |
| | Fade-out,<br>suspension | | |

| | | | |
|---|---|---|---|
| Autonomous segment 27″ Roubaud in the café; loses at cards | | Continuity | Café |
| | Cut, suspension | | |
| Seq. 14 3′22″ Lantier in the engine depot; goes to join Séverine | | Continuity with ellipses | Engine depot, night |
| | Fade-out, suspension | | |
| Seq. 15 2′9″ Roubaud comes home to fetch money; row with Séverine | | Continuity | Flat |
| | Dissolve, suspension | | |
| Seq. 16 5′7″ Lantier and Séverine; she describes Grandmorin's murder | | Continuity with ellipses | Flat, Paris |
| | Fade-out, suspension, indeterminate chrono. | | |
| Seq. 17 3′47″ Lantier cannot kill Roubaud | | Continuity | Engine depot, night |
| | Fade-out, suspension | | |
| Seq. 18 1′13″ Shunting on the engine | | Continuity | Engine |
| | Fade-out, suspension | | |
| Seq. 19 7′23″ Railwaymen's dance; Lantier tries to win back Séverine | | Continuity | Dancehall and garden |
| | Cut, chrono. | | |
| Seq. 20 7′30″ Lantier joins Séverine at her flat and kills her | | Alternation | Flat; dancehall |
| | Cut, chrono. | | |

| | | | |
|---|---|---|---|
| Seq. 21<br>1'45"<br>Lantier in street;<br>Roubaud discovers the<br>dead Séverine | | Alternation | Street; flat;<br>railway track |
| | Dissolve, chrono. | | |
| Seq. 22<br>3'53"<br>Just before the train<br>leaves, Lantier tells<br>Pecqueux what he has<br>done | | Continuity<br>with ellipses | Engine |
| | Dissolve, chrono. | | |
| Seq. 23<br>3'24"<br>Reverse journey of seq. 1;<br>Lantier's suicide;<br>Pecqueux stops the train | | Continuity<br>with ellipses | Engine |
| | Dissolve, chrono. | | |
| Pecqueux closes Lantier's<br>eyes; service resumes | | Continuity | Railway<br>track |

End

Up to the moment when Lantier and Séverine get involved with each other, at the time of the murder (which comes more than thirty minutes after the beginning of the film), two narrative threads unfold side by side, each successively interrupting the other: the breakdown of the locomotive, which is hinted at as early as sequence 2, explains why the two drivers stay in the engine depot (seq. 4) and why Lantier goes to see his godmother, who in turn tells him (seq. 5) to join Flore (seq. 6). Meanwhile, Roubaud's visit to his wife (seq. 3) follows, but is not determined by, his altercation with an 'important' passenger (seq. 2); and the decision to visit Séverine's godfather in Paris does not come into effect until sequence 7. The simultaneity of the two narratives is only briefly referred to by the dialogue in sequences 2 and 7. The whole series of sequences is all the more incoherent because this establishing phase comprises powerful punctuation marks which contradict possible continuities: for example, the locomotive's arrival at the station is disrupted because a fade-out and a pause in the music come between an impressionistic shot of an empty and mist-swathed Le Havre station and a close shot showing the engine at the platform.[26]

Detailed analysis of the mode of 'implication' shows the predominance of suspended sequences or sequences with a weak or indeterminate chronological relationship; the rupture effect is further accentuated by the frequency of fade-outs. Two very short segments (of 34 and 27 seconds), one showing Lantier on his engine, the other Roubaud in the café, sandwich the lovers' first nocturnal rendezvous and appear to be independent of the film's chronological development. Similarly, it is hard to ascertain the temporal relationship which might link sequences 14 and 15: is it the same night that Roubaud loses at cards (segment at the end of seq. 13) and goes home to get some money (seq. 15)? But then how is Séverine, whom we have just seen with Lantier (seq. 14), already there? A chronological thread is firmly established only during the last twenty-five minutes of the film, reinforced by the use of dissolves: it connects together the dance, the murder while the dance continues, Lantier's flight intercut with Roubaud's discovery of the body, the departure of the train, and Lantier's suicide. But the circularity caused by a repetition in reverse of the train's journey (seq. 23 repeats images from seq. 1) produces a loop and temporal condensation effect. This effect is all the more powerful because no indications of a chronological nature make it possible to measure the relative duration of the story's various episodes. The novel, by contrast, is firmly structured with indications of the date or the time at the beginning of each chapter; these establish precise causality which enables the story to be linearized and not to come to such an abrupt end as it does in the film.

At the same time, there are internal breaks in the sequential continuities – in sequence 2, for example, where Roubaud's altercation with the sugar magnate is sandwiched by two series of shots showing the activity of the men driving the locomotive; or in sequence 7, when the shot of the waiting husband is abruptly interrupted by some shots of Séverine at her godfather's. In both cases, the disruptive effect is accentuated by the editing: the high-angle close shot of the complaining passenger's dog and the façade of the Hotel Grandmorin, in sharp contrast with the buildings in the popular Saint-Lazare district, reinforce the fragmentation effect which can also be found, in a different way, in the 'episodic' structure of the segment that uses dissolves to link Gabin's and Carette's activities during their evening in the engine depot (seq. 4).

All this could explain the bewilderment of the critic quoted earlier, who said he sometimes lost the thread of the story. For the film to remain legible for the spectator, the latter has to take into account remote narrative clues and above all detect a whole network of repetitions/transformations which, by organising equivalences and substitutions, lend the narrative its compactness and coherence. This network is very dense, and I shall cite only two examples, leaving aside the train motif, which has been very thoroughly discussed elsewhere,[27] and which acts as a veritable 'binding agent' throughout the text.

My first example concerns the formation of the Lantier–Séverine couple, which is alluded to right at the start of the film (two shots of Lantier and Séverine are linked by a dissolve before the title of the film comes up), but which is postponed until sequence 8, more than half an hour into the film. In fact their meeting is already prefigured by the similarity in the way the two characters are shown at the end of sequences 6 and 7. Each sequence closes with a fade-out on a close-up shot of a face with a glazed expression: first Lantier's, after his row with Flore, then Séverine's, who has just been beaten up by Roubaud; Lantier is shown in a low-angle shot against an almost abstract sky, Séverine in a high-angle shot, but with her eyes looking up. They seem like fellow victims of their *fêlure*, whether it be the hereditary defect referred to explicitly in the quotation from Zola used as an epigraph at the end of the credits and mentioned again in the dialogue with Flore, or the mental block Séverine suffers from because she was raped as a child, which she reiterates later (seq. 12: 'I cannot love'). In this way the conjunction, at once plausible and impossible, of the two characters is heralded.

Two other networks of recurrences organize Roubaud's replacement by Lantier, and Lantier's replacement by Pecqueux. Although all three characters are seen together at the beginning of the film (seq. 2), they are subsequently shown only two at a time. The replacement of the husband by the lover materializes in sequence 12. In it, Roubaud encourages Lantier to come and see Séverine more often, while revealing himself to be fiercely jealous of an insignificant third man. The film plays on shifts in the positions of the characters, but more particularly on the two men's exits and entrances. After Lantier leaves, Séverine refuses to have any sexual relations with her husband, who in turn goes out. A general shot outside the building shows Lantier half cut off on the right of the screen, while Roubaud crosses the railway lines, stops for a moment (has he seen Lantier or not?), then continues on his way. Lantier goes back to Séverine, entering in exactly the same way as the amorous Roubaud did in seq. 3: he comes along the corridor and knocks on the door at the bottom of the stairs, down which a man is coming, just as when Roubaud arrived. This is immediately followed by the two autonomous segments whose chronological dysfunction I mentioned earlier. Finally, in sequence 16, Lantier joins Séverine in the same flat near Saint-Lazare station which was occupied by Roubaud in sequence 7. The two sequences work like exact replicas: the lover is shown waiting for the woman in exactly the same posture and framed in the same way as the husband. He gets up and goes to the door in exactly the same way, after the same ringing of the bell, and he puts the same care into preparing a snack (though it is a classier one, with cake and Malaga replacing pâté and red wine). Finally, and despite different framings, the dramatic content is similar: just as Séverine, when questioned by Roubaud, had admitted her relationship with Grandmorin, she describes, when egged on by Lantier, her feelings while the murder was being committed. Roubaud's threats ('You just wait and see what I'm going to do') are mirrored by Lantier's fantasy ('But we can't kill him'), and sequence 17 (the failed murder of the husband) refers back to sequence 8 (the murder of the ex-lover). Lantier's inability to carry out the act replaces Roubaud's actual violence, but the latter has already been contaminated by it since sequence 12, where he starts going to the cafe and sinking into apathetic resignation.

Pecqueux on the other hand is constantly represented as the shadow of the engine driver, but it is he who replaces him at the end, and who assumes his real power over the train. Lantier's face is replaced, in a dissolve, by his fireman's (the link between seq. 21 and seq. 22). It is he who helps his boss put on his work clothes, and he who stokes up the locomotive he later manages to stop after the driver's suicide. Of the four protagonists that Renoir retained from Zola's novel – 'the husband, his wife, her lover and the railway'[28] – the film erases the first three by replacing the ineffectual husband with an equally ineffectual lover, but retains the last protagonist through the replacement of Gabin by Carette.

The circularity of the film's course, its unwillingness to adopt a coherent, linear chronology, and the play of substitutions produce a condensed narrative which is riven with cracks, with *fêlures* that let the tragic flood in, but which also maintains possible openings on to the realm of the social. The very beginning of the film is echoed by its epilogue. The first three shots display a flawless coherence: the editing shows, in succession, the work of the men who feed and drive the engine (shot 1), its direct effect (shot 2: the axles of the driving wheels) and its final result (shot 3: the whole train moving along), and establishes a close link between action and reaction, man and machine. Pecqueux's action after the driver's suicide has the effect of stopping the train, but not rail traffic as a whole: a short epilogue, introduced by a dissolve, marks a pause by way of homage to the dead man, then work starts up again and the film ends with a general shot of the railway tracks. At this point the memory of the 'hereditary flaw' that was supposed to justify the story fades away and is replaced by a positive image of the railways.

## The fleeing gaze

Cracks and uncertainties are, however, maintained by the difficulty the spectator has in situating him/herself *vis-à-vis* the characters portrayed and the world represented. It is not a film in which it is easy to establish a subject of the gaze, as I shall try to suggest by making a few points about the interplay of gazes that takes place in it. I shall not dwell on it at length, partly because of lack of space, but also because it is a theme that has often been touched upon in discussions of *La Bête humaine*,[29] one of whose key scenes hinges on an intense exchange of looks. It comes in sequence 10, where a series of reverse-angle medium close-up shots of Lantier and Séverine enables Renoir to use Zola's sentence: 'Don't look at me like that, you'll wear your eyes out' – almost an echo of the contemporary *Le Quai des brumes* in which the hero, also played by Jean Gabin, pronounces the famous 'You've got beautiful eyes, you know.'

The first sequence of the film highlights the ambiguity of the place assigned to the spectator, despite an overall subjective effect. In the first three shots, the viewpoint remains external, while changing rapidly: the camera is placed, successively, behind the driver and the fireman, at the level of the driving wheels, and below the railway line. Very soon, as tracks, bridges and tunnels race past, we have the feeling we are at the front of the train in the position of the two drivers; this effect is all the stronger because several shots are apparently shown from their viewpoint. Yet we do not see things exactly through their eyes, which are anyway ostensibly masked by protective goggles: in actual fact, the way the shots are linked together does not allow 'internal focalization' to operate.[30] Thus, after the shot of Lantier leaning out of the door of his engine, the track is shown from the very front of the locomotive, and not from the supposed viewpoint of the driver; if that were so, the shot would be more to the side, with a part of the front of the engine in shot. That viewpoint is used several times during the film, but always independently of the driver's gaze; similarly, before the train arrives at the station, a sign marked 'Le Havre' is shown laterally, as if seen through a window. Unlike the novel (where everything is depicted through Lantier's eyes as he stands at the controls), the film both proposes and systematically denies the driver access to the gaze.

More particularly, in the novel, it is from the tunnel, where he has taken refuge, that Lantier sees the couple silhouetted against a window as they commit the murder; Renoir, on the other hand, puts Gabin in the corridor of the carriage where the crime is committed, so that neither he nor the spectator can witness an act which is hidden by blinds that are slammed down inside Grandmorin's private compartment, and which cannot be heard because of the roar of the train in the tunnel. Better even, Gabin gets a bit of smut in his eye, which entitles him to answer in the negative when asked by the police: 'Didn't you see anything?'

A network of recurrences emphasizes the central character's 'flawed gaze' – a series of close-ups of Gabin looking vacantly into the distance, all of which except the first are followed by a fade-out. This series, which begins with the last shot in sequence 5 (when Lantier's godmother has just reminded him of the effect his fits have on his behaviour), ties in with the closing shots of sequences 6 and 12 – first the already mentioned close-up that follows the row with Flore ('I think that women, for me . . .'), then the one showing that he accepts Séverine's rejection of his advances ('It's much better that way. . . . So let's just remain good friends . . .'). The series comes to an end with the last shot of sequence 17, where Gabin, framed from behind, leans his face against the side of a carriage and admits his powerlessness ('I can't do it') after failing to murder Roubaud. In the epilogue, after one last high-angle close-up of the dead Lantier, Pecqueux closes his eyes for good.

The point is that eyes are dangerous, as is shown by the remark of the magistrate Denizet just after arresting Cabuche: 'Did you see his eyes? I always recognize them from their eyes' (end of seq. 11). The reverse-angle shots of the interrogation scene did indeed give the tramp access to 'internal focalization'. On a less tragic plane, the gaze of the two voyeurs who first reveal Flore to us results in one of them being pushed into the water by the wild beauty, who later chides Lantier for looking at her 'like all the others do'. Finally, it is with her eyes that Séverine ensnares Lantier: both at their first meeting, in the carriage where the murder is committed, and at their first rendezvous, Lantier is caught in the vision that Séverine relays to the spectator. Although the reciprocity of the reverse-angle shots draws the man to his doom, the woman will have to die first. The gaze, when endorsed, is fatal: Cabuche, Séverine and Roubaud have internal focalization, and it earns them prison, death or decrepitude; but avoidance of the gaze, the refusal to see, is no protection. Lantier, when he sees Roubaud, cannot bring himself to strike him, and when he kills Séverine he does so with a knife he has not looked at but simply snatched in an unconscious movement (a high-angle shot just shows the murder weapon, harshly lit on the white tablecloth, and a hand quickly picking it up). However, after the murder, Lantier passes a mirror and is forced, between a hesitation (a lowered gaze) and a refusal (his eyes turned away), to look at himself at last. It is that reflection which commits him to killing himself.

Here we find Gabin in a role which he often took on – and which I and others have already analysed elsewhere (Lagny, Ropars and Sorlin 1986): that of a scapegoat, constituted as 'the object of the quest for the spectator, who delegates him to the function of subject', so that he dies in his/her place. Not only is that function confirmed in *La Bête humaine*, thus authorizing the reassurance of the spectator, but the film reinforces its effect by exhibiting the interplay of gazes thematically and at the same time undercutting their structural effectiveness, thereby placing the spectator in a position of ubiquity which enables him/her to see without running any of the risks that seeing involves.

It can be seen, then, that it is the moments of hesitancy in the film's textual system, involving breaks in 'implication' and a denial of the gaze, which take the *fêlure* on board while at the same time papering over it. True, Lantier carries within him a *fêlure* of sociological origin, produced by 'those generations of drinkers', but the brief descriptions of his fits are not very convincing, and it is clear that the main effect of his sacrifice is to destroy the oppressive social organization that turned the *petit-bourgeois* Roubaud and the pretty Séverine, 'dressed like a princess', into corrupt victims of the *grand-bourgeois* Grandmorin. True, too, the narrative dislocation and the weakness of the subject of the gaze (and many other clues which I have omitted to mention here) could be interpreted as reflecting the uneasy atmosphere of the late 1930s and their uncertainty about what the future held in store. But if Renoir regarded his film as a weapon against Hitler, could it not be because a number of disturbing fantasies are let loose in it? By keeping his spectators in the position of uninvolved voyeurs, but ones that are capable of asking themselves questions, Renoir offers them the shelter which makes a critical position possible.

The effectiveness of this protection answers a question put by Gilles Deleuze in his preface to Zola's novel: 'Why did Renoir shy away from

Lantier's vision on the railway track? . . . Why did he replace that scene with one where Lantier comes to the conclusion that the Roubauds are guilty, instead of sensing it instinctively through that vision, which is both certain and indeterminate?' (Deleuze 1977, 20). Reason, which *comes to a conclusion*, no doubt fails to save Lantier, but it is a challenge to what is none other than the death instinct that Deleuze analyses in Zola – not '*just one of many instincts*, but something like the *fêlure* personified, around which all the other instincts seethe' (Deleuze 1977, 14). In the process of *dédoublement* which I have outlined, Lantier's death leaves Roubaud, already corrupted, with (emotional) powerlessness but offers Pecqueux, the proletarian, (social) power. Thus we are brought to the 'vanishing point' which Deleuze again, in another text (Deleuze 1985, 115), regards as characteristic of Renoir, and through which 'something takes shape . . . which will succeed in emerging from the flaw and blossoming freely'. With its epilogue, where railway traffic starts moving again, the film succeeds better than the novel in turning the train into 'an epic symbol . . . which always has a future' (Deleuze 1977, 23), but the train is no longer driverless, and it is Renoir, rather than Zola, who is responsible for that 'socialist optimism . . . which implies that, through the *fêlure*, it is the proletariat that wins through' (Deleuze 1977, 23).

Perhaps this is why, in the late 1980s, despite the concerns of the engine driver faced with the new technology which transforms his living and working conditions, and provokes his revolt, *La Bête humaine* lives on after all.

*Translated from the French by Peter Graham*

## Notes

1 *Le Monde* (8 January 1987), 25.
2 Interview in *Ce Soir* (3 September 1938), in Renoir 1974a, 259.
3 Extract from a synopsis that Zola sent to a publisher, in Mitterand, Henri (1966), 'Etude' on *La Bête humaine*, in *Les Rougon-Macquart* IV, Paris, Gallimard.
4 Chardère 1962, 266–7. Extract from an article by the right-wing critic Jean Fayard in *Candide* (28 December 1938).
5 See Faulkner 1979, 113–14. The reason why the film did not feature among the big box-office successes of the end of the 1930s is probably that it was released too late to be included in the 1938 charts and *La Cinématographie française* figures for 1939 are no longer available.
6 Martin, Marcel, *Les Lettres françaises* (19 September 1966).
7 Cournot, Michel, *Le Nouvel Observateur* (28 September 1966).
8 *La Bête humaine*, cuttings files, Collection Rondel, Bibliothèque de l'Arsenal.
9 Interview with Renoir, *Cinémonde* (7 December 1938), in Renoir 1974a.
10 Mitterand, Henri (1981), 'Emile Zola en librairie', in *Catalogue général des ouvrages imprimés de la Bibliothèque Nationale, Auteurs*, CCXXXI, Paris, Imprimerie Nationale. In addition to the latest editon of Zola's *Oeuvres complétes* published by Maurice Leblond between 1927 and 1929, various individual editions were available at the time, notably in Fasquelle's 'La Bibliothèque Charpentier' series, but

also on the Flammarion list. Original 1890 printing: 55,000 copies; the 1949 edition carries the indication '179th thousand'.

11 For example: 'Le Passage à niveau' (extract from the derailment episode) in L. Dumas (1934) *Le Livre unique de français*, 15; 'Le Mécanicien et sa locomotive', in A. Souché (1936) *La Lecture expressive et le français*, Paris, Nathan, 46–7 (with an illustration); and, with the same title but a different extract (on the relationship between the driver and his locomotive, to which I have already referred, but here in a bowdlerised form: the sentence 'He loved it, then, with masculine gratitude' was excised, in Souché, Dard and Lamaison (1940) *Les Auteurs du nouveau programme*, Paris, Nathan, 1940.

12 Reproduced in *Cinémonde* (27 December 1938), in Renoir 1974a, 260.

13 See Vincendeau 1985a, 243–397; and 'Community, Nostalgia and the Spectacle of Masculinity: Jean Gabin in Two Films Made During the Period of the Popular Front', *Screen* (1985) 26 (6); Lagny, Ropars and Sorlin (1986).

14 Interview with Renoir, *Ce Soir* (24 July 1938).

15 *Cinémonde* (7 December 1938).

16 Renoir made many statements on this subject (e.g. in Renoir 1974a, 260; interview in *Ce Soir* (4 December 1938)), as did his set designer Eugène Lourié, quoted in Viry-Babel 1986, 108.

17 *Cinémonde* (12 December 1938), in Renoir 1974a, 267.

18 *Ibid*.

19 *Cinémonde* (4 November 1938), in Renoir 1974a, 262.

20 1969 interview in Viry-Babel 1986, 108; interview by Michel Ciment, *Positif* 173 (1975), 15–21.

21 In addition to Poulle 1969, see Gauteur 1980a, 119–130, and Renoir 1974a; Gauthier 1968, 30–2; and Serceau 1981.

22 For an exhaustive list of articles devoted to the film see Faulkner 1979, 112ff.

23 Extract from an article by Pierre Bost in *Les Annales* (10 January 1939, 111).

24 Christian Metz (1977) *Le Signifiant imaginaire*, Paris, UGE (10/18), 79.

25 The narrative unit is based on a 'diegetically based entity proposed by the narrative text'. A logical–diegetic 'implication' means that 'the second sequence comes not only after the first, but also because of it', whereas a chronological 'implication' restricts 'intersequential links to the interaction of before and after'. The 'implication' is described as 'suspended' when logical and temporal relationships remain indeterminate, thus producing a certain narrative imprecision. See Lagny, Ropars and Sorlin 1986, 24 and 26.

26 See the shooting script established in Gauthier 1968, 29, which turns the first two sequences into a single one, thus removing the break produced by the fade-out.

27 Notably in Gauthier 1968, 32–3, and Guillaume-Grimaud 1986, 72–3.

28 Interview with Jean Renoir in *Ce Soir* (24 July 1938), reproduced in *Ecran* (1974a), 31.

29 See, for example, Gauthier 1968, 33–4; Guillaume-Grimaud 1986, 75; and Viry-Babel 1986, 108.

30 I have retained the term used in *Générique des années 30*, despite the convincing analysis and concept of 'ocularisation' proposed by François Jost in (1987) *L'Oeil-caméra*, Lyon, PUL, 14–30.

## Selected bibliography

Bazin, André (1971) *Jean Renoir*, ed. François Truffaut, Paris, Editions Champ Libre. In English: (1974) *Jean Renoir*, trans. W. W. Halsey II and William H. Simon, New York, Dell.

Bertin, Celia (1994) *Jean Renoir, cinéaste*, Paris, Gallimard.

Beylie, Claude (1975) *Jean Renoir*, Cinéma d'aujourd'hui 2, Paris, Film Editions.

Chardère, Bernard (1962) *Jean Renoir*, Lyon, Premier Plan.

Ciment, Michel (1975) 'Interview with Jean Renoir (sur *La Bête humaine*)', *Positif* 173, 15–21.

Curot, Frank (1995) *Jean Renoir: nouvelles approches*, Montpellier, Université Paul Valéry.

Deleuze, Gilles (1977) 'Zola et la fêlure', preface to the Folio edition of *La Bête humaine*, Paris, Gallimard. This text had already appeared in Deleuze (1969) *Logique du sens*, Paris, Editions de Minuit.

Deleuze, Gilles (1985) *Cinéma 2 – L'Image-temps*, Paris, Editions de Minuit.

Durgnat, Raymond (1974) *Jean Renoir*, Berkeley and Los Angeles, University of California Press.

Faulkner, Christopher (1979) *Jean Renoir, a Guide to References and Resources*, Boston, G. K. Hall.

Faulkner, Christopher (1986) *The Social Cinema of Jean Renoir*, Princeton, Princeton University Press.

Gauteur, Claude (1974) 'Jean Renoir auteur de films (à propos de *La Bête humaine*)', *Ecran*, 31.

Gauteur, Claude (1980a) *Jean Renoir, la double méprise*, Paris, Editeurs Français Réunis.

Gauteur, Claude (1980b) '*La Bête humaine*', Image et Son, La Revue du cinéma 27.

Gauthier, Guy (1968) '*La Bête humaine*', Image et Son, La Revue du cinéma 227.

Guillaume-Grimaud, Geneviève (1986) *Le Cinéma du Front Populaire*, Paris, Lherminier.

Lagny, Michèle, Ropars, Marie-Claire and Sorlin, Pierre (1986) *Générique des années 30*, Paris, Presses Universitaires de Vincennes.

LoBianco, Lorraine and Thompson, David (eds) (1994) *Jean Renoir: Letters*, London, Faber & Faber.

Poulle, François (1969) *Renoir 1938, ou Jean Renoir pour rien? – Enquête sur un cinéaste*, Paris, Editions du Cerf.

Renoir, Jean (1974a) *Ecrits 1926–1971*, ed. Claude Gauteur, Paris, Belfond.

Renoir, Jean (1974b) *Ma vie et mes films*, Paris, Flammarion. In English: (1974) *My Life and My Films*, trans. Norman Denny, New York, Atheneum.

Renoir, Jean (1989) *Renoir on Renoir: Interviews, Essays and Remarks*, Cambridge, Cambridge University Press.

Serceau, Daniel (1981), *Jean Renoir, l'insurgé*, Paris, Editions du Sycomore.

Serceau, Daniel (1985) *Jean Renoir*, Paris, Edilig.

Sesonske, Alexandre (1980) *Jean Renoir, the French Films, 1924–1939*, Cambridge, Mass., and London, Harvard University Press.

Vincendeau, Ginette (1985a) 'French Cinema in the 1930s: Social Text and Context of a Popular Entertainment Medium', unpublished thesis, University of East Anglia.

Vincendeau, Ginette (1985b) 'Community, Nostalgia and the Spectacle of

Masculinity: Jean Gabin in Two Films Made During the Period of the Popular Front', *Screen*, 26 (6)

Viry-Babel, Roger (1986), *Jean Renoir, La Régle et le jeu*, Paris, Denoël.

Zola, Emile (1966) *La Bête humaine*, Paris, Gallimard.

Zola, Emile (1977) *La Bête humaine*, Harmondsworth, Penguin.

# Appendix

## *Jean Renoir (1894–1979): filmography*

1924  *Catherine (Backbiters)*
1924  *La Fille de l'eau (The Whirlpool of Fate)*
1926  *Nana*
1927  *Sur un air de Charleston (Charleston-Parade)*
1927  *Marquitta*
1928  *La Petite marchande d'allumettes (The Little Match Girl)*
1928  *Tire-au-flanc (The Slacker)*
1929  *Le Tournoi dans la cité*
1929  *Le Bled (The Back of Beyond)*
1931  *On purge bébé*
1931  *La Chienne*
1932  *Boudu sauvé des eaux (Boudu Saved from Drowning)*
1932  *La Nuit du carrefour (Night at the Crossroads)*
1933  *Chotard et Cie*
1934  *Madame Bovary*
1934  *Toni*
1935  *Le Crime de Monsieur Lange (The Crime of Monsieur Lange)*
1936  *Les Bas-fonds (The Lower Depths)*
1936  *Une partie de campagne (A Day in the Country)* released 1946
1936  *La Vie est à nous (The People of France)* released 1969
1937  *La Grande illusion (Grand Illusion)*
1938  *La Bête humaine (The Human Beast [UK]; Judas Was a Woman [USA])*
1938  *La Marseillaise*
1939  *La Règle du jeu (The Rules of the Game)*
1940  *La Tosca (finished by Carl Koch)*
1941  *Swamp Water*
1943  *This Land is Mine*
1944  *Salute to France*
1945  *The Southerner*
1946  *The Diary of a Chambermaid*
1947  *The Woman on the Beach*
1951  *The River*
1953  *Le Carrosse d'or (The Golden Coach)*
1955  *French CanCan*
1956  *Eléna et les hommes (Paris Does Strange Things)*
1959  *Le Déjeuner sur l'herbe (Picnic on the Grass)*
1959  *Le Testament du Docteur Cordelier (Experiment in Evil)*

1962  *Le Caporal épinglé* (*The Elusive Corporal* [UK]; *The Vanishing Corporal* [USA])
1970  *Le Petit théâtre de Jean Renoir* (*The Little Theatre of Jean Renoir*)

## Other films cited in the text

*La Bandera* (*Escape from Yesterday*), Julien Duvivier (1935)
*La Belle équipe* (*They were Five* [UK]; *A Fine Team* [USA]), Julien Duvivier (1936)
*Le Quai des brumes* (*Port of Shadows*), Marcel Carné (1938)

# 4

# POETIC REALISM AS PSYCHOANALYTICAL AND IDEOLOGICAL OPERATION

## Marcel Carné's *Le Jour se lève* (1939)

*Maureen Turim*

### Method of inquiry

Released two years after the demise of the Popular Front and just three months before the entry of France into war with Germany, Marcel Carné's *Le Jour se lève*, from a script by Jacques Viot with dialogues by Jacques Prévert,[1] is a film that more than most suffered from the way contextual factors apparently affected its reception in 1939. It was seen by some critics as a renunciation of the ideals of the Popular Front.[2] Then it was in fact banned by the military censor board as too 'defeatist'.[3] Judging the film from their racist, fascist ideological bias, Bardèche and Brasillach decried the 'judaïzing aesthetic' of *Le Jour se lève* which they compared to the German cinema before 1933.[4] It was not until ten years after its original release that the film's reputation was redeemed (partially owing to the efforts of André Bazin),[5] once it could be seen, not necessarily outside of the context of the late 1930s upheavals, but with more distance on the threat its tone implied to diverse groups at that time.

From our position of retrospection, there are many possible readings of the gloomy poetics of a film like *Le Jour se lève*, slightly different from the 1930s critiques, but using the same sort of symbolic approach: as an expression of the mood of despair after the collapse of the Popular Front on the eve of the Second World War; as the migration into French culture of Nietzschean philosophy; or as Carné and Prévert's personal fascination with and reworking of the US gangster film of the 1930s. All of these have some validity, and the historical thesis is particularly intriguing given the marked difference between the films from the end of the 1930s and those from earlier in the decade. What we will see, however, is that in addition to these readings *Le Jour se lève* prefigures the psychoanalytic narrative economy of the 1940s melodrama and *film noir*[6] in its configuration of a compulsive desire forcing repetitions that can be stopped only with death.

In the discussion that follows, I would like to continue the process of historical re-evaluation initiated by Bazin by proposing an analysis whose method takes into account polysemy, a weave of conflicting meanings, rather than unity of meaning and symbolism. Such a method considers the complexities of intertextuality and ideology in relationship to the multiplicity of meanings a film generates on several levels including psycho-analytical and deconstructive readings. This differs from symptomatic readings in which a given interpretation is said to reflect an assumed prevailing mood.

In the case of *Le Jour se lève*, symptomatic readings tend to emphasize the pessimism and fatalism dominant in the film. Such readings are largely thematic and tend to take these attitudes, as represented in the film, as the meaning of the film itself. If a working-class character or a Frenchman (the two ways of characterizing the hero pertinent to the 1930s critiques mentioned above) is shown to be driven to self-destruction, then the film is somehow seen as not offering the proper inspiration for class struggle or nationalist resistance or nationalist fascist collaboration, as the case may be. However, fictional suicides can also be part of a statement of protest or desperation. Two suicides from the 1930s, that of a friend of the Préverts, the surrealist Pierre Batcheff in 1931, and that of socialist Roger Salengro in 1937, Ministre de l'Intérieur under Léon Blum, were in fact seen at the time as just such acts of protest; Salengro's suicide was a major rallying point for the Popular Front, as he was perceived as having been driven to it by his political opponents. Further, if we allow that *Le Jour se lève* is more complex in its use of character than such thematic interpretation admits, the pessimism located within a character or within the trajectory of a character's life need not be taken as the singular 'message' of the film.

Instead, we can see how the film depicts characters whose desires and impulses are positioned as networks of conflicting forces. The tension is not only between characters representing different elements but within characters, with the protagonist, François (Jean Gabin), providing a central focus of this network. Ginette Vincendeau has analysed how characters played by Jean Gabin figure in the political imagination of the 1930s;[7] François, as one of the late incarnations of a continuing series of like personae, clearly does embody a mythic hero who, while marked as coming from the working class, rarely simply represents a typical constituent of it (his role in *La Grande illusion* is perhaps his most positive and also most typed working-class embodiment). Instead, this hero tends to represent the troubled aspect of a subject whose desires are poetically magnified as outside of control or compromise. The death act then takes a structural place in the narrative as a refusal of suffering and the danger of being further misunderstood or manipulated, as well as presenting psychic volatility as marking the construction of this hero.

As we shall see, this suicidal hero can be seen in relationship to a discourse on memory and the viewing of the past. The hero's focalization of his past serves the film's psychoanalytic unveiling, not merely at the level of psychology of character, but as meta-psychology. The social determination of this character then needs to be construed as an element in relationship to these other operations, symbolically inseparable from them. To retain the weight of an historical context while pursuing a process of reading beyond a symptomatic thematic interpretation into the psychoanalytical narrative economy – that is the goal of what follows.

## Double time and associative memory objects

In *Le Jour se lève* knowledge of the murder is first given the audience as an intertitle prefacing the frame story, one that was in fact added at the insistence of the producer to clarify the structure for the audience: 'A man has killed. Shut up and besieged in his room, he evokes the circumstances which made of him a murderer.'[8] The frame story then opens with the gunshot we hear, but do not see; the vision of the act of murder itself is withheld until the end of the final flashback. The frame story chronicles the degeneration of the hero's mood through the night towards dawn. The three flashbacks are offered within this frame as the subjective thoughts of this man, described as 'besieged by memories'. The flashbacks are 'causal' segments whose internal temporal structure is a linear progression narrating the jealousy, betrayal and villainous taunting that turns the promise of an ideal romance sour. Like many flashback films, the structure here reverses the cause and effect order, giving us the effect, murder, first, and the cause, an overwhelming psychic tension, following that. In a sense the past is offered to the audience as explanation and justification, though, due to this trope of interior thought, the narrative does not present itself as a courtroom trial, not even indirectly, as does the other famous 1930s French flashback film co-authored by Prévert and directed by Jean Renoir, *Le Crime de Monsieur Lange*. In fact, as the film progresses, the hero rejects the crowd's sympathy for him, misreading it as a perverse fascination, and will not acknowledge his friends who urge him to surrender in order to be given a real trial. Rather than directly appeal to the audience's judgement, *Le Jour se lève* shows us a man who rejects anyone who tries to help or understand him. It problematizes judgement before the inner workings of a psyche, but, paradoxically, it encourages our sympathy by proposing to show us how psychic tension can reach such an explosive level.

This double temporal organization of the film makes possible fascinating object associations which link the present to the past. These object associations are both an application of a notion of associative memory and a particular inscription of the object symbolism typical of Poetic Realism. The objects that will circulate through other segments, the mirror, the teddy bear and the brooch, are introduced within the first flashback. The scene of their introduction occurs three weeks after the hero's initial meeting with the young florist's assistant, Françoise, with whom he falls in love. He visits her in her room where, in the course of their flirtation, he holds her teddy bear next to his face as he looks in the mirror. This gesture marks his contemplation of Françoise's suggestion that the toy bear and he look alike, both have 'one happy eye and one sad'. The bear becomes a symbol of the ideal of happiness and the melancholy of defeat that coexist in François, and it is this bear that he takes with him upon being sexually rebuffed that evening. The taking of this souvenir, this emblem of himself as consolation, is a way in which the film marks its forces of narrative determination.

In the next return to the present, François repeats the gesture, the look in the mirror while holding a teddy bear, that he made in Françoise's room. The migration of this gesture from flashback to present gives us memory as a repetition of gestures and objects, doubling the sense of over-determination already located in the bear.

The brooch also makes its first appearance in Françoise's room, as one of the objects she puts on before leaving for her mysterious late night rendez-vous. The brooch figures in the complicated psychological torture Valentin devises for François in which he uses Clara's jealousy of Françoise to extract his revenge. Clara explains that the brooch signifies Valentin's sexual conquest of a new woman, that is, Françoise, and she now gives one like it to François as a souvenir of their affair which he has just ended. The brooch then serves as the visual symbol that will bridge the next transition between past and present. The brooch gets thrown by François at the *armoire* in the transitional shot that brings us back to the present.

The brooch inspires an on-going discourse on the relationship between objects and memory that thematizes the associative memory-links the film makes in its flashback structure. This is especially developed in the *double-entendre* in the French word *souvenir* (which means both a memory and a memento), which is developed in the dialogue between François and Clara. This word-play reminds us of how objects become invested with memories, for in Prévert's poetic condensation of *souvenir*, objects and memories are inseparable.

Objects are charged with meanings by the film and their recurrence is a key to the structure of the narrative. This circulation of symbolic objects can also be seen as forming the psychoanalytic narrative economy of the film. The objects provide a metaphorical rendering of imagination and the psyche in relationship to death. The room itself embodies the restriction of freedom through a limitation and closure of space. The response to this restriction is a withdrawal, an interiorization which has as its slogan François' shouts of 'Fous-moi la paix' and 'Fichez-moi la paix' ('leave me alone', but also 'give me some peace'). The window, mirror, door and *armoire* become symbolically rich elements of this architectonic shell. François' barricade against the world is destroyed element by element, first the shattering of the window, then François' breaking of the mirror which fragments his self-image, then the penetration of bullets through the door and then the *armoire* placed in front of it. The final penetration of his space, the ominous explosion of the tear gas occurs in ironic excess of good reason, as it explodes next to his corpse, yet reason enough exists in its imagistic purpose as this 'senseless' explosion, this puff of smoke, fills the space of the dead hero, underscoring the end of the *homme-récit*, the narrative process bound by the course of a fictional life.[9]

Let us take another look at how François' movement in the long take that begins the first return to the present links this shattered window with the mirror, which in turn will be shattered in a later sequence. As window and mirror are both frequent metaphors for cinema itself (for example, Bazin's 'window on the world'[10] and the widespread notion of cinema as mirror of society, the psyche or the author) these images gain meta-cinematic, theoretical signification. They place the character in the film as trapped not only by his temporal frame (the frame story) but by his cinematic frame (the image, its architectonics, its means of symbolization). The despair and the fatalism are not only pertaining to the social references, the failure of the Popular Front, they have permeated the language of expression, the controlling metaphors of the cinematic medium.

If these architectural elements become indicators of withdrawal, restriction and annihilation of the self in the present siege of the room, in the flashback past they had been imbued with other meanings. For example, the *armoire* shifts from being a treasure chest whose interior is decorated with photos of Françoise to being François' armour, shielding him from the police. The film plays on the near homonyms, *armoire, amour, armure* (chest, love, armour) visually and verbally.[11] Consider the dialogue between the commissaire of police and the concierge:

LE COMMISSAIRE: Dites donc. . . . Est-ce qu'il y a une armoire dans cette chambre? (Say. . . . Is there a chest in that room?)
LE CONCIERGE: Comment? (What?)
LE COMMISSAIRE: Je vous demande s'il y a une armoire dans sa chambre? (I'm asking you if there is a chest in his room?)
LE CONCIERGE: Naturellement, il y a une armoire. (Naturally, there is a chest.)
LE COMMISSAIRE: Une grande armoire . . . ? (A large chest?)
LE CONCIERGE: Une grande armoire? . . . j'sais pas, moi! . . . Une armoire comme toutes les armoires . . . (A large chest? I don't know . . . a chest like all the others . . .)

This dialogue calls attention to itself through obsessive repetitions, then begs for the substitution of *amour* for *armoire* in the phrase *une grande armoire*, especially when this is further modified by the concierge's answer. In this transposition, François' love, so obsessive as to be self-destructive, is said to be in fact like all other loves; in the transposition with armour, love, which once seemed an escape from an oppressive world, becomes an ineffective shield from a hostile one.

The exchange and contrast between the meanings objects had in the past and the ones they acquire in this new context of the present is so constant as to become an obsessive characteristic of the text. For example, when the bullet causes the door of the *armoire* to swing open, revealing the photos in the present, François slams it shut again, a metaphor for his attempt to not remember, which none the less triggers the next flashback. Each of the objects represents in microcosm this difference between two states of being, one in which there are restrictions, but also dreams and hope for change, and one in which hope is lost and death is inevitable. Objects also permit dialogues to be spun around them poetically, and here Prévert displays his similarity to his contemporary, Francis Ponge, in using the object as the basis for an ironic series of philosophical speculations.[12]

The recurrences of these objects also operate abstractly to engage structures of repetition and return. These structures contribute to the fatalism of the film, a film in which the past and the present join on the 'seam' of the murder, and once the murder is regained across this temporal fold, the suicide follows. Are we 'beyond the pleasure principle'? Is this film, sructured by deaths, an ode to the death drive?

## Melodrama: the hero, the villain and the two women

The answer to these questions must be postponed until we take another entrance into *Le Jour se lève*, the consideration of the melodramatic aspects of this narrative. French theatrical melodrama is an important intertextual force throughout the history of French film.[13] This is particularly evident in the collaborative work of Carné and Prévert, including *Jenny, Le Quai des brumes*, and *Les Enfants du paradis* as well as *Le Jour se lève* and Carné's *Hôtel du Nord* from a scenario by Henri Jeanson and Jean Aurenche. *Les Enfants du paradis* even thematizes this melodramatic proclivity on the part of Prévert and Carné by drawing directly on the life of Frédérick Lemaître and the Boulevard du Crime setting.[14] Although several of the films cited above do have novelistic rather than theatrical sources, these novels themselves are marked by the nineteenth-century theatrical melodrama.[15] Like other French films of the 1930s, *Le Jour se lève* concentrates on the male hero as central focus whereas melodramatic films of the 1920s were more likely to make the female central (*Jenny* is one of the exceptions, with its 1930s female focus). If the hero is central through his focalization, the melodrama develops a network of desire and rivalry that contains four principals, which can be diagrammed as follows:

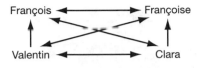

This diagram allows us to see the doubling of the couples and the crossing of the lines of desire. Above we have the hero and heroine, the couple of apparent charmed likeness, François and Françoise, who, except for the 'e', the signifier of sexual difference, share a name, a saint's day and memories of childhoods as orphans. Below, the couple meet at the point of rupture, the villain and the other woman. As close as it comes in many respects, this is not simply the melodramatic tale of the contamination of pure love by the impure. A look at each of the four characterizations will help show why.

If our hero is complexly drawn, this complexity is an amplification, through traits that construct a character psychology, of the traditional melodramatic hero. He is, on a more basic level, beneath all the elaboration of his subjective vision and his psyche, the romantic lead in a tale of morality, attempting to secure for himself and his love object an ideal life together. Valentin is a pure melodramatic villain, a cruel ringmaster who treats others in the melodrama like the dogs he trains for his *café-concert* act.

If the hero and villain follow the generic pattern of melodrama, the two women are harder to categorize. Françoise 'should' be the ideal innocent heroine and Clara, the other, fallen, woman, but here is where the film performs some of its most interesting play with character. The first flashback introduces both women, placing them in parallel roles in the working-class and marginal *café-concert* milieu of the film. The contrasts that melodrama might impose between them (a good/bad woman split) are mediated in a number of ways.

First, the opposition between the heroine and the other woman is modified by Françoise being far more worldly and far less innocent (in her attraction to Valentin) than she initially appears to François when he is interrupted at work by her confused attempt to deliver her flowers. Her chance appearance at his factory bearing azaleas on their mutual saint's day which begins his infatuation is painted as an array of symbols. In the protective suit of a sandblaster, François takes on the almost surreal appearance of the modem industrialized man, while Françoise appears as an ideal vision, innocence bedecked with flowers. The ideal image is destroyed soon thereafter, when François follows Françoise on her late night sortie to a *café-concert* where he discovers that she is enraptured by a rival, Valentin. François judges Valentin by watching the act, as does the audience; Jules Berry's exaggerated performative gestures as Valentin present him as self-aggrandizing and belittling others (Clara and the dogs who are presented by him as puppets rather than as intelligent performers).

*Le Jour se lève* – François (Jean Gabin).

The triangle (hero–innocent–villain) is doubled when François begins talking with Clara (Arletty), Valentin's co-performer and mistress who has just walked out on him. Clara's saucy rejection of Valentin, her refusal to continue to perform with/for him, given first as a flippant gesture, the purposeful missing of her cue to catch his top hat, aligns her with François' sensibilities, his distaste for Valentin's pseudo-elegance. François and Clara demonstrate from their initial meeting onward that indeed they speak the same language, a language without pretences at being anything other than what they are. The flashback ends with a confrontation between Valentin and François, not over Françoise, but over Clara. This uneasy substitution of Clara for Françoise continues throughout the next flashback.

If Clara's substitution for Françoise is a temporary compromise on François' part within the diegesis, it accrues a different reaction from most spectators. Arletty is so dynamic a performer in the role of Clara, and so winning not only in her independence, but also once she softens to admit her love of François, that it is actually difficult to accept emotionally the logic of the narrative by which François must break off with her to return to his doomed idealization, his infatuation with Françoise. We can analyse

*Le Jour se lève* – view of building where François (Jean Gabin) lives.

this intuitive discomfort not only in terms of a casting imbalance (the comparative weakness of Jacqueline Laurent's performance) that undercuts narrative determinations, but also as a longing, ultimately suppressed by the film, to step outside the overdetermination of the death drive as guarantor of narrative closure. The initial encounter between Clara and François at the bar of the *café-concert* is characterized by a revitalization of the romantic exchange of glances as a female-initiated sardonic volley. For example, in response to François' assertion that with all her make-up he cannot know if she is pretty, Clara, nonplussed, replies 'Make-up? I always take it off before I go to bed.' The film flirts with allowing a proletarian couple to evade the frame of pessimism of late 1930s French melodrama and reconstitute their lives on terms that offer a class-conscious, if personalized, alternative.

The glimmer of such an alternative is often suggested in the film, in ways that the dominant readings often ignore. We can understand this in terms of the affinities established between the two women that efface their opposition. Both women are presented as workers; though Clara is a performer, her job in the act is parallel to Françoise's role as service assistant to the florist. Discussions of representations of the working class in 1930s films tend to ignore

71

such representations of the female work force, focusing exclusively on the male factory worker.[16] Yet it is significant that, despite the romantic rivalry that will make them opponents, a solidarity between them, at least on Clara's part, will ultimately surface in the narrative. This occurs in the scenes surrounding the final flashback, when, in the present, Françoise shows up on the street below François' room in a state of hysterical delirium. It is Clara who takes Françoise away to comfort her, bringing Françoise to her room, and listens sympathetically while she rants of her love for François and, ironically, the insignificance of his tryst with Clara.

Clara and Françoise are also linked to the male workers, the comrades of François who form a kind of Greek chorus commenting on the action from their position beneath François' window. Unlike the bourgeoisie who assume a criminal or insane identity for François because he has committed a murder, the working-class representatives imagine that he must have had good reasons, that the killing was justifiable, something that Clara and Françoise know first-hand. Here the film joins the logic of *Le Crime de Monsieur Lange*, where the collective knows Lange's murder of Batala (also played by Berry) to be justifiable, and Lange's woman friend is able to communicate this to a group of strangers, also proletarians, whose sympathetic understanding and collaboration is attained at the film's end. If Prévert retells his *Le Crime de Monsieur Lange* in far less optimistic terms in *Le Jour se lève*, the traces of the earlier film's class awareness remain in this retelling.

Indeed, *Le Jour se lève* goes further than *Le Crime de Monsieur Lange* in its effort to depart from moral absolutes and either a happy or a retributive resolution. It is not just a more pessimistic film, but one less certain that the moral oppositions of early melodrama can serve a leftist ideological framework for narrative. Instead, the elements of melodramatic form are inscribed with considerable tension and reworking. If the villain remains a consummate villain, the hero, due to the complexities of his psyche, cannot simply defeat the villain without defeating himself, while the heroine and the other woman overlap rather than forming a neat opposition. The lines between self and other, so fixed in melodrama's character types, are here more ambiguous. The reason for this ambiguity is not just a greater political scepticism at the end of the 1930s, although that certainly plays a role, but a more subjective and intersubjective view of narrative.

The questions about the death drive with which the second section of this essay ended can now be reframed by this conclusion. We can see that the film's concern with subjectivity and intersubjectivity, especially as articulated through the depiction of memory, lends itself to this tendency towards a romance of the death drive. Pleasure, imagined as a bicycle ride to pick lilac by François or as a stay on the Côte d'Azur among the mimosas by Françoise, is always deferred and unattainable; identifying with bourgeois dreams will certainly not bring happiness, but neither, apparently, will acceptance of one's proletarian being.[17] The self contains its own debilitating contradictions, and romance with a proletarian existence is dissipated by a harsh look at what François' working conditions mean. The unhealthiness of the sand, the slow death it means to the blasters, the psychological toll the job extracts from François, are motifs introduced in the factory scene (a graphic image of work in a factory rare in this period of French film) and repeated throughout the film.

The murder and suicide which bring together the two temporalities at the end of the film join the other ironies developed earlier. For ultimately, when the final flashback unfolds, we learn, despite the film's seeming to present us with causes, that there is no reason for François to kill Valentin; Françoise has already pledged her love to François, and it is only through Valentin's goading François into shooting him that the young couple's future is foreclosed. François explodes irrationally in what amounts to a nervous breakdown. This is not just Gabin's famous short tempered scene of anger that is replayed from film to film, although it does culminate the development of that image.[18] François is a character who has unravelled.

The dual temporality of the film can be seen as the piecing together across past and present of this unravelled psyche we come to inevitably in the end. François' psyche is not just the subject of this interlacing of past and present, but is defined by the weave of retrospective linkages evoked in the film's imagery. Psychic functioning is presented primarily through external elements weighted with symbolic heuristic value. If the working-class hero destroys himself in the end, the film constructs not so much the causes of his behavior but the forces associated with objects and people which rage in a milieu and have no outlet, no place to simply dissipate. Valentin resurfaces to accomplish, through his provoked murder, the foreclosure of the promise of and nostalgia for peace and happiness in quite the same manner in which the brooch reappears. The torment of the inherently evil recurring object is a figuration of psychic temporality itself, non-linear and repetitious, a circulation of forces.[19]

## Realism, poetry and memory

In his article on *Le Jour se lève*, Bazin speaks of the realism of Alexander Trauner's sets, all built for studio production, crediting the great designer with the detailed touches that make the images of this film seem, in Bazin's view, like such an accurate 'social documentary'.[20] Yet Bazin also notes how Trauner has composed this little square in a working-class suburb 'as a painter would his canvas', and remarks continually on the dramatic role of the decor in the film, comparing it with Fritz Lang's *M*, while contrasting it with other works of German Expressionism.[21] If an element of contradiction appears to open up here in Bazin's insistence on social documentary on one hand, and poetic function on the other, this leads to his direct theoretical assessment of Poetic Realism. He argues that Trauner and Carné have infused this reality with poetry, and he praises Poetic Realism for founding its metaphors and symbolism, what he terms its 'metaphysical' signification, in the accurate depiction of a milieu.

We might well ask, however, if the textual strategy of Poetic Realism can any longer simply be seen in such terms. Recent work on the theory of realism in painting, literature and film demands a greater critical distance on the apparently real created through a weave of metonymic detail. We can recast Bazin's argument by acknowledging how the film's sets use metonymic elements as devices in which the codes of realism and analogy serve the codes of metaphor and the self-consciously poetic. Such incredulity before the real is all the more appropriate when looking at a film that renders the world as composed of metaphors. Poetics of the sort pursued by this film formulate a rhetoric that is quite different from a controlled documentation of the social. While Trauner (and the Carné–Prévert team in general), may have set out to recreate in the space of the studio a corner of a working-class suburb, such descriptive mimesis immediately becomes appropriated by the symbolic structuration and interior vision of this film. We should not let our desire to know the interior of a factory or a *café-concert* in 1939 let us substitute the image given to us in this film for that reality.

By extension, we should not allow our desire to know the interior life of a working-class man to permit us to substitute this film's treatment of memory and interiority for that which escapes our gaze. The images of the past the film gives us as François' memory are less like memory processes than the images of memories in the silent 1920s films of Louis Delluc, Germaine Dulac and Abel Gance. Here the only imagistic trope of memory is associative recall, the seeing of an object triggering the recall of a memory associated with that object. Even this device is presented less as part of a mimesis of memory *per se* than as part of the network of object symbolism and circulation discussed earlier. Perhaps unconsciously, the film marks in its treatment of memory its lack of concern with documenting the memory process; memory appears to be of interest as a dramatic trope, subjected to the discipline of the film's poetics rather than truly constructing the text.

In Poetic Realism, then, the accent is on poesis, on the trope deployed strategically, framed in a manner that sparkles with a simultaneous sense of design and imaginative play of thought and language. To move ever further into such poetics when the political climate chills in the way it did in 1939 is finally a quite comprehensible response on the part of artists who cared deeply about the working class their fictions represented. It is a response that sees fiction and the reality that is its context as complexly interactive. François' outrage and self-destruction are perhaps a displacement on to the working class of the self-portrait of the poets themselves.

# Notes

1 The question of authorship of this film (who is responsible for what) is not really my focus here. We know the film to be a collective effort, benefiting from the combined talents of a group who worked together repeatedly. While many discussions of the film assign a certain quality of the contribution to Viot, Carné, Prévert, Trauner, Maurice Jaubert, the actors and actresses, they tend to do so without any historical documentation of the process involved. For my purposes here, I am quite willing to accept that the work is a group project in which each of these strong personalities and talents interacted. At the end of the chapter, when I speak of 'the poets' I am referring to this collectivity.

2 Geneviève Guillaume-Grimaud (1986) *Le Cinéma du Front Populaire*, Paris, Lherminier.

3 Gérard Guillot (1966), *Les Prévert*, Paris, Seghers. The same source also says that later 'Vichy authorities held *Le Quai des brumes* accountable for the defeat of France before the Nazi regime'.

4 Maurice Bardèche and Robert Brasillach (1948), *Histoire du cinéma*, Paris, Martel, as quoted in *Avant-scène cinéma* 53 (1965). The anti-Semitism here seems aimed at Jacques Prévert.

5 André Bazin (1963), 'Fiche du *Jour se lève*', originally distributed as a leaflet at ciné-club presentations of the film, published in Jacques Chevallier (ed.) *Regards neufs sur le cinéma*, Paris, Seuil. Reprinted as part of the chapter 'Marcel Carné' in André Bazin (1983) *Le Cinéma français de la Libération à la Nouvelle Vague (1945–1958)*, Paris, Editions de L'Etoile, 53–69. John Mathews's (1970) English translation of extracts of Bazin's article appears in the 'Classic Film Scripts' translation of the script of *Le Jour se lève*, New York, Simon & Schuster, 5–12.

6 The pessimistic atmosphere, which has structural determinants in the film, is a strong prefiguration of the structure and tone of the American *film noir* flashback. *Le Jour se lève* did open in New York, under the tide *Daybreak*, but to less than completely enthusiastic reviews. A remake, *The Long Night*, Litvak, 1947, starring Henry Fonda, Barbara Bel Geddes, Ann Dvorak and Vincent Price, attests to the interest in *Le Jour se lève* by an émigré director known for *film noir* at the beginning of the peak period of production of this genre of film. Taken together these facts suggest that the film was perhaps historically influential in the development of American *film noir*. Even if this were not the case, however, a comparison of structure between *Le Jour se lève* and the *noir* genre would still prove intriguing.

7 Ginette Vincendeau (1985), 'Community, Nostalgia and the Spectacle of Masculinity: Jean Gabin in Two Films Made During the Period of the Popular Front', *Screen* 26 (6).

8 This and all other dialogue citations are taken from the script published in *Avant-scène cinéma*, 53 (1965).

9 Tzvetan Todorov (1971) *Poétique de la prose*, Paris, Seuil, 78–91.

10 André Bazin (1971) *What Is Cinema?* trans. Hugh Grey, Berkeley, Los Angeles and London: University of California Press, 111. It is also worth noting in the context of this analysis of *Le Jour se lève* that Bazin's use of the metaphor is in the context of a contrast drawn between theatre and film: 'we see that the basic aesthetic problem or filmed theater is indeed that of decor. The trump card that the director must hold is the reconversion in a window on to the world of a space oriented toward an interior dimension only, namely the closed and conventional area of the theatrical play.' Bazin's article on *Le Jour se lève* praises the film's use of windows and mirrors which I develop more thoroughly here.

11 Admittedly, the treatment of plays on words and objects that I analyse here

moves slightly beyond what is actually given in the text; it constitutes a reading between lines and images. I believe, however, that Prévert's work with wordplay and object symbolism in his poetry and film scripts (most notably for the poetry, *Paroles*, and for the film, *Un Oiseau rare* (1934), in which a parrot devises advertising slogans) justifies this play on my part, which at any rate in the context of the contemporary critical methods of Jacques Derrida or Jacques Lacan does not necessarily require such historical and intertextual evidence.

12  Francis Ponge (1942) *Le Parti pris des choses*, Paris, NRF.
13  See my discussion of this intertextuality in silent French cinema in Turim (1987) 'French Melodrama: A Theory of a Specific History', *Theater Journal* (fall).
14  See discussion of the melodramatic heritage of this film in Marcel Oms (1979) '*Les Enfants du paradis* ou la mutation cinématographique du mélodrame', *Cahiers de la cinémathèque*, 28, 141–8.
15  A point Peter Brooks (1976) makes in generalizing about the nineteenth-century French novel in his *The Melodramatic Imagination*, New Haven and London, Yale University Press.
16  As does François Garçon (1984) in his section 'Images de l'ouvrier à l'écran', *De Blum à Pétain*, Paris, Éditions du Cerf, 53–7.
17  Ginette Vincendeau has brought to my attention that this desire to identify with bourgeois dreams is a theme in French popular songs of the 1930s as in *Tout change dans la vie*, sung by Fréhel, where visions of the Côte d'Azur are opposed (albeit ironically) to the dreariness of everyday life on the *zone*. Similarly, flowers, and in particular lilacs, are a recurrent motif of the working-class version of the pastoral offered by popular songs, as in *Entre Saint-Ouen et Clignancourt*, an early Piaf song.
18  Bazin (1963), 70.
19  Let me suggest that this analysis differs markedly from that offered by Gilles Deleuze (1985) in *L'Image-temps*, Paris, Les Éditions de Minuit, 67, in which he argues that the flashback structure in *Le Jour se lève* does nothing more than assure a linear progression. His dismissal is dependent on a reading of the film, derived from Bazin, as using its flashbacks to merely represent the causes of François' behaviour.
20  (1963), 63.
21  (1963), 63.

# Selected bibliography

For a selected bibliography on Marcel Carné see Chapter 5, on *Les Enfants du paradis*.

# Script

Carné, Marcel and Prévert, Jacques (1965) *Le Jour se lève, Avant-scène cinéma*, 53.

# Appendix

## *Marcel Carné (1909–96): filmography*

1929  *Nogent, Eldorado du dimanche* (short)
1936  *Jenny*
1937  *Drôle de drame (Bizarre Bizarre)*

1938  *Hôtel du Nord*
1938  *Le Quai des brumes (Port of Shadows)*
1939  *Le Jour se lève (Daybreak)*
1942  *Les Visiteurs du soir (The Devil's Envoys)*
1943–5  *Les Enfants du paradis (Children of Paradise)*
1946  *Les Portes de la nuit (Gates of the Night)*
1950  *La Marie du port*
1951  *Juliette ou la clef des songes*
1953  *Thérèse Raquin (The Adulteress)*
1954  *L'Air de Paris*
1956  *Le Pays d'où je viens*
1958  *Les Tricheurs (The Cheaters)*
1960  *Terrain vague*
1963  *Du mouron pour les petits oiseaux*
1965  *Trois chambres à Manhattan*
1968  *Les Jeunes loups (The Young Wolves)*
1970  *La Force et le droit*
1971  *Les Assassins de l'ordre*
1974  *La Merveilleuse visite*
1976  *La Bible*
1992  *Mouche*

## Other films cited in the text

*Le Crime de Monsieur Lange (The Crime of Monsieur Lange)*, Jean Renoir (1935)
*La Grande illusion (Grand Illusion)*, Jean Renoir (1938)
*M*, Fritz Lang (Germany 1931)

# 5

# BENEATH THE DESPAIR, THE SHOW GOES ON

## Marcel Carné's *Les Enfants du paradis* (1943–5)

*Jean-Pierre Jeancolas*

The cinema which historians have definitively labelled Poetic Realism was, between 1935 and 1939, a cinema conjugated in the present tense. Jean Renoir, Julien Duvivier and Marcel Carné, Charles Spaak and Jacques Prévert, made their heroes dance to the music of their time: René Lefèvre, Jean Gabin, Charles Vanel and Jules Berry were contemporaries, even next of kin, of the viewers who were living the excitement of the emerging Popular Front in *Le Crime de Monsieur Lange*, its uncertainties in *La Belle équipe* or the bitterness of its disintegration in *La Bête humaine* or *Le Jour se lève*. The occupation of France in 1940, the control – direct or indirect – of its cinema by the German forces, condemned this use of the present tense. Fiction films were allowed, at best, to portray a kind of 'vague present day', a period which had the appearance of the present, but not its singular hardships: the cars or the costumes are of 1943, but the French are depicted in lighthearted romantic entanglements, stories that never show the daily problems of finding food, or the presence of Nazi uniforms. Even the rare 'realist' films of these bleak years, those of Jean Grémillon, or Clouzot's *Le Corbeau*, avoid any too obvious references to the hard times: the throb of civilian planes in *Le Ciel est à vous* has nothing to do with occupied France.

The type of realism associated with Carné and Prévert, in the era of *Le Quai des brumes* and *Le Jour se lève*, had less to do with a 'reality effect' than with the creative spirit of an exceptionally homogeneous team of artists: a designer who could reconstruct, in the Joinville studios, a street in Le Havre or a hotel on the outskirts of town so that street and building were quintessentially real, but at the same time planned with a view to lighting effects and camera angles; a director of photography, trained in the *noir* style of the Berlin studios, who knew how to juxtapose light and dark with a sense of drama that owed not a little to expressionism; a scriptwriter–poet whose highly literate dialogues escaped sounding like sententious aphorisms thanks to the talent and rigorous professionalism of the actors – Jean Gabin, Michel Simon, Jules Berry or Arletty; actors both popular and familiar to audiences who recognized Jean Gabin before they identified the deserter or the killer of the blackmailer . . . Carné's 'realism', more than Renoir's in the same prewar period, was in fact the orchestration of a myriad artifices controlled with exceptional talent by the director.

The realism which for half a century has been so lauded by devotees of Carné, by writers and historians, rests on a convention, a tacit agreement between the artist and his audience. Of course this is the case with all realism, but more so with Carné than with Renoir or the postwar film-makers who gave greater scope to, among other things, outdoor shooting and natural daylight. Renoir, in some of his silent films, as well as in *Toni* or *Une Partie de campagne*, purposely sets the camera at the water's edge, and accepts the rustic authenticity of occasional non-actors, and even the awkwardness (which we find endearing) of his own acting in *Une Partie de campagne, La Bête humaine* and *La Règle du jeu*.

However, they all avoid, not to say banish, the 'reality effect' that occurred fortuitously in the films of Feuillade and Antoine. When Feuillade filmed a car chase through the streets of Paris, he aimed his camera, mounted on top of a car hurtling along at top speed, at the convertible in which Inspector Juve was hot on the trail of the saloon which everyone knew held Fantômas. He filmed two cars, but he also caught the street, the pavements, the Paris façades racing past, the carriages and the occasional horse droppings. He captured the passers-by and the idle strollers, and it is not unusual to see one of these chance extras gazing with interest at what he has realized is the shooting of a film. When Antoine, in *Le Coupable*, places his main characters in one of the river buses that travelled along the banks of the Seine in 1917, he captures extraordinary documentary footage of wartime Paris, both of the real-life crowd and of the billboards that extol the true Frenchness of such-and-such a brand of soup. The screen fiction was loaded with a mass of information that had little to do with the original script. This practice, although not accidental (neither Feuillade nor Antoine were so naïve), brought an extra dimension to the filming. When Carné films the street in Le Havre where Michel Simon keeps shop, or the square in front of the hotel where Jean Gabin dies, he checks everything that appears on the screen: the cobbles, the railings, the Dubonnet advertisements, the lighting and the human beings, whether actors or extras directed by assistants under his orders. In the studio, nothing is left to chance: if a raised cobblestone catches the light from a streetlamp, it is because Trauner wanted the cobblestone and Schüfftan aimed a spotlight at it. Carné's cinema does not reproduce reality, it produces its own reality, by consensus.

Later, and elsewhere, the film-makers of the French New Wave were to rediscover the Feuillade effect (Godard's hidden camera in the Champs

Elysées sequence of *A bout de souffle*) but without the innocence of the father of *Fantômas*. The creators of *cinéma-vérité*, the 'cinéastes du réel' – in France Jean Rouch or, even more so, the Chris Marker of *Le Joli mai* – would no longer see it as an effect, but as the very nature of film-making. For them, the function of the camera became to seek out the 'reality effect', in the locations, the people, the words and the sound. Spontaneity of action counted for more than perfection of lighting.

The 'realists' of 1939, as embodied by Carné and Prévert, were the architects and builders of a fictional universe which they synchronized with the times, with real life. But they were better equipped than others to transpose their work into a temporal 'elsewhere', when the constraints of the occupation required them to do so.

After an abortive attempt at a futuristic film (it was not yet called science fiction) in 1941, *Les Evadés de l'an 4000*, Carné rejoined Prévert, who offered him the script of a film in the past historic mode, *Les Visiteurs du soir*. The film they made of it, produced by André Paulvé, was released in December 1942, to the acclaim we now know. Carné had regained a position in the profession which allowed him to propose a more ambitious and perhaps more personal project. This was to be, after a certain amount of trial and error, *Les Enfants du paradis*.

The French cinema of the occupation is in every respect a singular one. The catastrophe of 1940 had left deep wounds. Many were absent: some had been killed, like Maurice Jaubert, the musician of the great prewar films; many were prisoners in Germany; some left of their own accord (Jean Renoir, René Clair, Julien Duvivier went to Hollywood, as did Jean Gabin and Michèle Morgan); and others were outlawed under the anti-Semitic laws imposed in October 1940 by the Vichy government. Alexandre Trauner and Joseph Kosma, both Jews of Hungarian origin, were severely affected by these restrictions: they went into hiding in the south of France where the Italian occupation, more lax than the heavy German one in Paris, was more inclined to turn a blind eye to the presence of numerous Jewish refugees, particularly if they were associated with the cinema.

The cinema of the war years was hemmed in by a network of professional regulations, sometimes laboriously worked out by the last governments of the Third Republic before its defeat, and hastily instituted by Vichy at the end of 1940. The government of occupied France, an unstable mixture of clerical conservatism and technocratic modernism, created the COIC (Committee for the Organisation of the Cinematographic Industries) which had the ultimate authority over the profession, and which ruled it within the confines tolerated by the Germans.

These were years which paradoxically combined prosperity and poverty. French cinema was healthy: it was producing films, even big-budget films after a time, and they sold well. The market was dominated by national products: English-speaking films were prohibited because of the war, American films in particular becoming inaccessible. Italian films were rare, German films disdained by a proportion of the public. Yet these were years when the public queued at the box office. The cinema was cheap entertainment at a time when entertainment was sparse, it was also a safe place until the end of 1943. It provided the illusion and escape which were the necessary antidotes to daily misery – the difficulty of finding food, the queues in shops, the cold. Cinemas were heated, and you could also hide there. . . . The demand for films was pressing. The studios were active in 1942 and 1943. Producers were doing good business.

At the same time, film production (and especially for a weighty film like *Les Enfants du paradis*) came up against innumerable obstacles: finding wood and nails to build sets, fabrics for costumes, food to feed a troupe of famished technicians, actors and extras for weeks, electricity and, above all, film stock. Classified as a strategic commodity, film stock was granted only with the consent of the COIC and the German authorities. Production companies paid employees to besiege the offices that handed out the indispensable supply coupons or the 'goods coupons' which allowed them to buy all the necessary materials. Pathé even paid a worker to reclaim and straighten nails from disused sets.

So the adventure of *Les Enfants du paradis* was played out in a context of extreme tension (of which the finished film gives little hint). French cinema in 1943 had two capitals, Paris and Nice. André Paulvé, the producer of *Les Visiteurs du soir*, was quartered in Nice. Jacques Prévert and Alexandre Trauner lived a few miles away, at Tourettes sur Loup, Trauner in semi-hiding protected by solicitous friends. Carné joined them there. With Prévert, he was looking for the subject of their next film, which Paulvé had contracted to produce with a big budget. A chance encounter with Jean-Louis Barrault, on a café terrace on the Promenade des Anglais, was a turning-point: he told them a series of anecdotes revolving around the mime Debureau and the Boulevard du Crime at the time of the Restoration (1814–30). Carné returned to Paris to gather material, and came back with a sheaf of reproductions which he tossed on the table of Le Prieuré, the house at Tourettes which served as base camp for the entire team. There was enough there for several films, the more so as Prévert wanted to introduce and develop, within the story, the character of Lacenaire, the romantic murderer whose *Mémoires* and legendary exploits had fascinated generations of free thinkers since his execution in 1836.

Paulvé, when consulted, actually suggested making two films. According to Trauner, Prévert even envisaged a triptych, with the third section of the story devoted to the trial of Lacenaire: all Paris would have rushed to see it, as if to some rare spectacle, especially to hear the voice of Debureau in the witness box. . . . The script was written in the spring of 1943. Faced with the magnitude of the project, Paulvé took on as associate producer the Italian firm Scalera, with whom he had already produced L'Herbier's *La Vie de bohême*. The film would therefore be a co-production. The roles were assigned: Jean-Louis Barrault would obviously be Debureau, with Arletty as Garance, Marcel Herrand as Lacenaire, Pierre Brasseur as Frédérick Lemaître, Louis Salou as the Comte de Montray. Maria Casarès, making her film début, would play Nathalie, and Le Vigan would play Jéricho, the rag-and-bone man. It was agreed that Léon Barsacq would be in charge of building the big sets in the studios at La Victorine in Nice, from sketches which Trauner would send to him; and that Joseph Kosma, also a refugee in the area and banned from working, would write part of the music, the rest to come from Maurice Thiriet. Some of the interior scenes would be shot in Paris, where the editing and sound synchronization would later be done.

Shooting began in Nice in August. The big Boulevard du Crime set was not yet finished, so Carné started with the scenes at the Grand Relais, the boarding house where Baptiste and Frédérick Lemaître live. They had hardly started shooting on the Boulevard set when the war upset the production schedule: the Allies had landed in Sicily, Mussolini was overthrown. The order came from Paris to suspend filming. Scalera backed out of the contract that linked them with Paulvé. The entire company – apart from Trauner and Kosma, naturally – had to withdraw to Paris. Then another crisis occurred: Paulvé found himself banned by the Germans from producing films. Three months went by in attempts to save the film. Through the intervention of Louis-Emile Galey, head of COIC, Pathé was persuaded to take it on. Filming could start again. But without Le Vigan: too compromised by his active collaboration (an anti-Semite who denounced Jews, he sided with the writer Louis-Ferdinand Céline, with whom he would follow the defeated German armies), he abandoned the part of Jéricho, for which it seems he had done little more than a screen test. Carné replaced him with Pierre Renoir. In February 1944 authorization was granted to film again in Nice. Trauner's big set had been damaged by the winter and had to be restored, and the Germans refused to have it lit at night. Several scenes had to be cut, eventually to be replaced by cutaways and linking material shot in the studio in Paris.

The film was still not finished by the spring of 1944. Carné tells how, when he heard the news of the Allied landings in Normandy, he purposefully slowed down the post-production operations. He was marking time so as to release his film in a France at peace. He had, however, one more battle to fight, against the distributor, Gaumont. He wanted them to agree to screen the two parts of the film, *Le Boulevard du Crime* and *L'Homme blanc*, as a single programme lasting just over three hours. He got his way. On 9 March 1945, in an almost totally liberated France, *Les Enfants du paradis* was premiered at a gala evening at the Palais de Chaillot. A few days later, it was released in two first-run cinemas, and was received enthusiastically by both the critics and the public.

*Les Enfants du paradis* – above: the 'gods' (*paradis*, upper gallery) of the theatre; below: (from left to right) Frédérick Lemaître (Pierre Brasseur), Garance (Arletty) and Baptiste (Jean-Louis Barrault).

The film exists. Broad, complex, with a wealth of characters swept along by the action like the extras in the carnival scene on the Boulevard du Crime, *Les Enfants du paradis* marks a rare dimension in French cinema. Like some great novels, it is both dense and heterogeneous, fragmented into a plethora of heroes who reconcile history (Debureau, Lacenaire, Frédérick Lemaître) with the historical imaginary (the rag-and-bone man is a stock character from popular theatre) and with the contemporary imaginary of its creators: Garance is a creation of the Carné–Prévert duo.

Like many French films in the years between 1935 and 1950, *Les Enfants du paradis* is first and foremost a superb piece of scriptwriting. There has been much debate over the respective roles of Prévert and Carné in the writing of the films they made together. For *Les Enfants du paradis*, all accounts, including those of the two interested parties, are in agreement. The long task of developing the script, once Jean-Louis Barrault's initial idea had been adopted, evolved at Le Prieuré in an atmosphere of mutual agreement and collaboration. Prévert built on his own ideas, on those of Carné, on the documentation Carné had collected at the Musée Carnavalet in Paris, on the suggestions of Trauner. The isolation, amounting almost to sequestration, which the hard times imposed on them, helped the collective effort.

The script is Prévert backed by his small team. The dialogue, however, is Prévert alone, supreme master of his language, already close to many of the actors for whom he had etched superb lines in other Carné films, and his Frédérick Lemaître for Brasseur is also an extension of the already Shakespearean melodramatic actor created a year earlier in Grémillon's *Lumière d'été*. Jacques Prévert wrote to measure, for Brasseur, for Arletty, and especially for Marcel Herrand. Alexandre Trauner quotes his reply to Jean-Louis Barrault who insisted that the character of Debureau be mute: 'I understand. You don't want to talk! Never mind, I'll put someone else in who talks enough for two. That will restore the balance.'[1]

The script is divided into large blocks, which are closer to the chapters of a novel than to the normal sequence of a French film, the exceptional length of the film allowing it to develop in depth. The work of Carné and the director of photography, Roger Hubert, on Prévert's material has remarkable clarity. Anyone seeing the film and not knowing the vicissitudes surrounding its shooting, would never suspect the problems, the interruptions, the changes in lighting, the improvised linking material which the director had to contend with. Carné was at the height of his powers.

In his masterpieces of 1938 and 1939, Carné's vision was definitely in the *noir* mode. He depicted the end of a civilized world, the sordid, suicidal despair of a degenerating society. His heroes were crushed: Jean Gabin died on screen, betrayed by the vile cunning of the ultimate *salauds* (Pierre Brasseur, Michel Simon, Jules Berry) whose actions were inexcusable, and one could imagine the sad and solitary fate awaiting the hero's companion, whether Michèle Morgan or Jacqueline Laurent. It was irredeemably a dog's

*Les Enfants du paradis* – Garance (Arletty).

life. The sky was leaden, the streets slippery, society repulsive. These films bore the mark (the shadow) of the refugee German cameramen who had lit them. *Les Enfants du paradis* is less sombre. The 1943 film distils, sums up and surpasses French-style 'realism'. The characters imagined by the poet, Prévert, come alive, they are no longer 'acted upon' by an inhuman fate. All of them, even the minor characters and extras, have rare depth and complexity. With the exception of Jéricho, the rag-and-bone man who derives from the past and brings only misfortune, they are both manipulators and manipulated, at the same time or alternately; they have their reasons for what they do, and among these reasons there are some good ones. Even Lacenaire, the cold-blooded killer, is also a romantic rebel whom Marcel Herrand endows with a charm more sarcastic than perverse.

*Les Enfants du paradis* is also (again) a film about despair, about the impossibility of love, about living a dog's life. Its heroes are unhappy, their love affairs go wrong. But it doesn't leave that impression of the world coming to a sordid end that oppressed the films of 1938. There are moments of fulfilment in *Les Enfants du paradis* which in a way compensate for the fate of the protagonists. Beneath the despair, the show goes on.

And *Les Enfants du paradis* is a film about spectacle. It is the cinema in all its glory paying homage to the theatre. The curtain that rises on the Boulevard du Crime is a device reminiscent of Renoir. Carné and Prévert borrow it for the duration of one film to heighten the sense of illusion that makes reality bearable. In *Le Jour se lève* the spectacle was dire: Valentin humiliated his performing dogs in a degrading masquerade. In *Les Enfants du paradis* the actors are supreme, beautiful and strong – strong enough and clever enough in the practice of their art to turn a grotesque play to their advantage: *L'Auberge des Adrets* is no doubt a worthless drama, but Frédérick uses it as a springboard to release his creative energy, and he holds the delighted audience in the palm of his hand. It is surely not by chance that Carné's film shows us the whole spectrum of what the theatre can do: from the opening farcical pantomime of the Funambules – with Frederick trussed up in a lion's skin – to the poetic mime of Baptiste, 'Chand' d'habits'; from the serial melodrama of *L'Auberge des Adrets* to the inspiration of *Othello*. The cinema is paying homage to the theatre, to a theatre which is like its mirror: silent theatre, like silent film, loses nothing to the spoken word, even when the word is Shakespeare's. It is, among other things, a homage to the 'primitives' of theatre and of film.

The story of the theatre is also the story of the feverish activity backstage, the crush and the impatience. It is also the audience, whether in the stalls or the 'gods', the demanding, cheeky, public that makes the careers of Baptiste and Frédérick. It is even Paris, the most beautiful stage in the world, an idealized Paris, gilded by the nostalgic imagination of Parisians exiled in the countryside around Nice. Life is not much fun, especially in 1943. But for one moment, one evening, one night of love, life is redeemed.

*Les Enfants du paradis* occupies a unique place in French cinema. It is one of the rare films to have been genuinely popular – because of its subject, its roots and its history. It is a film which has become greater with the passage of time. Prévert and Carné together created, all of a piece, a world peopled by a half-dozen protagonists who, with their common, deep bond with a basic French culture, rank with the tremendous characters created by Victor Hugo and Emile Zola. The Jean Valjean of *Les Misérables* has had several screen versions; the adaptations of the best known of Hugo's novels by Henri Fescourt or Raymond Bernard are great films, both of which manipulate epic imagery. But that imagery pre-dated the cinema. The first viewers of *Les Misérables* on the screen compared the Jean Valjean interpreted by Gabriel Gabrio or Harry Baur with the original in the novel. Garance was created by the cinema. Imagined by Prévert, moulded by Carné, she is an original – a complex, astonishing and definitive heroine – which the seventh art has lodged in the collective imaginary for at least two generations. For the past twenty years, there has rarely been a week when *Les Enfants du paradis* has not been shown in some small Paris cinema,[2] and it is frequently broadcast on the (too small) television screen.

Like the great archetypal novels of the nineteenth century, *Les Enfants du paradis* is always alive to an audience that does not age. On 14 December 1984, an elegant cinema was opened in the Pompidou Centre in Paris. It is called the 'Salle Garance'.

*Translated from the French by Marianne Johnson*

## Notes

1 Alexandre Trauner, unpublished interview collected by Nicolas Bourdais and Véronique Guyot, 1987.
2 Likewise, *Les Enfants du paradis* is regularly screened in French film seasons in the UK and the USA, and ranks among top favourites (eds).

## Selected bibliography

Affron, Mirella Jona (1978) '*Les Enfants du paradis*: Play of Genres', *Cinema Journal*, 18 (1).
*A la rencontre de Jacques Prévert* (1987) Fondation Maeght.
Barsacq, Léon (1976) *Caligari's Cabinet and Other Grand Illusions: A History of Film Design*, Boston, Little, Brown & Co.
*Cahiers de la cinémathèque*, 5 (1972) special Carné issue.
*Ciné-Club* (1949) nouvelle série: special Carné issue.
Carné, Marcel (1975) *La Vie à belles dents*, Paris, Ollivier.
Chazal, Robert (1965) *Marcel Carné*, Paris, Seghers.
Jacob, Guy (1960) *Jacques Prévert*, Lyon, Premier Plan, 14.
Forbes, J. (1997) *Les Enfants du paradis*, London, British Film Institute.
Freadman, Anne (1986) 'Reading the Visual', *Framework*, 30/31.
Guillot, Gérard (1966) *Les Prévert*, Paris, Seghers.
Oms, Marcel (1979) 'Les Enfants du paradis ou la mutation cinématographique du mélodrame', *Cahiers de la cinémathèque*, 28.
Perez, Michel (1986) *Les Films de Carné*, Paris, Ramsay.
Queval, Jean (1952) *Marcel Carné*, Paris, Editions du Cerf.
Rachline, Michel (1981) *Jacques Prévert: drôle de vie*, Paris, Ramsay.
Sellier, Geneviève (1992) '*Les Enfants du paradis*': Marcel Carné et Jacques Prévert, Paris, Nathan.
Turk, Edward Baron (1979) 'The Birth of Children of Paradise', *American Film*, 4 (9).
Turk, Edward Baron (1989) *Child of Paradise, Marcel Carné and the Golden Age of French Cinema*, Cambridge, Mass., Harvard University Press.

## Scripts

Carné, Marcel and Prévert, Jacques (1967) *Les Enfants du paradis*, Paris, *Avant-scène cinéma*, 72–3.
Carné, Marcel and Prévert, Jacques (1968) *Les Enfants du paradis*, trans. Dinah Brooke, London, Lorrimer.

Carné, Marcel and Prévert, Jacques (1974) *Les Enfants du Paradis, album photo*, Paris, Balland (an illustrated book of the film).

# Appendix

## *Marcel Carné (1909–96): filmography*

See Chapter 4, on *Le Jour se lève*, for a full filmography

### *Other films cited in the text*

*A bout de souffle* (*Breathless*), Jean-Luc Godard (1959)
*La Belle équipe* (*They were Five* [UK]; *A Fine Team* [USA]), Julien Duvivier (1936)
*La Bête humaine* (*The Human Beast* [UK]; *Judas Was a Woman* [USA]), Jean Renoir (1938)
*Le Ciel est à vous* (*The Sky is Yours*), Jean Grémillon (1944)
*Le Corbeau* (*The Raven*), Henri-Georges Clouzot (1943)
*Le Coupable*, André Antoine (1917)
*Le Crime de Monsieur Lange* (*The Crime of Monsieur Lange*), Jean Renoir (1935)
*Les Enfants du paradis* (*Children of Paradise*), Marcel Carné (1943–5)
*Fantômas*, Louis Feuillade (1913–14)
*Le Joli mai*, Chris Marker (1963)
*Le Jour se lève* (*Daybreak*), Marcel Carné (1939)
*Lumière d'été*, Jean Grémillon (1943)
*Les Misérables*, Raymond Bernard (1933)
*Les Misérables*, Henri Fescourt (1925–6)
*Une Partie de campagne* (*A Day in the Country*), Jean Renoir (1936)
*Le Quai des brumes* (*Port of Shadows*), Marcel Carné (1938)
*La Règle du jeu* (*Rules of the Game*), Jean Renoir (1939)
*Toni*, Jean Renoir (1934)
*La Vie de bohême*, Marcel L'Herbier (1943)
*Les Visiteurs du soir* (*The Devil's Envoys*), Marcel Carné (1942)

# 6

# THE SACRAMENT OF WRITING

Robert Bresson's *Le Journal d'un curé de campagne* (1951)

*Keith A. Reader*

> these categories of salvation or loss or grace derive their strength only
> from this sense of the real, and not vice versa.
>
> (Arnaud 1986, 20)

Scarcely any other 'adaptation' of a major literary work for the cinema has
had the impact of Robert Bresson's filming of Georges Bernanos' *Le Journal
d'un curé de campagne*. The inverted commas are there to emphasize how little
Bresson's film owes to canonical concepts of filmic adaptation, which it did
much to challenge but which are still overwhelmingly dominant in the
world of television and largely so in that of the cinema. (An interesting
example is the international impact of Volker Schlöndorff's *Un Amour de
Swann* compared with the smaller-scale television and art-house success of
Percy Adlon's *Céleste*, another 'Proust film' which in its use of silences and
image/sound dialectic has much in common with the work of Bresson.) The
paring-away of many elements of Bernanos' text, the scrupulous – religious –
fidelity to what remains, the austerity of the filming and the avoidance of
star actors, even of actors *tout court* – these have been commented upon by
virtually every writer on the film, and in the French cinematic world of 1951
their contrast with what had gone before was particularly striking.

For *Le Journal d'un curé de campagne*, in the history of its making as well as
in its textuality, marked a radical break with the *'film de qualité'* characteristic
of much post-Occupation cinema, and of its literary adaptations in particular. Jean Aurenche and Paul Bost were the screenwriting team that established virtual rights of ownership over this area, notably through their scripts
for Jean Delannoy's *La Symphonie pastorale* and Claude Autant-Lara's *Le Diable
au corps*. The Aurenche and Bost 'recipe' involved the use of well-known
actresses and actors (Michèle Morgan, Gérard Philippe), carefully constructed
period atmosphere and often also the introduction of one or two elements

extraneous or marginal to the literary text, as if to append their authorial signature in between that of Gide or Radiguet and that of the director. (One example is the much greater stress given to the Armistice Day celebrations in the film of *Le Diable au corps*.)

Bresson's film is so clearly the antithesis of all this that it comes as a surprise to learn that the first adaptation of *Le Journal d'un curé de campagne* for the screen was by Jean Aurenche, in 1947. This was rejected by Bernanos himself, for reasons eloquently summarized by Michel Estève:

> the disappearance of characters essential to transcribing Bernanos' vision of the world (Torcy, Delbende, Olivier), the replacement of inner revolt by spectacular blasphemy (Chantal's spitting out of the host), and of 'everything is grace' by 'everything is death', were obvious betrayals of the spirit of Bernanos' novel.
>
> (Estève 1983, 26)

An attempt by the Dominican Father Bruckberger, which apparently translated the action into the resistance period, was likewise rejected. Bresson's adaptation in its turn was rejected by the initial producer, and it was not until 1950, with finance from the Union Générale Cinématographique, that he was able to begin filming. The result led André Bazin, in his fundamental essay 'Le Journal d'un curé de campagne and the Stylistics of Robert Bresson', to say: 'After Bresson, Aurenche and Bost are but the Viollet-le-Duc of cinematographic adaptation' (Bazin 1967, I, 143).

Viollet-le-Duc was best known for his architectural restorations of medieval monuments (such as the walled city of Carcassonne) in an idiom often a long way removed from the original, and characterized by anachronistic or superfluous flourishes. Bazin's remark is thus a direct thrust at the Aurenche–Bost conception of stylistic authenticity, which *Journal* (as it will hereinafter be referred to for brevity) did more to eradicate than any other film, except maybe Jean-Pierre Melville's *Le Silence de la mer*. Jean Lacroix, writing in *Le Monde* of 15 May 1954, distils well the specific quality of Bresson's fidelity to the text, a fidelity which is grounded in ascesis:

> The astonishing success of Bresson's film . . . is that it corresponds perfectly to Bernanos' text, not by being slavishly literal, but through a recreation that rigorously eliminates the psychological and the social alike, to centre everything on the spiritual drama.
>
> (in Estève 1983, 30)

Bernanos' novel abounds in sensory and social detail, excised or minimized in Bresson's film. Bresson shot, but eliminated in the editing, a number of scenes showing the priest in relationships with his parishioners (for instance, saying Mass), and the novel's descriptions of the village of Ambricourt, along with the touches of Flemish regional colour that are an important part of the character of the Curé de Torcy, all but disappear from the film.

This is not to say, however, that the film's ascesis makes of it a rarefied or dematerialized work. On the contrary; the sound of the gardener's rake gathering up the leaves, of the priest's pen as it moves across the page, of the bottle of wine as it falls to the ground has an impact as great as that of any visual image, and we are put in mind of Bresson's maxim: 'When a sound can replace an image, cut the image or neutralize it. The ear goes more towards the within, the eye towards the outer' (Bresson 1977, 28).

The sounds are 'realistic' (their place in the diegesis is clear, they do not come laden with pre-digested psychological or symbolic significance), yet that realism is precisely what bestows upon them, or reveals within them, a mystical or supernatural quality. In this respect the film itself can be seen as a *sacrament* – the outward sign of an inward grace, neither perceptible except with and through the other. Here there is an important analogy with post-Saussurean developments of the relationship between signified and signifier, seen (at least since Lacan) no longer as dissociable entities, but as indissolubly welded in their very difference from each other. If sacraments are linguistic, language is also sacramental.

The doubling-up of narrative in the diary scenes, where the text is pronounced by the priest's voice as we see his hand writing it, is the most striking instance of this sacramental view of language, at once Way of the Cross and way of salvation. *Journal* is not, however, a logocentric film, and the opening sentence of St John's Gospel would be a quite inappropriate epigraph to it; for the diary scenes make it impossible to decide which comes first, speech or writing, or indeed whether such a question is even meaningful. The first sentence that we hear and see ('I don't think I am doing wrong in jotting down, day by day, without hiding anything, the very simple trivial secrets of a very ordinary kind of life' (Bernanos 1956, 10)) is, precisely, language reflecting on itself – the voice destroying the myth of its own origin and authorship not only through what it says, but also through the trace of the writing hand across the paper. The sacrament of writing does not, for Bresson as for Derrida, give access to a metaphysics of presence.

This is most graphically illustrated by the film's final image – the (empty) Cross filling the screen as the priest's friend Dufréty recounts his final moments and dying words: 'Tout est grâce.' The last diary scene, immediately before, has shown the priest writing with great difficulty and without a voice-over, as though to figure the imminent disappearance of his body. Just as the social body of Ambricourt and of the Church has disappeared from the film, so the priest's body and that of Christ disappear, or are not present, at the film's climax. This needs to be borne in mind as an important corrective to Dudley Andrew's statement that 'his rigorous instrument of self-knowledge – his writing – has brought him into focus with his image and, therefore, has made him one with Christ' (Andrew 1984,

91

130). The oneness with Christ, suggested in a host of ways throughout the film (as when Séraphita, Veronica-like, wipes the priest's exhausted face with her kerchief), can achieve its apotheosis only through absence, and in this way the film seems to me closer than the novel to the notion of Godhead as kenosis or emptying-out – as renunciation, that is to say, rather than as plenitude.

Related to this is Bresson's almost legendary antipathy to the use of 'actors' on the one hand and to any taint of psychology on the other. 'The thing that matters is not what they show me but what they hide from me and, above all, what they do not suspect is in them' (Bresson 1977, 2); Bresson's remark shows how alien to his concerns any view of actors 'understanding' their part is. The weeding-out of all non-believers before Claude Laydu was cast as the priest, Laydu's spending time fasting and meditating in Normandy before filming started, Bresson's use of real live coals in the fire from which the priest plucks the Countess's medallion – these are superficially akin to the tricks and techniques of Stanislavsky or the Actors' Studio, but Bresson's 'method' is quite other. Psychology, for him, intrudes between surface and soul, between matter and spirit, seeking to explain what can only be shown. Here again we find echoes of Lacanian psychoanalysis, in the resolute antipathy to rationalization and the stress on engaging with language as material process. Lacan, in *The Four Fundamental Concepts of Psychoanalysis*, speaks of sacraments as operative (much as for J.-L. Austin in *How to Do Things with Words* they would be examples of performative speech-acts) and as 'struck by a kind of oblivion' (Lacan 1977, 265). The 'oblivion' in question is – for Bresson at least – *inter alia* that of the world of ego-psychology and of understanding, whether rational or intuitive. Lacan's definition of desire in/of analysis as 'a desire to obtain absolute difference' (Lacan 1977, 276) presents analogies with Bresson's attitude towards his models (he refuses the term 'actors'), and the oneness of which Andrew speaks is achieved in the end only through – is perhaps paradoxically the 'same' as? – the absolute difference figured by the absences – of voice-over, of bodies, of Body, almost of image – in which *Journal* culminates.

Jean Sémolué, in his monograph *Bresson*, sees the film as following the overall pattern of the novel in its division into three unequal parts, each organized around three fundamental themes relating to the priest's solitude – sickness (the 'solitude of the body'), sacerdotal or spiritual solitude, and social solitude (his alienation from his parishioners). The film's opening sequences – the first writing of the diary, the priest mopping his brow, the glimpse through the château gates of the Count and his mistress Louise embracing furtively, the priest entering the presbytery – give us these three forms of solitude in a way that immediately suggests a world without wholeness or totality. Ambricourt is nowhere presented as a community, and the priest's speaking of 'my parish, my first parish' is thus a poignant, almost nostalgic utterance – an aspiration towards a transcendental unity that will

*Le Journal d'un curé de campagne* – above: the priest (Claude Laydu); below: the priest and Séraphita (Martine Lemaire).

be achieved only with his death. The priest's end, like the film's, is implicit in its/their beginning.

It very quickly becomes impossible to view the priest's ill-health in purely medical terms. When we not only see, but hear his voice describing the 'meals' of stale bread dipped in wine that are his sole sustenance, the sacramental dimension could hardly be plainer. Paul Schrader, author of a major essay on Bresson but better-known as the scriptwriter of the Scorsese films *Taxi Driver* and *Raging Bull*, both strongly Bresson-influenced, alludes to this when he has taxi-driver Travis Bickle – a tormented 'priest' of a quite different kind – feed himself on bread and apricot brandy. To persist in drinking the cheapest of *gros rouge* when subject to agonizing stomach pains runs counter to any conceivable verisimilitude, and thereby warns us from an early stage not to read the film too referentially or 'realistically'. When a bottle of wine falls from the table and breaks, much later in the film, the dark rivulets across the floor inevitably remind us of blood – the blood the priest will cough up more and more as his agony reaches its end. . . . The important point is that this is done without pathos, that the wine and the blood signify the priest's sufferings rather than inviting some impossible empathy with them. The sacramental quality of the text is once more plain beyond the comparatively obvious level of its subject-matter.

The priest's social solitude – needless to say not given any 'psychological' justification – is plainest in his relationship with the Curé of Torcy. The Curé – played by Armand Guibert, a psychoanalyst acquaintance of Bresson – represents a robust, combative type of priesthood seemingly at odds with the country priest's, but in fact its necessary complement. The Church Suffering requires the Church Militant that it may become the Church Triumphant, just as neither the active nor the contemplative life is conceivable without its counterpart. The Curé of Torcy's understanding of his colleague is thus of a spiritual rather than a psychological kind, and – by stressing the two priests' reciprocal otherness – paradoxically reinforces the very loneliness it might appear to alleviate.

Psychological incomprehension and spiritual understanding (however shadowy) characterize the attitudes of many of the other inhabitants of Ambricourt towards the priest. Séraphita Dumouchel, his brightest catechism pupil, says that she listens to him only because 'he has very beautiful eyes', yet she will be there when he faints at the climax of his agony in Ambricourt. Chantal, the daughter of the Count and Countess, pours forth her hatred – of her father and his mistress, but also of herself and (thus) of God – in tones that cruelly mock any exhortations to love, yet when the priest divines her deeper intentions and asks her to hand over the suicide note he realizes she is carrying, she does so with a whispered: 'Are you then the Devil?' This may put us in mind of Bernanos' *Sous le soleil de Satan* (filmed in 1987 by Maurice Pialat with Gérard Depardieu), in which Satan is invoked to raise a child from the dead. Good and evil, and often in both Bernanos and Bresson, exist as complements rather than opposites – as so to speak allotropic variants of one spiritual state – in a way distinctly Catholic rather than just 'Christian' (Chabrol, Graham Greene, Hitchcock, Mauriac, Scorsese all display a similar tendency in their work). If the major 'epistemological break' between Catholicism and Protestantism was that between justification by works and justification by faith, it needs to be added that the works by which, in a Catholic perspective, we are justified may 'belong' to us only in a seemingly arbitrary, even random, manner. This evokes the disturbing rhetoric of grace constantly present in Bresson, and distilled in the memorable *pensée* of one of his major pre-texts, Pascal: 'Be comforted; it is not from yourself that you must expect it, but on the contrary you must expect it by expecting nothing from yourself' (Pascal 1966, 95).

It also presents striking parallels with the Freudian psyche, most significant precisely where it escapes the subject's control – for Lacan, 'là où ça parle', where 'it' but also the id (*ça* in French) speaks, in the text of the unconscious.

That unconscious, structured like a language, thereby returns us again to the materiality of the linguistic – thus also sacramental – sign. This is most strikingly apparent in the film's – literal and spiritual – centre, the long dialogue between the priest and the Countess. It is here that the dialectic between psychological and spiritual affinity is given its fullest development, reinforced in its insistent materiality by the sound of the gardener's rake gathering up the leaves – an echo of the priest's pen moving across the diary pages, a suggestion that what is going on inside the château, on the screen, is some kind of raking bare or gathering up of souls, the rhythmic *archiécriture* of grace? . . . Bazin describes the dialogue as 'the opposite side of the coin, if one dare to say so, of the Divine Countenance' (Bazin 1967, I, 137). This formulation will obviously pose problems for non-believers, or at any rate for those to whom the soul is a concept at best nebulous, at worst obscurantist. One way of dealing with this is to view the soul not as some primary essence, whose very antecedence makes it necessarily unsayable, but rather as that which remains as a signifying absence after 'everything else' – the bodily, the psychological, the gestural – has been stripped away. (There are parallels here with Lacan's notion of the necessary-but-unsayable 'real'.) If, that is to say, the soul is viewed differentially rather than as the apogee of a metaphysics of presence, the dialogue can be seen as leading into the final conversation with Chantal, immediately before the priest leaves for Lille, in which he counters her defiant threats of evil-doing with the phrase: 'I answer for you, soul for soul.' This transposes the Pascalian wager on the existence of God on to the plane of difference and exchange; what is important is not the plenitude of the two souls but their interchangeability, in accord with the Catholic notion of transferability of grace and redemption. The ascetic quality of the film is thus spiritually as well as aesthetically significant, reaching even to that ineffable innermost essence that is for orthodox Christianity the soul.

It is immediately before this dialogue that the film introduces a diegetic ambiguity absent from the novel, and one whose theological implications seem to me so fundamental that I am surprised that no writer on the film known to me has commented on them. The priest, on his rounds to far-flung parishioners, walks, or stumbles, with great difficulty, eventually to faint and be discovered by Séraphita Dumouchel. The Bernanos text describes what is clearly, depending on one's faith or lack of it, a mystical vision or the hallucination of one very close to death: 'I feared, in opening them [my eyes] to look upon the face before which all must kneel. Yet I saw it. And it was the face of a child, too – or a very young girl – only without the spark of youth' (Bernanos 1956, 184).

This is followed, after he has picked himself up and walked a little further, by his second fainting and the intervention of Séraphita. What Bresson does – and of all the myriad ways in which he stresses the insistence of the spiritual in the material this is perhaps the most remarkable – is to conflate the two losses of consciousness. The screen goes dark (though emphatically not empty) as the voice-over recounts the priest's vision, and this runs into a close-up of Séraphita wiping his face. In the novel, the vision of the face of God precedes the encounter with Séraphita; in the film, it seems to me that we are invited to identify the two, that the 'face before which all must kneel' is quite literally Séraphita's. The divine permeates and is permeated by the human, rather than being transcendentally set against it. Paul Schrader speaks of a hypothetical 'irate viewer' antagonized by the film's refusal to allow her or him place for intellectual or emotional judgement. For Schrader, 'he [*sic*] has mistaken the everyday for transcendental style and has only seen a fraction of the film' (Schrader 1972, 70). I would qualify this, at least for certain key points in the film, by saying that there is a sense in which the transcendental re-immanentizes itself – most notably in the diary-writing, but most audaciously perhaps in the episode to which I have just referred.

The process of ascesis and stripping away that is the aesthetic and spiritual dynamic of the film reaches its climax, as I have suggested, at the end, beginning when the voice-over disappears from the final diary-writing sequence. This does more than suggest the priest's terminal exhaustion; it also focuses our desire as spectators upon the trace of the written characters. Jacques Derrida's contention in *Of Grammatology*, that the traditional primacy of speech over writing rests upon a delusive metaphysics of presence, has by now acceded to the rank of a post-structuralist commonplace. Here, in a film whose concluding words, and their theological context, would seem to point towards just such a metaphysics, the disappearance of speech at such a key moment acts to undercut such a presupposition. Presence is always–already impregnated with absence, in the filmic text far more than in the novel, as though Bresson's weaving of doublings-up, ellipses, and silences added even as it appears to take away.

We are reminded too of Lacan's stress on the importance of the scopic drive – the desire to look. It may appear difficult to transpose this into the world of Bresson's film, apparently as desexualized as any text-to-be-looked-at ever can be; but if we at the same time return to the notion of writing as sacrament, and think of the successive holding-up of the host and the chalice in the Catholic Mass as they are consecrated, the difficulty will become less. Writers as different as Georges Bataille (in *Histoire de l'œil*) and Annie Leclerc (in *Hommes et femmes*) have spoken of the erotic charge carried by the sacrament of Communion; we may think too of the work of Buñuel, the 'Beggars' banquet' parody of the Last Supper in *Viridiana* and the mysterious First Communion photograph of Séverine in *Belle de jour*. The holding aloft – erect – of the chalice, so evident a vaginal symbol, by a celibate male to a congregation that will not partake of its contents (Catholics receiving only the host at Communion) is a striking example of the Roman Church's *nonpareil* choreography of desire and denial. E. M. Forster, being a humanist, could ground an ethics that was also an aesthetics in the phrase 'Only connect'; Bernanos, and after him Bresson, knew that for Catholic mysticism and the post-Freudian psyche 'Only cathect' would be nearer the mark.

The Cross that fills the screen at the end takes the dialectic of presence to its furthest conceivable point. The absence of the body (of the priest from the screen, of Christ from the crucifix as from the tomb on the third day) is a conventional theological signifier of an eternal, because no longer material, presence. Yet that presence is dissipated and disseminated by the words that accompany the visual image: 'Tout est grâce.' Claude Laydu did not realize until he had watched the final version of the film that he had been playing a saint. Sanctity and grace, Laydu's experience and the final shot alike suggest, are process not telos, their presence diffused and deferred throughout the film and its ultimate recognition (as process), as Harold Bloom would say (Bloom 1975 and 1982), belated. That which hostile critics of the film singled out as its most profoundly uncinematic aspect turns out to be a supreme meditation, not merely on film as textuality, but on the whole dialectic of presence and absence in which theodicy is grounded. It is virtually a commonplace nowadays that film-makers such as Eisenstein or Godard were able to write political essays in film; Bresson, with *Journal d'un curé de campagne*, produced not merely a qualitatively new type of literary adaptation, but probably the first theological essay to be written in the film medium.

*Where readily available published translations of the original French texts exist, I have used these. All other translations from the French are my own.*

## Selected bibliography

This is necessarily brief and selective, concentrating on major or widely available texts, mostly in book form.

Andrew, Dudley (1984) *Film in the Aura of Art*, Princeton, Princeton University Press.

Arnaud, Philippe (1986) *Robert Bresson*, Paris, Cahiers du cinéma, Paris, Editions de l'Etoile.

Bazin, André (1967) *What Is Cinema?*, trans. Hugh Gray, Berkeley, Los Angeles, London, University of California Press.

Bernanos, Georges (1956) *Journal d'un curé de campagne*, trans. Pamela Norris, London, Collins/Fontana.

Bloom, Harold (1975) *A Map of Misreading*, New York, Oxford University Press.

Bloom, Harold (1982) *Agon: Towards a Theory of Revisionism*, New York, Oxford University Press.

Bresson, Robert (1977) *Notes on Cinematography*, trans. Jonathan Griffin, New York, Urizen Books, London, Pluto Press. Reprinted, London, Quartet Books, 1986.

Durgnat, Raymond (1969), 'Le Journal d'un curé de campagne', in Cameron (ed.) (1969) *The Films of Robert Bresson*, London, Studio Vista, 42–50.

Estève, Michel (1983) *Robert Bresson – la passion du cinématographe*, Paris, Editions Albatros.

Hanlon, Lindley (1986) *Fragments: Bresson's Film Style*, n.p., Associated University Press.

Lacan, Jacques (1977) *The Four Fundamental Concepts of Psychoanalysis*, trans. Alan Sheridan, London, Hogarth Press.

Païni, Dominique (1997) *Robert Bresson: éloge*, Paris, Mazzotta.

Pascal, Blaise (1966) *Pensées*, trans. A. J. Krailsheimer, London, Penguin Books.

Reader, Keith (1986) ' "D'où cela vient-il?" Notes on Three Films by Robert Bresson', *French Studies*, XI (4), 427–42.

Schrader, Paul (1972) *Transcendental Style in Film: Ozu, Bresson, Dreyer*, Berkeley, Los Angeles, and London, University of California Press.

Sémolué, Jean (1959) *Bresson*, Paris, Editions Universitaires.

Sémolué, Jean (1993) *Bresson ou l'acte pur des métamorphoses*, Paris, Flammarion.

Sloan, Jane (1983) *Robert Bresson: A Guide to References and Resources*, Boston, Mass., G. K. Hall.

Sontag, Susan (1966) *Against Interpretation*, New York, Farrar, Straus & Giroux.

# Appendix

## *Robert Bresson (1907–): filmography*

1934  *Les Affaires publiques* (short), co-director, Pierre Charbonnier
1943  *Les Anges du péché* (*Angels of the Street*)
1945  *Les Dames du Bois de Boulogne* (*Ladies of the Park*)
1951  *Le Journal d'un curé de campagne* (*Diary of a Country Priest*)
1956  *Un Condamné à mort s'est échappé* (*A Man Escaped*)

1959 *Pickpocket*
1962 *Le Procès de Jeanne d'Arc (The Trial of Joan of Arc)*
1966 *Au hazard Balthazar (Balthazar)*
1967 *Mouchette*
1969 *Une Femme douce (A Gentle Creature)*
1971 *Quatre nuits d'un rêveur (Four Nights of a Dreamer)*
1974 *Lancelot du lac (Lancelot of the Lake)*
1977 *Le Diable probablement*
1983 *L'Argent*

### Other films cited in the text

*Un Amour de Swann (Swann in Love)*, Volker Schlöndorff (France/Germany 1982)
*Belle de jour*, Luis Buñuel (1967)
*Céleste*, Percy Aldon (1983)
*Le Diable au corps (Devil in the Flesh)*, Claude Autant-Lara (1947)
*Raging Bull*, Martin Scorsese (USA 1979)
*Le Silence de la mer*, Jean-Pierre Melville (1949)
*Sous le soleil de Satan (Under Satan's Sun)*, Maurice Pialat (1987)
*La Symphonie pastorale*, Jean Delannoy (1946)
*Taxi Driver*, Martin Scorsese (USA 1976)
*Viridiana*, Luis Buñuel (Spain 1961)

# 7

# A BREATH OF SEA AIR

Jacques Tati's *Les Vacances de Monsieur Hulot*
(1952)

*Pierre Sorlin*

*Les Vacances de Monsieur Hulot* turned out to be a success the very first week of its release. Not a *big* hit: the 300,000 seats sold in Paris put it in seventh position in the 1953 box office. Hollywood had lost its predominance, and the winners of the year were French–Italian co-productions – *Le Retour de Don Camillo* and *Le Salaire de la peur*, two expensive, cleverly made, well photographed pictures. An American movie as lavish as the former, *The Greatest Show on Earth*, came third. As for the other three films the difference with *Hulot* was small: Tati could easily have been in fourth place. At least, his was the first French film on the 1953 list (Centre Nationale de la Cinématographie, 1954).

The picture was poorly advertised. The cast was not impressive: outside the director (and screenwriter) Jacques Tati, who plays the part of Hulot, it was made up of little-known stage actors, most of whom would never make a brilliant career. Among the technicians, only the chief editor was highly experienced,[1] and the producer had made only two other movies. Notwithstanding these shortcomings, the film was praised by all critics and movie buffs and met with a good response. The unexpected had happened four years before when *Jour de fête*, a hastily completed movie with almost no dialogue and an ill-defined plot, made a great deal of money and was awarded significant national and international prizes.[2] *Jour de fête* was something totally new in French cinema. *Hulot*, which made another step in the same direction, is more famous. This may be due to the fact that *Jour de fête* is a picture of the postwar Reconstruction era and manifests typical features of the period. Postman François, the main character, is greatly excited by the projection of an American picture, one of those naïve propaganda works which introduced Europe to the 'superiority' of American management. François tries to adapt American methods to his deliveries. The setting of the film is a village at a time when many French movies emphasized the importance of the rural tradition and of the revival of the countryside in postwar France. *Hulot* is (seemingly) exempt from these connections with the spirit of the times. It is a blast of fresh air, a pleasurable moment outside the ponderous conventions of current production, a floating story with shaky characters and a humour distinct from the wordy theatrical comedies or the clumsy slapsticks which were usually offered on French screens.

*Hulot* is still a highly enjoyable piece of cinema, but film studies cannot be content with simply expressing appreciative statements. There is always something in films which escapes easy evaluation, but we must continue to analyse pictures in so far as they are structured combinations of perceptible data.

Narrative categories become ineffective where *Hulot* is concerned: there is no coherent, logically organized plot. We are in a French seaside resort on the Channel. Tourists arrive at the beginning of the summer vacation at the outset of the picture. They leave at the end. There are scenes on the beach, in a hotel and a boarding-house, on a tennis court and in a small harbour. Is it then a documentary? Not in the least, since we lack certain necessary information: the precise location of the resort, a description of the surroundings, etc. The movie-camera seems to have been placed at random in more or less convenient corners. Consider the first shots on the beach. People merely pass by. Then there are several short scenes: a man who has just lain down is called and has to scramble up quickly. A woman is cross because she has not brought the right things. A boy burns the strings of a tent with a sun-lens. Another unfastens a boat which is swept away by the waves. Funny though they are, these snapshots are hardly likely to make viewers cry with laughter. Spectators enter a different, bizarre atmosphere; jokes raise only distant smiles and actions are not tied together, not even by Hulot, who is personally unaware of what is happening around him.

This very lack of co-ordination gives the picture part of its charm: we are sometimes left in ignorance of where the scene is taking place, we are in no hurry and do not anticipate the unexpected or the sensational. But the ostensible looseness is a trick: the film is in fact carefully, deliberately constructed. There are no sequences, in the common meaning of the word, but rather 'moments', identified less by incidents (of which there are few) than by the time of the day, the location, or meeting with people. The film may be summarized as follows:

1  A railway station; moving trains on a summer day;
2  Cars driving towards the sea;
3  Martine's arrival at her boarding-house;[3]
4  Hulot's arrival at his hotel;
5  Evening meal at the hotel;
6  The beach; Hulot takes a walk among the bathers;
7  Lunch at the hotel;
8  Arrival of Martine's aunt;

9  Evening at the hotel;
10  The beach; Hulot hits a bather (Smith) and hides in a dinghy;
11  Hulot dripping wet re-enters the hotel at lunch time;
12  Hulot in a cemetery;
13  Hulot plays tennis;
14  Evening at the hotel;
15  Hulot's abortive attempt to ride a horse;
16  Fancy-dress ball;
17  Jaunt in the countryside;
18  During the night Hulot accidentally sets fire to the fireworks;
19  End of the holiday.

This summary allows us to see how well crafted the film is. 'Moments' 1 to 4 introduce the situation (holiday) and the characters – or at least the people who will recurrently be seen on the screen. An opposition outside/inside is then used in 5 to 12 and interplays with an alternation of meals and leisure. From 13 to 16 the same contrast operates, but the relationship is reversed. The seven last 'moments' expand upon possibilities opened in 6 to 12, in other words amusements offered to tourists on a beach. 'Moments' 5 to 12 could also be understood as: the first evening, the first day, the second day; but they might also just as well be every morning, every lunch, every afternoon, etc.

Most viewers miss this extremely cohesive, almost exaggerated regularity and see the picture as a free variation on the theme of vacations. They are not wrong in that: every 'moment' is made up of a collection of small, unrelated details which could be inserted in another part of the filmic concatenation. A man wants to photograph his family but he is called to the telephone, and the others have to wait for him. The scene opens 'moment' 8 but would not be out of place in 6 or 10. The structure, rigid on paper, is constantly blurred on the screen by many of the moments' fungibility. The boundaries between moments dissolve with the intrusion of images taken from another filmic space. At the end of 6, Hulot is in the street; at the beginning of 7, he enters the dining room: outdoors/indoors. But it is hard to decide when 7 ends: some shots are taken outside, while the soundtrack still conveys the unmistakable noises of the dining room. Subsequent shots show the street as seen from the hotel, or picture the candy-seller, whom Hulot looks at at the end of 6, at lunch (the meal is a staple theme). The candy-seller is one of the many people, possibly inhabitants of the village, foreign to the cast, who intervene fleetingly as if they were going to become characters in the fiction and then vanish for ever. By mixing up space and by focusing short scenes around different people, the film never stops undermining its own ability to follow a well-defined order.

From a formal point of view, the film is to be read as a conflict between necessity and chance. Yet the clash neither disconcerts the audience nor gives it the impression it is being offered an 'absence of film'. Antagonistic elements are of different nature and strength. While necessity is deeply rooted in a systematic use of conventions with which filmgoers are familiar, chance is limited to an erratic depiction of settings or a temporary fading of characters. All the night-time 'moments' are enclosed by a fade – probably the tritest of all cinematic devices. 'Moments' 1 and 2 are firmly linked by an identity of motion inside the frame: 1 closes with a train arriving from the left background and turning towards the left foreground; 2 begins with a car driving in the same direction. 'Moment' 2 is devoted to the road but its last shot, by panning on to a beach from a car-window, ties up 2 (cars) to 3 (the seaside resort). What is more, the film obeys the rule of coherent structure by creating its own references so that the audience can interpret the relationship between people and surroundings. *Hulot* 'arrows' the spectators' itinerary throughout the film with recurring images which reintroduce already known, therefore reassuring places. Although there is no delineation of the whole village, the audience is rapidly acquainted with a few locations. Provided the guide-marks are noticed, the cyclical disappearance of characters presents no difficulty for the audience.

The above might be taken to mean that Tati is not innovating in the field of cinematic expression. If a film is considered as a system in which signs are articulated by certain rules of combination, the assumption is correct, since *Hulot* operates according to well-established patterns. Certainly, the editing is perfectly classical, there are no brutal transitions or 'cheat cuts' between images, the shots are assembled in relation to the framing, lighting and tonality of the whole 'moment', and the advance from image to image is visually linear. On the other hand, in most films formal arrangement is utilized to guarantee the progression of the story. As there is neither story nor narrative progression in *Hulot*, viewers meet with routine stylistic figures but do not have to use them to make sense of a missing plot. In that lack lies one of the film's original features.

Instead of providing its audience with uninterrupted information, the film creates blanks. None of the characters is 'the hero', and it is hard to develop a story-line without one or two people who focus the attention. Yet the sophisticated deployment of the characters unveils another of Tati's originalities. Nearly all the characters in *Hulot* are stereotypes: *the* Commandant, a retired officer who never stops recounting his deeds and giving orders, *the* small, black-haired, touchy South American, *the* chattering, bustling English spinster, *the* fat English businessman, unpleasant with everybody and quick to peep through the holes of the women's beach huts. Being nameless (the businessman has a name which is a non-name: Smith) and caricatural as social identities they can change neither themselves nor the fictional world of the film. They are a mere background against which the film builds up Hulot and Martine. Unlike the rest, the latter have proper names but cannot be assigned social positions: where they come from and where they will go after their vacation are equally a mystery. In contrast with the rest of the characters, they do not speak. When he enters the hotel, Hulot introduces himself to the landlord: 'Hulot, Monsieur Hulot.' These are the only words he utters. Martine's few words are unintelligible. Their case is puzzling, and there is deep ambiguity in the highly calculated cleverness (or perversity) with which Tati simultaneously suggests that they are different and prevents his audience from identifying them as 'heroes'.

Take Martine first. She gets out of the coach and enters the boarding-house, where there are three nice shots, classically edited, of her discovery of her room. She arrives in a leisurely fashion. We think we are looking at her through the window from the right, but when she moves from the left we understand that the supposed window was a mirror-wardrobe (an extremely trite cinematic trick which has no specific purpose in the circumstance); she laboriously opens drawers and arranges her belongings. Finally, she opens the window. There is something reassuring in these shots. We believe we are grasping elements of a portrait to be, but we shall never be granted another scene of the same length. Later we see her talking with three young men and we wonder whether she is a flirt. At another time we witness her putting a record on a record-player: is she fond of music? Needless to say, there is no answer.

There is more consistency on the side of Hulot. He is remarkably tall, awkward, and gangling. He is forever clumsily greeting people. He tries to be helpful by carrying a boy's rucksack or giving a lift to a man who has missed the coach. Is he then 'a nice guy' or a fool who intervenes at the wrong moment? He looks polite and friendly; but on the other hand he never addresses his tablemate and does not hesitate to disturb the man in an extremely irritating manner. When he sees Smith peeping through a hole in the side of a cabin, he kicks him in the backside before running away and spending a long time trying to hide. However, if he wanted to protect someone's privacy, surely it is Smith who should be ashamed; perhaps Hulot himself was tempted by an attractive bottom? The question is of course meaningless. It is vain to try and put together aspects of Hulot's personality, every episode being developed for itself with no reference to the others. Hulot sees a new arrival greeting her hosts. He picks up the suitcase, which is too heavy for him. Its weight carries him into the house, drags him across the ground floor, and out into the courtyard where he collapses. The guest, of course, believes that her suitcase has been stolen. The scene is built around the gag of the space traversed and of the false robbery. It would thus be futile to interpret the details as psychological hints of Hulot's character.

Are Hulot and Martine then empty forms, moving images deprived of any fictional personality? Partially, but not entirely. Imprecise clues give Martine some sort of relief. She goes in for tennis and horse-riding, she dances, she can laugh: there is nothing precise, only fragments of a sketch. She has her

*Les Vacances de Monsieur Hulot* – above: M. Hulot (Jacques Tati); below: Monsieur Hulot's car.

own musical theme, however, since she is connected with the leitmotif of the film, a slow, quite unexpressive melody which is first heard when she arrives at the boarding-house and is afterwards mostly associated with her.[4] More importantly she is 'Martine'. This relates more to the context than to the text. Although not exceptional, the name Martine was not in current use after the War. In 1953, whenever it was pronounced in the world of movies it referred to the only undisputed female star of the moment, Martine Carol. There was no other actress whom popular or movie magazines called simply: 'Martine'. *Hulot*'s Martine is not meant to look like Carol. Yet she is blonde, slim, pretty, easy-going like her famous counterpart, quite unlike the smaller, sexier, whimsical star-to-be Brigitte Bardot. Even the least-informed spectator could hardly miss the reference to *the* cinematic female name – and hence make the assumption of Martine's 'star' status in the film.

Hulot is best defined by the tremendous noise of his old rattletrap and the outlandishness of everything associated with him – his car, his outdated bathing-costume, and strange, baggy clothes. By playing the part himself, Tati accentuates these characteristics. Unknown before 1948, the director–actor sprang to fame in *Jour de fête.* Miming rather than acting, he took advantage of his six feet and more to establish a clumsy, touching figure, a gigantic silhouette. In *Hulot*, his hat seems to bob above most heads, and he moves with a curiously mechanical, bent-backed gait, geometrically across the surface of the screen. His awkwardness reaches it apotheosis in the legendary tennis scene. Hulot buys a racket. Having (presumably) never played before, he improvises: racket horizontal, elbow backwards, wrist forward, bang! Even experienced players give up as Hulot repeats his absurd gesture again and again. Hulot's blunders point to a general inadequacy. He is forever nowhere or somewhere else – at any rate never where the others are. This is not a positive description so much as a definition by absence.

In so far as fictional characters are collections of peculiarities which spectators more or less organize into a 'personality', Martine and Hulot are not characters. Subjective glances exist in *Hulot*, but they are attributed to secondary or even unknown characters. Hulot is deprived of his own viewpoint; we never watch what he watches.[5] Analysis of narration also defines characters as producers of events. In this respect, Hulot and Martine are different. Martine is passive while Hulot takes decisions or triggers events. Yet his actions have no long-term effects. Unlike orthodox characters, Hulot does not tie motifs together throughout the film.

Although the film lacks plot and characters, most spectators credit it with a meaning or a message. Recent research puts the emphasis on the function of the spectator in making sense of a film: thanks to her or his previous awareness of fictional convention and the clues given by the text, the viewer organizes the internal relationships into a narrative. Although Tati was probably completely unaware of this theory, he applied it to perfection. Many people perceive a love-affair in the film and bewail Hulot's loneliness.

Are there elements of a love-story? Love can be suggested by words, looks, or attitudes, and we have seen that the former are missing. As for attitudes, Hulot and Martine are only twice in close proximity – once for a short talk in the street, secondly when they dance at the fancy-dress ball.[6] Their hypothetical interaction is inferred from the fact that they are a man and a woman, i.e. the unavoidable constituents of romance in most films. A close analysis shows that in some 'moments' shots of Martine and shots of Hulot alternate; if there is no meeting in the actual shot, the spectator is quick to bind together independent images and to interpret them in classical narrative terms. Hulot never complains. His impassive face does not allow us to decide whether he feels lonely. It is the strong contrast between him and the others, the permanent cumbersomeness of his behaviour which make us feel sorry for him. The unaccountable seductiveness of *Hulot* derives significantly from the intensive work performed by the viewer himself or herself. Neither love-affair nor loneliness are unambiguously indicated in the film. But it is impossible to say that audiences are wrong if they apply their fictional experience to create them in the film.

*Hulot* is a wonderful combination of the ordinary and the unexpected. Although elements of its material are borrowed from classical cinema, it firmly rejects established patterns. Its bizarre humour, quite unlike that of contemporary comedies, is nevertheless well-rooted in tradition. A streak of macabre humour, linked to the absurd, has always existed in French films and was revived in the 1950s with works such as *Jeux interdits* which gain their effect by ridiculing death or mourning. In *Jeux interdits*, for example, while the Germans are overrunning France (in 1940), two families fight for the control of a grave in a churchyard. That farcical vision of burials appealed to Tati. An important moment of his film takes place in a cemetery where Hulot is trying to mend a flat tyre. The crowd is more interested in his efforts than in the graveside liturgy. The inner-tube is mistaken for a wreath and put on the grave where it goes merrily flat. People mistake Hulot for a relative. Some start crying, more begin laughing, and presently Hulot's rattletrap joyously delivers back home a few of the mourners. Tati prefers understatement to outrage and, unlike in *Jeux interdits*, the joke is not taken to extremes; but the inspiration is identical.

Tati's adherence to previous models, especially to comics of the silent era, has often been noted, and it would be all too easy to list the gags adapted from a pre-existing stock – such as the banging door in the restaurant which gets in the way of the waiters. Familiar jests from old movies are generally performed quickly and in succession. Tati innovates by repeating the best jokes as if to get more out of them: Hulot is twice dragged down by heavy luggage, he comes back twice to his hotel dripping wet trying to escape the waiters, etc.

Whether borrowed or invented, all the jokes are screened with the same avoidance of haste. As we follow Hulot's drive towards the beach, the camera momentarily leaves him and films a village street where a dog lies down in the road. We know that Hulot will arrive, stop, and spend a long time before the lazy beast moves; and indeed he does exactly as expected. Later the old car starts popping. We conjecture it will break down. Not yet. It climbs the hill, making more and more noise. Now it has reached the top. Pop pop again. We insist: it must have engine trouble. At last, here we are, the roar dies away, the gag happens, as a reward for our long anticipation.

Spectators are challenged in various ways, and their deep involvement runs at curious odds with the limited commitment of the film: the audience tends to find more in it than is offered. By preventing the full development of actions or effects, *Hulot* creates a sense of the hiatus and inconsequentiality of holiday time, a period of leisure and ephemeral encounters. Hulot has gone on vacation and, as he is not a real protagonist, we can freely enjoy the flavour of vacant days.

*Hulot* was neither the first nor the only picture about summer holidays, but its relationship to the social context is particular; it in part accounts for the film's popularity when it was first released. To a certain extent, we might consider it a documentary rather than a fiction, provided we assume that documentaries, far from being purely factual, are frequently fictionally made. The countryman or the miner we see on screen are not 'real' people, their long hours of work have been reduced to a few minutes, we are shown a synthesis of their activities. *Hulot* is an outline of summer vacations such as people could imagine them in mid-century France. Wage-earners had only two weeks' annual holiday (the third was not granted until 1956), and most of them spent it at home. There were of course financial reasons. In 1952, the Club Méditerranée was just two years old. Its cheapest holiday package was set at 25,000 francs, the equivalent of the monthly salary of an unskilled worker. But as recent research has proved,[7] it was the very conception of time off which was the determining factor: holidays were not conceived of as a time for travelling but as a time for rest – vacation, *vacances*, are derived from the latin *vacare*, 'to be empty'.

Since the end of economic reconstruction (1947), wages had been rising and the tendency was to save money to improve domestic equipment – the most urgent purchases being gas cookers and fridges. Cars came much behind. Only one Frenchman in twenty-five had a car, the same proportion as in 1939. The production of vehicles was drastically limited and, if Hulot's banger was an exception, the old cars depicted in the film were typical of the period. It is true that the country was on the verge of a revolution: Citroën announced their 2CV in 1953, but buyers were warned that the first cars would not be available before 1955. An advertisement (in fact the only one which dealt with vacations in the summer of 1953) read: 'They really are happy because they chose a motorbike for their holidays.' Popular though motorbikes were, they hardly allowed for a family trip to the sea.

The two initial 'moments' of the film provide amusing information about travelling. The first moment, with its crammed-full trains and its speaker announcements which, twice, mislead the passengers, is an allusion to the bad reputation of French railways. In the second moment we see but a few cars running on narrow roads: July and August were not yet the months of the ritual rush away from towns that they would later become. Other details that contemporaries did notice suggest the backwardness of a country which was still predominantly rural. Television was broadcasting from 1949, but there is no television set at the hotel. The film makes fun of Smith, the English businessman, who seems to be tied up to the hotel telephone; but it must be recalled that only one French household in thirty had a telephone, that there were no telephone booths and that, in a village, the only telephone was at the hotel. So Smith had no choice.

The most interesting, in this unwitting testimony on archaic France, is the population of holidaymakers. The French baby-boom began in 1942 and ten years later the beach would be jammed with kids. In fact there are very few children present in this film, the only large family being the Smiths. Does that mean that English people can afford what is beyond French people's means? Maybe, but there is another reason. Mountains or seaside resorts were not automatically associated with the idea of holidays. In the nineteenth century, these locations had been reserved for very affluent people. After the First World War, they were swamped by the middle classes and, after 1945, the situation had not changed. The young people who flirt with Martine or play tennis do not live in the hotel or live in boarding houses. They are probably rich boys and girls who own a weekend cottage. Apart from Martine, the holidaymakers are all above 35 years old, childless, not in the money but well-off enough to be pretentious. In order to boast that they have spent some time on a beach, they make do with uncomfortable rooms: we visit Martine's, it is small, ill-furnished and has been so badly cleaned that she finds in the cupboard a pair of worn-out shoes.

Hulot does not belong to that conformist circle. In fact, he is given no social personality and no individual psychology. By contrast, his oddity reinforces the strangeness of the people in the film: they belong to a bygone age, the era of individual holidays, quiet beaches, unobtrusive record-players, the era when a village and its beach were two unconnected worlds and when the inhabitants had little to gain from tourism. And yet there is a glance at the future. One evening, campers pass by the hotel. They are young, they carry all that they need in their rucksacks and they climb a rock where they are going to spend the night: the years of collective holidays are at hand.

Nowadays the decline of the old customs described in the picture is probably more perceptible than it was in 1953. But *Hulot*'s fascination has always been found less in its consonance with the period than in its contradiction between strong structure and absence of overt message. Unlike avant-garde films, *Hulot* does not distort cinematic forms to tell viewers they are looking at a movie. It is classically built, but spectators find less in it than what they bring – hence their enjoyment.

## Notes

1 Tati formed his crew from young people he knew well and with whom he had already worked. *Jour de fête* and *Hulot* are *'films de copains'* made at low cost and with profit-sharing.
2 Cady-Films, which had only made shorts previously, associated with Fred Orain, a noted producer, for *Jour de fête*. The film was sixth at the box-office with 260,000 tickets sold in Paris: the result was about the same for *Hulot* which suggests that the same people saw both films. Cady-Films financed *Hulot* with the returns of *Jour de fête*.
3 She does not get her name before 'moment' 8, but in this short abstract it is simpler to call her Martine from the beginning.
4 The melody became a hit in the mid-1950s with the title of 'What's the Weather Like in Paris?'
5 Martine is conceded a 'subjective vision' when she is presented in 'moment' 3, but her temporary capacity to 'see' results in nothing.
6 In an early version of the film, before the final view of the empty beach, Martine and her aunt are filmed in a train. The aunt alludes to Hulot, and Martine answers scathingly: 'Oh, Monsieur Hulot . . .'. Her scorn means that she has an opinion. In the final version the shot has been dropped, so that we do not know whether Martine has ever taken notice of Hulot.
7 Alain Corbin (ed.) (1995) *L'Avènement des loisirs*, Paris, Aubier.

## Selected bibliography

Agel, Geneviève (1955) *Hulot parmi nous*, Paris, Editions du Cerf (a moralistic, sentimental book, which illustrates the response of the first spectators of the film).

Carrière, Jean-Claude (1958) *Les Vacances de M. Hulot d'après le film de Jacques Tati*, Paris, Robert Laffont.

Cauliez, Armand-Jean (1962) *Jacques Tati*, Paris, Seghers (documents well Tati's early films and the genesis of *Hulot*).

Dondey, Marc (1989) *Tati*, Paris, Ramsay.

Gilliat, Penelope (1976) *Jacques Tati*, London, Woburn Press (the most reliable biography of Tati).

Thompson, Kristin (1977) 'Parameters of the Open Film: Les Vacances de M. Hulot', *Wide Angle*, 1 (4). (This excellent paper has exempted me from attempting a structural analysis and has led me to look more at the feelings and reactions of the film's contemporaries.)

## Appendix

### *Jacques Tati (1908–82): filmography*

1947 *L'Ecole des facteurs* (short)
1948 *Jour de fête*

1952  *Les Vacances de Monsieur Hulot* (*Mr Hulot's Holiday*)
1953  *Mon oncle* (*My Uncle*)
1968  *Playtime*
1971  *Trafic* (*Traffic*)
1974  *Parade*

## Other films cited in the text

*The Greatest Show on Earth*, Cecil B. De Mille (USA 1952)
*Jeux interdits* (*Forbidden Games*), René Clément (1952)
*Le Retour de Don Camillo* (*The Return of Don Camille*), Julien Duvivier (1952)
*Le Salaire de la peur* (*The Wages of Fear*), Henri-Georges Clouzot (1952)

# 8

# CASQUE D'OR, CASQUETTES, A CASK OF AGEING WINE

## Jacques Becker's *Casque d'or* (1952)

*Dudley Andrew*

> There's the sentimental [*fleur bleue*] side to yourself. You think of
> your youth [the further you get from it the more you think back]
> with a limitless tenderness, so much so that tears can well up in your
> eyes at nearly any moment.
>
> (Jacques Becker, interview in *Cahiers du cinéma*, 1954, 32)

The sheer surface appeal of *Casque d'or* necessarily increases every year; not as compound interest on the capital of its signification, but through the slight chemical agitation that thickens the texture across and through which such signification must be realized with each viewing. The wine (a Bourgueil) that Leca peddles to the owner of L'Ange Gabriel deepens in color and fragrance for us. It already attracted the film's first viewers in 1952 with its cool musk, preserved in crafted wooden barrels. The thirty-five years since the film's première doubly ages the wine, redoubling the appeal of the film.

Let us name this appeal: professionalism, forthrightness, sincerity; and to these let us append nostalgia. Jacques Becker surely traded on nostalgia in imagining the decor, the gestures and the codes of the *belle époque.* In France's postwar crisis of values where 'ambiguity' clouded personal and political motives and acts, the apparently limpid moral codes of 1900 must have felt like a tonic, a restorative rebuke. No qualms qualify Leca's duplicity or the police commissioner's routine corruption. No speeches motivate their venery; no anguished self-doubt crosses their confident worldly faces. Such villains belong on screen next to Simone Signoret with her flushed cheeks and Serge Reggiani with his deep, unblinking eyes. This was an era that knew what it wanted out of life, and pressed unapologetically to attain it. The sureness of Manda's strokes as he planes fine boards in the cabinet shop defines both his ability and his determination; they define the competence of an era for a later, degenerate era at the brink of losing its skill in carpentry and in living.

112

Becker kept before himself a representation of that way of life: Auguste Renoir's *Le Déjeuner des canotiers* (1880–1),[1] Early on he provides us this painting as a tableau vivant, staging at the airy *guinguette* the buoyant dancing, drinking, and fighting that Renoir's shimmering colours and mobile composition suggest. If he felt capable of mimicking the unself-conscious integrity of Renoir's lusty yet social painting, it was because he had imbibed that spirit from Jean Renoir during the flourishing cinema of the Popular Front.

And so Becker's is an earned nostalgia, neither vague nor sentimental. He displayed for his generation exactly what the modern world and modern art lack: professionalism, forthrightness, and sincerity. We now experience this lack at a double remove, for Becker's own era, as troubled as it was, seems incomparably more professional and sincere than our own. Hence the aroma of the images is more luxuriant for us.

This is not the solemn aura of high art disposed of by Walter Benjamin, but the tobacco flavour of a bygone populism where solid artisanship stands above fine art.

Pride in artisanship returns us to the 1930s, to Jean Renoir's vision of film-making, to the subjects of films like *La Belle équipe. Casque d'or* in fact was first envisaged in this period. Renoir purportedly looked at Henri Jeanson's scenario of the subject in 1939 and Julien Duvivier was in pre-production for producer Robert Hakim when the Second World War opened. Hakim then tried to mount the film in Hollywood with Jean Gabin as Manda. As a project, *Casque d'or* comes through the Occupation and Liberation preserving the Poetic Realist sensibility.

The tale, taken from lurid newspaper accounts of the lives and deaths of romantic *apaches* at the turn of the century, is related most closely to the swan song of Poetic Realism, *Les Enfants du paradis.* Itself a romanticized evocation of the nineteenth-century Parisian *demi-monde*, *Les Enfants* stages a multi-layered Oedipal struggle at the center of which is the mysterious Garance, flower of the underworld, whose welcoming glance at the mime Baptiste precipitates the longing, the intrigues and the disasters that carry the film across its marvellous three hours. Those intrigues involve the misanthropic poet and assassin Lacenaire, whose vendetta against society makes him the most perverse avatar of Oedipus in the film. A healthier Oedipus, Frédérick Lemaître directs his limitless ambition so as to rise atop the world of theatre. Unscrupulous, talented, and truant, he finally and literally rewrites a drama during its performance, outraging its authors to the point of precipi-tating a sunrise duel. Meanwhile Baptiste displaces his hatred of his father and the prison of his domestic life on to his mute masterpieces that mesmer-ize immense popular audiences at the Théâtre des funambules, the little child-theatre set opposite the magnificent house where the garrulous Lemaître plays before the dandies of society.

Jacques Becker began to work on *Casque d'or* in 1946, the year following the triumph of *Les Enfants du paradis*. It would take him five years to find his Arletty in Simone Signoret, five years to reshape a scenario that had been, like that of *Les Enfants*, packed with subplots, thrillingly contorted coincidences, and flowery language. Becker mercilessly slashed scenes, characters, and dialogue but only so as to stage more purely and directly the film's mythic theme. In their lengthiest, most ebullient love scene, a promenade in the forest covered in ten shots, Marie utters two brief sentences, Manda utters none. The film as a whole, like Baptiste and like Manda, is modest, reticent, yet full of romantic longing. In 96 minutes of screen time, Serge Reggiani recites a total of only 78 sentences, more than the '60 words' Becker was fond of bragging, but fewer than any other hero in the history of French sound cinema (Truffaut and Rivette 1954, 13; Couturier 1957, 10). Language is the privilege of fathers, of the eloquent Lacenaire, the strident Frédérick Lemaître and, in Becker's film, the dandy Leca. Language seduces and lies. The mime Baptiste, the taciturn Manda distrust it. The film's directness and sincerity cut through the overwrought, loquacious 'cinema of quality' whose frothy costumes and sets, whose romanticized plots and flowery language, filled French screens in a vain attempt to replicate the Carné–Prévert masterpiece. Indeed, Carné and Prévert were the first victims of this decadent postwar aesthetic in their much reviled *Les Portes de la nuit*. In the history of French cinema, then, the production of *Casque d'or* is itself the drama of Oedipus, Becker wrestling the cinema of quality to the ground in his desire to attain whatever the cinema is capable of. Golden Marie, like Garance, is that very cinematic treasure figured directly within the cinema. A goddess who rows up to the napping man and bestows herself upon him, she is both the ideal of beauty French cinema has flirted with all century long, and the fickle public for whose favours, for whose attention and gaze, film-makers have betrayed one another. She is the mythical destiny of popular romance, over whom father and son will lose their lives. Becker was devoted to her.

There is something legendary in this film's title, in its production, and in the tale it tells. It inspired the *enfant terrible*, that self-declared Oedipus, François Truffaut, to set it off against that 'tendency' of French cinema he mercilessly excoriated as 'le cinéma de Papa' (Truffaut 1954). And its star, Simone Signoret, likewise saw it as a rebuke to the established order. The film submitted to its poor reception, she suggests, 'murdered by the critics and at the box office', as though this were the law of the father, just as a law beyond even Leca's power commands Manda's ultimate castration at the guillotine. Despite the cold response it received from those who ruled French cinema, Signoret would call it a production graced by good fortune, by good will, and by the supreme effort of all concerned. It was, she declared, her greatest role, as the British would have to prove to the French (Signoret 1978, 107–10).[2]

It is certainly her most mythic role. She is introduced immediately as the golden treasure of Leca's band, rowing her snivelling boyfriend to the shore. He is never anything more than an errand boy, escorting and amusing Marie in the absence of Leca. They are all Leca's boys, farming out in Belleville to find her and bring her to him. 'Pauvre mec', Marie sighs in the film's first scene. 'Pauvre Roland', Manda follows in the next scene. Confined to the antechamber, Roland truly is pathetic as he listens to his boss proposition Marie, then send him packing when he complains. Thinking to win Marie by imitating the 'father', Roland thereby renounces the Oedipal drama and dies for it, sent as the father's substitute out into the cul-de-sac behind L'Ange Gabriel, there to do battle with the real son, the rebel Manda who has shown up to carry off Marie.

Serge Reggiani's character is truly Oedipal. An orphan in the original script, an ex-convict for Becker, his identity is immediately at stake when Raymond recognizes him at the *guinguette*. For Raymond's old cellmate, 'Jo', has re-emerged baptised 'Manda', an apprentice to the Belleville carpenter played by Gaston Modot. The action at the picturesque *guinguette* is a quaint miniature of the deadly drama that will unfold. Manda leaves his *patron*, lured by the welcoming gaze of Marie, 'Casque d'or'. Set off from the rowdy band in medium shot, they are all seated as Raymond makes the introductions. Each member has an epithet, each a girl (ignored in the introductions). Manda instead has his *patron* and his work. 'Monsieur travaille', Raymond quips, offering him a mug of beer. And it's true. Manda, sweaty from constructing the music platform, was amused to watch these boys waltz each other, amused till he saw Marie dance with Roland. Now she asks him to dance, 'Ils savent danser, les charpentiers?' How simple it is to displace Roland, outdancing, then outboxing this poor pretender. The worker's conquest has been too swift; a greater rival will have to be met, Leca, under whose authority and at whose pleasure this band and this woman strut the streets of Belleville.

The historical Manda broke off with Leca to lead a splinter gang, precipitating the violent jealousy over a beautiful woman. Becker's Manda, at ease in the underworld, nevertheless presents himself as a worker. He proudly wears the casquette that Leca's middle-class pretension scorns. How close Becker has come to the most classic of Poetic Realist films, *Le Jour se lève*, where the worker François, likewise an orphan, stands up to, then cuts down the corrupt dandy, Valentin, both 'father' and lover to the beautiful Françoise. Jean Gabin, like Serge Reggiani, refuses to flee, dying in the sight of a great public among whom is the girl at the core of the drama. In a complex but nevertheless clear echo, Reggiani is guillotined in the prison courtyard, while Marie looks on from a top-floor room in what could be Gabin's fleabag hotel. Recall that Gabin lost his life in the top floor, while a crowd looked on from the street. Becker seals the citation when he matches Carné's famous camera angle looking down flights of concentric railings as Marie ascends.

As in Poetic Realism, the romantic purity of characters and motives in *Casque d'or* is tempered by modesty and stylistic rectitude. Manda is no knight errant in search of adventure. His silent integrity he inherits from Gabin. Manda belongs to the 1930s. He belongs with the solid carpenter Danard and with his old buddy Raymond, for whom he is ready to die. Serge Reggiani even belongs with Gaston Modot and Raymond Bussières, the two veteran actors Becker chose to take on these characters. They carry the 1930s in their blood, having worked with the surrealist Buñuel, with Prévert, and above all with Renoir. These actors carry forward the virtues of the workers' theatre tradition.[3]

We might say that the drama of *Casque d'or* pits this older world against modern life. When Manda leaves his *patron*'s care to seek Marie at L'Ange Gabriel, he abandons his patrimony, both the little shop and the plain, long-suffering daughter he is in line to possess. Marie makes him take on the modern world, the one that has grown up while he was in prison, just as Becker must confront the cinema of dandyism that flourished during the occupation and that replaced the Poetic Realism it nevertheless claimed to have inherited. But Becker is the true inheritor; and the real 'casque d'or' is the little *casquette* Becker placed on Manda's head. It is a challenge thrown quietly but directly at the pretensions of postwar cinema, a challenge that comes from the cinema of the pre-war days when films were made like good cabinets. Becker and Manda walk right into the gangsters' den to walk off with what they alone know how to love, the golden beauty of L'Ange Gabriel.

An exquisite period piece, suspended in the warmth of the Popular Front atmosphere for a dozen years, what sort of relation can *Casque d'or* maintain with its age and its audience? Becker always declared himself a 'social *cinéaste*' (Truffaut and Rivette 1954, 8); he has been likened to Renoir and through Renoir to Zola and Maupassant (Sadoul 1952a). His previous six films had zeroed in on various classes and locales in French life, specifically avoiding the *recherché*. *Rendez-vous de juillet* was hailed as a first-class inquiry into the Saint-Germain youth culture during the existentialist days after the war. *Edouard et Caroline* used the lightness of comedy to batter the *grand monde*. And now suddenly Becker's most meticulous and expensive production throws us into a world of *apaches* at the turn of the century. What has happened?

To what shall we lay the difficulty we have in linking the film to the social issues of the day? Shall we fault Becker? Georges Sadoul, a great supporter of Becker whom he put alongside Renoir and Clair, complained that Manda's love affair betrayed the mission of every working man (Sadoul 1952b). The film he found to be well crafted but its subject was insignificant, disappointing all those who had invested their hopes in Becker. He even refused *Casque d'or* entry on the list of the key films of 1952. Only three films out of

100 merit his favour that year: Christian-Jaque's *Fanfan la Tulipe*, Clément's *Jeux interdits*, and naturally André Cayatte's *Nous sommes tous des assassins* (Sadoul 1962, 266). But Becker, it appeared in the early 1950s, had shucked off the social temperament and aptitude that marked him in some quarters as France's answer to Italian Neo-Realism. Beginning with *Casque d'or*, he 'oriented himself toward "entertainment cinema" toward which nearly all the major French cinéastes have rallied in reaction against the *film noir* of the past few years and also against the "problem film"' (Leprohon 1957, 387).

If in the 1950s French cinema as a whole turns toward mere entertainment, as Pierre Leprohon believed, *Casque d'or* becomes a brilliant emblem of a weak age. Not in every era do the arts touch the pulse of a nation. Compare Italian Neo-Realism, so often in touch with the sensibility, if not the issues, of the day, with that of the French cinema of the occupation which understandably produced films whose cool distance provided a place of refuge for a beaten audience. *Casque d'or* struck critics in 1952 as a film cut off from social life and even, on account of its deliberate rhythm, cut off from the sensibility of what was becoming the jazz age.[4]

But what artworks responded directly or adequately to the 1950s in France? Cynicism ruled the theatre, probably the form that drew most attention to itself. Beckett's *En attendant Godot* was staged in 1950, Ionesco's *La Cantatrice chauve* in 1951 and *Les Chaises* in 1952 (Tint 1970, 187–9). Critics read these plays as hardened rejections of the optimism that greeted the liberation. Sartre's call for a new humanism, for an extension of anti-fascist solidarity into socialist communality had been dashed by the Cold War, by Indochina, by Korea, and by the return to political power of the moneyed class. Although the cinema of the late 1940s had tried to foster solidarity (one would have to mention Becker here, but also Clément, Grémillon, Le Chanois, Daquin), by 1950 films like *L'Ecole buissonnière* or *Le Point du jour* must have seemed naïve.

One might go further and suggest that the nationalist enthusiasm attending the liberation was, from the first, tainted with self-interest. In the sector of the cinema, the term 'quality', employed in the very first issue of *Le Film français*, was a term rife with business sense. Quality films aimed to recapture the authenticity of Poetic Realism which had won over an international audience; instead they exhibited only good taste and advanced moral values in a paternalistic fashion. The populism of *Les Portes de la nuit*, *Les Amants de Vérone*, *Au-delà des grilles*, and even *Le Diable au corps* was visibly calculated, just as Yves Allégret's dark *Dédée d'Anvers* and *Une si jolie petite plage* appear disingenuous and forced against the more natural pessimism of *La Bête humaine* or *Le Jour se lève* a decade earlier.

*Casque d'or*, scheduled for production in 1946, based on a romantic prewar script, was a postwar project in the quality image. Yet the finished film assiduously avoids association with that school of film-making. A costume drama it was, but one in which Mayo's understated costumes were worn, not

117

strutted, and where the sparse dialogue is never edifying but serves instead as an index to each character's style. Truffaut (1954) was right to mention *Casque d'or* as a film incomprehensible to those raised on the anodyne 'psychological realism' of the tradition of quality. *Casque d'or* strips cinema down to its purest, seeking to distil emotions and codes of behaviour that the loquacious, pretentious, paternalistic, and flamboyant postwar culture has sold off.

And so one might say of *Casque d'or*, as one says of the Theatre of the Absurd of the times, that its refusal of political and social relevance shouts out a political and social message. *Casque d'or*'s contribution to the politics of the culture that surrounds it, then, is as discreet as its style. One looks in vain for an allegory of the Fourth Republic or of the Cold War. The broadcast of the film, like that of most films of the day, reaches no further than the sphere of the cinematic. The film does not speak to the literary concerns of the day, nor to those of the theatre. It is a film-maker's film, one Truffaut thought must be seen, because of its great candour, as an indictment of reigning approaches to period pieces, indeed as an indictment of the reigning 'tendency' in the industry altogether. *Casque d'or* concludes with an image of two lovers dancing alone into a future that has already been cut short. It offers neither programme nor project, merely an unforgettable emblem, a 'legend' (in the strongest sense) of real love that we, who are fated to live in this era of compromises, must never forget.

And Becker makes certain we cannot forget it. He has his title character row the film directly to us. In the first scene she deposits a worthless companion, exchanging him in dance for Manda. The film's second act begins when the boat she rows alone floats gently to a similar shore, and to Manda sleeping in the grass. A halo floods around her head which eclipses the sun as she descends from heaven to wake him with a kiss. A dissolve to them naked in bed, her hair unhinged, figures their wordless union and our blind acceptance of a cinematic love. Other dissolves use the buffer of our mind to interlace the fragments of disjointed drama. When Manda leaves Danard, the godfather – who has watched over his life of calm routine – fades and is reshaped into Mère Eugène, the peasant godmother, guardian of the dreamy rural hideaway. These kindly, legendary oldfolk divide the world into country and city, a symbolic opposition of values that is utterly undisguised. When Manda and Marie lie down in the soft grass, the camera tilts up to mime their passion. At its height the sky imperceptibly changes and the subsequent tilt back finds us in front of L'Ange Gabriel in Paris. Such punctuation of sequences insists on the clarity of values alive in the world of the *apaches*. Likewise Becker's *mise-en-scène* compels us to register the similarity of the cul-de-sac where Manda kills Roland and the one where, mercilessly, he guns down the terrified Leca.

Compositions are often boxed tightly as in cartoons. The lovers happen upon a country wedding, which they can scarcely glimpse from the back of

*Casque d'or* – above: Manda (Serge Reggiani) and Casque d'or (i.e. Marie, played by Simone Signoret); below: Casque d'or with group of men including Leca (Claude Dauphin, situated to her immediate right).

the church. Yet Becker frames the comic organist and choir close up and straight on. Then comes a solemn portrait shot of the stiff couple getting married that carries with it simultaneously the tint of old photographs and an air of mockery. The gendarmes who show up so often yet so ineffectually in the film seem likewise to have stepped from the pages of a comic book or, better, from the old serials of Louis Feuillade that captivated Becker as a youth (Sadoul 1962, 117). Even the gang, when first introduced to Manda, affect attitudes as caricatural as the epithets by which they know one another. When Leca approaches to slap Fredo for palming 300 francs, the frightened toughguy sticks out his forearm rigidly to protect his face. The gesture is a pose from a lost repertoire we are asked to bring to mind. In scenes like these Becker achieves his wish to avoid the painterly and arrive instead at a look straight out of those magazines of his youth such as *Le Petit journal illustré* (Sadoul 1952a). Once, gratuitously, Becker tracks away from a scene to fade out on a nearby poster, an art nouveau girl advertising *Triple Sec.*

Becker's search for clarity of presentation is less defensible when we catch him helping us with the plot. Do we really need the newspapers that inform us of Raymond's incarceration? Worse, do we need the photo of Anatole brought out at L'Ange Gabriel to help us identify the waiter rubbed out as a police informer? In case we still had trouble understanding that his 'accident' had been pre-arranged, Leca whispers between his teeth to one of his henchmen. 'Did it go OK?' 'A piece of cake' is the reply, as they all make contributions for Anatole's grandmother.

But while playing up to his audience, Becker finds one occasion to rebuke us and make us rethink our role. We first enter L'Ange Gabriel with a party of bourgeois carousers who, after a fine dinner no doubt, have dared to cross the tracks to sample the atmosphere at one of Belleville's most notorious *boîtes.* The regulars recognize this contrast of lifestyles, and they recognize it as condescending. First they stage a thrill to mock these voyeurs, when Roland presses one to dance with him, then pulls her roughly around the floor in a gesture of rude eroticism. The thrill is soon multiplied when the police invade the place and Roland's body is carried out past them.

If we are to be voyeurs, it will not be the sort that safely sit on the outside. Instead Becker makes us track forward with Manda in his desperate search for Marie. We push Fredo aside and climb the stairs to Leca's apartment. With him we lean down to find Marie's slippers beneath Leca's fine sheets. Becker forces this primal scene upon us, fastening us to Manda's side till we wind up with him in the cul-de-sac of the gendarmerie, Leca's corpse at our feet. Without missing a note, the music carries us through a fade out/fade in to Marie's silhouette in a carriage. It's the dead of night as she pulls up to the cheap hotel beside the guillotine. This transference from the spent energy of Manda to the vigil Marie keeps for him struck François Truffaut (1964) as one of the most brilliant strategies of scriptwriting he had ever encountered. Not only do we flow with the music from the internal perspective of one character to that of another (his lover), we are carried by this movement past the vengeance we have desired to its immediate consequence, the guillotine. The quaint set-ups taken from *Le Petit journal illustré* have given way to a mode of viewing which is utterly tied to the characters, indeed which their love permits to be passed between them. Marie has brought us this film, has rowed it to us from the lovely waters of the Marne. We now watch with her. As the big knife falls, her own head nods forward. We track in to an enormous closeup of that head and of its magnificent hair. As the music comes up, the film's final image wells up as though within Marie's mind: the couple whirling eternally in love. Is this her final vision? Or is it his last thought (for he had promised her in bed, 'I never stop thinking of you, Marie'). Or is it our vision, we who carry this legend on?

The merging together of Manda and Marie in total identification lures us to merge into them and into the film as well. The beams of reflected light fall to us from the screen, as we lie daydreaming; the film presses up to our eyes and lips, and asks us to embrace it. But something restrains us and interrupts this ageless dream of fusion. The pictorialism of the style, its search for a lost means of popular representation, is something to appreciate rather than merge with. *Casque d'or* tempts us with its alluring purity but continually asserts its temporal distance from us, its pastness. Hence its calculated and clever nostalgia.

The tone Becker achieves can be better appreciated by setting the film alongside another major work of 1952, Max Ophuls' *Le Plaisir*. Similarities between the films immediately arise.[5] The sets of both were designed by Jean D'Eaubonne who sought to bring alive a world like that of Maupassant. But the nostalgia Becker tenders a modern audience is explicitly mocked by Ophuls, or rather by his chosen narrator, Peter Ustinov, who wryly introduces each of the three episodes that comprise the film. Ophuls' usual cynicism makes his vision of the past truly sophisticated in its artifice. We moderns can indeed laugh but only if we are prepared to laugh at ourselves. In the final episode of *Le Plaisir* ('La Maison Tellier') the camera creeps up the wall of Madame Tellier's notorious house. It moves from window to window, framing vignettes of the members of the human species at their pleasures. The distance of viewer and viewed is spatial. We are blocked from the image by its frame, by the window, and by the screen Ustinov repeatedly reminds us of.

On the other hand, the distance of viewer from viewed in *Casque d'or* is temporal. We are encouraged to enter the image but are made to realize that it fades as we watch. In the final shot, the couple dances away from us, then evaporates to leave us alone with a sad song, 'Le Temps des cerises'. Becker's nostalgia is a rebuke to a present that has failed to live up to the image he casts of the past. The past looks *different* from the present, and this difference keeps us, despite our boundless admiration, from complete identification with it.

Raymond's role is a figure of this difference, a third term prising us away from uncritical immersion in the lovers and in love. While Raymond brings Manda to Marie, first at the *guinguette*, then later, through his handwritten message, to the tryst at Mère Eugène's, allegiance to Raymond is what pulls Manda from his embrace with Marie, and back to the city, to arrest, and to decapitation.

Although he mocked Manda's staid and virtuous life in the carpenter's shop, Raymond maintains this same old-fashioned virtue even within the gang. 'Don't touch Manda', he tells Leca threateningly, 'I can count on him and that doesn't happen very often.' Clearly he cannot count on the band he has joined, for all of them are Leca's tools, morally unformed little boys. Thus the film upholds the strength of the natural and the heterosexual. You can see the health of it on Marie's face. Manda is worthy of her, having passed beyond the adolescence that binds the other boys to Leca.

Another Prévert film now rises to view, *Quai des brumes* where the moral strength of the deserter, Jean Gabin, shatters the puerile bravado of Pierre Brasseur and his gang of thugs. The apparently respectable but depraved Michel Simon controls this gang from his basement where he also tries to rape his 'daughter', Michèle Morgan, before Gabin bashes his head in. Prévert and Becker lean on the popular psychological account of the fascist sensibility as being one of arrested adolescence and displaced homosexuality. The fascist leader, on the other hand, has no excuse and is pictured as unregenerate, cruel and duplicitous. When caught stealing from the gang, Fredo not only whimpers as he takes his punishment, he then meekly goes to buy his boss some cigars. Instead of rebelling, Fredo completely introjects this 'father'; he abjures all interest in women, and bullies his mates. Leca recognizes a miniature of himself in Fredo, making him his right-hand man.

Ultimately Leca's strength, like that of Fredo and Roland, is shown to be pure bravado, a façade that crumbles as he pleads, 'Don't shoot, Manda. Don't shoot.' Manda not only shoots; he empties his gun into Leca. But even before this, we learned that Leca's power rests on that of the commissioner of police, who in turn jokingly claims to take orders from his wife, a woman Leca buys off with gifts of port wine. In this world of slaps and favors, no one is at the top. To belong to the system is to kneel before another man, weakly, childishly, in hopes of replicating within oneself the power that disciplines.

Raymond refuses the narcissism of this economy, insisting on the difference of a kind of friendship that 'doesn't happen very often'. In his undemanding affection for Manda, Raymond offers an alternative to the film's presentation of the oblivious union of heterosexual passion and the pathological infantilism of homosexual dependency. This difference is that of a chosen brotherhood, established in, and as, history.

With such sentiments in mind, Raymond returns us once more to the era of the Popular Front, the 'temps des cerises' of the title song. This famous song recapitulates in its lyrics and its history the complications followed out by the allegory of the plot. Composed in 1866 by Jean-Baptiste Clément, this romantic ditty expresses the sentiments of passion and regrets that at first blush carry the film (Buchsbaum 1983, 289). Yet immediately there accrued to it direct revolutionary overtones when Clément published it along with other songs in his *Chansons révolutionnaires* in 1868. He became a member of the Paris Commune (Belleville district) and was exiled to England and Belgium for a decade after that. A celebrated socialist, he stands alongside Eugéne Pottier, who wrote the *Internationale* at just this time.[6] It was in Belgium that Clément re-published his little masterpiece, belatedly dedicating the songs to a female ambulance driver of the Commune (Noel 1971, 75; Brunschwig, Calvet and Klein 1981, 361). After his death, but in harmony with his life, this tune would sport radical new lyrics and a small but radical shift in title, 'Le Temps des crises' (Berbier 1959, 80). Overtaking France during the end of the *belle époque*, performed by Montéhus, the great 'anarchist crooner of the world of the *apaches*' (Brunschwig, Calvet and Klein 1981, 74), this now utterly political anthem would persist into the 1930s when it was sung along with the *Internationale* as an antidote to *La Marseillaise* which tended to be appropriated by the right.

The political intent behind the use of this song as the major leitmotif in *Casque d'or*, is ratified by a powerful 'coincidence'. In 1937, as Jean Renoir was seeking to wrest *La Marseillaise* from its adoption as theme-song by the right, his co-director at Ciné-Liberté, Jean-Paul Le Chanois, was busy making a communist feature film the title of which was indeed *Le Temps des cerises*. Becker had worked with Le Chanois the year before on Renoir's *La Vie est à nous*, a film edited by *Casque d'or*'s editor Marguerite Renoir. As in *Casque d'or*, the action of *Le Temps des cerises* begins at the very end of the nineteenth century. Like *Casque d'or* it features Gaston Modot playing a carpenter who grows old in the course of the film.

The song's simultaneous expression of joy and regret is given a political referent in Le Chanois' film, which hailed a lost past (the Paris Commune of 1871) while pointing to a utopia where social injustice and economic privation will have vanished. Thus the mixture of tones that Truffaut (1964) found so exhilarating in *Casque d'or* (and which later he specifically imitated in *Tirez sur le pianiste*, especially in the back alley fight scene) is embedded in the film's theme, in its theme-song, and in the history of both. Nor has that history run its course. In 1975 one of the politically enlightened heroes of Alain Tanner's *Jonas qui aura 25 ans en l'an 2000* takes a job caring for the aged. He leads them in a reprise of *Le Temps des cerises*, whose theme Tanner, like Becker, continues to employ to underscore a lost political utopia. The fact that a now aged Raymond Bussières takes a major role in Tanner's film links it even more closely to *Casque d'or* and through it to the Popular Front. Indeed Bussières continues to proclaim to the disillusioned veterans of 1968 who populate Tanner's movie that life was better in 1936.

And so it must have been for Jacques Becker who once exclaimed, 'I have a horror of my own generation' (Queval 1962, 46). *Casque d'or* looks back to its version of a better time and finds it precisely in the era of the Popular Front, which in its turn had looked back to the Commune in search of political direction. The difference this time is that *Casque d'or* displays no hope of a better future. The 'temps des cerises' was but a brief moment of fraternity and love in a world dedicated to smashing both. If the film strikes us as delicate and vaguely otherworldly in its feeling and design, then Becker has delivered the film he had in mind, one which, because of the discouraging impasse of the postwar years, must be read as both social and tragic in its ineluctible confrontation of the possible and the impossible. We are further than ever from establishing a world where human work and love prevail, and so this is a film whose delicacy grows rarer each day. *Casque d'or* has become an image for us of a better era, or at least a better cinema, one based on solid craft and direct sentiment, a real 'temps des cerises'. The genius of the film is that it predicted, understood, and thematized this inevitable process of decay and nostalgia. It made of it a legend.

## Notes

1 The opening of *Casque d'or* in fact recalls a half-dozen Renoir canvases, including *Bal du Moulin de la Galette* (1876), *La Seine à Asnières* (1879), *Déjeuner au bord de la rivière* (1879), *La Dance à la campagne* (1883), *Le Bal à Bougival* (1883). Rowboats, dancers, drinking boatsmen, trellised dance-floors, and a riverside setting certify the reference to the great painter.
2 André Bazin confessed that he should have known better and that it was Lindsay Anderson who had pointed to the film's brilliance (Bazin 1971, 91).
3 Raymond Bussières has pursued this vocation from the 1920s into our own era, appearing most recently in another film evoking the Popular Front ethos, Alain Tanner's *Jonas qui aura 25 ans en l'an 2000*, a film we shall have occasion to return to in this chapter.
4 Although Sadoul in his already cited review mentions *Bicycle Thieves* as a precursor for the tight dramatic logic and the lack of fatalism in *Casque d'or*, Queval and Bazin both point to the effect of destiny produced by 'the encounter of the possible with the impossible' (Bazin 1955; Queval 1962)
5 The link between Becker and Ophuls would be sealed five years later when, upon the latter's death, Becker completed *Montparnasse 19*, another film of *belle époque* Paris.
6 Clément and Pottier are often linked. In 1924 their songs were published together in a German translation, *Französische Revolutionslieder* (Berlin, Malik Verlag).

## Selected bibliography

Bazin, André (1955) 'Autocritique', *Cahiers du cinéma*, 35.
Bazin, André (1971) *What Is Cinema? II*, Berkeley, University of California Press.
Berbier, M. (1959) 'Vers la belle époque', *Histoire de France par les chansons*, 3, Paris, Gallimard.

Beylie, Claude and Buache, Freddie (1991) *Jacques Becker: études, textes et scénarios inédits, entretiens*, Paris, Editions du Festival

Brunschwig, C., Calvet, L.-J. and Klein, J.-C. (1981) *Cent ans de chanson française*, Paris, Editions du Seuil.

Buchsbaum, Jonathan (1983) 'Left Political Filmmaking in France in the 1930s', Doctoral dissertation, New York University.

Couturier, Jean (1957) *Fiche filmographique*, 113.

Leprohon, Pierre (1957) *Présences contemporaines: Cinéma*, Paris, Debresse.

Noel, B. (1971) *Dictionnaire de la Commune*, Paris, F. Hazan.

Queval, Jean (1962) *Jacques Becker*, Paris, Seghers.

Sadoul, Georges (1952a) 'Interview with Jacques Becker', *Les Lettres françaises* (10 April).

Sadoul, Georges (1952b) 'Puissance de la Sobriété' (review of *Casque d'or*), *Les Lettres françaises* (17 April), reprinted in Sadoul (1979) *Chroniques du cinéma français*, Paris, Union Générale d'Editions, 120–4.

Sadoul, Georges (1962) *Le Film françaises*, Paris, Flammarion.

Signoret, Simone (1978) *Nostalgia Isn't What it Used to Be*, New York, Harper & Row.

Tint, Robert (1970) *France Since 1918*, New York, Harper & Row.

Truffaut, François (1954) 'Une certaine tendance du cinéma français', *Cahiers du cinéma*, 31.

Truffaut, François (1964) 'De vraies moustaches' *Avant-scène cinema*, 43.

Truffaut, François and Rivette, Jacques (1954) 'Entretien avec Jacques Becker', *Cahiers du cinéma*, 32.

Vey, Jean Louis (1995) *Jacques Becker ou la fausse évidence*, Lyons, Aléas.

## Script

Becker, Jacques (1964) *Casque d'or*, in *Avant-scéne cinéma*, 43.

## Appendix

### *Jacques Becker (1906–60): filmography*

1935  *Le Commissaire est bon enfant* (short)
1935  *Le Gendarme est sans pitié* (short)
1935  *Tête de Turc* (short)
1942  *Dernier atout*
1943  *Goupi mains-rouges* (*It Happened at the Inn*)
1945  *Falbalas* (*Paris Frills*)
1947  *Antoine et Antoinette* (*Antoine and Antoinette*)
1949  *Rendez-vous de juillet*
1951  *Edouard et Caroline* (*Edward and Caroline*)
1952  *Casque d'or* (*Golden Marie*)
1953  *Rue de l'estrapade*
1954  *Ali Baba et les quarante voleurs* (*Ali Baba*)
1954  *Touchez pas au grisbi* (*Grisbi*)
1957  *Les Aventures d'Arsène Lupin* (*The Adventures of Arsène Lupin*)

1958  *Montparnasse 19 (Modigliani of Montparnasse)*
1960  *Le Trou (The Night Watch)*

## Other films cited in the text

*Les Amants de Vérone (The Lovers of Verona)*, André Cayatte (1948)
*Au-delà des grilles (The Walls of Malapaga)*, René Clément (1948)
*La Belle équipe (There Were Five* [UK]; *A Fine Team* [USA]), Julien Duvivier (1936)
*La Bête humaine (The Human Beast)*, Jean Renoir (1938)
*Dédée d'Anvers (Dédée)*, Yves Allégret (1947)
*Le Diable au corps (Devil in the Flesh)*, Claude Autant-Lara (1947)
*L'Ecole buissonnière (Passion for Life)*, Jean-Paul Le Chanois (1949)
*Les Enfants du paradis (Children of Paradise)*, Marcel Carné (1943–5)
*Fanfan la Tulipe*, Christian-Jaque (1952)
*Jeux interdits (Forbidden Games)*, René Clément (1952)
*Jonas qui aura 25 ans en l'an 2000 (Jonah who will be 25 in the year 2000)*, Alain Tanner
    (1975)
*Le Jour se lève (Daybreak)*, Marcel Carné (1939)
*La Marseillaise*, Jean Renoir (1927)
*Nous sommes tous des assassins (We Are All Murderers)*, André Cayatte (1952)
*La Plaisir*, Max Ophuls (1952)
*Le Point du jour*, Louis Daquin (1948)
*Les Portes de la nuit (Gates of the Night)*, Marcel Carné (1946)
*Le Quai des brumes (Port of Shadows)*, Marcel Carné; (1938)
*Une Si jolie plage (Riptide)*, Yves Allégret (1949)
*Le Temps des cerises*, Jean Paul Le Chanois (1937)
*Tirez sur le pianiste (Shoot the Pianist)*, François Truffaut (1960)
*La Vie est à nous*, Jean Renoir (1936)

## 9

# NO PLACE FOR HOMOSEXUALITY

## Marcel Carné's *L'Air de Paris* (1954)

### *Richard Dyer*

*L'Air de Paris* is a film with a strong pedigree: directed by Marcel Carné, starring Jean Gabin and Arletty, with a title song sung by Yves Montand. Yet although a moderate commercial and critical success in the period (with Gabin winning the best actor award at the Venice Film Festival), it is a largely forgotten film. Even Edward Baron Turk in *Child of Paradise* (Turk 1989), his fine rescue of Carné from critical neglect, has little to say for, or indeed about, *L'Air de Paris*; it does not figure among those films that have made Gabin and Arletty icons and its song did not become a fixture of Montand's repertoire.

If it draws attention now it is for two opposed reasons that this chapter in part seeks to interrelate. On the one hand, it is an example of high quality popular French studio production of the postwar years, simply an instance of that wealth of mainstream production that it has taken film (especially European film) history so long to pay attention to. On the other hand, it is also, startlingly for its period, a film about homosexuality. What is fascinating is this conjuncture of the mainstream and the marginal, suggesting both what could and could not be said within the former about the latter. This chapter then is less a rescue of a film that is unjustly neglected (though it is) than a study in the dynamics of cultural expression.

In *L'Air de Paris*, a boxing trainer, Victor (Gabin), takes on a young man, André (Roland Lesaffre), whom he believes he can make into a champion. Victor's wife, Blanche (Arletty), resents the time and care he lavishes on André. She says to a friend that, when Victor gets as serious as this about one of his *poulains* (trainees), she'd rather it was for *une poule* (a girl). When she says to Victor that André is 'the only thing that interests you – it's disgusting', he tells her she's jealous and she says yes and why not? Meanwhile, André meets and has an affair with a woman, Corinne (Marie Daëms), a model – much to the annoyance of Victor and of Chantal (Simone Paris), an antique-shop owner who shares her flat with Corinne. Corinne realizes the harm she's doing André (to his training and to his relationship with Victor) and leaves town. Outside Corinne's flat, Victor comforts André, throws a bracelet charm, symbol of André and Corinne's relationship, into the river, and the two men walk off together into the dawn.

The film displays Roland Lesaffre's athletic body to a very unusual degree: in singlet and short boxing shorts, in the shower, in pyjama bottoms only and, for a massage scene with Gabin, bikini briefs. By contrast, it hardly displays Marie Daëms's body at all. Lesaffre is also the focus of glamorizing lighting and of the explicitly libidinal looks in the film, not only from Corinne but from a neighbourhood girl, Maria (Maria-Pia Casilio), and a camp couturier, Jean-Marc (Jean Parédès).

Presented like this in terms of narrative and visual pleasure, *L'Air de Paris* sounds like an obviously gay film. Yet almost no one at the time commented on it in these terms.[1] The reasons why, which I shall discuss first, are partly production circumstances, partly the strategies of the closet. They are also, though, to do with the construction of an impossible conception of desire between men. This relates, as I shall discuss finally, to the uncertainty of the film's representation of Paris, of how the film cannot place its homosexuality in Paris, accounting for the fascination of what André Bazin felicitously described as a film 'out of kilter, disoriented, and somehow untrue to itself'.[2]

The year 1954 was not a propitious one in which to produce a gay film. We may think of the publicly famous relationship of Jean Cocteau and Jean Marais in the 1940s and of *Un Chant d'amour* (1950), of the line of remarkable gay representations in French cinema of the 1930s – *Le Sang d'un poète* (1932), *Paris-Béguin* (1931), *Zéro de conduite* (1933), *La Kermesse héroïque* (1935), *Hôtel du Nord* (1938), *La Règle du jeu* (1939) – and of lesbian representation not only then, in for example *Club de femmes* (1936) and *Hélène* (1936), but also through and beyond the 1950s: *Quai des Orfèvres* (1947), *Au Royaume des cieux* (1949), *Olivia* (1950), *Huis-clos* (1954), *Les Collégiennes* (1956), *La Garçonne* (1957), *La Fille aux yeux d'or* (1960), *Thérèse Desqueyroux* (1962). However, anything approaching the latter grouping for gay male representation would have to wait until 1964 for *Olivia*'s equivalent, *Les Amitiés particulières*, even though the source novel had been published in 1943. The only gay filmic representations in the period are *Un Chant d'amour*, virtually unknown, Cocteau's extremely indirect films, Michel Auclair's magnetic queer Nazi criminal in *Les Maudits* (1947) and a sprinkling of marginal, comic queens (to whom I shall return).

The apparent isolation[3] of *L'Air de Paris* in terms of gay representation should not really surprise. The postwar period was markedly homophobic. The anti-gay legislation introduced under Vichy in 1942[4] was maintained, and the Paris police began cracking down on homosexuality from 1949 on; anti-gay laws were to be strengthened under Charles de Gaulle (Girard 1981; Copley 1989; Martel 1996). With the occupation fresh in the memory, male homosexuality might be seen as a product of Nazism (*Les Maudits*) or a form of collaborationism, as one may read Daniel in Jean-Paul Sartre's *Les Chemins de la liberté* (1945–9)[5] and either way excoriated: it was not about to be openly celebrated in a mainstream film.

Aspects of the production also had the effect of hiding *L'Air de Paris'* homoeroticism. One of the backers, Cino del Duca, published photo romances and insisted on the inclusion of 'a real love story', i.e. that of André and Corinne (Billard 1995, 557). The casting of Gabin also took away any queer taint. According to the film's openly gay director, Marcel Carné, Gabin was 'terribly frightened of that':

> When at the end of [the film] he meets up with the young boxer, I told him to put his hand on the back of his neck and lead him off: 'No way, I don't want to look like a queer.' He wasn't happy at all. Gabin queer, come off it, really!
>
> (Grant and Joecker 1982–3, 14)

Yet the very incompatibility of Gabin's essential image as 'the decent bloke' ('*l'honnête homme*' (Vincendeau 1993, 146)) with queerness may well have been what made *L'Air de Paris'* audacity possible, whilst simultaneously making a more overt gay representation impossible. As Victor is Gabin, he can't possibly be queer, which lets the film get away with suggesting just that in the relationship between him and André, but makes it hard for it to go too far beyond suggestion.

Carné's position is fascinatingly unclear. At the time (cf. Marrot 1962, 4) and in his autobiography, *La Vie à belles dents* (1979, 331), he maintained that what he wanted to do with *L'Air de Paris* was to make a film about boxing, of which he was, like Cocteau, a fan. In a later interview for the gay journal *Masques* (Grant and Joecker 1982–3, 14), he says that it is 'obvious' that Corinne and Chantal (see below) 'sleep together', but is equivocal about Victor and André, evoking the suggestiveness of the massage scene ('there's no point him [Gabin] denying it') while also saying that all the same he hasn't really ever made a film centred on a male love story.

I will return to the exact terms in which he says this in a moment. First though I want to begin considering *L'Air de Paris* and homosexuality in relation to Carné's work more widely. Turk (1989) shows, with a scrupulous refusal to over-interpret, the persistence of gay themes and images throughout Carné's work, and even Pierre Billard, who is warier of Turk's gay readings, agrees that *L'Air de Paris* is about 'a profound affective relationship between two men' (1995, 615). Billard however feels that, given Carné's age and his roots in popular culture, he wasn't in 1954 'up for the slightest public display of his sexual life' (*ibid.*). Perhaps so, but in *Hôtel du Nord* he already had at any rate portrayed a gay man, Adrien (François Périer), who is not only sympathetic and apparently integrated into the community of the hotel but who also, as we might say now, comes out in the course of the film. This occurs when he is out walking with Renée (Annabella) one evening. A soldier passes by, glancing at Adrien. When Adrien calls him by name, Fernand, saying 'Didn't you recognize me?', Fernand replies, 'I didn't even look at you when I saw you with Mademoiselle'. But he had (looked at him): Adrien insists on their acknowledging each other in public and they then go off together (presumably to Adrien's room which he had earlier told the hotel owner, Mme Lecouvreur, he had been getting ready for a visit from his 'mate'). 'Never again', as Turk puts it, 'would Carné be so direct and unmannered in his treatment of homosexuality' (1989, 140). This may have much to do with the increasingly homophobic climate in which he found himself, but it may also be more deeply rooted in his conceptualization of homosexuality.

If circumstances (legality, the need for a heterosexual love story, the presence of Gabin) closeted *L'Air de Paris*, the film also bears two of the hallmarks of closet expression. First, the in some ways astonishing treatment of Lesaffre's body is none the less within the codes of the 'alibis' Thomas Waugh (1996) discusses in his history of gay erotic photography and film: showers, heterosexuality, massage as sports therapy. In *Thérèse Raquin* a year earlier, Carné's treatment of Lesaffre, in an important but secondary role invented for the film, is less body-baring but, in one telling sequence, much more gay iconographic: a striped sailor top is torn to reveal a nipple and a bicep flexed to hold a hand mirror, imagery that could come straight from Cocteau's *Le Livre blanc* (republished with said imagery in 1949) or much 1950s gay pornography. *L'Air de Paris*, though centrally homoerotic, places its potentially homosexual imagery firmly within less declarative bounds.

A second, but paradoxical, strategy of the closet is the presence in the film of a very obviously gay character and (*pace* Carné) a less obviously lesbian one, Jean-Marc and Chantal. The former, whose first words on greeting Corinne are 'j'ai passé une nuit complètement folle',[6] is virtually identical not only to the same actor's captain in *Fanfan la Tulipe* (1951) but also to Alain, one of five twin brothers played by Fernandel in *Le Mouton à cinq pattes* (1954): large men with rather small, manicured moustaches (rather like Marcel Proust's M. de Charlus), walking with short steps and hands held out the side, given to too many fussy gestures and a shriek in the voice. Parédès, who specialized in such roles, makes his camp characters livelier, warmer and wittier than those of Fernandel, and more unequivocally gay,[7] but there is not a lot in it. Chantal fits the less sharply defined stereotype of the rich lesbian in the world of fashion and antiques (cf. *Club de femmes*, *Quai des Orfèvres*, *Olivia*, *La Garçonne*, *La Fille aux yeux d'or*, *Les Biches* (1967), *La Fiancée du pirate* (1969), to name only French examples): single, elegant, cold, with a large, ornately furnished dwelling. Corinne tells André that Chantal, the older woman, 'formed' her, itself a trope of lesbian representation (Dyer 1977, 33–34);

Daëms' pause before telling André that Chantal is 'a friend' is virtually a wink to the audience that there is more to it.

Jean-Marc and Chantal represent the world of smart high style to which Corinne, a model from the provinces, aspires. Though André and Corinne have seen each other before, it is Jean-Marc who brings them together for an impromptu photo shoot (they are eating in a restaurant in Les Halles and notice André who is working there); Chantal prevents André and Corinne from making love the first time by arriving back too early (to the flat where she and Corinne live) and it is she who tells André with undisguised contempt that Corinne has left him (and her). In short, these queer characters' function is to take André from Victor and then also to break up André and Corinne. They represent a negative view of homosexuality in the film, but also its only explicit representation. By in effect attacking queers, *L'Air de Paris* may hope to ensure that its central vision of homosexuality remains in the closet.

Production circumstances and the closet do then account for much of the missability of *L'Air de Paris'* homosexuality. However, it also arises from the conceptualization of . . . And here we have a problem. I have used a variety of terms above to characterize the central relationship in this and other films, but in many ways there is no term for it. *L'Air de Paris* aspires to represent something without naming or indeed really representing it.

One senses the problem in Carné's brief discussion of the film alluded to above. He has been asked why he has 'never shot a male love story'. First he replies that he has perhaps indeed never shot an 'histoire d'amour entre hommes', but, after talking about the homosexual elements in *Hôtel du Nord*, *Les Enfants du paradis* (Lacenaire and Avril) and *L'Air de Paris*, he affirms, 'Mais histoires entre homos, non' (Grant and Joecker 1982–3, 14). The slippage from '*hommes*' to '*homos*' is crucial. Though he then acknowledges that he may simply not have had the nerve, it does also seem that he wants to say that the 'evocative' relationship in *L'Air de Paris* is, all the same, not gay because it is about men, not queers. But how then is this relationship to be conceptualized?

In Carné's last feature film, *La Merveilleuse visite* (1974), the main character, the angel Jean (Gilles Kohler), tells Delia (Deborah Berger), the young woman who befriends him, that love can take many forms, that it 'can take thousands and thousands of colours'. 'What colour is yours?', asks Delia, to which the angel replies, 'Transparency'. The homoerotic tones of *La Merveilleuse visite* are if anything even stronger than those of *L'Air de Paris* and validation of the many forms of love is standard pro-gay rhetoric. It is very hard not to hear in this exchange a message about homosexuality – but the really symptomatic element is the representation of the angel's love as transparency. Later Delia tries to explain the feelings between herself and the angel to her jealous boyfriend, François (Jean-Pierre Castaldi); it's not sex nor even really like sibling closeness, she says, 'I really don't know what it's called – there must be a word for it, but not in our language – you'd have to look elsewhere'. Transparency and namelessness – this is the ideal of love proposed by *La Merveilleuse visite* and, I'm now going to argue, *L'Air de Paris*.

*L'Air de Paris'* homoeroticism comes close to that proposed by the journal *Arcadie*, the first number of which appeared in the same year.[8] There had already been the short-lived journal *Futur*, from 1952 to 1955, but *Arcadie* was much more successful (though banned from display in kiosks), leading in 1957 to the establishment of social clubs in the French-speaking world. Its founder, André Baudry, was very well connected in the arts and politics, but his message also astutely judged the temper of the times. He proposed the notion of homophilia, stressing the erotic ('understood in the widest sense of the word: physical, psychological, affective and intellectual' (*Arcadie* 71; quoted in Girard 1981, 49)) rather than the merely sexual; as Jacques Girard puts it, 'homosexual' was seen as 'designating precise, localizable and easily identifiable acts', whereas 'homophile' related to 'a global attitude which takes in the thousand nuances of human being' (*ibid.*, 49–50).

Two things relevant here mark the conception of homophilia. One is the insistence that it 'must not be confused . . . with prostitution and effeminacy' (*Arcadie* 3, quoted in *ibid.*, 53). The Victor–André relationship could not be so confused – the film refuses the tarty iconography used on '*mauvais garçon*' Lesaffre in *Thérèse Raquin* and implies the relationship's distinctness from the likes of Jean-Marc.

Second, as the quotes above suggest, there is something vague, evasive and intangible about just what homophilia is, not least in the equivocation about sex. This is caught in the use of the word '*amitié*', *Arcadie*'s key term for defining homophile relations, at times a euphemism but also an attempt to define something between lust and comradeship. The term was also important to Carné: Turk (1989, 60) quotes from his praise of friendship in his autobiography, linking it to Carné's oblique representation of homosexuality in such friendships as Xavier and Lucien in *Jenny* (1936). The ambiguity of the term is caught in a remark of Victor to Blanche in *L'Air de Paris*, that men's 'friendship pisses women off'. Throughout the film Blanche knows what the real erotic story is between Victor and André;[9] he presents as asexual camaraderie what she recognizes as an erotically charged commitment.

The film, though, is not doing what Victor is doing. It may have counted on being misread as doing so. Male bonding, including the male couple, is a staple of French cinema (cf. Vincendeau 1993, Burch and Sellier 1996): as with the casting of Gabin (star of many such films, of course), the homophilia of *L'Air de Paris* may have assumed it was thus gaining some generic protection. However, it is instructive to compare it with two male couple films released shortly before, *Le Salaire de la peur* (1953) and *Touchez pas au grisbi* (1954). Both of these if anything make even more of the central male relationship. In *Le Salaire de la peur*, Mario (Yves Montand) effectively dumps

Luigi (Folco Lulli), who has looked after him like a wife, for the fake glamour of Jo (Charles Vanel); there is an emotionally charged reconciliation scene between Mario and Luigi, hugging and kissing when the former realizes the latter has not been killed in an explosion, but the strongest emotion is reserved for Jo's death in Mario's arms at the end of their long, perilous journey. In *Touchez pas au grisbi*, people remark on the fact that professional criminals Max (Gabin) and Riton (René Dary) 'have been together for twenty years'; the heart of the film is Max's sacrifice of his loot (the *grisbi* of the title) to save the kidnapped Riton, who in the process is fatally wounded.

All three films put the emotional weight on the male couple relationship, although the men all have wives or girlfriends. However, there is much greater heterosexual conviction in *Le Salaire de la peur* and *Touchez pas au grisbi*. In the former, Mario and Luigi contrast with Jo and also Luigi's co-driver, Bimba (Peter Van Eyck), who both explicitly say they are not interested in women; Mario not only has a girlfriend, Linda (Vera Clouzot), but he is constantly eyeing women in the street and the film ends with his delirious (and fatal) drive home, cross cut with Linda dancing in anticipation of his arrival, a clear suggestion of libidinal enthusiasm on both sides. Similarly in *Touchez pas au grisbi*, Max has a girlfriend, Betty (Marilyn Bufferd), and they both clearly take pleasure in their regular lunch and sex trysts. Linda and Betty are undoubtedly emotionally secondary to Jo and Riton, but there is genuine affection for and definite sexual satisfaction with the women in both cases. The same is not true of *L'Air de Paris*. The pointed absence of children in the Victor–Blanche household (underlined by having Blanche holding a baby, someone else's, the first time we see her in the film) and the fact that Victor's only mode of expressing affection is a light, mock punch to Blanche's chin both suggest this is a sexually undynamic marriage.[10] André and Corinne do clearly make love, though (partly for reasons of class difference) it seems not to have crossed his mind as a possibility when he first drives her home: he is all wide-eyed innocence, she worldly libidinousness when they stop outside her flat and she has to propose that he comes up. A later scene makes him more sexually forward, but opinions differ about how convincing Lesaffre's performance is at this point.

In short, if *L'Air de Paris* might just pass as an ungay male friendship film, it is certainly in no hurry to suggest the friends' heterosexuality. Moreover, unlike *Le Salaire de la peur* or *Touchez pas au grisbi*, *L'Air de Paris*' treatment of its central male couple draws much of its rhetoric from the treatment of heterosexuality in film. Lighting especially – both in two shots and in shot/reverse shot editing – reproduces the dynamics of screen heterosexuality. One scene, for instance, has Victor and André talking together on the latter's bed. Victor is screen right, wearing a black jacket, sitting turned towards us on the edge of the bed, elbows on his knees, looking down at his clasped hands. Light catches the top of his hair, his forehead and left leg, but André, who is stretched out on the bed, wearing a white shirt, is fully in the light. Victor talks about why he and some of the others love boxing, then asks André if he knows why he does. There is a cut to a different, closer angle: Victor's dark hair and jacket fills the right third of the screen; André, propped up one elbow now, turned towards us, catches to the full the frontal light that illuminates only Victor's turned-away-from-us profile; he also has a strong light, coming from behind Victor, on his right shoulder, a top back light that catches and blondes his hair and, when he looks up into Victor's face, the light flashes in his eyes. This kind of differentiated disposition, used throughout the film with the Victor–André couple, is exactly that used for heterosexual couples in film (cf. Dyer 1997, 132–140), with one qualification: the light on André is not softened. Whereas women in such set-ups are glowing, André is brilliant.

This brilliance may simply be a more 'masculine' lightness than soft glamour lighting, but it also relates to angel imagery. There is a long tradition of representing gay desire in the figure of the (male) angel in the international high gay culture that was very much a reference point for *Arcadie*. A French locus classicus of this is the early work of André Gide (discussed in a classic 1950s study by Jean Delay (1956: 492–519)), while in cinema we may note *Vingarne* (Sweden 1916), *Mikael* (Germany 1924), *Le Sang d'un poète*, *Lot in Sodom* (USA 1930), *Teorema* (Italy 1968), *Looking for Langston* (GB 1989), related films like *Billy Budd* (USA 1962) and *Morte a Venezia* (Italy 1971), and, most relevant here, the work of Carné himself: the sexually and morally ambiguous emissaries of the devil in *Les Visiteurs du soir*[11](1942), the diaphanous clothes and white, white face of the pure lover Baptiste in *Les Enfants du paradis* (1943–5) and, most explicitly, the blond, almost permanently half or completely naked angel of *La Merveilleuse visite*.[12] The whole tradition, and especially its denial of any compatibility between lust and innocence, is wickedly sent up in Lionel Soukaz' short film, *Le Sexe des anges* (1978).[13]

It is above all the brilliant light on André in *L'Air de Paris*, emphasizing at once his physicality and his ingenuousness, that puts him clearly in this line of images of gay desire. This is reinforced by his not being socially located. Like Roland Lesaffre himself (as publicity emphasized), André is an orphan and has learnt boxing in the rootless anonymity of the military. He is first encountered on the railway line in Paris, rather, that is, than in a Paris neighbourhood. There is something strange about the way the film introduces him the first time he and Victor meet. They have both gone to a hospital where a mutual friend, one of Victor's boxers, has just died; Victor is standing talking to a registrar, when suddenly André's voice is heard and the camera moves back to reveal his presence – almost as if he has just landed there rather than having been physically present all along. The brilliant light and the lack of social location reinforce the overriding angelic characterization: intense sexual appeal yet apparent lack of sexual awareness.

*L'Air de Paris* – above: André (Roland Lesaffre, facing, inside the ring) and Victor (Jean Gabin, his back turned to us); below: (from left to right) Victor (Jean Gabin), André (Roland Lesaffre) and Blanche (Arletty).

Vivid and sensual, the angel is unimpeachably spiritual. He may sometimes be another Waughian alibi, but he also expresses a longing for a form of sexual desire that is sinless and pure. He is the fantasy resolution of a conflict between lust and morality endured by generations of gay men. In some cases, he can also be the site for playing out the ambiguities and deceptions of this resolution, but where this is not so, as with *L'Air de Paris*, his brilliance and vividness at once expresses the keenness of homophile longing and betrays its impossibility. After all, he does not exist. At the end of *La Merveilleuse visite*, the angel, besieged by uncomprehending townsmen, falls off a cliff and becomes a seagull. It is the only place for such unsulliable sensuality. *L'Air de Paris*' angel, André, is of course not literally one, any more than the film is generically a fantasy. This creates especial problems for a film on the face of it so much about place.

*L'Air de Paris* seems to be a film insistently about Paris. Even before the credits, a song, 'La Ballade de Paris', is sung in the darkness by Yves Montand. He had introduced it with some success a year earlier; both it and the film's title told the first audiences that they were going to see a film about Paris. The credits reinforce this, with a series of postcard images of Paris to the accompaniment, mainly, of instrumental versions of 'La Ballade' and another Montand success, 'Toi tu n'ressembles à personne', played by accordion and orchestra: nothing could be more 'Parisian'. The two main stars, Gabin and Arletty, have indelibly Parisian images (and accents), the first shot of the film is a railway sign indicating 'Paris 2 kilomètres', locations (some studio recreations) include the area round the boulevard de Grenelle, the Iles de la Cité and Saint-Louis and Les Halles, all very familiar, there is an interspersed montage of postcard Paris and the films ends with Victor and André walking off towards Notre-Dame.

Yet the film also seems to undermine this Paris project. Blanche/Arletty spends most of the film saying she wants to leave Paris, André speaks with bitter irony about it ('it's got everything you need, the good Lord, cops . . . and if that's not enough, you can always throw yourself in the Seine'), and when Corinne tells André she is marrying a rich man to help her career and, not least, Chantal's ailing antiques business, she says, 'That's life, that is, that's Paris.' Some of this may be generic: people in Paris films are always complaining about Paris.[14] Equally, some aspects of the faltering view of Paris – as compared to the Paris of accordions and postcard views – might be seen as in part registering changes in contemporary Paris, notably in its ethnic mix: Victor and Blanche live next door to an Italian family, André initially lives in an Arab hotel, and one of Victor's boxers, often prominent in the frame and especially fondly treated by Blanche, is black.

What makes these elements more unsettling is the way the film seems set on making Paris somehow insubstantial. The song sung in the dark at the beginning concentrates the audience on Paris, but also leaves it ungrounded

136

in any imagery, while its gist is the problem of singing a song about Paris ('So many poets have written songs about Paris that I don't know what to say to sing its praises').[15] The accordion and postcards credits seem too insistently Parisian, especially when it turns out they have so little to do with the Paris of the film. The film's opening sequence takes place two kilometres from Paris (a sign tells us) on a railway track (as Corinne and André see each other for the first time, he working on the line, she looking down from a halted train), a moment of standstill in a site of transition, not quite yet in Paris proper.

One especially telling index of this undermining representation is the treatment of Victor/Gabin in relation to food. As Vincendeau points out, food is central to Gabin's image, as a man and as French (1993, 167–8, 177–8). *L'Air de Paris* denies him this. He is only once seen in a café (just after he first meets André); it is deserted and he is not known there, in other words, an impersonal space. Meals are often taken with the neighbouring family, where they eat Italian food; without telling Blanche and much to her annoyance, Victor uses their anniversary meal to celebrate André's victory in the ring, except that André doesn't come and we don't see the meal. The only meal properly shown in the film is that of Corinne, Jean-Marc, Chantal and their associates in a bistro in Les Halles, a sequence that does not include Victor/Gabin and which contrasts strikingly with the opening scene of *Touchez pas au grishi*, where bourgeois slummers like Jean-Marc *et al.* are expressly excluded from the restaurant that is virtually Max/Gabin's home. The very thing that grounds Gabin in his world – and archetypally Paris – in his other films is taken away from him here.

This desubstantializing representation of Paris goes hand in hand with the film's focus on a homophilic relationship. *L'Air de Paris* eschews showing us the gay Paris that did exist, despite the homophobic climate, the Paris described in Paul Reboux' open-minded survey *Sens interdits* of 1951, a Paris 'taken over by a pederastic elite', according to one commentator in 1953.[16] Even the homosexually obvious Jean-Marc is not placed anywhere in the city. In the racy sequence featuring Lesaffre in *Thérèse Raquin* discussed above, the proximity of the most important gay area of Paris, Pigalle, is rammed home by the sight of Sacré Coeur through the window, but Pigalle does not figure at all in *L'Air de Paris*.

Refusing to document this non-homophilic Paris, the film also cannot imagine any other locus for homosexuality. The film ends with Victor and André walking together towards Notre-Dame. It is a strange shot. Notre-Dame figures quite late in the credits sequence, seen in the distance, the frame dominated by a modern bridge; it appears in the sequence at the moment the music changes to a new melody in a jazzy arrangement, one that becomes associated in the film with the Paris of high fashion that the film rejects. Thereafter, Notre-Dame is shown only in order to place the flat where Corinne lives with Chantal. In other words, it has no meaning for the men or the film except a negative one. Moreover, it is shot, in this final image, with its flying buttresses fully lit and light flooding out of all the doors and windows of the Ile Saint-Louis quayside street down which the men walk – a magical look that at the same time underlines the impossibility of this happy ending. In short, the shot suggests that for Carné there is no place for Victor and André, for homophilia, in Paris – or, this must mean, anywhere else.

## Notes

1 Pérez (1994, 130) notes this. The main exception seems to be the right-wing journal *Aspects de la France*, whose critic, Georges Hellio, referred to Victor being in the grip of 'a demon a teensy weensy bit equivocal' (1 October 1954; in Pérez 1994, 133). Marcel Carné, in the context of a discussion of the lesbianism in the film, says that he was much attacked at the time, *Paris-Presse* referring to '*L'Air de Paris*, an unbreathable air', evoking, so Carné presumably understands, the image of the airless decadence of lesbian milieux (Grant and Joecker 1982–3, 14).
2 'déséquilibrée, désorientée, et comme intérieurement trahie', *Le Parisien Libéré*, 30 September 1954 (in Pérez 1994, 133).
3 It is possible that we are simply ignorant about gay representation in French cinema. There is as yet for the latter no equivalent to Vito Russo's *The Celluloid Closet* (1981) and recent research suggests that there is more to find out than even he knew about gay representation in Hollywood (let alone elsewhere). The French language books on homosexuality and film (Garsi 1981, Philbert 1984) in fact have very little in them about French film (especially before the 1970s). It's possible that research will reveal that *L'Air de Paris* is less isolated than it appears.
4 The first such legislation since decriminalization in 1791.
5 Burch and Sellier (1996) note that the issue of collaborationism commonly focused on questions of sexual relations between French women and German men; it would not be surprising if the same trope applied to gay men. One of the key witnesses in Marcel Ophuls' *Le Chagrin et la pitié* (1969) is a respected underground militant who emphasizes the importance for him of coming out as gay in the film to counter the idea that gay men were all collaborationists.
6 Literally 'I've had a completely mad night'. However, 'folle', the feminine form of 'fou' (mad), is also slang for a camp gay man.
7 Alain in *Le Mouton à cinq pattes* seems to live with a woman, whom he addresses with extravagant terms of endearment – but he also calls her 'vous' and they have separate bedrooms. Jean-Marc on the other hand goes into raptures when he sees André and his mates at Les Halles – 'They are splendid! Young Hercules!' – while the captain in *Fanfan la Tulipe* says that he'd love to see Fanfan (Gérard Philipe) do his swashbuckling stuff, throwing 'Wouldn't you?' to Fanfan's beloved (Gina Lollobrigida) with a distinctly libidinal moue.
8 Given *Arcadie*'s founder's wide connections, and the involvement in it of, among others, Cocteau and the film critic Jacques Siclier, it is unlikely that Carné did not at least know about *Arcadie*. Frédéric Martel notes that in 1968 some break-away members of *Arcadie* 'took the view that the allusions to homosexuality in the films of Marcel Carné were no longer sufficient' (1996, 71), indicating at any rate the perception of a link between the world views of Carné and *Arcadie*.
9 Women's perceptiveness about sexuality between men is a recurrent motif in Carné: cf. Renée and Adrien in *Hôtel du Nord*, Garance and Lacenaire in *Les Enfants du paradis* and Delia and the angel in *La Merveilleuse visite*.

10  Absence of children in a couple would certainly not indicate sexual coldness in contemporary cinema, but it did by and large before the 1960s.
11  Cf. the discussion in Turk 1989, 206–12.
12  This would have been even more obvious had Carné been able to shoot the ending he wanted, in which the camera would be shown and on it the crew, all 'young and beautiful, just wearing trousers with a little heart on them [like the angel] and all of a sudden the camera flies off into the infinite . . . as if to say, even if no-one believes in this story, at least the crew did'. However, he couldn't film it because he couldn't get hold of any 'M. Muscle' types from Paris in time (Grant and Joecker 1982–3, 10).
13  Briefly described in Dyer 1990, 225–6.
14  I'm grateful to Ginette Vincendeau for pointing this out.
15  Vincendeau (1993, 151–2) points out that Paris songs (with accordion) are often important in Gabin films, either sung to an audience within the film or direct to camera. Here not only is it not Gabin singing in a Gabin film, but the voice is disembodied, not visually addressed to anyone.
16  Frédéric Hoffet in his *Psychanalyse de Paris*, referenced in Copley 1989, 193. 'Pederasty' (notably in the slang term 'pédé') was often used in the period to refer to all male homosexuality, not just that involving boys.

## Selected bibliography

Billard, Pierre (1995) *L'Age classique du cinéma français*, Paris, Flammarion.
Burch, Noël and Sellier, Geneviève (1996) *La Drôle de guerre des sexes du cinéma français*, Paris, Nathan.
Cadars, Pierre (1982) *Les Séducteurs du cinéma français*, Paris, Henri Veyrier.
Carné, Marcel (1979) *La Vie à belles dents*, Paris, Editions Jean Vuaret.
Chirpaz, François and Jeanine (1956) 'Carné, ou la rencontre impossible', *Esprit* 244, 716–23.
Copley, Antony (1989) *Sexual Moralities in France, 1780–1980*, London, Routledge.
Delay, Jean (1956) *La Jeunesse d'André Gide*, Paris, Gallimard.
Dyer, Richard (1977) 'Stereotyping,' in Richard Dyer (ed.) *Gays and Film*, London, British Film Institute, 27–39.
Dyer, Richard (1990) *Now You See It: Studies on Lesbian and Gay Film*, London, Routledge.
Dyer, Richard (1997) *White*, London, Routledge.
Garsi, Jean-François (ed.) (1981) *Cinémas homosexuels*, Paris, Papyrus (*CinémAction* 15).
Girard, Jacques (1981) *Le Mouvement homosexuel en France 1945–1980*, Paris, Syros.
Grant, Jacques and Joecker, Jean-Pierre (1982–3) 'Rencontre avec Marcel Carné: Cinéaste Fantastisque (sic)', *Masques* 16, 6–16.
Marrot, Henri (1962) '*Air de Paris*', *Image et Son* 153–4, 3–4.
Martel, Frédéric (1996) *Le Rose et le noir: les homosexuels en France depuis 1968*, Paris, Editions du Seuil.
Pérez, Michel (1994) *Les Films de Carné*, Paris, Editions Ramsay.
Philbert, Bertrand (1984) *L'Homosexualité à l'écran*, Paris, Henri Veyrier.
Reboux, Paul (1951) *Sens interdits*, Paris, Raoul Solar.
Russo, Vito (1981) *The Celluloid Closet*, New York, Harper & Row.
Turk, Edward Baron (1989) *Child of Paradise: Marcel Carné and the Golden Age of French Cinema*, Cambridge, Mass., Harvard University Press.

Vincendeau, Ginette (1993) 'Gabin unique: Le pouvoir réconciliateur du mythe', in Claude Gauteur and Ginette Vincendeau, *Jean Gabin: anatomie d'un mythe*, Paris, Nathan, 93–205.

Vincendeau, Ginette (1997) 'Paradise Regained', *Sight and Sound*, 7 (1) (NS), 12–16.

Waugh, Thomas (1996) *Hard to Imagine: Gay Male Eroticism on Photography and Film from Their Beginnings to Stonewall*, New York, Columbia University Press.

# Appendix

## *Marcel Carné (1909–96): filmography*

See Chapter 4, on *Le Jour se lève*, for a full filmography.

### *Other films cited in the text*

*Les Amitiés particulières*, Jean Delannoy (1964)
*Au Royaume des cieux*, Julien Duvivier (1949)
*Les Biches*, Claude Chabrol (1967)
*Billy Budd*, Peter Ustinov (USA 1962)
*Un Chant d'amour*, Jean Genet (1950)
*Club de femmes*, Jacques Deval (1936)
*Les Collégiennes*, André Hunnebelle (1956)
*Les Enfants du paradis* (*Children of Paradise*), Marcel Carné (1943–5)
*Fanfan la Tulipe*, Christian-Jaque (1951)
*La Fiancée du pirate*, Nelly Kaplan (1969)
*La Fille aux yeux d'or*, Gabriel Albicocco (1960)
*La Garçonne*, Jacqueline Audry (1957)
*Hélène*, Marie Epstein and Jean Benoît-Lévy (1936)
*Hôtel du Nord*, Marcel Carné (1938)
*Huis-clos*, Jacqueline Audry (1954)
*Jenny*, Marcel Carné (1935)
*La Kermesse héroïque*, Jacques Feyder (1935)
*Looking for Langston*, Isaac Julien (UK 1989)
*Lot in Sodom*, James Sibley Watson and Melville Webber (USA 1930)
*Les Maudits*, René Clément (1947)
*La Merveilleuse visite*, Marcel Carné (1974)
*Mikael*, Carl Dreyer (Germany 1924)
*Morte a Venezia* (*Death in Venice*), Luchino Visconti (Italy 1971)
*Le Mouton à cinq pattes*, Henri Verneuil (1954)
*Olivia*, Jacqueline Audry (1950)
*Paris-Béguin*, Augusto Genina (1931)
*Quai des Orfèvres*, Henri-Georges Clouzot (1947)
*La Règle du jeu* (*Rules of the Games*), Jean Renoir (1939)
*Le Salaire de la peur*, Henri-Georges Clouzot (1953)
*Le Sang d'un poète*, Jean Cocteau (1932)
*Le Sexe des anges*, Lionel Soukaz (1978)
*Teorema* (*Theorem*), Pier Paolo Pasolini (Italy 1968)

*Thérèse Desqueyroux*, Georges Franju (1962)
*Thérèse Raquin*, Marcel Carné (1953)
*Touchez pas au grisbi* (*Grisbi*), Jacques Becker (1954)
*Vingarne*, Mauritz Stiller (Sweden 1916)
*Les Visiteurs du soir*, Marcel Carné (1942)
*Zéro de conduite* (*Zero for Conduct*), Jean Vigo (1933)

# 10

# THE SCRIPT OF DELINQUENCY
## François Truffaut's *Les 400 coups* (1959)

*Anne Gillain*

Throughout his career, François Truffaut expressed some degree of displeasure when critics labelled his work autobiographical. His ambivalence on this record is apparent as early as 1959 when his first film, *Les 400 coups*, was released to worldwide acclaim. His interviews at the time reveal two types of contradictory statement. He first adamantly claimed that nothing in the film was an exaggeration and that he had experienced as a child all the hardships endured by Antoine Doinel in the film. He also flatly denied that *Les 400 coups* was his biography (Truffaut 1959). For this there were of course reasons of a personal nature. The film was after all a violent indictment of his parents, particularly of his mother. Both were alive when the film came out and Truffaut had been trying to establish a normal relationship with them during his years as a film critic for *Cahiers du cinéma.* But, more importantly, this denial was prompted by reasons pertaining to aesthetics.

Autobiographies, even the least sophisticated, involve elements of stylization. By turning experience into language, autobiographical narration injects it with meaning. The need to understand oneself better, the desire to establish one's unique identity or the urge to interpret one's life – all these motives account for the autobiographical impulse. In order to treat the self as a narrative object, the author must select the facts that he or she recalls to reconstruct the unity of his or her life. The author must also impose an order on its individual events and bestow upon them narrative coherence, as well as achieve the creation of an imaginary self. These constraints explain Sartre's remark in *Les Mots* (Brooks 1984, 114) that autobiographical narration is obituary in its nature. Such narration entails the creation of a space between the narrating and the narrated selves in order to allow for the former to objectify and look back on the latter. In Truffaut's case this distancing is made particularly complex and fascinating by the fact that his autobiography is not enclosed within one given film but spread over twenty-one full-length features, each of them attacking the problems of genre, narrativity, authority and closure from a fresh perspective. While each picture is entirely self-contained, it can also be read as a piece of a puzzle to be inserted within the wider image formed by the whole body of his works. The open-ended nature of this process seems infinite and there is no doubt that, had he lived another thirty years, Truffaut could have extracted many more films from his life experience. In this creation *Les 400 coups* evidently occupies an exceptional place, not only because it is the most universally admired of his films but because it unleashes, in a literal way, Truffaut's imaginary world, with a passion, a vigor and a mastery which set the model for all his future works.

In his interviews Truffaut described *Les 400 coups* as the chronicle of the thirteenth year, the most difficult since it marks the passage from childhood to adolescence. Born in 1932, Truffaut reached that age in 1945 during the turmoil of the liberation of Paris after four years of German occupation. In the picture, the time period is transposed to 1958 when the actual filming took place. This temporal distortion is counterbalanced by the documentary exactitude of the spatial background of the film. Most of the exterior shots were set in the exact neighborhood where Truffaut grew up, chiefly rue des Martyrs, a lively popular street that runs down from Montmartre towards the grands boulevards. The Doinels' cramped apartment was certainly reminiscent of Truffaut's modest lodging in rue Navarin. His young parents had met at the French Alpine Club and were both fervent mountaineers. They would often leave their son alone on weekends to go rock-climbing in the Fontainebleau forest. In the film, this sporting activity is replaced by the passion of Antoine's stepfather for automobile rallies. Truffaut's mother worked as a secretary for a magazine and does not seem to have ever displayed much interest in a child she had never wished to have. Neglected at home, the young Truffaut soon retaliated by skipping school and running away from home. Cinema and his friend Robert Lachenay (René in the film) were his only companions. From 1942 on, the situation progressively worsened until in 1947 Truffaut was arrested at his father's request, not for stealing a typewriter as in the film, but for running the cine-club he had created with stolen funds. After two nights in the central jail, the boy was sent to a center for delinquent minors at Villejuif which was part insane asylum, part *maison de correction* (reform school) (Walz 1982, 3). Truffaut's legendary friendship with André Bazin saved him from this tragic situation. The adolescent had met the film critic when he had opened his cine-club and had much impressed Bazin with his encyclopedic knowledge of films and his fervour for cinema. Bazin would rescue him a second time from jail in 1951, when Truffaut went AWOL after enlisting in the French army to fight in Indochina. Bazin and his wife sheltered the young man in their home, where he wrote his first articles as a journalist. By 1954 he had become the most famous film critic of his generation and by 1958 he had joined the ranks of the French New Wave film-makers. Sadly enough, Bazin died on the first day of shooting of *Les 400 coups*. Truffaut dedicated the film to his memory.

This brief outline confirms Truffaut's declaration that his first film reflects the bare facts of his own existence as a child. It also shows how close to destruction the experience of delinquency brought his life in his formative years. This experience has, in my opinion, been underplayed in the analysis of his work as a film-maker. Incarcerated twice, Truffaut was to remain profoundly marked by a sense of exclusion from society, which accounts for his sympathy for outcasts. Most of his heroes will be misfits. My contention is that, not only *Les 400 coups*, but all of Truffaut's films offer a complex variation on the same hidden and repressed scenario of childhood, or what I will call 'the script of delinquency'. 'A man is formed between seven and sixteen', Truffaut once remarked, 'later he will relive all his life what he has acquired between these two ages' (Sand 1968, 13). This comment can be applied to the films, but to understand Truffaut's use of autobiography, one must discard the facile notion of a direct transposition from life to films. If the director's youth informs his stories, it is as an atemporal matrix structure which each film replays in a different vein, on a different tone. The constant quality of the script of delinquency relies on affects not on events. In this light, *Vivement dimanche* is as autobiographical as *Les 400 coups*. This script generates a phantasmatic matrix which gives form and content to the relations of desire played out in the films. In *Les 400 coups*, this script unravels for the first time the figural and narrative patterns for the films to come.

Essential to the script of delinquency is first a peculiar quality of space. Visually *Les 400 coups* is built on an elegant binary opposition which is maintained throughout the film. Inside, at home or at school, the narration is dominated by static shots and close-ups, while outside, long and mobile shots prevail. These alternations give the film its powerful rhythm of tension and release. A prisoner indoors, Antoine becomes in the streets a child free to roam, play and explore. The examples of this dual regime are numerous but one of its most effective uses occurs after Antoine's first attempt to run away from home, following his encounter with his mother and her lover in the street. When his mother has brought Antoine back to the apartment, she gives him a bath and undertakes to win back his affection, and probably to buy his silence, by reminiscing about her own youth. She also proposes a contract to him: if he writes a good essay, she will reward him with money. This tense exchange is filmed in a shot/reverse shot pattern, reflecting each character's guarded position. The next image abruptly presents an exterior scene where the gym teacher leads the column of schoolchildren through the streets. All of them will progressively scatter and disappear in the course of this exercise. First shot at eye level from a standard angle, this vignette suddenly switches to a bird-like point of view where the dynamics of the group appear to be watched by a distant and ironic observer. This striking visual effect, in sharp contrast with the preceding scene, injects this episode with mythic significance and makes it one of the most memorable moments of the film. A tribute to a similar scene in Vigo's *Zéro de conduite*, it captures the boundless energy of childhood and becomes an allegory of its dispersion within the currents of life. In the same vein, the credits of *L'Argent de poche* present a crowd of schoolchildren cascading down the narrow streets of a village as a free, joyful and irrepressible flow. In *Les 400 coups* this scene also programmes Antoine's final escape from the columns of young delinquents in an attempt to assert his own separate and unique identity.

Another important characteristic of the street scenes lies in the scarcity of their information content. In fact, an episode such as the gym lesson could be placed anywhere in the narrative. It is not linked by any cause–effect relationship to what precedes or follows. It appears as a pure interlude when all the constraints of the plot are suspended. In the streets, Antoine benefits from an amnesty which relieves him from the steady flow of disaster besieging him at home or at school. An obvious example of this occurs when Antoine accidentally meets his mother and her lover. This momentous encounter will have surprisingly few effects on the plane of reality. The spatial alternations coincide in effect with a dual temporal regime: a cyclical time, built on the repetition of the same, and devoid of information, is opposed to a linear time that nourishes the plot with events and carries forward the story. These two temporalities are typical of Truffaut's films, where the narrative process often seems to be a struggle to delay the revelation of some dismal truth.

This spatial and temporal freeze/flow effect is reinforced by another set of oppositions in the film between the photographs and the rotor in the funfair. The image of the pin-up will start Antoine's ordeal, the picture of Balzac will set the house on fire and Antoine's face will be brutally entrapped in the mug shots at the police station. Photographs are always for Truffaut pieces of evidence, pointing to some inaccessible secret. They are the indicators of time marking the path towards death. The enigmatic value of the famous last shot of the film carries the weight of these associations. In contrast, the rotor, one of the most commented-upon figures in *Les 400 coups*, has long been associated with cinema by the critics. Its circular and playful space is also clearly a maternal one where the child curls back in a foetal position while time is suspended. Cinema as a place of affective compensation for parental neglect played such a role in Truffaut's own experience.

In order to understand fully the connection between these spatio-temporal structures and the script of delinquency, it is helpful to invoke D. W. Winnicott's theories on anti-social behaviours and, in particular, his concept of the transitional space. Briefly stated, the transitional space is the area which allows the child to approach external reality in the first years of his/her life and to adjust successfully to it. By creating a world subjected to the infant's desire, the mother gives him or her the necessary trust to discover the outer reality and to explore its boundaries: 'The mother's adaptation to the infant's needs, when good enough, gives the child the illusion that there is an external reality that corresponds to the infant's own capacity to create'

(Winnicott 1975, 22). His or her first creation will be what Winnicott calls the transitional object, a favourite toy which embodies all the positive values of the transitional space and allows him or her to tolerate the threat of separation. The paradox of this object is that in order to be *created*, it has first to be *found* in the external world. It is both a subjective and objective phenomenon and bridges the gap between outer and inner reality. Later on, the transitional space will become the area for playing and creativity, and the transitional object will be replaced by cultural experiences. But if the child is deprived for too long of maternal care in his or her youth, he or she will lose his or her ability to relate to the external world and suffer what Winnicott calls an 'unspeakable agony'. A sense of danger will replace trust. The transitional space will fill with persecutive elements and change into a carceral space. Delinquency is one of the less damaging outcomes to this predicament, which can also lead to autism – as *L'Enfant sauvage* shows. *Les 400 coups*, like most of Truffaut's films, focuses on this critical situation and presents the hero's attempts to recapture, after the breakdown of his environment, the transitional space of communication, creativity and shared experience. An analysis of the first two sequences of *Les 400 coups* will demonstrate how Winnicott's views help to enlighten the interconnection of the themes developed in the narrative.

By setting his opening scene in a classroom, Truffaut immediately denounces the failure of an institution designed to facilitate the child's adaptation to social reality. He also makes clear that Antoine is an exceptionally creative youth. The fatal pin-up picture will quietly circulate among his schoolmates until he decides to draw a moustache on it. Punished and isolated in a corner, which is the first representation of a carceral space, he will not remain passive but will compose a poem on the wall. In the decline and fall of Antoine throughout the film, writing evidently plays the role of the original sin. Whenever writing is involved, disaster will strike. In this vein, the absurd choice made by Antoine to steal a typewriter makes perfect sense. There is no point insisting on the overwhelming importance of language in Truffaut's films. Within the sphere of the transitional activities, verbal expression is one of the most effective ways to reach and master the external world or, to use Lacanian terminology, language represents the passage from the Imaginary to the Symbolic, from past to present, from a dual relationship dominated by the mother, to a reality mediated by the paternal law. In *Les 400 coups*, this primordial activity is shown from the start to be hopelessly hampered.

While Antoine is writing his fateful poem, two inserts show the other children playing in the schoolyard. This filmic construction points to the similarities between these two forms of expression. If writing is doomed to failure throughout the film, playing will assert in contrast the indomitable spirit of childhood. Antoine will share many games with René and will even play at the *centre d'observation* (the centre for delinquent minors). The redeeming nature of this activity is made particularly clear by one scene. When Antoine spends his first night at the police station, a long silent sequence reveals the nocturnal routine in this carceral space. Two pan shots (the second of which is filmed from Antoine's point of view) show a couple of policemen absorbed in a silly child's game played with plastic horses and dice.[1] This sequence, which constitutes the most desolate episode of Antoine's exclusion from society, is much lightened by the insertion of these images where a transitional activity injects a note of hope within the carceral space.

Antoine's resilience in the face of adversity is made obvious by a third activity: stealing. It is first mentioned when René and Antoine leave school in the first scene and ask the sinister Mauricet where he stole the money to buy the goggles he is proudly wearing. Stealing is, in *Les 400 coups*, as in most of Truffaut's films, indeed a pervasive habit. Antoine and René will devote to it most of their energies, and both their mothers will prove adept in this art. A thug in the streets, a child in the school corridors, will also try their hand at it. In his study of anti-social behaviours, Winnicott (1957, 159–73; 1971, 279–304; 1975, 119) characterizes stealing as a gesture of hope on the part of a child who feels he or she has been deprived of the care and love to which he or she was inalienably entitled. The young robber is not looking for objects but trying to re-establish contact with a maternal figure who failed to recognize his or her needs. In this sense, stealing and delinquency represent positive behaviours endowed with healing powers. Instead of renunciation, the youth demands reparation. Stealing constitutes an attempt to avoid withdrawal from reality and to recapture the transitional space. An elliptic and beautiful scene illustrates this process in the film, when Antoine and René make the momentous decision to steal the typewriter during a puppet show in the Luxembourg gardens. This conversation is framed by numerous shots of young children enthralled by the spectacle. This odd association suggests an analogy between both activities. Stealing, in this context, appears as a desire to claim back, in a forceful and destructive way, the passionate involvement with reality generated by transitional experiences. Finally, it is characteristic that, in the film, the only person to be robbed is Antoine's stepfather who keeps lamenting the loss of his Michelin Guide. This points to the obvious failure of his authority and of the law he should represent.

After this magisterial opening where all the symptoms of Antoine's inner conflicts are revealed, the second sequence will unveil the source of his discontent. The first three actions he performs in the Doinels' deserted apartment are gestures of anger and destruction: opening the stove, he lets high flames surge in the room; wiping his dirty hands on the curtains he soils them, a tribute to Renoir's *Boudu sauvé des eaux*, and he then proceeds to steal some money.

In contrast with this display of violence, the bedroom scene that follows expresses an elegiac nostalgia for an absent mother. Antoine smells her perfumes and toys with the strange contraptions designed to enhance her beauty. Three mirrors capture his lonely figure and reflect the painful fragmentation of his self in search of an identity. Commenting on Lacan's 'stade du miroir', Winnicott (1975, 153) simply observes that 'the precursor of the mirror is the mother's face'. The child staring at his image tries to catch back in his reflection his mother's glance. Antoine is a youth who longs to be seen, to be acknowledged and, within the visual dynamics of the narrative, looks will play an essential role. They will always, however, be hostile and bring him reprimands, slaps, denunciations. Antoine will only manage to attract the icy stare of the law. When Madame Doinel arrives home, she will not even glance at her son but will display, with a stark contempt for his young sexual awareness, her silky legs. This shot is seminal in Truffaut's films, and legs will remain forever linked to maternal exhibitionism and sexual appeal. In *Baisers volés*, the 'magic' Fabienne Tabard will first meet Antoine when she is trying on a pair of shoes. In *L'Argent de poche*, Madame Riffle will be painting her toes when an enamoured Patrick brings her red roses. The examples are too numerous to all be reviewed. These legs frighten the child as much as they seduce him. Directing his glance towards the 'mystery' of female sexuality, they generate anxieties which account for the systematic fragmentation of the woman's image in Truffaut's films. *L'Homme qui aimait les femmes* presents a deep and lucid account of the pathological structures which develop from this early fixation on the maternal body. In this film, an eloquent scene shows the young hero, Bertrand Morane, reading a book while his mother walks around in an elegant négligé indifferently exhibiting her legs. The unmediated fixation of the adolescent's desire on her body will result in his future inability to resolve his Oedipal crisis. In his adult life, women's legs and books (both strongly connected in his early experience with the maternal body) will function as fetishes allowing him to maintain a regressive and painful situation of pre-Oedipal fulfilment.[2] The position of a maternal figure is central to the script of delinquency, and each film will offer a solution to the conflict-relationship between mother and son.

Madame Doinel is, throughout the narrative, the principal generator of textual energies. Whether he sees her with her lover, declares her dead, or sets the house on fire, Antoine's actions are always determined by his Oedipal pulsions towards her. It is important that his most significant attempt at creativity is directly linked to maternal attention. As mentioned earlier, after his first flight from home, Madame Doinel proposes a contract to her son. This scene is followed by an evening at the movies which represents the only joyful evocation of family life in the film. But Antoine fails to fulfil his part of the contract by involuntarily plagiarizing a text by Balzac. The narrative makes plain that Balzac is in fact a transitional object for the young hero (Antoine organizes a sort of cult around the novelist's image) and his problem arises from a confusion between finding and creating, outer and inner worlds. Misunderstood in his attempt to reach external reality, he will end up a delinquent.

But *Les 400 coups* would not have retained its relevance over the years if it were simply a story of deviance and despair. It is essential to see that behind the realistic plot linked to linear time, lies a second scenario, The script of delinquency involves a powerful phantasmatic component which, in all the films, relies chiefly on what the psychoanalysts Laplanche and Pontalis have defined as 'primal phantasies', i.e. on phantasies which are inherent in the development and maturation of any human being. In *Les 400 coups*, the underlying plot expresses a passionate desire for fusion with a maternal figure. This desire is not presented as real, for Madame Doinel will never fulfil it, but as the expression of a haunting nostalgia.

Nostalgia runs high in Truffaut's films and always represents the precarious hold an individual can have on the inner representation of a lost object. Nostalgia points to an archaic past, and Antoine, like many of Truffaut's heroes, seeks the realization of his desires in the reproduction of indestructible signs of infantile satisfaction. The yearning to fuse with a maternal figure is expressed by images of a mythic nature for the first time in the introduction and then again in the conclusion of the film. The credits unroll on shots evoking an impatient attempt by the camera to be reunited with the Eiffel Tower. Similarly at the end the child will be followed by a long tracking shot until he reaches the exact point where the waves touch the sand. Freud is barely needed here to validate connotations of birth. Poets have said long before him that the shore is the mother's body where the child is born: 'On the seashore of endless worlds, children play.'[3] Truffaut freezes this last image, blending the evocation of birth with a threat of death. This brilliant synthesis is typical of the ambivalence of his imaginary world. But within the film itself, the wish for fusion is expressed by Antoine's love affair with Paris. The city is a maternal space which shelters the child, protects his games, hides and feeds him. The moving episode of the night in Paris shows Antoine stealing a milk bottle and stealthily drinking it in the deserted streets. The only time he displays grief and cries is when he is separated from this symbolic maternal body.

At the centre for delinquent minors, a powerful scene will actualize these nostalgic images of reunion with a maternal figure when Antoine, facing the camera, engages in a free and lively conversation with the psychologist. In this scene, it is essential to note, first, that the psychologist is a woman, and second, that this woman is represented as a disembodied voice.[4] As a woman, the psychologist clearly evokes a positive maternal figure (contrary to Madame Doinel, a sexual taboo is cast on to her body: another young delinquent warns Antoine not to look at her legs), and Antoine trustfully converses with her. He looks relaxed, playful and happy. This exchange where the child is allowed for the first time to formulate a lucid account of his problems, attests to his inner resilience and to his capacity for analysing his predicament. In

*Les 400 coups* — above: Antoine Doinel (Jean-Pierre Léaud) at his mother's dressing table; below: (from left to right) Mme Doinel (Claire Maurier), Antoine (Jean-Pierre Léaud) and M. Doinel (Albert Rémy) in the family car.

*Les 400 coups* – above: Mme Doinel, M. Doinel and Antoine; below: Antoine stealing a bottle of milk.

this scene, a successful communication is established with a maternal substitute. However, the absence of the psychologist from the filmic space and her representation as a disembodied voice points to the limits of this communication. The maternal body for which Antoine yearns, which both fascinates and frightens him, remains absent and seemingly inaccessible. Antoine is in fact addressing the spectator through the indirect mediation of the filmic apparatus. Cinema, as the ultimate representation of transitional activities in Truffaut's own personal development, will compensate for parental neglect and allow for an approach of external reality.

In contrast to these evocations of the child's yearning for a reunion with a maternal figure, the film also imposes on the viewer a complementary phantasmatic reading focusing on Antoine's profound ambivalence towards his actual mother. Truffaut achieves this effect by cultivating an elliptic and disconnected mode of narration. Certain scenes, as it was observed earlier, seem not to bear any relationship to the main plot and to slow down the story. A close analysis reveals, however, that they are designed to feed the phantasmatic vein and that they form a closely knitted network within the narrative. Two examples of these subterranean signifying chains will demonstrate their common concern with a definition of Madame Doinel.

In the first scene at school, an ironic vignette shows a little boy struggling to copy down a poem. He will end up lost in an ocean of ink and crumpled paper. This episode metonymically refers to Antoine's own difficulties with writing. But it also metaphorically introduces in the film the important theme of trash, dirt and mess. Antoine soils the curtains and seems for ever unable to wash. He is also officially in charge of the garbage at home. A scene describes his trip down the stairway and his disgusted handling of a pestilential looking trashcan. Stairs, a prevalent figure in Truffaut's work, are often associated with womens legs. Monsieur Doinel will invite his son to admire his mother's legs when they climb the stairway after the movies. Interestingly enough, Truffaut cut a scene from the US commercial version of the film (it is present in the UK version) which casts some light on these associations. Situated in the second sequence of the film, it shows Antoine arriving at a store to buy flour for his mother. There, he is seen overhearing a conversation which centers around the description of a difficult and bloody birth and ultimate hysterectomy. He almost vomits. Truffaut may have removed this scene because it pointed too clearly to the phantasmatic content of the film. To be effective, the content of the phantasy must remain latent and not trigger on the spectator's part a possible reaction of censorship. In this process of indirect revelation, repetition under the form of displacement and condensation represents a major operative factor. The repetitive network linking trash, women's legs and stairways discloses the deep anxiety the feminine body inspires in Antoine. This body constitutes for him a frightening mystery generating visions of chaos, dirt and blood.

Melanie Klein (1980, 279–83) in her analysis of epistemological disorder in adolescents observes that learning disabilities spring from an inability on the child's part to form an image of the interior of the woman's body and in particular to understand its special functions such as conception, pregnancy and birth. In the film, the associative network we have examined evokes these sexual fears and their consequences, but in an indirect way, through a system of displacement and condensation which does not threaten the spectator's psychic apparatus with crude images of violence. During his night in Paris, Antoine will throw the milk bottle into a sewer. A similar scene will be found both in *L'Argent de poche* and in *L'Homme qui aimait les femmes*. This odd gesture points to an attempt to probe the bowels of the city. In *Baisers volés*, the famous episode describing the trajectory of a letter through the *pneumatiques*, an underground mail system (now discontinued), displays the same curiosity and concern. There again, we find metaphoric expressions of the constant fascination with the mother's body which all of Truffaut's films reflect. Spatial representations in his work often reproduce an intricate maze of corridors, stairways, trapdoors and caves. All of these allude to the labyrinth the female body constitutes for the child's imagination. *Le Dernier métro* is, in this respect, exemplary.

The second example involves one of the most enigmatic scenes in the film. Set at the centre for delinquent minors, it presents three little girls being locked up in a cage. To account for this fragment, two complementary scenes must be invoked. In the first one, Madame Doinel comes back home late one night. The noise of the car that brings her back wakes up Antoine in his bed. His stepfather will angrily accuse his wife of sleeping with her boss. At the police station, Antoine will also be awakened by a car. This time, it is a van bringing in three prostitutes to be locked up behind bars. In an interview (Gillain 1981, 33), Truffaut declared that, in this segment, he had deliberately adopted the style of a fairy tale, the three prostitutes speaking in turn as do fairies in children's stories. The three little girls in their cage are obvious references to them. Antoine's ambivalence towards his mother is all inscribed within this signifying chain. The noise of the engine suggests that she is a whore; the three prostitutes say that she is a fairy; the shot of the little girls adds that she is, like her son, an imprisoned child who longs to roam the streets of Paris with her lover.

The script of delinquency is a useful model to account for the common features all of Truffaut's films share. Applied to *Les 400 coups*, it serves to illuminate the deep and complex work of stylization to which the director subjected his life experience. Among his films, it is certainly the most directly autobiographical. Its beauty, however, springs from Truffaut's ability to create a system of representation which transmutes the private data of an individual destiny into a universal language. Truffaut's goal was never to reveal anything about his own life but rather to make his life narratable by structuring his personal memories into a construction of mythic significance.

## Notes

1 In several other films by Truffaut, we see grown men engaged in professional activities which resemble children's games. For instance, in *Domicile conjugal* or *L'Homme qui aimait les femmes*, Antoine Doinel and Bertrand Morane work with miniature boats. This obsession with toys and regressive behaviours points, in a humorous vein, to Truffaut's male characters' inability to adjust to social (and sexual) maturity. The only adult activity available to them will be creative expression: both Antoine and Bertrand write a novel. This makes evident once more the link between transitional activities and artistic realizations.

2 For a more extensive discussion of transitional phenomena and fetishism in Truffaut's films, see Gillain 1985, 114.

3 R. Tagore quoted by Winnicott 1975, 132.

4 It is worth mentioning that for this role, Truffaut (Wilderstein 1959) had chosen a young actress, Annette Wademant, who happened to be absent from Paris when the scene was filmed. Truffaut decided to take the shots with Jean-Pierre Léaud and intended to add at a later time the reverse shots with the psychologist. Jean-Pierre Léaud was given only a few vague indications as to what the questions would be and invited to improvise the answers. There was no written script. The result of the rushes was so striking that Truffaut and his operator, Henri Decae, gave up the project of filming the reverse shots with Annette Wademant and simply added her voice to the images.

## Selected bibliography

Allen, Don (1974) *Truffaut*, New York, Viking.

Allen, Don (1985) *Finally Truffaut*, revised and updated edition of *Truffaut*, London, Secker & Warburg.

Baby, Yvonne (1959) 'Les Quatre Cents Coups: Une chronique de l'adolescence nous dit François Truffaut' (interview), *Le Monde*, 21 April, 12.

Billard, Pierre (1959) '*Les 400 coups* du pére François' (interview), *Cinéma*, 59, 37, 136–7.

Bonnafons, Elizabeth (1981) *François Truffaut*, Lausanne, l'Age d'Homme.

Brooks, Peter (1984) *Reading for the Plot*, New York, Vintage.

Capdenac, Michel (1967) 'Tour d'horizon avec François Truffaut: Des *400 coups* à *La Mariée était en noir*', *Les Lettres françaises* 1179, 18.

Ciment, Gilles, Fievez, Sylvie and Vallet, Stéphane (1988) *Les 400 coups de François Truffaut*, Paris, Les Cahiers du Septième Art.

Collet, Jean (1977) *Le Cinéma de François Truffaut*, Paris, Lherminier.

Collet, Jean (1985) *François Truffaut*, Paris, Lherminier.

Crisp, V. G. (1972) *François Truffaut*, New York, Praeger, London, November Books.

Crowther, B. (1977) '*The 400 Blows*', in *Vintage Films*, New York, G. P. Putnam's Sons, 175–8.

Dalmais, Hervé (1995) *Truffaut*, revised edition (first published 1987), Paris, Payot et Rivages.

Desjardins, Aline (1973) *Aline Desjardins s'entretient avec François Truffaut*, Ottawa, Leméac.

Dixon, Wheeler Winston and Hoffman, Cassel (1993) *The Early Film Criticism of François Truffaut*, Bloomington, Indiana, Indiana University Press.

Doniol-Valcroze, Jacques (1959) '*Les 400 coups*', *Cahiers du cinéma*, 16, 96.

Dupont, C. (1974) 'François Truffaut et l'enfance' (interview), *Ciné Jeunes*, 78, 1–7.

Durgnat, Raymond (1963) *Nouvelle Vague: The First Decade*, Loughton, Essex, Motion Publications.

Fanne, D. (1972) *L'Univers de François Truffaut*, Paris, Editions du Cerf.

Fiesehi, Jacques (1975) 'L'Enfance', *Cinématographe*, 15, 10–13.

Gillain, Anne (1981) 'Reconciling Irreconcilables: An Interview with François Truffaut', *Wide Angle*, 4 (4).

Gillain, Anne (1985) 'The Little Robber Boy as Master Narrator', *Wide Angle*, 7 (1 and 2).

Gillain, Anne (1988) *Le Cinéma selon François Truffaut*, Paris, Flammarion.

Gillain, Anne (1991) *François Truffaut: le secret perdu*, Paris, Hatier.

Guérif, François (1988) *François Truffaut*, Paris, Edilig.

Holmes, Diana and Ingram, Robert (1998) *François Truffaut*, Manchester and New York, Manchester University Press.

Insdorf, Annette (1989) *François Truffaut: Le cinéma est-il magique?*, Paris, Ramsay.

Insdorf, Annette (1995) *François Truffaut*, revised edition (first published 1978), Cambridge, Cambridge University Press.

Kinder, M. and Houston, B. (1972) 'François Truffaut', in *Close Up: A Critical Perspective on Film*, New York, Harcourt Brace Jovanovich, 183–97.

Klein, Melanie (1980) *Essais de psychanalyse*, Paris, Payot.

Le Berre, Carole (1994) *François Truffaut*, Paris, *Cahiers du cinéma*.

Lopez, A. (1985) 'An Elegant Spiral: Truffaut's *The 400 Blows*', *Wide Angle*, 7 (1 and 2).

Maillet, D. (1984) 'François Truffaut' (interview), *Cinématographe*, 105.

Maraval, P. (1975) 'Antoine Doinel', *Cinématographe*, 15, 14–17.

Mardore, Michel (1962) 'Les Aveux de Jekyll Truffaut' (interview), *Les Lettres françaises*, 911, 25–31.

Monaco, James (1976) 'Truffaut', in *The New Wave*, Oxford and New York, Oxford University Press, 13–97.

Mouren, Yannick (1992) *François Truffaut: L'Art du récit*, Paris, Lettres Modernes/Mina.

Murray, E. (1978) '*The 400 Blows* 1959', in *Ten Film Classics*, New York, Frederick Ungar, 121–33.

Nelson, J. R. (1985) 'The Rotor: Elements of Paradigmatic Structure in Truffaut's *The 400 Blows*', *Wide Angle*, 7 (1 and 2), 137–43.

Nicholls, David (1993) *François Truffaut*, London, Batsford.

Parinaud, A. (1959) 'Truffaut: Le Jeune cinéma n'existe pas' (interview), *Arts*, 1, 9.

Petrie, Graham (1970) *The Cinema of François Truffaut*, New York, Barnes, London, A. Zwemmer.

Philippe, Claude-Jean (1988) *François Truffaut*, Paris, Seghers.

Prédal, René (1976) 'Images de l'adolescent dans le cinéma français', *Cinéma*, 76, (214), 19–28.

Rabourdin, D. (1985) *Truffaut par Truffaut*, Paris, Editions du Chêne.

Rabourdin, Dominique (1995) *Truffaut, le cinéma et la vie*, Paris, Mille et Une Nuits.

Rhode, Eric (1961) '*The 400 Blows*', *Sight and Sound*, 29 (2), 89–90.

Sadoul, Georges (1959) 'Je crois à l'improvisation' (interview), *Les Lettres françaises*, 775, 1, 6.

Salachas, G. (1959) '*Les 400 coups*', *Télé-Ciné*, 83, 1–11.

Sand, L. (1968) (interview), *Jeune cinéma*, 31, 10–15.

Thiher, Allen (1979) *The Cinematic Muse: Critical Studies in the History of French Cinema*, Columbia, University of Missouri Press, 143–64.

Truffaut, François (1959) 'Je n'ai pas écrit ma biographie en *400 coups*', *Arts*, 715, 1–5.

Walz, E. P. (1982) *François Truffaut: A Guide to References and Resources*, Boston, G. K. Hall.

Wilderstein, P. (1959) 'Conversation avec François Truffaut' (interview), *Télé-Ciné*, 83, 2–8.

Winnicott, D. W. (1957) *L'Enfant et le monde extérieur*, Paris, Payot.

Winnicott, D. W. (1971) *La Consultation thérapeutique et l'enfant*, Paris, Gallimard.

Winnicott, D. W. (1975) *Jeu et réalité*, Paris, Gallimard.

## Scripts

Moussy, M. and Truffaut, F. (1959) *Les 400 coups, récit d'après le film de François Truffaut*, Paris, Gallimard.

Truffaut, F. (1969) *The 400 Blows*, in Denby, D. (trans. and ed.), New York, Grove Press.

Truffaut, F. (1971) *The Adventures of Antoine Doinel: Four Autobiographical Screenplays*, trans. H. G. Scott, New York, Simon & Schuster.

## Appendix

### *François Truffaut (1932–84): filmography*

1954  *Une Visite* (short)

1957  *Les Mistons* (short)

1958  *Histoire d'eau* (short)

1959  *Les 400 coups* (*The 400 Blows*)

1960  *Tirez sur le pianiste* (*Shoot the Pianist*)

1961  *Jules et Jim* (*Jules and Jim*)

1962  *Antoine et Colette* (sketch in *L'Amour à vingt ans*)

1964  *La Peau douce* (*Silken Skin*)

1966  *Farenheit 451*

1967  *La Mariée était en noir* (*The Bride Wore Black*)

1968  *Baisers volés* (*Stolen Kisses*)

1969  *La Sirène du Mississipi*.

1970  *Domicile conjugal* (*Bed and Board*)

1970  *L'Enfant sauvage* (*The Wild Child*)

1971  *Les Deux anglaises et le continent*

1972  *Une Belle fille comme moi*

1973  *La Nuit américaine* (*Day for Night*)

1975  *L'Histoire d'Adèle H.*

1976  *L'Argent de poche* (*Small Change*)

1977  *L'Homme qui aimait les femmes* (*The Man Who Loved Women*)

1978  *La Chambre verte* (*The Green Room*)
1978  *L'Amour en fuite* (*Love on the Run*)
1980  *Le Dernier métro* (*The Last Métro*)
1981  *La Femme d'à côté*
1983  *Vivement dimanche* (*Finally Sunday!* [UK]; *Confidentially Yours* [USA])

## *Other films cited in the text*

*Boudu sauvé des eaux* (*Boudu Saved from Drowning*), Jean Renoir (1932)
*Zéro de conduite* (*Zero for Conduct*), Jean Vigo (1933)

# 11

# 'IT REALLY MAKES YOU SICK!'
## Jean-Luc Godard's *A bout de souffle* (1959)

### *Michel Marie*

Jean-Luc Godard shot *A bout de souffle* (*Breathless*) in four weeks, from 17 August to 15 September 1959, on location in Marseilles and on the 'Nationale 7' highway, but principally in various parts of Paris. His modest budget was only 40 million francs at 1959 value (50 million according to *Le Film français*), half the average budget for the period (Godard 1980, 26).

By 1959, Godard had made five shorts, the first in 1954, *Opération béton*, which he produced himself, the second in 1955 in 16mm, *Une Femme coquette*. Pierre Braunberger produced the three 35mm shorts he made for Pléiade Films: *Tous les garçons s'appellent Patrick, Charlotte et son Jules*, and *Une Histoire d'eau*. But by August 1959, Godard had become one of the last of the *Cahiers du cinéma* critics to embark on a feature-length film. Shortly before, Rohmer had begun shooting *Le Signe du lion* (July–August 1959), produced by Claude Chabrol for AJYM Films. As for Chabrol himself, he had just made his third feature, *A Double Tour*, which was to be released on 4 December 1959. In it, Jean-Paul Belmondo plays a friend of the son of the family, a young sponger called Lazlo Kovacs. *Le Beau Serge* and *Les Cousins* had come out on release in February and March 1959. *Les 400 coups*, François Truffaut's first feature, which had been selected for the Cannes Festival where it was awarded the prize for *mise-en-scène*, came out on 3 June 1959, followed by *Hiroshima mon amour* by Alain Resnais on 10 June. And Jacques Rivette had begun filming *Paris nous appartient* in 1958, to be finished in 1961. Godard knew that Sergei Eisenstein and Orson Welles had made their first films at the age of 26 years; he had just turned 29 years old and desperately needed to get into the swim and, like his hero Michel Poiccard at the beginning of the film, forge ahead: 'After all, I'm an idiot. After all, yes, I must. I must!' This convergence between the director's position and that of the central character was to be a determining factor in the film's rhythm. It was absolutely essential that this first attempt should prove to be the work of a master. 'Afterwards I felt nothing but terror, the terror of not being able to make another film, like not being able to get food' (Godard 1985, 16). Truffaut wrote later,

'While he was making *A bout de souffle*, Godard didn't have enough money in his pocket to buy a metro ticket, he was as destitute as the character he was filming – more so, really' (Godard 1985, 28).

*A bout de souffle* was produced by Georges de Beauregard. Born in 1920 in Marseilles, he was not yet 40 years old and already had five features to his credit. A former journalist, Beauregard specialized in the overseas distribution of French films, especially in Spain, which had led him to produce two of Juan-Antonio Bardem's best-known features, *Muerte de un Ciclista* and *Calle Mayor*. He then produced *La Passe du diable*, co-directed by Jacques Dupont and Pierre Schoendoerffer, then two Pierre Loti adaptations directed by Schoendoerffer (*Ramuntcho* and *Pêcheurs d'Islande*). At this juncture, Godard was editing documentaries for Pierre Braunberger and travel films for the publisher Arthaud, and he also wrote dialogues for Edouard Molinaro and Jean-Pierre Mocky, for two films that were never made. In 1958 he worked on the dialogue for *Pêcheurs d'Islande* and was present at the beginning of the shooting. His experience in editing and dialogue was to be decisive for *A bout de souffle*. Pierre Schoendoerffer had been a cameraman in the armed forces film unit, then a war correspondent in Indochina. Schoendoerffer's cameraman on his three features had also himself been a cameraman for the armed forces in Indochina, then a great reporter, and Beauregard insisted that Godard should use him for his film: it was of course Raoul Coutard.

The script for *A bout de souffle* was written by François Truffaut:

> a month after the premiere of *Les 400 coups*, he asked me to lend him the scenario of *A bout de souffle* so he could give it to Beauregard to read. It was a story I had written several years earlier. I had been following an incident that took place over one weekend and made a deep impression on me.
>
> (Truffaut, in Collet 1963, 171)

Beauregard had turned down an earlier proposal from Godard: *Une Femme est une femme*; although, in fact, Godard had published the original script of this film in August 1959 in *Cahiers du cinéma* (98), a few weeks before making *A bout de souffle*. And that same year Philippe de Broca made *Les Jeux de l'amour* based on a script developed by Godard (from an idea by Geneviève Cluny). *A bout de souffle*, as directed by Godard, is reasonably faithful to the way the narrative develops in the script by Truffaut (Truffaut, in Godard 1968, 47–9). The opening quotation from Stendhal, 'We are going to speak of dreadful things' is replaced by a dedication to Monogram Pictures, a small American company specializing in low-budget Westerns and horror films, and crime series like *Gun Crazy*. Truffaut's Stendhalian 'Lucien' was rechristened Michel, the name of the friend at the Inter-Americana Agency in Truffaut's version, who was renamed Tolmatchoff in the film. But most significantly, Godard took complete responsibility for the dialogue and reworked many details of the script. The most fundamental change was the development of the very long sequence in the hotel room (more than twenty-five minutes) which was only ten lines in Truffaut's script; similarly, the second long sequence in the Swedish woman's flat was scarcely hinted at in the original text. The last change was the ending, which was much less tragic in Truffaut's version where Lucien was allowed to escape, calling Patricia names:

> Lucien is furious. But he has to get away. He starts up the car which Berruti has driven over in. From the car-door, he hurls insults at Patricia. The last shot shows Patricia watching him drive off, not understanding a word because her French is still not good enough.
>
> (Truffaut, in Godard 1968, 49)

According to Truffaut,

> Jean-Luc chose a violent end because he was by nature sadder than I. He was in the depths of despair when he made that film. He needed to film death, and he had need of that particular ending. I asked him to cut only one phrase which was absolutely horrible. At the end, when the police are shooting at him one of them said to his companion: 'Quick, in the spine!' I told him, 'You can't leave that in.' I was very vehement about it. He deleted the phrase.
>
> (in Collet 1963, 174)

Michel Poiccard is played by Jean-Paul Belmondo. In 1959 the actor was 26 years old. From 1953 to 1956 he had been a student at the Conservatoire d'Art Dramatique in Paris. He then joined a little theatre company with Annie Girardot and Michel Galabru. In 1955 he had a part in a film about Molière (by Norbert Tildian) and began to appear in comedies: *Sois belle et tais-toi, A pied, à cheval et en voiture.* He made an impression as one of the gang in *Les Tricheurs*, but Laurent Terzieff was the star of the film. In a review of *Un Drôle de dimanche*, Godard was highly critical of both screenplay and actors:

> The script is lamentable, so are the actors. . . . but you can't save much of a Serge de Boissac script with Bourvil, nor Jean Marsan dialogue with Cathia Caro. With Jean-Paul Belmondo you just might, since he is the Michel Simon and Jules Berry of tomorrow; even so this brilliant actor would have to be used differently and elsewhere.
>
> (Godard, in Milne 1972, 99)

160

This is what Godard did himself by giving the actor the central role in his short film *Charlotte et son Jules*, dubbing it with his own voice:

> For Jean-Luc's friends, there is something particularly precious in this film, in that Belmondo, who was doing his military service, was dubbed in by Jean-Luc. Jean-Luc's intonations make this little film more moving, less relaxed than it would have been had Belmondo dubbed himself.
>
> (Truffaut, in Collet 1963, 170)

The theme of this little sketch is well known. Charlotte returns briefly to the home of her old boyfriend (her 'Jules'), who proceeds to bombard her with words, in turn scornful, moralizing, protective, loving, begging, not allowing Charlotte to open her mouth, until the final moment when she confesses that she has come back to fetch her toothbrush. This film, dedicated to Jean Cocteau, and a real homage to the film-maker Guitry, prefigures in more than one way the manner in which words function in *A bout de souffle*, especially Michel and Patricia's two long parallel monologues; and it was fortunate that Godard was able to use Belmondo again for his first feature rather than Jean-Claude Brialy, the eponymous hero of *Tous les garcons s'appellent Patrick*, who was considered briefly for the role of Poiccard (Salachas 1960, 8).

Jean Seberg, twice Otto Preminger's leading lady, in *Saint-Joan* and *Bonjour tristesse*, was the only possible choice for Patricia. Godard declared on many an occasion,

> For some shots I referred to scenes I remembered from Preminger, Cukor, etc. And the character played by Jean Seberg was a continuation of her role in *Bonjour tristesse*. I could have taken the last shot of Preminger's film and started after dissolving to a title, 'Three Years Later'.
>
> (Godard, in Milne 1972, 173)

There is a certain physical resemblance between Jean Seberg and Anne Colette, the heroine of Godard's two previous shorts who was dressed like Patricia in a T-shirt with horizontal stripes, and had ultra-short blonde hair and a rounded figure. In a letter to Pierre Braunberger written during the shooting of *A bout de souffle*, Godard wrote,

> I would like to be the only person to like this film, I'd like everyone [except Melville and Anne Colette] to detest it. . . . Even the film stock, you'll see, will be breathless. Seberg is panicking and wishes she hadn't agreed to do the film. I start shooting with her tomorrow. I'll say goodbye because I must work out what to film tomorrow.
>
> (in Braunberger 1987, 184)

The atmosphere of the shooting was fairly tense. Seberg was at her wits' end and Jean-Paul Belmondo felt as if he was working on an amateur silent film. The technical crew were not very enthusiastic either.

> At the rushes, the entire crew, including the cameraman, thought the photography was revolting. Personally I like it. What's important is not that things should be filmed in any particular way, but simply that they should be filmed and be properly in focus. My main job is keeping the crew away from where we're shooting. . . . On Wednesday we shot a scene in full sunlight using Geva 36 film stock. They all think it stinks. My view is that it's fairly amazing. It's the first time that the maximum has been expected from film stock by making it do something it was never intended for. It's as if it was suffering from being pushed to the limit of its possibilities.
>
> (in Braunberger 1987, 183–4)

Raoul Coutard has given a lengthy explanation of Godard's technical requirements involving the use of Ilford H.P.S. film stock which he usually used for photographic journalism in natural light (Coutard quoted by Courtade 1978, 277). Godard refused artificial light; he also refused the machinery of the studio. 'If we used a hand-held camera, it was simply for speed. I couldn't afford to use the usual equipment, which would have added three weeks to the schedule' (Godard, in Milne 1972, 173). But why all these technical innovations, why this intransigence towards the dominant practices of French cinema in 1959, to the point of using a type of film stock hitherto used only in photography and which had to be spliced end to end in rolls of 17.5 metres? It was because Godard, filming after Chabrol, Truffaut and Resnais, wanted to make *A bout de souffle* the standard-bearer of a new aesthetics, that of the French New Wave of 1959. His film was to explore a hitherto unknown continent in the aesthetics of cinema, smash the boundaries of the conventionally 'filmable' and start again from scratch:

> *A bout de souffle* was the sort of film where anything goes: that was what it was all about. Anything people did could be integrated in the film. As a matter of fact, this was my starting-point. I said to myself: we have already had Bresson, we have just had *Hiroshima*, a certain kind of cinema has just drawn to a close, maybe ended, so let's add the finishing touch, let's show that anything goes. What I wanted was to take a conventional story and remake, but differently, everything the cinema had done. I also wanted to give the feeling that the techniques of filmmaking had just been discovered or experienced for the first time. The iris-in showed that one could return to the cinema's sources; the dissolve appeared, just once, as though it had just been invented.
>
> (Godard, in Milne 1972, 173)

In this sense, *A bout de souffle* set out to secure a position in the history of the cinema analogous to that of the monumental *Citizen Kane*, a megalomaniac 26-year-old director's first feature and another manifesto issued some twenty years earlier in defiance of the cinema industry. The similarity between the two title sequences, or rather the absence of a title sequence in both films, confirms the wish for an explicit reference. After the dedication to Monogram, two vigorous notes of music by Martial Solal accompany the title, which is displayed full frame in white letters on a black background, foreshadowing as in *Kane* the later inserts of newspaper headlines. Welles's film begins with the death of the eminent citizen whose biography is then reconstructed bit by bit through newsreel, eye-witness accounts and press headlines. At the start of *A bout de souffle*, Poiccard is a man living on borrowed time, whose tragic progress is punctuated first by the editions of *France-Soir* and then by the neon lights flashing, 'The net is closing in around Michel Poiccard', then 'Michel Poiccard, arrest imminent', just as neon lights had announced to the world the death of the American press magnate.

First of all, everything was possible technically. The signifying potential of editing was to be pushed to the limits, in the manner of *Citizen Kane*. Godard thus did not hesitate to follow a very high angle establishing shot with a big close-up (Patricia runs to give Michel a kiss at the end of their first meeting; the next shot is an insert of a poster saying 'Live dangerously till the end', while Michel crosses the frame in medium close-up); nor did he hesitate to alternate hyper-fragmentation of the image and rapid montage (the series of shots of Patricia's face in profile in the car as Michel declares 'I love a girl who has a pretty neck, pretty breasts, a pretty voice', etc.) with a long continuous take (when Michel finds Tolmatchoff at the Inter-Americana Agency, the camera tracks back in front of them all the time they're walking, the first metaphor of the labyrinth and of the trap in which the tragic hero is caught).

Right from the beginning of the film, the 'Nationale 7' sequence ruthlessly violates the moribund codes of spatial and graphic continuity editing which were so scrupulously observed by professional editors in 1959. It cuts in quick succession between a number of rapid panning shots from side to side of the road, close-ups of the driver framed from the passenger seat or the back seat, intercut shots of the road flashing by, inserts of headlights or of the central white line which the driver transgressively crosses, up to the famous sequence in extreme close-up detailing the cylinder and barrel of the colt, with a cutaway in the opposite direction to the motorcycle cop collapsing. Godard could not have found a more devastating way of reviving the dynamics of Eisensteinian montage and the deconstruction of the revolutionary machine-guns in *October.*

At the other end of the scale, when Michel finds Patricia in the Champs-Elysées the camera tracks the couple as they walk up and down, refusing the classic shot/reverse shot alternation in order to avoid any ambivalent identification with the characters and to underline the parallel progression of the two monologues, or rather of the soliloquy which Michel began in the opening sequence, and which Patricia's replies merely bounce off, without any real communication ever being established. The motif of the labyrinth, where two parallel paths never meet, is taken up again when Michel and Patricia find themselves in the Swedish woman's flat, the final trap: the camera follows first Michel, then Patricia, as they pace up and down the room. Michel says, 'Whenever we talked, I talked about myself, and you talked about yourself. . . . But you should have talked about me, and me about you.'

This dynamic conception of editing first and foremost has a rhythmic function. As we have seen, Poiccard, like Godard, sets the ball rolling by throwing himself behind the wheel of his 1950 Oldsmobile. The diabolical rhythm of his race to the finish must not lose its hold on the spectator, and the moments of respite based on continued takes are as breathtaking in their movement as the bursts of shots in discontinuous sequences. The important thing is to keep the pace up and not stop until the very last breath, the last grimace, when all the spectator sees of Patricia is the nape of her neck, hiding her soul, as Bruno Forrestier, the little soldier (in *Le Petit soldat*), and Nana, the prostitute (in *Vivre sa vie*), were to say.

As Michel and Patricia kiss to get their breath back, in the darkness of a cinema auditorium two voices, one male, one female, call them to order amid the pandemonium of a Western shoot-out. The man (Godard's voice) says,

> Méfie-toi Jessica.
> Au biseau des baisers – les ans passent trop vite –
> Evite, évite, évite – les souvenirs brisés.

> Beware, Jessica.
> With the sharp cut of kisses – the years pass too quickly –
> keep away, away, away – from shattered memories

an extract from a poem by Aragon, the alliteration of which, in French, echoes the title of the film, as Marie-Claire Ropars has indicated (1982, 59–81). The woman rejoins:

> Vous faites erreur, Shériff . . .
> notre histoire est noble et tragique comme le masque d'un tyran.
> Aucun détail indifférent ne rend notre amour pathétique.

> You are making a mistake, sheriff . . .
> our story is as noble and tragic as a tyrant's mask.
> No insignificant detail brings pathos to our love.

(extract from the poem *Cors de chasse* by Apollinaire in the collection *Alcools*).

*A bout de souffle* – above: Michel Poiccard (Jean-Paul Belmondo); below: Michel and Patricia (Jean Seberg).

The most fundamental innovation of *A bout de souffle* is the dialogue, which constitutes the most revolutionary use of language since the coming of sound. We know that the film was made entirely without sound. Godard edited a first, post-synchronized, version which was an hour too long. Then he decided to make cuts in the middle of sequences, eliminating particular fragments (shots of Van Doude telling a story about going to bed with some girl) or series of shots (countershots of Michel accompanying the views of Patricia, framed in profile in the car while he is enumerating her charms). This deliberate opting for visual discontinuity goes hand in hand with the general autonomy of the soundtrack, which has its own time, regardless of its links with the image. Thus, at the beginning of the film, while Michel is talking to himself at the wheel of his American car, the image track cuts between fragmented images of his journey with very obvious spatial ellipses, while the language, however nonsensical, operates in a relatively continuous way.

> La, la la, la (he hums). Buenas noches, mi amor, . . . If he thinks he's going to get past me in that bloody car. . . . Pa, Pa, Patricia! Patricia! So, I'll get the money, I'll ask Patricia for a yes or a no . . . and then. Buenas noches, mi amor . . . Milano! Genova! Roma!

Michel Poiccard is the one who is cursed, the one who brings bad luck ('la poisse'). According to the *Littré* dictionary, from the beginning of the seventeenth century, 'poissard' (Poiccard) was the name given to the slang of the lower classes. Despite the distinctive language used by Henri Jeanson and his disciples, Poiccard was the first film character to violate the refined sound conventions of 1959 French cinema by using popular slang and the most trivial spoken French. The 'Nationale 7' sequence, in itself a demonstration of what the film as a whole sets out to do, piles up sweeping examples of spoken French, of contemporary slang which was to be heard even within the intellectual microcosms of the Champs-Elysées and Saint-Germain des Prés, and of a language reminiscent of Céline, which scriptwriters in French cinema had never before rendered on screen except via the conventions of *série noire* slang. To come back a moment to the opening monologue quoted briefly above, it offers: the humming of an onomatopoeic tune, the chorus of a popular song ('Buenas noches, mi amor'), a fixed slang expression ('sa frégate à la con'/'his bloody car'), provocative pseudo-sentences and gratuitous aphorisms of an ideological nature ('Women at the wheel are the epitome of cowardice'), made-up quotations ('And as old Bugatti said, cars are made to go, not to stop'), and frequent spontaneous interjections of slang ('Yes, shit, roadworks, shit, the fuzz'). There is no point in giving more examples, the whole linguistic texture of the film is shot through with a wealth of popular and slang terms and expressions.

Through his use of language Godard was clearly showing what he had learnt from the central character of *Moi, un noir*, filmed and recorded by the ethnologist Jean Rouch at Treichville in the suburbs of Abidjan (made in 1958, winner of the Prix Louis Delluc in 1959 and released on 12 March 1960, a week before *A bout de souffle*). He wrote two very appreciative articles on Rouch's film in *Cahiers du cinéma* in March and April 1959. Jean Rouch's film portrays an unemployed youth from Abidjan nicknamed 'Lemmy Caution' and his friends 'Eddie Constantine' and 'Dorothy Lamour'; Rouch used a handheld camera to follow the half-improvised adventures of the characters. Even more remarkably, the actor Oumarou Ganda (who plays 'Edward G. Robinson') dubbed himself, improvising a monologue as he viewed the edited version of the image track. At one point in the film when 'Eddie Constantine' meets 'Dorothy Lamour' in the street, the voices are those of the two actors who improvised *a posteriori* a conversation which is very approximately synchronous with the image. Later on in the film, 'Robinson' , both narrator and character, mixes simultaneous dialogue with subjective comments added later.

> One must take it at its word when it comes from the mouth of Lemmy Caution, American federal agent and unemployed of Treichville, as he waits for girls at the church door, or tells P'tit Jules why France lost the match in Indo-China in a speech which is part-Céline, part-Audiberti, part nothing at all ultimately, because the conversation of Rouch and his characters (whose resemblance to persons living or dead is absolutely not coincidental) is as new and as pure as Botticelli's Venus, as the black rising from the waves in *Les Statues meurent aussi.*
>
> (Godard, in Milne 1972, 129)

> And when Eddie Constantine, American federal agent, is arguing with P'tit Jules in a staggering flow of words along the lines of *Bagatelles pour un massacre*, and Rouch, kneeling beside them with the camera on his shoulder, suddenly straightens up slowly and lifts *à la* Anthony Mann, his knees serving as the crane, to frame Abidjan, O! Abidjan of the lagoons, on the other side of the river, I love it.
>
> (*ibid.*, 134)

*A bout de souffle* even contains a direct reference to a brief moment in *Moi, un noir* which illuminates Poiccard's offhand manner when, having seen the body of the pedestrian knocked over by the Renault 4CV, he merely crosses himself and continues on his way, reading his paper. At the beginning of *Moi, un noir*, 'Robinson' is wandering through the streets of Treichville when he sees a crowd of people idly staring at a motorcyclist who has been knocked down. He merely remarks in a detached voice, 'Oh! Another accident! There are such a lot of accidents in Treichville! Cars here last two months at the most. . . . That's why it's such a shambles.'

There can be no doubt that 'Robinson's' long monologue at the beginning of the film had a direct influence on Poiccard's soliloquy at the wheel of his car. Similarly, the constant film references in *A bout de souffle* which everyone has commented on, and which have since been detailed by Dudley Andrew (1986, 11–21), the reworking of American B movie *film noir* (the homage to Bogart, the posters of *The Harder They Fall*, the quotation from *The Enforcer* when Poiccard knocks out the customer in the toilets, the sound-track and photos from *Whirlpool*, etc.) originated in the fanciful imagination of Rouch's young Africans who identified with American *film noir* actors and their parodic French imitations to such an extent that they had only assumed names: 'Eddie Constantine', 'Edward G. Robinson' and 'Dorothy Lamour' never use any other name, whereas when Poiccard finds himself face to face with the picture of Bogart, he murmurs to the actor's nickname (Bogie) but retains his own identity.

In *A bout de souffle*, Godard was exploring every facet of verbal language. So far, the opening monologue and the false dialogue which characterizes the confrontations between Michel and Patricia have been discussed. These examples alone do not do justice to the wealth and diversity of the verbal material used in the film. First there are the innumerable literary, cinematographic, pictorial and musical quotations exchanged by Michel and Patricia; then there are the little stories that Michel recounts, like the one which Van Doude also tells about the bus conductor who had stolen five million francs to seduce a girl, obviously a *mise-en-abyme* of the film ('I'd known this girl for two years', etc.). There is a play on the variety of different languages: the international Americanese that Michel uses ('As you like it baby'), the odd words of Italian ('ciao', 'buon giorno') and Spanish ('amigo', 'buenas noches'); stereotyped plays on words ('Maintenant, je fonce, Alphonse!'), alternation between the formal and the familiar words for you ('tu' and 'vous'), the use of ambiguity and misunderstanding ('qu'est-ce que c'est dingue?' 'qu'est-ce que c'est dégueulasse?'). To sum up, *A bout de souffle* is a tragedy of language and of the impossibility of communication.

This allows us to tackle the question of the subject which Godard talks about in relation to the film:

> *A bout de souffle* is a story, not a theme. A theme is something simple and vast which can be summed up in twenty seconds: vengeance, pleasure. A story takes twenty minutes to sum up. *Le Petit soldat* has a theme: a young man is mixed up, realizes this, and tries to find clarity. In *Une Femme est une femme*, a girl wants a baby right away. In *A bout de souffle* I was looking for the theme right through the shooting, and finally became interested in Belmondo. I saw him as a sort of

block to be filmed to discover what lay inside. Seberg, on the other hand, was an actress whom I wanted to see doing little things which amused me.

(Godard, in Milne 1972, 177)

However, it is easy to sum up the 'subject' of *A bout de souffle* in the way that director did for *Une Femme est une femme*. A young small-time hoodlum and car thief goes up to Paris to find the young American girl he is in love with, cash a fat cheque and leave with her for Italy. But this synopsis merely reduces the subject to the initial situation of the story, the hero's 'project'. When Poiccard hot-wires the car to get it started in the first few seconds of the film, he sets in motion an infernal machine. The goal of his quest is his desire to sleep with Patricia again. As soon as he finds her, he says quite clearly, 'Are you coming to Rome with me? Yes, it's stupid, but I love you . . .' and later, 'Are we sleeping together tonight?' Before that, he refuses the more or less direct advances of several dark-haired young women: the girl on Marseilles' Vieux Port who asks him to take her away with him, his former mistress whom he wakes up at seven o'clock in the morning. Just as he makes the observation that the two girl hitch-hikers are not fanciable enough, he finds the colt in the car glove compartment, after switching on the radio for a few moments to let us hear Brassens' famous song 'Il n'y a pas d'amour heureux'/'There is no such thing as happy love'. Immediately afterwards, Michel defies destiny by shooting at the sun, and this playful act evokes both the revolver shot fired at the sun by the German engineer at the end of the first part of *Le Tigre du Bengale* by Fritz Lang (released in France on 22 July 1959) and Meursault getting blinded by the sun on the Algerian beach at the beginning of Camus' *L'Etranger*. Indeed, quite unconsciously Poiccard is defying the gods and performing an absurd act, since it is destiny which pulls the trigger at the end of the cutaway travelling shot framing the barrel of the colt.

Michel's stations of the cross are marked by the signs of destiny. When Patricia offers him the *New York Herald Tribune*, he refuses it because it does not have a horoscope; throughout the film, once he has left Marseilles, he keeps asking the time, making telephone call after telephone call, buying the paper, then lighting up cigarette after cigarette, like the hero of *Le Jour se lève*, imprisoned in his hotel room and also destined to die in a hail of police bullets (although he shoots himself in the end). Patricia, the object of his desire, a little girl with a handbag and a teddybear (another obvious reference to Carné's film) is the agent of destiny. The caricature of her in the opening shot (the 'pin-up' on the issue of *Paris-Flirt* that Michel is reading) indicates as much right from the start: Michel '*must*' go on until death. When she goes to ring the police at the end of the film, she in her turn buys *France-Soir* and goes past a kiosk with a woman selling lottery tickets who calls out, 'Your lucky day! Try your luck, buy a ticket!' As for Michel, he commits act after

169

act of provocation as if they were gratuitous acts proving that he was free to exercise his freedom; but 'between sorrow and nothingness' he knows that he has chosen nothingness. He knows that destiny is waiting for him at the end of the road (rue Campagne Première) just as Godard knew that he had to get to the end of the film, to keep going come what may. Poiccard's death, despite the concession made to Truffaut, is still agonizing: the camera follows Michel's crazy attempt to run down the street until he collapses on the pedestrian crossing, murmuring with his last breath and with a last grimace, 'C'est vraiment dégueulasse'/'It really makes you sick'. Here Godard is making a direct reference to the spectacular death-scene of a character in *Man of the West* which he had just reviewed, under the title 'Super Mann', in *Cahiers du cinéma* (1959, 92). It's the death-scene of a dumb man, a member of the gang led by a megalomaniac old bandit played by Lee J. Cobb, who makes his way down a seemingly endless street in the middle of a deserted village with a bullet in his back, as Poiccard was to do, until he finally collapses, uttering his first cry and drawing his last breath as he does so.

*A bout de souffle* was to be Godard's first cry, the only one in his long early career to be heard by a fairly large public: almost 260,000 people saw the film in seven weeks of its first run in Paris from 16 March 1960. Poiccard knew that he was playing double or quits, as Patricia says. He also observes near the end, 'I'm fed up, I'm tired, I want to sleep'. As for Godard, he was to move on immediately to an even more personal second film, *Le Petit soldat*, and despite the fact that the film was completely banned by the censor until 1963, in 1961 he was able to direct the film he had first proposed to Georges de Beauregard, *Une femme est une femme*. Since then he has never stopped making films, even in the 1970s when he decided to adapt the technical conditions of his projects (16mm films, video) to the nature of his discourse. He's still not breathless.

*Translated from the French by Carrie Tarr*

## Selected bibliography

Andrew, Dudley (1986) 'Au début du souffle: le culte et la culture d'*A bout de souffle*', *Revue belge du cinéma*, 16 (special Godard issue).

Bellour, Raymond and Bandy, Mary Lea (eds) (1992) *Jean-Luc Godard: Son et Image, 1974–1991*, New York, Museum of Modern Art.

Braunberger, Pierre (1987) *Cinémamémoire*, Paris, Centre Georges Pompidou, Centre National de la Cinématographie (CNC).

Brown, Royal S. (1972) *Focus on Godard*, Englewood Cliffs, New Jersey, Prentice-Hall

Cannon, Steve (1999) *Jean-Luc Godard*, Manchester, Manchester University Press.

Cerisuelo, Marc (1993) *Jean-Luc Godard: Au-delà de l'image*, Paris, Lettres Modernes.

Collet, Jean (1963) *Jean-Luc Godard*, Paris, Seghers.

Collet, Jean (1970) *Jean-Luc Godard*, trans. Ciba Vaughan, New York, Crown Publishers.

Collet, Jean and Fangien, Jean-Paul (1974) *Jean-Luc Godard*, Paris, Seghers.

Courtade, Francis (1978) *Les Malédictions du cinéma français*, Paris, Alain Moreau.

Dixo, Winston Wheeler (1997) *The Films of Jean-Luc Godard*, New York, State University of New York Press.

Douin, Jean-Luc (1994) *Jean-Luc Godard*, Paris, Rivages.

Godard, Jean-Luc (1980) *Introduction à une véritable histoire du cinéma*, Paris, Albatros.

Godard, Jean-Luc (1985) *Jean-Luc Godard par Jean-Luc Godard*, Paris, Cahiers du cinéma, Editions de l'Etoile.

Goldmann, Annie (1971) *Cinéma et société moderne: le cinéma de 1958 à 1968*, Paris, Editions Anthropos.

Lesage, Julia (1979) *Jean-Luc Godard: A Guide to References and Resources*, Boston, G. K. Hall.

Loshitzky, Yosefa (1995) *The Radical Faces of Godard and Bertolucci*, Detroit, Wayne State University Press.

Milne, Tom (ed.) (1972) *Godard on Godard*, London, Secker & Warburg.

Milne, Tom and Narboni, Jean (eds) (1986) *Godard on Godard*, New York, Da Capo (revised edition of Milne (1972), with preface by Annette Michaelson).

Monaco, James (1976) *The New Wave*, New York, Oxford University Press.

Ropars, Marie-Claire (1982) 'L'Instance graphique dans l'écriture du film', *Littérature*, 46, Paris, Larousse, 'Graphies'.

Salachas, Gilbert (1960) '*A bout de souffle*', fiche filmographique 36, *Télé-ciné*, 89.

## Scripts

Godard, Jean-Luc (1968) '*A bout de souffle*', *Avant-scène cinéma*, 79 (contains Truffaut's original script).

Godard, Jean-Luc (1974) *A bout de souffle*, Paris, Balland, 'Bibliothèque des classiques du cinéma' (illustrated book of the film).

For other works on Godard, see bibliographies in Chapters 12 on *Le Mépris*.

## Appendix

### *Jean-Luc Godard (1930–): filmography*

1954 *Opération béton* (short)
1955 *Une Femme coquette* (short)
1957 *Une Histoire d'eau* (short)
1957 *Tous les garçons s'appellent Patrick* (*All Boys Are Called Patrick*) (short)
1958 *Charlotte et son Jules* (short)
1959 *A bout de souffle* (*Breathless*)
1960 *Le Petit soldat* (*The Little Soldier*)
1961 *Une Femme est une femme* (*A Woman is a Woman*)
1961 *La Paresse* (sketch)
1962 *Le Nouveau monde* (sketch)
1962 *Vivre sa vie* (*It's My Life* [UK]; *My Life to Live* [USA])
1962–3 *Les Carabiniers* (*The Soldiers* [UK]; *The Riflemen* [USA])

1963  *Le Grand escroc* (sketch)
1963  *Montparnasse-Levallois* (sketch)
1963  *Le Mépris* (*Contempt*)
1964  *Bande à part* (*Band of Outsiders* [UK]; *The Outsiders* [USA])
1964  *Une Femme mariée* (*A Married Woman* [UK]; *The Married Woman* [USA])
1965  *Alphaville*
1965  *Pierrot le fou*
1966  *Anticipation* (sketch)
1966  *Deux ou trois choses que je sais d'elle* (*Two or Three Things I Know About Her*)
1966  *Made in USA*
1966  *Masculin–féminin* (*Masculine–Feminine*)
1967  *L'Amour* (sketch)
1967  *Caméra-oeil* (episode in *Loin du Vietnam*)
1967  *La Chinoise*
1967  *Weekend* (*Week-End*)
1968  *Un Film comme les autres* (*A Movie Like the Others*)
1968  *Le Gai savoir*
1968  *One Plus One* (*Sympathy for the Devil*)
1968–9  *One American Movie 1 A.M.*
1969  *British Sounds*
1969  *Pravda*
1970  *Jusqu' à la victoire* (*Till Victory*) (short, unfinished)
1970  *Luttes en Italie* (*Struggle in Italy*)
1970  *Vent d'est* (*East Wind*)
1970  *Vladimir et Rosa*
1972  *Letter to Jane*
1972  *Tout va bien*
1974  *Ici et ailleurs*
1975  *Numéro deux*
1976  *Comment ça va*
1976  *Six fois deux*
1978  *France/tour/détour/deux/enfants*
1980  *Sauve qui peut* (*la vie*) (*Slow Motion* [UK]; *Every Man for Himself* [USA])
1981  *Passion*
1982  *Scénario du film Passion*
1982  *Lettre à Freddy Buache*
1982  *Prénom Carmen*
1983  *Je vous salue Marie*
1984  *Detective*
1987  *Soigne ta droite*
1987  *Aria* (episode *Armide*)
1987  *King Lear*
1990  *Nouvelle vague*
1990  *Qu'est-ce que le cinéma?*
1991  *Allemagne neuf zéro* (*Germany Year 90 Nine Zero*)
1991  *L'Enfance de l'art: How Are the Kids?*
1992  *Contre l'oubli* (*Lest We Forget*)
1993  *Hélas pour moi* (*Woe Is Me*)

1993  *Momentous Events: Russia in the 90s*
1993/1997  *Histoires du cinéma*
1993  *Les Enfants jouent à la Russie (The Children Play Russian)*
1994  *Autoportrait de décembre*
1994  *Film de l'intranquillité*
1995  *2 × 50 Years of French Cinema: The Century of Cinema*
1996  *For Ever Mozart*

## *Other films cited in the text*

*Le Beau Serge*, Claude Chabrol (1958)
*Bonjour tristesse*, Otto Preminger (1957)
*Calle Mayor (The Lovemaker)*, Juan-Antonio Bardem (Spain 1956)
*Citizen Kane*, Orson Welles (USA 1941)
*Les Cousins*, Claude Chabrol (1959)
*Un drôle de dimanche*, Marc Allégret (1958)
*The Enforcer*, Raoul Walsh and Bretaigne Windust (USA 1951)
*Gun Crazy*, J. H. Lewis (USA 1949)
*The Harder They Fall*, Mark Robson (USA 1956)
*Hiroshima mon amour*, Alain Resnais (1959)
*Les Jeux de l'amour*, Philippe de Broca (1959)
*Le Jour se lève (Daybreak)*, Marcel Carné (1939)
*Man of the West*, Anthony Mann (USA 1958)
*Moi, un noir*, Jean Rouch (1959)
*Muerte de un Ciclista (Death of a Cyclist)*, Juan-Antonio Bardem (Spain 1955)
*October*, Sergei Eisenstein (USSR 1927)
*Paris nous appartient*, Jacques Rivette (1958)
*La Passe du diable*, Jacques Dupont and Pierre Schoendoerffer (1956)
*Pêcheurs d'Islande*, Pierre Schoendoerffer (1959)
*A pied, à cheval et en voiture*, Michel Delbez (1958)
*Les 400 coups (The 400 Blows)*, François Truffaut (1959)
*Ramuntcho*, Pierre Schoendoerffer (1958)
*Saint-Joan*, Otto Preminger (USA 1956)
*Le Signe du lion*, Claude Chabrol (1959)
*Sois belle et tais-toi*, Marc Allégret (1957)
*Les Statues meurent aussi* (short), Alain Resnais (1953)
*Le Tigre du Bengale (Tiger of Bengal)*, Fritz Lang (Germany 1959)
*Les Tricheurs (The Cheaters)*, Marcel Carné (1958)
*Whirlpool*, Otto Preminger (USA 1949)

# 12

# THE FALL OF THE GODS

## Jean-Luc Godard's *Le Mépris* (1963)

### *Jacques Aumont*

Thirty-three is, quite literally, a crucial age for any western male, the age of crucifixions and triumphs. The 33-year-old Jean-Luc Godard who made *Le Mépris* was no beginner since he had already directed five features, five shorts, and three episodes for 'omnibus' films, and long since put behind him the period of his masterly first attempts. But in the course of a career that had consisted solely of climaxes, each more powerful than the last, 1963 was the year in which he made not only *Les Carabiniers*, his most resounding flop and most provocative movie, but also *Le Mépris*, the film that came closest to the prevailing models of the time, from both an aesthetic and an industrial point of view.

Let me immediately remove any possible ambiguity: although *Le Mépris* was a more 'normal' production than Godard's previous films (big budget, international co-production, cast of stars) it is above all, in retrospect, the prototype of a configuration that often recurred subsequently in his career – the wholesale destruction of an apparently traditional screenplay, the misuse (or abuse, or non-use) of stars, a stylistic impertinence. This is a configuration that can be found, to varying degrees, in *Pierrot le fou*/Belmondo, *Sauve qui peut (la vie)*/Dutronc/Baye, and *Détective*/Halliday. It has become a common-place to say, but it is none the less true, that Godard was extraordinarily successful in integrating himself into the film industry, but in a totally idiosyncratic manner (involving, very early on, the crediting of his own name as film-maker *on an equal footing* with any other name or body).

Itself a big-budget movie, *Le Mépris* can thus be regarded – and today should be regarded – as a commentary, at once ironic and nostalgic, on the big-budget movie. Of all the French films made in 1963, it was one of the most costly,[1] both thanks to and because of Bardot's presence: 'It was the only time I had the feeling I was going to be able to make a big film with a big budget. In fact it was a small budget for the film, as all the money went to Brigitte Bardot, Fritz Lang and Jack Palance' (Godard 1980, 73). But of all 'Bardot's' films it was the one which made the least money, along with

Louis Malle's *Vie privée*. It is impossible not to be reminded, while making all due allowances, of another 1963 movie, Joseph Mankiewicz's *Cleopatra*, a bottomless pit that swallowed up so many millions of dollars it hastened the demise of the studio system. Godard was certainly not responsible for any such disaster, and one of the admirable qualities of *Le Mépris* is that, first, it forewarns us of that demise, and then poeticizes, *ante factum*, its infinite sadness. If one excepts the first two shots in the film (the sequence against which the credits are spoken, and the celebrated shots of the naked Bardot, which were imposed by the producer), the movie opens with views of Cinecittà and Francesca's remark: 'The Italian cinema's doing very badly.' Now Francesca, the 'go-between', as Marie so rightly calls her (1986, 35), is played by Georgia Moll, an actress who made a career in Italian *peplum*[2] films, but who was also noticed in Mankiewicz's *The Quiet American* – and who is thus in an ideal position to remark on the demise of Cinecittà and, at the same time, to prophesy that of Hollywood.

If *Le Mépris* is a film which lays itself open, almost too easily, to feverish intercultural interpretation, it is chiefly because it is a kind of melancholia for the cinema, a lucid *mise-en-abyme* of the 'death' of the cinema that was marked once and for all by the end of Hollywoodian classicism. Indeed, from that angle the film can be interpreted in many ways: as a '*politique des auteurs* in the flesh' (Marie 1986, 29), but flesh doomed, alas, to the frailty of old age – or, correlatively, as a veritable lampoon against blind and deaf producers, a kind of '*J'accuse . . . !*' which portrays them as dealers of death. That Jeremy Prokosch is a satirical character could not be more obvious; Godard's choice of Palance to play the part leaves no room for ambiguity, and the man with the sardonic grin, the sadistic black-gloved killer of *Shane*, does not inject any superfluous subtlety into his portrayal of the man who 'draws his chequebook' whenever he hears the word culture, the producer who makes up for his semi-culture and semi-competence by repeatedly 'humiliating and offending his employees or friends' (Godard 1985, 243). He is the only character in the film (except perhaps for the character played by Godard himself) who is treated as a puppet, and above all as someone who has an extremely naïve view of the cinema: when three naked young women swimmers appear on the viewing theatre screen, he has the same besottedly lecherous, adolescent leer as Michel-Ange in *Les Carabiniers* before he tries to leap into the bath-tub projected on the screen.

Not all that many films portray the movie world. In that respect, *Le Mépris* lies somewhere between Minelli's, *The Bad and the Beautiful* and Truffaut's *La Nuit américaine* – between totally mythical self-congratulation, with a central character (a producer) wracked by a desire for Art, and the family film that affectionately recounts the harmless intrigues of people in the movie world (under the stewardship of a benign director). In Godard's film, the basic idea is simpler: the director, Fritz Lang, is a conscience and a victim, while the producer's ambition (which is worthy of Kirk Douglas in the Minnelli movie) degenerates into sadistic madness. What is certain is that the film is a somewhat embittered discourse on the film *industry*, unlike another film, *8½*, also made in 1963, where the anxiety of creation seems in the end to shake off all material constraints. That is surely no coincidence: by siding with poor Lang against the villainous Prokosch, Godard takes revenge a hundred times over for the humiliation he suffered at the hands of Carlo Ponti and Joseph Levine[3] – and, more generally, gives vent to his customary feelings about producers, which could hardly be described as overflowing with the milk of human kindness.[4] Godard clearly cannot bear the idea that, in the conflict which always pits the producer against the director, he should fail to get the upper hand, or at least have the last word. The famous second shot of *Le Mépris* is a fine example of the art of how to have the last word: at the insistence of Levine, who thought the film did not show enough of Bardot as Bardot (i.e. 'sexy'), Godard added a long take of the naked star, but what might have been a fetishistic reification of a body in box-office terms is instead an affectionate, almost awestruck moment of contemplation (even *Positif*, which loathes Godard, admired the shot). What is more, Godard somehow manages to make that last-minute addition tie in with the rest of the film – with that other, briefer shot of the lower part of B.B.'s body against a background of red velvet (a strident, fleeting allusion to Marilyn Monroe's celebrated calendar), and, of course, with an already mentioned scene, where Prokosch smirks at the sight of the naked young women he has clearly forced Lang to include in the film. Godard, obviously, is a past master at falling on his feet.

By the time *Le Mépris* was released, there was already an image – and an already stereotyped image – of Godard and his style. Critics harped on two or three aspects of that style: its jerky rhythm, its 'crossings-out', its frequent quotations, and above all the casual way such quotations are introduced. *Le Mépris* is no exception really, and any list of the quotations it contains would be lengthy; what makes them different, perhaps, from the excessively ludic quotations in *Les Carabiniers* and *Une femme est une femme*, is that they both accompany and are based on the 'materialist' discourse on the art of film which I have already mentioned. *Le Mépris* quotes *both* the film industry *and* the history of the cinema, which is why it is, among other things, a sort of compendium of classical cinema (cinema of the kind which was loved, defended and dreamt of by the young *Cahiers du cinéma* critics). The film's interweaving of references and filiations has often been noted, not least by Godard himself. Jack Palance, Georgia Moll and Fritz Lang are vehicles, in the flesh, of part of the past, of history. They are living quotations and, already, survivors of a vanished world (one is reminded of the book-people in *Fahrenheit 451*): through them, Godard quite consciously evokes not only his own immediate past as a *cinéphile* – *The Barefoot Contessa*, *The Quiet American* – but a more distant, already heroized and mythicized past (Lang's legendary

meeting with Goebbels). But this wealth of direct quotation is comple-
mented in the film by a dense nexus of indirect quotations, not all of them
equally profound. Sometimes Godard simply raises his hat to favourite
movies like *Some Came Running*[5] (which is itself, up to a point, a tragedy of
cowardice and contempt) or *Hatari!*, which Godard rated 'the best film of
1962', and a poster of which, curiously, is stuck up on the Cinecittà set (it is
perhaps worth mentioning that it appears just before Camille first feels contempt for Paul; 'hatari', incidentally, means 'danger'). More essentially, there
is the subterranean but powerful presence of another reference, a reference to
Europe, to Italy, and more particularly to one film, Roberto Rossellini's
*Viaggio in Italia*.

It can never be emphasized too much that Rossellini was the film-maker
who had the most direct influence on the *Cahiers* group, at least as much
because he met them regularly and urged them amiably, but insistently, to
make films themselves, as because of his 'Bazinian' mantle of glory as the
inventor of Neo-Realism. Shooting *Le Mépris* in Italy, Godard could hardly
have failed to think of Rossellini, but there was nothing to suggest that his
film would take its cue as directly as it did from Rossellini's. In fact the
subject is the same: how misunderstanding (*méprise*) can lead to contempt
(*mépris*), cross-purposes to cross exchanges. The story-line is the same: a
couple of foreigners, who have married almost by chance and come to Italy,
quarrel fiercely and realize they have already grown apart and will have to
separate – there is even the same final intervention of chance (the miracle in
one film, the fatal accident in the other). Lastly, both films give the same
feeling of an almost physical presence of the gods, and not just because
Godard films his plaster reproductions with the same majesty as Rossellini
does the statues in the Naples Archaeological Museum.

So *Le Mépris* bristles with references, and insistent ones at that; again and
again acts of homage are paid, and models hinted at. This is hardly surprising, as Godard has always been, ever since he wrote for *Cahiers*, the recognized master of the quotational genre (even in his later films, he still prides
himself on the fact that not a single line of the dialogue in *Détective* or in
*Soigne ta droite* was written by him). However that may be, the striking thing
about *Le Mépris* is the way such references are concentrated on the cinema, its
history and its philosophy, whereas in Godard's earliest films, still typically
those of the young *cinéphile*, it is commoner to find literature rubbing shoulders with *film noir*, or painting, and drama with comedy. *Le Mépris* is one of
the rare films by Godard where we never glimpse the familiar, and in a sense
reassuring, figures of Klee, Matisse, Renoir or Picasso. It is also one of the
few where literary quotation is used, precisely, as a quotation – i.e. spoken, in
quotes, by one character to another, instead of being an integral part of the
movie like, for example, the quotation from Poe's *The Oval Portrait* in *Vivre sa
vie*. (Surely the absence of Godard's customary references must be regarded
as one of the most visible aspects of Rossellini's influence? If Moravia's

*Il Disprezzo*, on which *Le Mépris* is based, is, as Godard generously put it, a *roman de gare* – the kind of cheap novel you buy at a station bookstall – then *Viaggio in Italia* is a *roman-photo* entirely improvised by Rossellini from stock situations; in *Le Mépris*, Godard relies much less on improvisation than in any of his other films, and exploits stereotypes as well as psychological and dramatic conventions to an unaccustomed degree.)

What of it? Doubtless, as I pointed out at the start, Godard's aim with *Le Mépris* was to take his bearings *vis-à-vis* history, to accentuate a sense of history as an escape, a loss, to intensify a delectable anxiety about the end of history. That concern was shared by the whole generation of the New Wave, and more particularly the *Cahiers* group, and centred on the important notion that film-making was but an extension of the critic's or aesthetician's activity, and that each individual film would therefore be a re-reading, a re-writing, of the entire history of the cinema (a very particular kind of history, of course, polarized by strongly voiced likes and dislikes). In that respect, Godard was very typical of his generation, and he does not really go much further than, on occasion, Truffaut, who prided himself on *Jules et Jim*'s forty-odd quotations and acts of homage. Godard was simply more systematic, and above all more persistent, gradually elaborating, from film to film, something that came to be seen by the end of the 1960s as an aesthetics of the fragment (people at the time were less interested in the actual insistence of Godard's use of quotation than in the almost detachable nature of the quotations themselves and, correlatively, in his masterly use of collage and the cut-up technique).

It was precisely Godard's persistence and systematic obstinacy that lent him an affinity, not found in any other New Wave director (with the possible exception of Rivette, but on a completely different register), with what can only be termed the literary 'avant-gardes' of the 1950s and 1960s. The use of the second degree, self-reflexivity, specularity and other 'defamiliarizing' techniques was characteristic of what came to be known as the *Nouveau Roman* group, which was just as loosely structured as the New Wave. Much sarcasm was directed at such 'novelties' (they were even accused of conforming too closely to the 'modernizing' ideology and phraseology of the Gaullist Fifth Republic). The sarcasm turned to scorn when, taking the practical premises of Butor's *La Modification*, Ollier's *La Mise-en-scène* and Robbe-Grillet's *Les Gommes* to their logical conclusion, Barthes and the Tel Quel group erected them into a theory. To be quite accurate, this intellectual terrain was not, directly or at first hand, that of Godard himself (who was more familiar with such precursors of the *nouveau roman* as Joyce, Faulkner and Céline). All I am attempting to do here is, if you like, to point to a cultural coincidence. But it is well known that as far as culture goes no coincidence is the fruit of pure chance: in this particular case, Godard (and some members of the New Wave), the *nouveau roman* (and those sometimes

linked with it like Le Clézio, whom Godard met in 1966)[6] and, more generally, a large section of the French intelligentsia of the 1960s did at least share
one basic notion: that any work worthy of the name must contain its own
keys. Their complicity was not only formal, but ideological: modernity, this
'novelty' so often foolishly derided and violently denigrated, also resides in a
rejection of naïvety, a wish to show that one knows what one is doing (a wish
which, towards the end of the decade, and more particularly in Godard's case,
naturally took on a directly political form).

Thus, to return to *Le Mépris*, it contains other references, which are given a
varying degree of prominence, and through each of which the film seems to
be looking back on itself. The painted eyes of the statues supposedly filmed
by Lang call to mind other painted eyes, those of Cocteau, a poet whom
Godard admired, and another first-person film-maker, who constantly
explored and pointed up the powers of the cinema. The way Godard films the
Villa Malaparte in Capri, and the very idea of using its rectilinear architecture, outdo Antonioni at his own game – which is of some relevance in a
film which Godard wanted to be 'a successful Antonioni, in other words
filmed by Hawks'. In short, *Le Mépris* is a movie in which the film-maker's
'authorial' self-awareness is never far below the surface and a deliberate
reflexivity constantly asserts itself.

That reflexivity was something that 'art' films of the 1960s seized upon
with relish, particularly through the specific stylistic figure – also found in
*Le Mépris* – of the 'film within the film'. By about the middle of the
decade, any movie with ambitions would systematically, but not always
very subtly, exhibit the whole paraphernalia of its own shooting, e.g.
*Persona*, and *La Chinoise*, or at least refer to itself as a film, for instance
*L'Amour fou*, and *Belle de jour*. The presence of the film equipment, technicians and actors in *Le Mépris* remains, as in its Hollywoodian predecessors,
unobtrusively confined to the diegesis, and thus does not possess the disruptive impact of the appearance of the camera and clapperboard in *La
Chinoise*. Even so, the existence of the film within the film does tend to
have an effect of disruption, of tearing the fabric of the narrative. In this
respect the credit-title sequence of *Le Mépris* works to perfection, as it
combines the principal modes of 'distancing' and of interpellation of the
spectator (voice-over, film equipment shown on the screen, the camera
pointing at 'us') with what is already the beginning of a narrative: in that
first shot of the film, Georgia Moll – or should she already be referred to as
Francesca Vanini? – is tracked by the camera as she walks down a studio-
built street in Cinecittà which, in the third shot, she walks up in the
opposite direction, now accompanied by Paul Javal/Piccoli as well as the
camera (on the same rails).

This credit-title sequence is remarkably striking, as well as being famous – at least in France, where it was long used for the credits of a now
defunct television programme on the cinema. It is also, as Jean-Louis

Leutrat has shown (1986, 68), totally representative of a film in which 'the characters are affected' by a certain 'indecision'. I myself would even go so far as to contend that not only the characters but the whole story and the whole diegesis are affected by that indecision. What is basically at issue here is Godard's conception of the cinema, which attempts to combine and to embrace both the classical heritage (the conception of the open, transparent window) and something which can now clearly be seen to be modernity (distancing, the play on shifters). It is of course no coincidence that Godard here quotes from André Bazin, the champion of Italian neorealism and Rossellini, and defender of the kind of cinema which respects 'the ambiguity inherent in reality'. But the Bazin quotation is itself not unambiguous, first because it comes at the precise moment when the camera lens (the monstrously large CinemaScope lens) tilts down towards us, and we cannot clearly see, at that point, what 'replaces our look', unless it is the look at another look that is looking at us, and secondly because Godard has here somewhat shortened the quotation: Bazin's words, as heard on the record in *Une femme est une femme*, are 'the cinema replaces our look in order to offer a world which matches our desires' (Godard 1985, 211), whereas the credit-title sequence of *Le Mépris* tells us that 'the cinema replaces our look with a world which matches our desires'. To say that the cinema replaces our look is to pinpoint its essentially *documentary* nature, whereas if it does propose to replace our look with anything it is with an intellectual, *imaginary* construction. This may be only a minor point, but it is anyway symptomatic of the film's key position – its intermediary position (which is paradoxical, like any intermediary) between a belief in documentary revelation and an unavoidable knowledge of the imaginary nature of film ('Just an image', as Godard was to theorize in 1970).

This duplicity is, moreover, evident in the very style of the film. The long scene in the apartment consists mostly of an almost didactic demonstration of the 'ambiguity inherent in reality', since it involves turning the space, which is explored from every angle, into a place where 'the misunderstanding that gives rise to contempt will occur' (Faux 1986, 105): the scene is a translation, in the film, of the characters' curious opacity (as if they really existed in their own right) which comes across in the '*Scénario*' published by Godard (1985, 241). On the other hand, Godard, the great inventor of forms, has left traces of his intervention throughout the film. Taken at random, they include: violent ellipses (the accident at the end), rhythmical editing (the to-ing and fro-ing around the lamp), 'the longest tracking shots in the history of the cinema' (the credit-title sequence, but also the tracking shot of the naked Bardot), sound editing effects (e.g. the arbitrary cutting off of the song during the variety turn, so the dialogue is heard against a background of total silence), and even – though less characteristic of Godard's style – two or three quick montages of subjective flashes.

*Le Mépris* – above: (from left to right) Jeremy Prokosh (Jack Palance), Camille (Brigitte Bardot) and Paul (Michel Piccoli); below: (from left to right) Francesca (Georgia Moll), Jeremy Prokosh and Camille.

How are we, then, some thirty-five years later, to determine the place which this film, and the paradoxical conception of the cinema it points up and puts into practice, should occupy in the history of film? On this point as on others, I am loath to give the impression of seeing too much significance in the coincidence of dates. But the following brief chronology is surely eloquent enough: on the death of Bazin, at the end of 1958, Eric Rohmer took over as editor of *Cahiers* and gave it the rather extreme orientation that might have been expected from his earlier theoretical articles (a somewhat rigid and doctrinaire defence of a cinema of 'pure' *mise-en-scène*). His aesthetic extremism, which was accompanied, on occasions, by a similar political extremism, resulted in Rohmer being ousted by Jacques Rivette and Jacques Doniol-Valcroze in 1962. The *Cahiers* line then became more hesitant, but under the influence of Jean Douchet and newcomers brought in by him (Jean-Louis Comolli, Jean Narboni) it gradually began to call into question the *politique des auteurs* and to show a very keen interest in the 'new cinema' and 'young auteurs'. In the articles he wrote in the 1950s, in particular 'Le Celluloïd et le marbre', Rohmer the aesthetician placed the cinema on a higher plane than the other arts, because the latter had already entered their period of decadence whereas the cinema, paradoxically taking advantage of its innate backwardness, had yet to experience its 'classical' age. What happened instead, with the sudden emergence of new Czech, Brazilian, Canadian and British directors in the mid-1960s, was an explosion of the baroque, almost as if – and that was rather the feeling one had at the time – the classical age in question were already over and done with.

In a sense, the rapidity of that process has no parallel in the history of the arts, and there is some significance in the fact that *Le Mépris* was made when the upheaval was at its height. By 1963 Godard had already parted company with Rohmer (who influenced him considerably when he started out as a critic), because he no longer – or no longer solely – espoused the credo of *mise-en-scène;* and most of his subsequent movies up to *Weekend* (1967) marked a gradual shift towards another kind of *écriture*, one based on greater prominence being given to editing. Godard's situation in general, and more particularly in *Le Mépris*, was highly original: he was constantly tempted by classicism, but also, to an equal degree, by another, very different desire for mastery – a kind of mastery which, precisely, can be engendered only by a reflection on classicism. Indeed, that originality, that duplicity of the position of *écriture* in *Le Mépris*, now seems to go without saying, but this is largely because of the subsequent evolution of a movement which Godard initiated.

What has undoubtedly changed in the perception critics may now have of this kind of position as film-maker are the references they attribute to it and the parallels they draw. They would certainly feel happier using the word 'mannerism' rather than *écriture*, because everyone nowadays likes to compare the cinema to painting, and also because a movie like *Le Mépris* invites such a

*Le Mépris* – above: Paul and Camille; below: (from left to right) Michel Piccoli, Fritz Lang, Jack Palance and Jean-Luc Godard.

comparison, since it illustrates one of the principles of stylistic duplicity – 'making a hole in the wall' while at the same time indicating its surface – which lay at the roots of pictorial mannerism (the film also displays equally manneristic secondary tactics, such as the off-centred presence of the film-maker in his own work, which acts as a signature). And although crude historical parallels between painting and the cinema are always highly suspicious (their respective histories do not interlock sufficiently), the fact remains that over the last ten years or so Godard has built up an image of 'painter/film-maker' which undoubtedly prompts a re-examination of his 'first manner' from a plastic – and, if the word needs to be used, pictorial – viewpoint. So here goes.

*Le Mépris* is in Technicolor. This must come as a surprise to anyone who remembers the flamboyant Technicolor of the Kalmus[7] era, during the 1940s and 1950s. While the charm of early Technicolor now seems to reside in its very flashiness, in the brilliance, even garishness, of its colours, the colour of *Le Mépris* appears on the whole much more pastel-like, much more 'moderate', much more 'natural' (it is in *Une femme est une femme*, *Pierrot le fou*, *Made in USA* and other films Godard shot in Eastmancolor that violent colours are to be found in abundance, and increasingly so as his taste for flat-tints became more pronounced – viz. *La Chinoise*). Colour is not absent from *Le Mépris*, but, put simply, it could be said that it seems to have been used not as a purely plastic material, but almost always for its emotional or symbolic impact. The strongest impression left by the shots of the trees, rocks and sea around Capri is one of light – the dazzling, relentless light of the Midi (of 'midi le juste', as Paul Valéry puts it in *Le Cimetière marin*; and, as in that poem, what the light accompanies and signifies is the presentation of a tragic world under the constant gaze of the gods). In the other parts of the film, it is the colour red that plays the most important role: it is initially associated with contempt, through the red Alfa-Romeo, because it is when she is forced to get into that car that Camille first feels contempt for Paul, but also because its facile and vulgar phallic symbolism embodies the contemptuous attitude the film shows towards the producer, himself a vulgar and macho character. The colour red seeps from the car into other scenes, and it is, for instance, when she rolls up and unrolls her red bath towel, in the apartment scene, that Camille comes to realize her mounting contempt for Paul. (The end of the film, of course, sees the return of the most basic signification of red – blood and death.) There is unfortunately no space here to discuss the blue stains on the statues (a pre-echo of Belmondo's face at the end of *Pierrot le fou*), or the saffron-yellow of Camille's and Francesca's bathrobes in the last scene in the villa.

Side by side with this work on colour, the other main plastic constituent, the frame, is similarly employed in two different ways – as a *cadre-fenêtre* (the frame as a window on the world) and as a *cadre-limite* (everything composed within the frame). Examples of the first mode include the film's (few)

landscapes (the sea, the countryside around Rome), the extraordinarily flex-
ible way the camera explores the space of the apartment, and the virtuosity of
the tracking shots. But, in contrast to that, there are elements which obstruct
the straightforward and natural functioning of the 'window' and tend, for
example, towards the 'compositional', towards the frame as a plastic boun-
dary. First of all there is the format of the picture itself, CinemaScope, which
as everyone knows – whatever Bazin may have thought of it, and despite the
rather naïve notion that more surface means more reality – is the most
unrealistic format there is. As Fritz Lang rightly says to Paul Javal, it is a
format that is no good for anything except, at a pinch, filming snakes
and funerals (a quip which, oddly enough, cites one of the examples – the
snake – given by Eisenstein in his argument in favour of changing the
format from shot to shot). So Godard repeatedly uses Cinemascope here in
such a way that it becomes a caricature of itself, as in the celebrated scene
around the lamp, or, more obviously, in the scenes 'from *The Odyssey*' (I am
thinking in particular of the shot where two statues are banished to the far
left and right of the screen). But Godard exploits the frame in other ways as
well. Mention must at least be made, because it recurs more than once, of the
way he films viewing theatres from the proscenium, so as to show the spectators looking (or not looking) towards the screen, in a reversal of the 'normal'
point of view – a 'defamiliarizing' mode of filming, and one of the manifestations of a Griffith-like archaism in Godard, where excessive transparency
destroys transparency.

My last few remarks need enlarging upon, but there is no space to do so
here. What I have tried to suggest is that there may be an extension, in the
actual way the visible material is exploited, of the fundamental stylistic
characteristic of *Le Mépris*, which is duplicity. Something finally should be
said about one of the essential features of the film – the fact that it is an
adaptation. In this respect as in many others, the film occupies a special
position in Godard's *oeuvre*, since it is the only one of all his 'adaptations'
where the plot, the characters, the situations and even some dialogue from
the original novel have been retained (Godard's casual approach to the 'adaptation' of literary works is an integral part of his brand image as an icono-
clast). It is in fact the only one of his films where the novel is treated as it
would have been by a Hollywood director. It is consequently of some interest
that the story of the film within the film itself centres almost exclusively on
problems of adaptation (of *The Odyssey*): Paul Javal is hired by Prokosch to
rework that adaptation, and, more importantly, most of the discussions
between Lang, Prokosch and Javal are about the meaning that should be
given to a modern reading of *The Odyssey*. Lang's professional and moral
principles prevent him from seeing it as the story of a 'modern neurotic',
while Javal, partly out of eagerness to please and partly from sincerity, ends
up believing not only that this is a possible interpretation, but that he is
himself a kind of unhappy Ulysses, despised by the impenetrable Penelope/

Camille. But the most remarkable thing is that *Le Mépris* does not come down in favour of either of these two points of view (the third, held by the producer Prokosch, is discounted); it maintains both of them. It is as if the film accepted, pragmatically, the possibility of two or more interpretations not only of Homer's work, but of the cultural heritage in general, depending on the interpretative approach – and always supposing that it is coherent. Lang distances himself (through quotations from both Dante and Hölderlin) from any 'archaeologizing' approach to the story of Ulysses, because for him the gods are dead; but there is nothing to prevent Javal from projecting himself into a dramatic situation which, with a few minor adjustments, seems tailor-made for him – perhaps because, as Godard says, he is 'an anguished dreamer who is searching for an identity, without wishing to admit as much' (1985, 242).

*The Odyssey* is an epic, but also a tragedy, in the sense that it shows how the fate of mankind is sealed in advance by superior forces. *Le Mépris*, too, is a tragedy, even if the forces that grip Camille and Paul are not divine, but all too human (or socio-psychological, to use the terminology of the period). In the movement from one of these tragedies to the other, the task of the film-maker is one of rewriting – in a way that respects the original, instead of a massacre *à la* Prokosch. It is a simple, ambitious task, which must get across the notion that even if our culture is nothing but a gigantic and interminable process of rewriting we shall always have to go back to our sources – that even after their twilight, we must still speak of the gods.

*Translated from the French by Peter Graham*

## Notes

1 About 500 million francs. I obtained this information from the best article so far published on *Le Mépris*, by Michel Marie (1986).
2 A popular Italian genre of the 1950s and 1960s, consisting of costume epics set in Antiquity (eds).
3 Even Leonard Maltin noticed: 'Producer Joseph E. Levine didn't seem to understand that Godard, who appears here as Lang's assistant, held *him* in contempt, making the film a highly amusing "in" joke' (1987, 186) – though to me the joke seems acerbic rather than funny. 'Before May 1968, Godard used to send telegrams addressed to "Mussolini Ponti" and "King Kong Levine" ' (Piccoli 1970, 91).
4 See, for example, his letters to such an understanding and agreeable producer as Pierre Braunberger, which, although friendly in tone, show Godard maintaining a certain directorial aloofness (Braunberger 1987, 180–9).
5 Paul's celebrated hat, too, comes straight out of *Le Doulos* (J.-P. Melville, 1962), in which Piccoli got his first really major film part; Godard was friends with Melville at the time – 'doulos' is a slang word for 'hat'.
6 *L'Express*, 9 May 1966 (reproduced in Godard 1985, 286–91).
7 Herbert T. Kalmus was a pioneer in colour technology and the founder of the Technicolor Company. Here, however, 'Kalmus' refers principally to Nathalie Kalmus (his former wife), a formidable character most dreaded by directors

of photography, who, as 'technical advisor for color', made her mark on *all* Technicolor films from the 1930s to the 1950s.

## Selected bibliography

Aumont, Jacques (1986) 'Godard peintre', *Revue belge du cinéma*, 16, 41–6.

Braunberger, Pierre (1987) *Cinémamémoire*, Centre Georges Pompidou, Centre National de la Cinématographie.

Eisenstein, Sergei (1930) 'Le Carré dynamique', French trans. *Au-delà des étoiles*, Paris, UGE, 1974, 209–23.

Faux, Anne-Marie (1986) 'Quelque chose à entendre et à regarder', *Revue belge du cinéma, 16.*

Godard, Jean-Luc (1980) *Introduction à une véritable histoire du cinéma*, Paris, Albatros.

Godard, Jean -Luc (1985) *Jean-Luc Godard par Jean-Luc Godard*, Paris, Editions de l'Etoile, 241–8.

Leutrat, Jean-Louis (1986) 'Il était trois fois', *Revue belge du cinéma*, 16.

Maltin, Leonard (1987) *TV Movies and Video Guide*, New York, New American Library.

Marie, Michel (1986) 'Un monde qui s'accorde à nos désirs', *Revue belge du cinéma*, 16.

Piccoli, Michel (1970) 'Rencontre avec Michel Piccoli', *Cinéma*, 70, 147.

For additional Godard bibliography, see Chapter 11, on *A bout de souffle*.

## Appendix

### *Jean-Luc Godard (1930–): filmography*

See Chapter 11, on *A bout de souffle*, for full filmography.

### *Other films cited in the text*

*L'Amour fou*, Jacques Rivette (1968)
*The Bad and the Beautiful*, Vincente Minnelli (USA 1952)
*The Barefoot Contessa*, Joseph Mankiewicz (USA 1954)
*Belle de jour*, Lois Buñuel (1967)
*Les Carabiniers* (*The Soldiers* [UK version]; *The Riflemen* [USA version]), Jean-Luc Godard (1963)
*La Chinoise*, Jean-Luc Godard (1967)
*Détective* (*Detective*), Jean-Luc Godard (1985)
*Le Doulos*, Jean-Pierre Melville (1962)
*Fahrenheit 451*, François Truffaut (1966)
*Une femme est une femme* (*A Woman is a Woman*), Jean-Luc Godard (1961)
*Jules et Jim* (*Jules and Jim*), François Truffaut (1961)
*Made in USA*, Jean-Luc Godard (1966)
*Le Mépris* (*Contempt*), Jean-Luc Godard (1963)
*La Nuit américaine* (*Day for Night*), François Truffaut (1973)

*8½ (Otto e Mezzo)*, Federico Fellini (Italy 1963)

*Persona*, Ingmar Bergman (Sweden 1966)

*Pierrot le fou*, Jean-Luc Godard (1965)

*The Quiet American*, Joseph Mankiewicz (USA 1957)

*Sauve qui peut (la vie)* (*Slow Motion* [UK]; *Every Man for Himself* [USA]), Jean-Luc Godard (1980)

*Shane*, George Stevens (USA 1953)

*Soigne ta droite*, Jean-Luc Godard (1987)

*Viaggio in Italia* (*Voyage to Italy* [UK]; *Strangers* [USA]), Roberto Rossellini (Italy 1953)

*Vie privée* (*A Very Private Affair*), Louis Malle (1962)

*Vivre sa vie* (*It's My Life* [UK]; *My Life to Live* [USA]), Jean-Luc Godard (1962)

*Weekend* (*Week-End*), Jean-Luc Godard (1968)

# 13

# *MISE-EN-SCÈNE* DEGREE ZERO

## Jean-Pierre Melville's *Le Samouraï* (1967)

### *Colin McArthur*

## Melville: surrealism/existentialism/Americanophilia

Attempting to define the particular kind of *noir* sensibility which emerged in post-Second-World-War Paris, James Naremore (1996, 14) lights on Boris Vian (aka 'Vernon Sullivan'). Several facets of Vian connect with Melville: the adoption of an American pseudonym (Melville was born Jean-Pierre Grumbach); a deep involvement with American culture (in Vian's case jazz and in Melville's primarily cinema); the capacity to oscillate between, perhaps to meld, high culture and mass culture; and the association with both surrealism and existentialism.

The citing of this last point illustrates the extent to which the interpellative discourses open to the postwar Parisian intelligentsia were dominated by surrealism and existentialism. Both surrealism and existentialism partook of American culture, it being probable that the surrealists were particularly taken with American cinema and the existentialists with American literature. André Breton's favourite film was Henry Hathaway's *Peter Ibbetson* (1935) and James Naremore has demonstrated (1996, 18) that, although the term *noir* had to some extent been applied by the French to their own prewar cinema, the application of the term *film noir* to certain American films in post-Second-World-War Paris by critics such as Raymond Borde and Etienne Chaumeton — especially in their *Panorama du film noir américain* (1955) — came from within surrealist circles. If surrealist-inspired Borde and Chaumeton saw in the American *film noir* all that was 'oneiric, bizarre, erotic, ambivalent, and cruel' (quoted in Naremore 1996, 19), the existentialists drew other lessons from the novels of Dashiell Hammett, Raymond Chandler and James M. Cain, 'pulp' writers whom they bracketed with 'serious' novelists like Ernest Hemingway, William Faulkner and John Dos Passos. The existentialists were entranced by a particular kind of American hero driven to action in a meaningless universe.

Jean-Pierre Melville (1917–73) was very close to being of the generation of Jean-Paul Sartre (1905–80) and, apart from a brief brush with surrealism through his association with Jean Cocteau in the making of *Les Enfants terribles* (1949), the philosophical basis of Melville's work was to remain throughout his life Americanophile existentialism or, perhaps more accurately, Americanophilia later bolstered by pre-*engagé* existentialism. This is particularly true of his great gangster trilogy *Le Doulos* (1962), *Le Deuxième souffle* (1966) and *Le Samouraï* (1967). The rubrics which introduce these films resonate with the sense of ontological solitude central to existentialism. In the case of *Le Doulos* the rubric is

One must choose . . . to die or to lie

(which may be a quotation from Céline) and with *Le Deuxième souffle* it is

At birth man is offered only one choice – the choice of his death. But if this choice is governed by distaste for his own existence, his life will never have been more than meaningless.

In the case of *Le Samouraï* it is ostensibly a quotation from the Book of Bushido, but in fact was written by Melville himself

There is no greater solitude than that of the Samurai, unless perhaps it be that of the tiger in the jungle.

With their recurrent vocabulary of solitude, choice and death and their underlying theme of the necessity of integrity, of – in Sartrean terms – avoiding 'bad faith', the rubrics might be passages from a Sartre novel of the 1930s or 1940s. As will be demonstrated, the same existentialist concerns are realized in a recurrent range of haunting images in Melville's films, culminating in the austere beauty of *Le Samouraï*.

Melville's philosophical and political attitudes seem to have become 'frozen' as a result of his experience of the outbreak of the Second World War. A Communist in the 1930s, he was, by his own account, overcome with a profound sense of national shame over the surrender. He has indeed spoken of contemplating suicide for the only time in his life at that moment (Nogueira 1971a, 159). His politics remained frozen round wartime anti-fascism and his postwar life was marked by a retreat into an apparently 'pure' cinephilia, although his films remained profoundly existentialist and, as will be argued, deeply shaped by the experience of the surrender and the resistance.

Taking his philosophical position very largely from pre-*engagé* existentialism and his politics from wartime anti-fascism, Melville's Americanophilia, like that of the surrealists, centred very largely on cinema. A cursory look at the *noir*-ish quality of his *oeuvre* would suggest that the defining cinematic moment for Melville was the delirious reconnection with American films, with critical attention focusing particularly on five films of the 1940s: *The Maltese Falcon*; *Double Indemnity*; *Laura*; *Murder, My Sweet* and *Lost Weekend*. This is, however, to some extent misleading. Although Melville's love affair with American cinema was to continue well into the postwar period – he is on record as saying that John Huston's *The Asphalt Jungle* (1950) is the greatest film ever made (Nogueira 1971a, 67) – he had already acquired a deep love and encyclopaedic knowledge of prewar American cinema.

Melville's Americanophilia, however, goes beyond cinema into a kind of mystical relationship with America itself. Several interviews (Breitbart 1964/ 5, 15; Nogueira and Truchaud 1968, 122) reveal a kind of ecstatic response to the American landscape. Melville's mystical Americanophilia is strongly present in *L'Aîné des Ferchaux* (1962), most particularly in the hypnotic car rides through New York and New Orleans and in the 'pilgrimage' to the house in which Frank Sinatra was born. More generally, the intensity with which Melville experienced both America and its cinema helps explain why – at a conscious level at any rate – they, rather than contemporary France, seem to be the major shaping influences on his work.

## Melville and the 'cinema of process'

In his long interview with Melville, Nogueira recalls a description of him as 'the Francis Ponge of cinema' (Nogueira 1971a, 54), Ponge being a poet noted for his detailed descriptions of objects. To indicate the extent to which Sartrean existentialism hovered over all intellectual and artistic endeavour in postwar Paris, Ponge's poetic preoccupations clearly connect with one strand of existentialism, that sense of the brute facticity of objects in the real world. Melville, understanding how Ponge's poetry comes out of this tradition, correctly links it to the *nouveau roman* which, despite its practitioners' critiques of Sartre, was very much concerned with the same phenomenon.

With due allowance for the differences between the existentialists and the *nouveau romanciers*, clearly they both insisted on the *materiality* of the real world. Melville also addressed this question in relation to cinema by evolving what might be called a 'cinema of process', a cinema which went some way to honouring the integrity of actions by allowing them to happen in a way significantly closer to 'real' time than was formerly the case in fictive, particularly Hollywood, cinema. If one film should be singled out as influential on Melville's evolving style in this regard, it is probably Jacques Becker's *Le Trou* (1960 (although Jules Dassin's *Du Rififi chez les hommes* (1954) may also have been important). Strikingly similar thematically to Melville's own work (it is about loyalty and betrayal among convicts in a prison cell), it is at the level of its handling of action in relation to 'real' time that *Le Trou* connects with the literary and philosophical concerns 'in the air' in France at that time and inaugurates the 'cinema of process'. What this means can best be illustrated by one particular scene. Putting the escape plan into effect, one of the convicts detaches the iron leg from his bed and begins to strike the raw concrete. In a 'normal' Hollywood prison picture there would then have been a cut away to the men in the cell and a return to the floor when the hole had been made. Becker's camera, on the contrary, remains remorselessly fixed on the concrete floor as the iron hits it again and again and again until, after multiple blows, it slowly begins to chip and crumble. It is only after this lengthy action, carried on within one unblinking shot, that Becker permits himself a dissolve to the completed hole.

This 'cinema of process' is a recurrent feature of Melville's work, particularly in the gangster movies, but two examples will suffice. The enigma which drives *Le Doulos* (1962) is whether Silien (Jean-Paul Belmondo) has betrayed his friend Faugel (Serge Reggiani). The answer is given in an intricately plotted sequence, described in detail by Murray Smith (1995, 216–23), in which Silien manufactures the evidence which will reveal his loyalty. This sequence, cinema of process *par excellence*, centres on virtually wordless attention to physical actions. The twist in the tail is that by the time Faugel learns of Silien's loyalty, his contract killer is already in place at Silien's house waiting for him. The film ends, in typically Melvillian style, with everyone dead.

The second example of Melville's 'cinema of process' comes from *Le Deuxième souffle* (1966). One of the most intriguing figures in that film is Orloff (Pierre Zimmer). In many respects Orloff is a dry run for the figure of Jeff Costello in *Le Samouraï*. As with so many of Melville's films, the action turns on the possibility of betrayal by one of the gang members. Orloff and Antoine (Denis Manuel) have developed a certain mutual antipathy. When the film's hero Gu (Lino Ventura) is captured and made to seem as if he has betrayed the rest, Orloff arranges a rendezvous with Antoine and two others. Some time before the meeting, Orloff goes to the scene and systematically explores the room for places he might conceal a weapon. Melville, in a superb example of the 'cinema of process', follows Orloff's extended 'casing' of the room, finally showing him concealing a gun, which he ascertains he can reach with a quick upward movement, on a shelf by the window. Satisfied that he can now control the meeting to come, he leaves. Melville then shows Antoine going to the room after Orloff and 'casing' it in his own terms in the course of which he finds the gun Orloff has planted. When the meeting takes place and Orloff takes up his position by the window, the audience expectation is that at some point he will reach for the gun he has planted, find it gone and be killed by Antoine. Orloff does not do this. Ignoring the shelf, he takes a gun from his overcoat and is able to dictate the terms of the meeting. By not reaching for the gun Antoine has removed, Orloff reveals that his calculations have included the realization that Antoine, professional that he is, will have gone to the rendezvous and discovered the weapon. By taking a trope much favoured by both existentialists and new novelists – the detailed perusal of actions and objects – Melville 'thickens the soup', so to speak. He raises the valency of the process, by locating it within the intensely professional *amour propre* of the characters and the intricacy of his own narrative plotting.

More than anything in Melville's work, it is his 'cinema of process' which makes him both an *auteur* and an entertainer, a mainline filmic craftsman and an artist of profound seriousness.

## Melville and the resistance: the return of the repressed

Rui Nogueira's book (1971a) includes two photographs juxtaposed on the same page. One shows Lino Ventura as Gu Minda, the gangster from *Le Deuxième souffle*, the other Lino Ventura as Philippe Gerbier, the resistance fighter from *L'Armée des ombres*. There is a curious similarity between the photographs. What explanation can there be for an image from a gangster movie and an image from a film about the resistance being virtually identical? Could it be that, throughout his several gangster films, Melville has indeed been obliquely addressing the resistance?

Susan Hayward (1993) has talked about the 'unsignifiability' of the war period in postwar French cinema. In contrast to the lack of historical consensus with regard to the cinemas of Vichy and of occupied France, Hayward points to the consensus among film historians *vis-à-vis* French films about the period made *after* the war that the reality of the occupation was left unspoken until Marcel Ophuls' *Le Chagrin et la pitié* (1970) and that 'the sacrosanct image of the resistance was untouched until Jean-Pierre Melville's *L'Armée des ombres*' (Hayward 1993, 189). Hayward explains this primarily in terms of the need for national unity repressing the messy contradictoriness of the resistance.

The issue of the public evasion of the war years and their psycho-social legacy in postwar France has been most fully addressed in Henry Rousso's *The Vichy Syndrome* which uses psycho-medical terminology such as 'syndrome', 'repression' and 'neurosis' to explore the phenomenon (Rousso 1991). More recently, Sylvie Lindeperg has suggested that, among other things, attention to certain postwar comedies might provoke a revision of the view that the reality of the occupation was not adequately dealt with (Lindeperg 1997). In essence, Melville had been able to address the resistance directly in 1947 with *Le Silence de la mer* and again after a period of twenty-two years with *L'Armée des ombres*, on both occasions securing the approval of some at least of the *résistants*.

An active member of the resistance himself for two years before joining de Gaulle's Free French forces in London, Melville was in his early twenties when these events took place. The surrender, the occupation, the betrayal of Vichy, and the resistance, these were the key, formative political influences on Melville's generation. What became, then, of the repressed of Melville's resistance over the two decades of officially imposed silence from 1947? It seems reasonable to speculate that it returned in the displaced form of the obsessive preoccupation with comradeship, integrity and betrayal in his gangster films, particularly *Le Doulos* and *Le Deuxième souffle*.

Just as Melville's existentialism is discernible in his *mise-en-scène* in the recurrent images of figures alone in empty rooms or walking deserted corridors and streets, so too is the question of solidarity worked into the fabric of the *mise-en-scène* of *Le Deuxième souffle*. There are recurrent images of (primarily) men embracing each other, touching each other gently, and gazing at each other. Although this account mobilizes this ensemble of touchings and gazings as evidence of a concern with solidarity and, arguably, with the (repressed) resistance, the ensemble gives a powerful homoerotic charge to *Le Deuxième souffle* which is present also in *Le Doulos* and, in particular, *L'Aîné des Ferchaux*. The other side of the coin of this concern with loyalty and solidarity in *Le Deuxième souffle* is its detestation of betrayal. When Gu is tricked by the police into revealing Paul Ricci's participation in the armoured car robbery and the lie of his betrayal is circulated to the press, Gu's response is to slash his wrists. It is not unreasonable, in this context, to recall the young Melville's contemplating suicide at the moment of France's wartime surrender.

This central concern with loyalty and betrayal appears to wane in *Le Samouraï* which is an altogether more bleak and austere film than the other two, although it certainly connects with them in other ways. However, at least one critic (Buss 1988, 143–4) has suggested that a concern with truth and lies, appearance and reality, unites all three films. To be speculative, through reworkings of the gangster movie the repressed tropes of the resistance might have forced their way on to French screens in a period in which they were officially discouraged.

## Melville and *Le Samouraï*

It is now time to gather together the general arguments made thus far about Melville's work and life – ideas about the centrality of existentialism and Americanophilia, the 'cinema of process' and the (repressed) resistance – and assess their applicability to *Le Samouraï*.

The film can usefully be divided into three parts. The opening section covers the introduction to Jeff Costello (Alain Delon), his theft of a car, his construction of an alibi in advance of deploying it, and his carrying out of a contract killing. In the middle section Jeff is hauled in with other suspects to take part in an identity parade. The last section shows him pursued both by the police and the figures who originally contracted him, culminating in his being shot by the police. Each section is, in itself, an extended example of 'the cinema of process' and, within each, there are individual scenes which are themselves local realisations of the same. The other strands of *l'univers*

*Le Samouraï* – above: Jeff Costello (Alain Delon); below: Jeff Costello (centre) and the
Inspector (François Périer, left).

*melvillien* – the existentialism, the Americanophilia, the (repressed) Resistance – are woven into the fabric of the overall structure.

The opening section of *Le Samouraï* is generally conceded to be breathtaking in its boldness – barely a word is spoken for the first ten minutes of the film – and its austerity. It begins at night, with Jeff lying on his bed in a darkened room, the only sound, apart from the ambient noise of passing traffic, being the chirping of a canary. As the credits cease and plaintive music rises, Melville deploys a curious technical procedure, a simultaneous track back and zoom forward, but in a staggered, stop-go way, which has a profoundly disturbing effect on the spectator. Melville has spoken of this as a signal to the audience of Jeff's 'schizophrenia', but such psychologizing of the character is not illuminating. Jeff is readable primarily as the existentialist Melvillian hero taken to its furthest point. This is partly achieved by the lengths Melville went to in order to drain any vestiges of colour from this opening scene, despite the film being in colour. Apparently Melville replaced banknotes, a cigarette packet and the label of a bottle of mineral water with black and white photocopies of the originals in order that there would be no splash of any colour in the scene. The muted decor, the stillness and the (by the standards of Hollywood narrative cinema) inordinate length of the scene combine to produce an overwhelming sense of solitude. This sense of solitude is reinforced by the (on the face of it, narratively 'unnecessary') scenes of Jeff walking alone in streets and corridors and standing alone in areas of cinematic space unrelieved by any furnishings. Most of all, however, it is the astonishing performance of Alain Delon which defines Jeff as the Melvillian hero *par excellence*. Several of Melville's heroes have been solitary and relatively wordless, for example Silien and Faugel in *Le Doulos* and Gu and Orloff in *Le Deuxième souffle*. Indeed, as already mentioned, Orloff looks in retrospect like a dry run for the figure of Jeff, although Orloff's solitude is softened by the respect and affection of other gangsters. Jeff Costello, incarnated in the hard-eyed impassivity of Alain Delon, is metaphysically alone.

At a conscious level it is clear that Melville's films are made out of cinema rather than out of 'life'. This is evident in the extent to which he deploys the same iconography as the classic American gangster films: cars, guns, telephones, rain-soaked streets at night, art deco nightclubs in which progressive jazz is played and in which women dance with top hats, canes and long cigarette-holders, the particular shape made on the screen by a certain kind of hat and raincoat. The latter is ritualized to an incredible degree in *Le Samouraï*, with the camera lingering over Jeff's enrobing before the mirror each time he leaves his apartment, complete with the characteristic running of his fingers over the hat brim which Delon is said to have appropriated from Melville himself. To illustrate the extent to which *Le Samouraï* connects iconographically with American gangster movies of the 1930s and 1940s, simply compare its 'look' with that of American gangster movies contemptuous with it (apart, of course, from such historical reconstructions as *Bonnie and Clyde*). Films such as *Gunn* (1967) and *Point Blank* (1967) are suffused with light, exploit the entire range of the colour spectrum, and both their hoodlums and their investigators, in line with changing fashions in American life, are without hats or overcoats.

Additionally, Melville's Americanophilia may make itself felt in the actual structure of his films. Although they are extremely 'French' in their philosophical underpinning and tone and in the 'inordinate' length of certain scenes and sequences, their narratives are very direct, like those of Hollywood movies (despite their often intricate plotting), and are constructed round actions rather than states of mind. Melville himself has spoken often about the necessity of delivering 'spectacle' and 'pleasure' in the cinema and of working out of feeling rather than intellect, positions more readily associated with Hollywood popular cinema than European art cinema where the watchwords are likely to be social concern and/or intellectual seriousness. *Le Samouraï*, despite its philosophical bleakness and its stylistic austerity, delivers many of the traditional pleasures of action in line with classical gangster movies. Indeed, measured against the three-act structure which is at the centre of what might be called 'story-structure discourse' (Field 1978), *Le Samouraï* conforms very closely to the Hollywood narrative paradigm.

It has been suggested that Melville's gangster movies, with their obsessive returning to issues of comradeship and betrayal, might be read as displaced renderings of the French wartime experience. Such an argument is well-evidenced by *Le Doulos* and *Le Deuxième souffle*. Superficially, it seems to fit less easily with *Le Samouraï* since the male solidarity and detestation of betrayal so evident in the earlier films is entirely absent. However, on closer inspection, it can be seen that questions of loyalty and betrayal have not vanished from *Le Samouraï* , they have been ceded to the two women in the film, Jeff's 'fiancée' Jeanne (Nathalie Delon) and the nightclub pianist Valérie (Caty Rosier) on whose account Jeff in effect commits suicide. Jeanne's devotion to Jeff is dog-like to the extent of being prepared to lose her 'sugar daddy' Weiner (Michel Boisrond) and risk the threat of the vice squad to maintain Jeff's alibi which she knows to be false. It is not entirely clear in the film itself, but Melville has described Jeff as having fallen in love with Valérie and thereby, for the first time, having become vulnerable. She is clearly the lover of the gang boss Olivier Rey (Jean-Pierre Posier) who has given Jeff the initial contract to kill the nightclub owner. Jeff finds out about their relationship and, concluding that the second contract he is given, to kill Valérie, is part of an elaborate plan to lure him back to the club (a plan he believes she is party to), he points an empty gun at her and is shot by the police. The critic seeking to locate this act – suicide in the face of betrayal – in relation to Melville's displaced (and perhaps not altogether conscious) handling of his wartime experience, might again link this to Gu's attempted suicide and to Melville's own response to the wartime surrender.

As mentioned above, the three 'acts' of *Le Samouraï* can themselves be seen as extended examples of the 'cinema of process' and, within each are to be found local realizations of this equal to anything in Melville's *oeuvre*. When Jeff leaves his apartment for the first time in the film, there occurs the scene in Melville's work most reminiscent of that in *Le Trou* where the 'real' time of breaking a hole in the cell floor is to a large extent allowed to be seen unblinkingly on screen. In a busy Parisian street, Jeff enters a car he wants to steal. In an analogous Hollywood movie the thief would have tinkered with the wiring and quickly jump-started the car. In *Le Samouraï*, however, Jeff sits impassively in the driver's seat, takes out a ring carrying about a hundred ignition keys, and slowly and deliberately begins to try each one in sequence. He succeeds with the fifth key.

In a later example of the 'cinema of process' from the third 'act' – the police placing a 'bug' in Jeff's room – Melville has the police enter Jeff's place by an exactly similar procedure, a large ring of diverse house keys, a characteristically Melvillian conflation of the moral universes of police and criminals. Many other sequences in *Le Samouraï* might be discussed in terms of 'the cinema of process'. Jeff's intricate construction of a two-part alibi in advance of his fulfilling the first contract killing (like the sequence from *Le Doulos* discussed in detail above, a process which the audience will understand only retrospectively) is such a sequence, as is the masterly scene in the second 'act' in which Weiner unwittingly backs up Jeff's alibi by recreating the 'composite figure' he saw in the foyer of Jeanne's building: Jeff's face; Jeff's hat, worn by another figure in the identity parade; and Jeff's coat, worn by yet another figure. The term 'cinema of process' might also be applied to Jeff's bandaging of his wounded arm and the celebrated chase through the Paris métro with Jeff being picked up and lost by a succession of plainclothes police figures while the Inspector (François Périer) follows the chase, Mabuse-like, on a giant illuminated map of the métro system.

Melville's work, to the chagrin of many critics and on his own recurrent insistence, is hermetically sealed, has no direct purchase on the 'real' world, is ultimately (in its conscious dimensions at any rate) about *cinema* rather than 'reality'. This is brought sharply home by the figure of Valérie in *Le Samouraï*, who is black. Melville has talked about her rather vaguely as representing Death, which Jeff is so manifestly seeking. In common with the other characters in the film, nothing is revealed about her background and her motivation. Although she is black, there is a certain ambiguity about her territorial origin and, indeed, her ethnicity (similarly beautiful, non-white women hover round the edges of both *L'Aîné des Ferchaux* and *Le Deuxième souffle*). Valérie could be of African, West Indian or Asian origin. The point is that the film offers nothing about her that would encourage a social or political reading. True to Melville's stated policy, at the conscious level of its construction *Le Samouraï* is an exercise in the sophisticated reworking of

American generic forms. However, as the argument of this essay makes clear, this does not preclude it from serving unconsciously as a vehicle for Melville's deepest philosophical and political values.

## Melville and the critics

Jacques Zimmer and Chantal de Béchade argue that 'the long love affair between Jean-Pierre Melville and the critics, which saw a honeymoon, quarrels, fierce discords and reconciliations, ended in irredeemable divorce' (Zimmer and de Béchade 1983, 111). They regard *L'Aîné des Ferchaux* (1962) as the film which marked Melville's entry into the critical pantheon of French *auteurs*, but in the four-year gap between that film and *Le Deuxième souffle*, Melville's critical reputation had begun to unravel, producing an extraordinary effect of critical polarization. On the one hand, *Le Deuxième souffle* provoked an ecstatic essay by Gilles Jacob in *Cinéma 66* in which he placed it alongside *Le Trou* ('that jewel in the firmament of the *film policier*'). On the other hand, it was this film which was to mark the widening gulf between Melville and *Cahiers du cinéma*, in which Jean Narboni described *Le Deuxième souffle* as a 'dishonest and aimless meander'. A year later, *Cahiers* dismissed *Le Samouraï* with a brief review, grudgingly judging Delon's performance as 'the only truly moving aspect of the film'.[1]

Like most Melville films, then, *Le Samouraï* divided the critics, producing some of the most crassly blinkered responses to his work. However, Jacques Zimmer's evaluation of the film (quoted in Zimmer and de Béchade 1983, 109), in its insistence not only on *Le Samouraï*'s stylistic excellence, but on its moral seriousness, provides a fitting epitaph both for *Le Samouraï* and for Jean-Pierre Melville: 'Le Samouraï is a Picasso canvas: three strokes of vivid simplicity, fifty years of work, a hundred sketches . . . and a masterly talent. It is the culmination of doggedness, style . . . and morality.'

As Melville increasingly becomes a point of reference for makers of *films noirs* in diverse cultures (Martin Scorsese, Quentin Tarantino and John Woo are the most recently identified disciples) and as, within France, questions of (film) culture and ideology become more and more divergent, there are signs that Melville's cinematic excellence is coming to be appreciated unanimously in his own country. Two simultaneous events signal this emergent consensus. The November 1996 issue of *Cahiers du cinéma* contained an extensive reassessment of Melville's work under the appropriate title 'Le deuxième souffle de Melville' and alongside this, the Cinémathèque Française ran an extensive Melville retrospective. His rightful place in the pantheon has at last been assured.

## Notes

1. See *Cinéma 66*, 111 (December 1966), 88; *Cahiers du cinéma* review of *Le Doulos*, 141 (March 1963), 46; *Cahiers du cinéma* review of *Le Samouraï*, 196 (December 1967), 72.

## Selected bibliography

Andrew, Dudley (1987) *Breathless*, New Brunswick, Rutgers University Press.

Borde, Raymond, and Chaumeton, Etienne (1955) *Panorama du film noir américain, 1941–1953*, Paris, Editions de Minuit.

Breitbart, Eric (1964/5) 'An Interview with Jean-Pierre Melville', *Film Culture*, 35, 15–19.

Browne, Nick (1990) *Cahiers du cinéma 1969–1972: The Politcs of Representation*, London, Routledge/British Film Institute.

Buss, Robin (1988) *The French Through Their Films*, New York, Ungar

Case, Brian (1994) 'Cinefile: Brian Case on *Le Samouraï*', *Time Out* (16–23 November), 161.

Field, Syd (1978) *Screenplay*, New York, Dell Paperbacks.

Forbes, Jill (1992) *The Cinema in France After the New Wave*, London, British Film Institute.

Gille, Vincent (1993) 'The Writers', in Morris (1993).

Harvey, Sylvia (1978) *May '68 and Film Culture*, London, British Film Institute.

Hayward, Susan (1993) *French National Cinema*, London, Routledge.

Hillier, Jim (ed.) (1985) *Cahiers du cinéma, the 1950s: Neo Realism, Hollywood, New Wave*, London, Routledge & Kegan Paul/British Film Institute.

Jousse, Thierry and Toubiana, Serge (1996) 'Le deuxieme souffle de Melville', *Cahiers du cinéma*, 507 (November), 63.

Lindeperg, Sylvie (1997) *Les Ecrans de l'ombre, La seconde guerre mondiale dans le cinéma français (1944–1969)*, Paris, CNRS Editions.

Morris, Francis (ed.) (1993) *Paris Post-War: Art and Existentialism 1945–1955*, London, Tate Gallery.

Naremore, James (1996) 'American Film Noir: The History of an Idea', *Film Quarterly*, 49 (2), (winter), 12–28. A version of this article is included in Naremore (1998).

Naremore, James (1998) *More Than Night: Film Noir in its Context*, Berkeley, University of California Press.

Nogueira, Rui and Truchaud, Francis (1968) 'A Samurai in Paris', *Sight and Sound*, 37 (3) (summer), 119–23.

Nogueira, Rui (ed.) (1971a) *Melville on Melville*, London, Secker & Warburg.

Nogueira, Rui (1971b) 'Jean-Pierre Melville Talks to Rui Nogueira about *Le Chagrin et la pitié*', *Sight and Sound*, 40 (4) (autumn), 181.

Rousso, Henry (1991) *The Vichy Syndrome: History and Memory in France since 1944*, trans. Arthur Goldhammer, London, Harvard University Press.

Smith, Murray (1995) *Engaging Characters: Fiction, Emotion, and the Cinema*, Oxford, Clarendon Press.

Zimmer, Jacques and de Béchade, Chantal (1983) *Jean-Pierre Melville*, Paris, Filmo.

# Appendix

## *Jean-Pierre Melville (1917–73): filmography*

1946  *Vingt quatre heures de la vie d'un clown* (short)
1947  *Le Silence de la mer*
1949  *Les Enfants terribles*
1953  *Quand tu liras cette lettre*
1955  *Bob le flambeur*
1958  *Deux hommes dans Manhattan*
1961  *Léon Morin, prêtre*
1962  *Le Doulos*
1962  *L'Aîné des Ferchaux*
1966  *Le Deuxième souffle*
1967  *Le Samouraï*
1969  *L'Armée des ombres*
1970  *Le Cercle rouge*
1972  *Un flic*

## *Other films cited in the text*

*The Asphalt Jungle*, John Huston (USA 1950)
*Bonnie and Clyde*, Arthur Penn (USA 1967)
*Le Chagrin et la pitié*, Marcel Ophuls (1970)
*Double Indemnity*, Billy Wilder (USA 1944)
*Du Rififi chez les hommes*, Jules Dassin (1954)
*Gunn*, Blake Edwards (USA 1967)
*Laura*, Otto Preminger (USA 1944)
*Lost Weekend*, Billy Wilder (USA 1955)
*The Maltese Falcon* (USA 1941)
*Murder, My Sweet*, Edward Dmytryk (USA 1944)
*Peter Ibbetson*, Henry Hathaway (USA 1935)
*Point Blank*, John Boorman (USA 1967)
*Le Trou (The Night Watch)*, Jacques Becker (1960)

# 14

# EYE FOR IRONY

## Eric Rohmer's *Ma nuit chez Maud* (1969)

### *Norman King*

You can say that my work is closer to the novel – to a certain classic
style of novel which the cinema is now taking – than to other forms
of entertainment, like the theatre. And that, for me, is significant.

(Eric Rohmer 1971)

How faithless film-makers, critics and audiences can be. In May 1969, the
first anniversary of certain celebrated events, the French entry at Cannes was
*Ma nuit chez Maud* which, after a highly favourable reception there, was
quickly released in Paris, instantly drawing big houses both on the Right
Bank and in the Latin Quarter. It was as if May '68 had not existed, or at
least as though audiences could simply overlook it in a nostalgic glance back
towards less troublesome times. That, to a great extent, was the secret of
*Maud*'s success. It was not mindless, but it made you think in a comfortable
way. Whether God was in his Heaven or not, all was not irredeemably wrong
with the western world's traditional views on politics and morality. *Maud*
was a film which happened on the cinematic scene at the right moment. It
turned over an old leaf.

For once the critics were almost unanimous.[1] Here was a film that went
against the grain but which was intelligent, admirably subtle, psychologically rich and captivating. It was actual in that it was in tune with 'the true
morality and the true sensibility of the France of today'.[2] Yet it was also a
continuation of great literary traditions: the psychological novel in its analysis of states of mind, its rigour and its economy; the realist novel in its
attention to time and place, to the influence of environment on behaviour.
Critics writing in conservative or progressive papers cite different examples
but their standpoint is basically the same.

What is at stake, though, in this rehabilitation of the traditional is not
just a hearty appeal to well-tried values after an upheaval which could still
not be properly understood. It was not only the abortive revolution of
May 1968 that was being effaced but great swathes of political, moral and

aesthetic history. When Henry Chapier, reviewing *Maud* in *Combat* (a radical daily) compares Rohmer to Flaubert, it is as if everything back to Zola and the Paris Commune is taken out of play. And when Jean-Louis Bory, film critic of the *Nouvel Observateur*, sees *Maud* as a brilliant dialogue within which Diderot occasionally hands over to Marivaux, it is almost as though 1789 had not happened either. Indeed, if *Maud* had appeared in 1790, 1871 or 1888 (the year after the violent split between naturalists and psychological realists), the critics would possibly have used similar arguments, more abrasively perhaps, but no less complacently. One critic does extend the literary analogy to a musical one, but only to compare *Maud* to a Mozartian cadence, a small clear note breaking through the cacophony which surrounds it. Having already described it as the opposite of a revolutionary cry and praised its classical virtues, he is like Jean de Baroncelli, valuing the film because it sets aside the troubles and obsessions of the present.[3]

Rohmer, hitherto so unfashionable, was now in favour because he made it possible to forget about so much, so many frustrating disturbances and drastic upheavals. *Maud's* immediacy was that it offered a return to pre-revolutionary situations, to humanist values and pre-modernist aesthetics.

In one of his many interviews, Rohmer claims to be apolitical, quickly adding that whether or not he is a right-winger, he is certainly not a man of the left.[4] That is exactly how *Maud's* spectator appears to be constructed, as intelligent abstentionist who can take discreet pleasure in the charms of bourgeois democracy, in discussions about good and bad faith, and how to make tea.

The point is not, of course, to berate Rohmer, *Ma nuit chez Maud*, its reviewers or its audiences, but to begin to understand its historical inscription, what made *Maud* so appealing to audiences in the France of 1969 and in the western world of the early 1970s. And why, in spite of Rohmer's attentiveness to the cinematic, the film has continued to be discussed in terms derived from literary debates. The reference to the past with its assurance of the permanence of value systems involves not just the denial of the actual. It evacuates in one blow the politically controversial and the blatantly commercial. It also improvises a direct line between immediate desires and the literary concerns of a hundred, two hundred or three hundred years ago.

*Maud* seems then to belong to a category of reactionary films which seek to efface the impingement of more urgent debates. It proposes a world of continuity rather than of radical change. While the characters talk about the actuality of Pascal, the critics refer to Diderot, to Marivaux and to Flaubert, as if they could be assimilated into one great unified tradition. Yet the equation of reaction and tradition is too neat. *Maud* cannot be explained away quite so easily.

In 1966–7, when Rohmer claims the screenplay was written, *Maud* would have been set alongside *Deux ou trois choses que je sais d'elle*, and perhaps found wanting both in terms of the study of environment and of cinematic language. But in 1968–9, while Godard was struggling with *Vent d'est*, it was time to return to something safer, to the sweetness and light of *L'Enfant sauvage* and the melodramatic *La Femme infidèle*. In that context *Maud* may not seem quite so reactionary. Its challenges may appear to be gentle – but appearances in Rohmer's films are deceptive. There is always more at stake than we can initially guess. And the tradition the reviewers refer back to may not be so barren in that it does at least escape the sentimentalism of Truffaut and the self-indulgence of Chabrol. Rohmer's literariness may in fact signal a way ahead in the development of the cinematic, in the shifting of spectator position, in the construction of a cinema which does indeed feed upon tradition, arguing from the inside while gnawing away at the structures it apparently supports. In short, a cinema of irony.

There are of course other reasons for considering Rohmer's films as deriving from the literary, not least the choice of 'Moral Tales' as generic title for the series which includes *Maud*, plus the insistent references to written texts as well as the process of writing: Aurora as novelist in *Le Genou de Claire*, Bougainville as lure in *L'Amour l'après-midi*, Rousseau and Pascal as centres of debate in *La Collectionneuse* and *Ma nuit chez Maud*. Yet these are all traps in which we are invited not to be caught. Whether they hark back to early written projects formulated before Rohmer's involvement with cinema or are merely convenient structuring devices demonstrating how the characters fictionalize (or mythologize) their day-to-day existence, they are only pre-texts. It does not much matter either that Rohmer, in his own idiosyncratic way, subsequently published the Moral Tales as a series of short and not very interesting novels, or that his shooting scripts gave him the impression that he was re-working pre-existent material. What does matter is a process of conversion which draws on the literary as source for the transformation of the cinematic, redefining it and expanding its language. Or rather its signifying system, since the late 1960s were also a crucial moment in the development of a semiotics of cinema. By exploring the ironic within what had been considered a literal medium, Rohmer was, however derivatively, staking out a claim for new territory, making a film which undercut all the discourses it contained and, to an extent, its own. That, after all is what irony is about. While arguing for changes, it does not usually tell us how we can make them happen.

The literary analogies are thus more relevant than they might seem. In spite of their apparent contradictions, the examples quoted are nearly always the same ones: the psychological novel, or rather the 'roman d'analyse', since its exponents argue that it is a specifically French genre (even though its exemplar, Benjamin Constant's *Adolphe*, was written by a Swiss protestant); and the 'roman réaliste', typified by Flaubert's *L'Education sentimentale*.

The two genres appear at first to share few characteristics. *Adolphe* is a short first-person narrative with few characters and virtually no description.

*L'Education sentimentale* is on the other hand as concerned with environment and the meticulous study of historical events as with the behaviour of the numerous characters. But both, like most of their counterparts, are novels of misapprehension. Adolphe as narrator may seek to criticize and to justify his behaviour as protagonist, but the reader, distanced by ironic strategies, can fully accept neither the criticisms nor the justifications. In *L'Education sentimentale* the characters seek always to control their social and political environment but are unknowingly motivated and manipulated by it. Their thoughts and actions are always undercut by narrative strategies such as Flaubert's celebrated free indirect style. A double irony, then, in both instances: one which we could think of as appertaining to the intrigue, and one which is integral to a narrative discourse. We could add a third one, an irony which undermines the position of the reader, leaving him/her in a state of uncertainty, trying to resolve the enigma but unable to do so, being sent back to the beginning to try again.

*Maud* is also a tale of misapprehension and its strategies of irony closely resemble those of the literary genres which *Adolphe* and *L'Education sentimentale* have come to represent. Both the novels and the film foreground speech rather than action: the protagonists spend much of their time talking about, and trying to explain their actions in terms which are never quite convincing. The attempt to control via language is always illusory. The unsaid 'speaks' more clearly, undermining all certainty, except one that can be found only outside the fiction in a changed apprehension of the real.

This does not mean that we can simply assimilate *Maud* into a tradition which has such impeccable credentials, nor that we can integrate the literary analogy by shifting its terms of reference. It does not in that sense matter whether Rohmer had read Constant and Flaubert, or Diderot and Marivaux . . . or Jane Austen and Henry James. The literary, as subject matter, tradition or analogy, provides a lead rather than a source. It can suggest different ways of analysing irony and perhaps reflect back on the way the literary is often discussed. In other words, *Maud* as example of a cinematic irony may impose a redefinition of how it functions in written texts, diverting attention away from its classification as rhetoric towards the study of a practice, towards a notion of irony as being as historically inscribed as any other mode of discourse.

Since irony has a habit of cropping up in the most likely circumstances, signalling a disjuncture, a displacement of problems which cannot be resolved, it might be defined as pervasive discrepancy. It is less a set of rhetorical devices than a discourse which articulates the presence/absence of power, which attempts to impose power from an apparently powerless position and ultimately undercuts the illusory control of the reader/spectator. The positioning process, in filmic terms, creates a distance between the protagonist's 'I' and the viewer's eye, while providing the ambivalent pleasure of challenge, of the unresolved, and insoluble. Irony is recognition of a lack and its transferral.

*Maud's* narrator claims to have a hold on his life, to be in control of his luck, but from the outset he is, like Adolphe, misplaced. Returning from Valparaiso (or is it Canada?) to the Michelin tyre factory, to Clermont-Ferrand, catholicism, Pascal, Chanturgues and a rented house in Ceyrat, he has no 'territory'. He does not even have a name. That might be called the first level or irony, a situational one. However much our narrator may seem to be the organizer of his life, events do not occur quite like that. If he does find himself in the right place at the right time, it is apparently by chance and like Flaubert's Frédéric Moreau, he attributes this to his good fortune or, more precisely, to the imperatives of the laws of fortune.

That is why the plot is so obviously contrived. If it were not, there would be no story to speak of, for when our No Name (N for short) sets off in search of something – or someone – he encounters something or someone else, an edition of Pascal, Vidal or Maud. Françoise is seen by chance in Clermont cathedral, N's attempts to meet up with her fail, and it is only by the most outrageous of coincidences that they bump into each other, twice in the same day, after visits to Maud.

Although fundamental to the plot, this structuring irony, or irony of circumstance, is not, taken on its own, especially remarkable. Its impact derives from a combination with a second ironic level. The shooting script and the novelistic version of *Ma nuit chez Maud* are both written in the first person. Although there is a shift from the future tense at the begin-ning ('Je ne dirai pas tout dans cette histoire') to the past historic at the end ('Je la pris par la main et courus vers les vagues') the narrative is almost all in the present tense. More importantly, the narrator's intentions are spelt out, cutting out almost entirely the distance between the two 'I's in *Adolphe* and the use of free indirect style in Flaubert's novels. In the film the first-person, present-tense narrative has almost entirely disap-peared and is replaced by an image which is discrepant. N's persistent attempt to control the event is undercut by what we see. Thus many of his seemingly haphazardous encounters are in fact motivated by unavowed intentions. N, we increasingly realize, is in the right place at the wrong time, looking for what he does not find. That is why he spends so much time exploring the centre of Clermont-Ferrand after work. He is, without admitting it, looking for Françoise. Hence his visit to the bookshop where he rediscovers Pascal, his entering a bar frequented by students only to chance upon Vidal, his acceptance of Vidal's invitation to Léonide Kogan's concert where instead of listening to the music – Mozart of course – he spends his time scanning the audience, looking to see if Françoise is there. At Midnight Mass he does the same, while Vidal, a committed Marxist, seems as genuinely interested in the ritual and the homily as he was in the sonata.

In literary terms this second level might be called the distance between engagement and estrangement, the slippage between first and third person. Its importance for cinema is that it presents a filmic equivalent of free indirect style. It is an irony which privileges the attentive spectator who is cast in a position of intelligence, whose understanding surpasses that of the characters. It establishes a complicity between the spectator and the image at the expense of the protagonists.

But irony also operates against the spectator. During the long sequence in Maud's apartment, after Christmas has been celebrated a second time and Vidal has left, Maud talks about her life, her estranged husband and her lover who died in a car crash. It is one of the few really emotional moments in the film. There is a pause, a shadow passes across the lamp and we assume, correctly, that N has changed places. But our desire, mobilized by Maud's confusion and our look at her, is that N has got up from his armchair to comfort and embrace her. In the film there is an abrupt cut. Suddenly N is standing at the window, looking at the weather conditions to see if he can go home instead of participating in Maud's distress. Along with Maud, but in a different way, we have been caught out. We already knew that the characters were not what they seemed. Now we find that the image cannot be relied upon either. In the novelistic version there is just a gap. Perhaps that shadow was not even intended to be interpreted that way. But irony is not necessarily intentional, as readers of Daisy Ashford's *The Young Visiters* (*sic*) will know.

There is the epilogue too, with its voice-over, again in the past historic, closing off the narrative in a way we cannot accept. Once again the audience has been taken in. We could have guessed that Françoise's lover was Maud's husband and, indeed, as in *Adolphe, L'Education sentimentale* and myriad detective stories, we are sent back to look for clues we missed or misinterpreted – and have in consequence to reflect on what has been happening to us, on how we have been misled by the layering of ironies (fortune, *mauvaise foi*, manipulation). Unlike detective stories, however, the problem is not neatly resolved by an imagined re-reading. N, as we already know, lied to Françoise in order to gain her confidence. Now he compounds that lie, putting himself in the wrong in a doubly ironic way, sinning in his own catholic terms against the Holy Spirit while she repeats her sin of omission by not at last taking the opportunity to recount that vital episode in her past life. The rest is a silence founded on an illusory confidence, on untruths which undermine all that we have just seen and everything we have witnessed previously. There is no place here for complacency, just for discrepancy, in time as well as action. Everyone is deceived, including ourselves.

When, after all, is this epilogue taking place? The main action of the film looks for all the world as if it is set in Clermont-Ferrand in December 1968 (even though there are no references to current events, no apparent attempts are made in the location shooting to put us back a few years in time). Yet the epilogue takes place several years later (five in the novelistic version and the

*Ma nuit chez Maud* – above: Maud (Françoise Fabian) and Jean-Louis (Jean-Louis Trintignant); below: Maud and Antoine (Antoine Vitez).

*Ma nuit chez Maud* – Maud (Françoise Fabian) and Jean-Louis (Jean-Louis Trintignant).

shooting script), and Rohmer's meticulously realist signalling of days of the week and dates cannot, according to the calendar, correspond to 1968. They could be 1964 but in that case the epilogue has to be situated after the film has been completed, and after its release. That is its final irony, as text which gives us no secure place from which to start or finish. It is like Flaubert's 'Vers le début de cet hiver' in the final chapter of *L'Education sentimentale* (is it *this* or *that* winter? – 1869 or 1867 – probably the former, the one which implicates the reader).

This third level is both pernicious and crucial as an ultimate undermining of the spectator's confidence, whether we realize it or not. Without it, the other levels would hardly be worth analysing except as rhetorical devices. With it, it becomes possible to begin to sketch out a politics of irony and of its historical incidence which could, in the examples quoted here, be considered as displacement of the political to the moral and of the moral to the aesthetic.

Constant, by setting the main strand of his narrative in late eighteenth-century Germany and Poland, completely effaces the political as actuality. Instead he transfers the terms of the debate to morality, even suppressing the sections of his preface which did indeed link the moral to the political. In the end he resorts to the aesthetic as the only possibility of change. Flaubert described *L'Education sentimentale* as the moral history of a generation which, living in a world of misapprehension, had no hold on its time. Like N, the characters never quite get their act together, blaming fate for good or bad luck without realizing that there are other factors at work. Flaubert does not efface the political, as Constant and Rohmer do. On the contrary, he upfronts it, but only to subject it to his heaviest ironies, unmasking it as the determinant of a suspect morality (there are no moral politicians and those who believe there might be are deluded). Only the artist can speak the unpalatable truth.

Both novels thus foreground the moral as yet another trap. It provides no answers whereas the political should and the aesthetic could, if only in the Imaginary. The displacement is in effect a sabotaging of the moral, using it as a passage from one instance to another. It is an attempt to reassert power.

Constant sketched out *Adolphe* during the First Empire but completed it only during the Restoration. In both instances he was marginalized, unable to pursue the political career he valued more than literature. Flaubert in his insistence on art was even more out of sympathy with his time. If the moral was a pretext, the aesthetic was a refuge from the political. Irony in both cases is a specific response to a historical moment. It is political because it can respond in only an aesthetic way. It asserts a power which it does not really have.

That punctuality of irony, always there when there is nothing else to be done, is what makes *Maud* distinctive. The world we are confronted with is patently provincial France of the late 1960s. It looks and it sounds tremendously convincing. Yet the political, that unavoidable issue in 1960s France, has apparently been evacuated and the moral centred. But yet again the moral is undermined. The aesthetic reigns not as content or form but as a discourse founded upon traditions which are both upheld and challenged. The film's ironies are only a feigned absence of power, giving the momentary impression that the protagonist, the environment or the reader might possibly be in control of meaning. Its object is to construct the author-in-the-text as sole incidence of true knowledge.

Irony also negates that attempt to impose a discourse of control. In one of his many interviews Rohmer expressed a desire to create a cinema in which the camera would be absolutely invisible. Whether he was aware of it or not, he was paraphrasing and updating Flaubert's remarks on authorship and style. The book (or the film) would seem to be unauthorized, to be coming from nowhere. What this implies, however, is the construction of a text which exempts the author from a level of irony which would include him. Like a deist God, he has just set things in motion, leaving his imperfect creatures to sort things out for themselves.

Flaubert, in his other most quoted remark, said that he would so much like to write a book that would not be about anything at all, a book without 'content'. Perhaps, relatively speaking, Rohmer succeeded there more than

Flaubert. Hardly anything happens in *Maud.* People meet up for various reasons, they eat, drink, go to concerts and masses – and Marie insists on seeing the Christmas lights. But mostly they just talk or look. They are just there, imagining that they know why. Or sometimes admitting that they do not.

It is a response to the actual that is always relevant, but only as statement of inadequacy. That, ultimately, is the point of references to literary analogies. They make us rethink both the novelistic and the cinematic. They make us think again about the classic realist text, imposing a reinsertion of irony and how it functions politically within a hierarchy or discourses, recognizing its presence when there is, authorially speaking, nothing else to be done. For all his aestheticism, we can thank Rohmer for that. He signals a gap which moral pretentions and pious thoughts can never fill.

## Notes

1  There is a well-chosen selection of reviews in *Avant-scène cinéma*, 98, 1969.
2  Pierre Billard, writing in *L'Express*, 9 June 1969.
3  Gilles Jacob, *Les Nouvelles littéraires*, 22 May 1969.
4  *Le Monde*, 7 June 1969.

## Selected bibliography

Bonitzer, Pascal (1991) *Eric Rohmer*, Paris, Éditions de l'Etoile.
Clouzot, Claire (1972) *Le Cinéma français depuis la nouvelle vague*, Paris, Nathan.
Collet, Jean (1972) *Le Cinéma en question*, Paris, Éditions du Cerf.
Crisp, Colin (1977) 'The Ideology of Realism. Eric Rohmer: *Celluloid and Marble* and *My Night with Maud*', *Australian Journal of Screen Theory*, 2, 3–32.
Elsaesser, Thomas (1974) 'The Cinema of Irony', *Monogram*, 5, 1–2.
*Etudes cinématographiques* (1985–6), 146–52 (Eric Rohmer I and II).
Magny, Joël (1986) *Eric Rohmer*, Paris, Rivages.
Monaco, James (1976) *The New Wave*, New York, Oxford University Press.
Rohmer, Eric (1974) *Six contes moraux*, Paris, Lherne.
Showalter, English (ed.) (1993) *'My Night at Maud's': Eric Rohmer, Director*, Rutgers, Rutgers University Press.
Vidal, Marion (1977) *Les Contes moraux d'Eric Rohmer*, Paris, Lherminier.

For a more complete bibliography and for details of Rohmer's writings and interviews, see Magny, Vidal and *Monthly Film Bulletin*, December 1976.

## Script

Rohmer, Eric (1969) *Ma nuit chez Maud, Avant-scène cinéma*, 98.

# Appendix

## *Eric Rohmer (1920–): filmography*

1950  *Journal d'un scélérat* (short)
1951  *Charlotte et son steack* (short)
1952  *Les Petites filles modèles* (short)
1954  *Bérénice* (short)
1954  *La Sonate à Kreutzer* (short)
1958  *Véronique et son cancre* (short)
1959  *Le Signe du lion*
1960  *La Boulangère de Monceau* (short)
1963  *La Carrière de Suzanne* (short)
1964  *Nadja à Paris* (short)
1965  *Paris vu par* (episode)
1966  *Une étudiante à Paris* (short)
1967  *La Collectionneuse*
1968  *Fermière à Montlaucon* (short)
1969  *Ma nuit chez Maud* (*My Night with Maud*)
1970  *Le Genou de Claire* (*Claire's Knee*)
1972  *L'Amour l'après-midi* (*Love in the Afternoon*)
1976  *La Marquise d'O*
1978  *Perceval le Gallois*
1980  *La Femme de l'aviateur* (*The Aviator's Wife*)
1982  *Le Beau mariage*
1983  *Pauline à la plage*
1984  *Les Nuits de la pleine lune* (*Full Moon in Paris*)
1986  *Le Rayon vert* (*The Green Ray* [UK]; *Summer* [USA])
1986  *Quatre aventures de Reinette et Mirabelle*
1987  *L'Ami de mon amie*
1989  *Conte de printemps* (*contes des quatre saisons*)
1992  *Conte d'hiver* (*contes des quatre saisons*)
1993  *L'Arbre, le maire et la médiathèque*
1995  *Les Rendez-vous de Paris*
1996  *Conte d'été* (*contes des quatre saisons*)
1998  *Conte d'automne* (*contes des quatre saisons*)

## *Other films cited in the text*

*Deux ou trois choses que je sais d'elle* (*Two or Three Things I Know about Her*), Jean-Luc Godard (1966)
*L'Enfant sauvage* (*The Wild Child*), François Truffaut (1970)
*La Femme infidèle*, Claude Chabrol (1968)
*Vent d'est*, Jean-Luc Godard (1970)

# 15

# SEX, POLITICS AND POPULAR CULTURE

## Bertrand Blier's *Les Valseuses* (1973)

### *Jill Forbes*

Based on his best-selling novel of the same name,[1] Bertrand Blier's *Les Valseuses* was the French box-office hit of 1974. It owed its immense success to its controversial subject-matter, its energy and verve and, above all perhaps, to the extraordinary performances of its three stars, Gérard Depardieu, Patrick Dewaere and Miou-Miou, and while it continues to be attacked as vulgar and misogynist it has also been considered representative of a generation,[2] and over the years it has acquired the status of a cult movie.

Critical opinion in France was strongly divided on the film's release. The Catholic newspaper *La Croix*, for example, called it a 'rubbish tip' and wanted it censored; in *L'Ecran* Jean Domarchi described as 'authentically Nazi'; *Minute* referred to its 'sordid eroticism'; *Le Figaro* worried about the possible copycat effects of the petty crimes depicted and called on a child psychologist to assess its likely impact on society; *France-Soir* disliked its 'complacent display of cynicism, brutality and unbridled triviality'; and *Le Point* deplored 'the way it attacked the audience with its constant vulgarity and sexual exhibitionism'.[3] The film's evident iconoclasm meant that it was better received by the centre and left-wing press which laid stress on its comedy and good humour; only *Libération,* at the time, protested at the way women were represented in the film. Reaction was more muted in the English-language press, where it was compared to Roger Corman's *The Wild Angels* (1966) and Stanley Kubrick's *A Clockwork Orange* (1971), which Blier acknowledged as an important influence on his film.[4] Much of the criticism was directed against the sympathetic depiction of a couple of 'hooligans'[5] whose crimes, though on the whole unsuccessful, were not adequately punished as well as against the dialogue whose slang and obscenities struck the first viewers as outrageous though they seem banal today.

## *Les Valseuses* as social document

The first viewers of the film were certain that it was an important social statement. For Jean Chevalier, writing in *Image et Son*, the film's strength resides in its 'authenticity'. Jean-Claude (Depardieu) and Pierrot (Dewaere) are characters whom viewers have themselves encountered or at least read about in the crime section of the newspapers.[6] The protagonists roam the streets of their bleak housing estate looking for amusement and the action of the film is initiated by a car theft perpetrated by the two youths because they have nothing better to do on a Sunday afternoon. Right from the justly famous opening sequence in which Pierrot is seen pushing Jean-Claude in a shopping trolley across the concrete piazza of a high-rise estate, attempting to goose a middle-aged woman shopper and then snatching her handbag, and being pursued across an urban wasteland against a backdrop of ugly tower blocks, *Les Valseuses* appears firmly anchored in the problematic of modernization and its socially undesirable effects.

The postwar period in France was, of course, marked by a massive rural exodus, by vast construction programmes which spawned new towns and housing estates on the outskirts of large cities, and by a huge rise in the ownership of cars, the 'central vehicle of modernisation'. Indeed, Kristin Ross invokes car manufacturer Louis Renault's dictum 'vivre c'est consommer' (to live is to consume),[7] to emphasize that the consumption which drove French postwar expansion was essentially that of the automobile and that 'the augmentation of French buying power after 1949 was used principally to buy cars'.[8] It is therefore no accident that the car features as a central element in the plot of *Les Valseuses* – not just any car, moreover, but a Citroën DS ('déesse', that is 'goddess') – and that cars are sexualized and feminized, metaphorically fused with women by the protagonists as well as by the marketing department of Citroën. Stroking the bonnet of the DS they are about to joyride, Jean-Claude refers to it – 'elle' – as nicely warmed up ('encore tiède'), and therefore ready to accept his penetration. Indeed the pair make no distinction between their twin objectives of acquiring cars and women.

The film provides a fascinating, if obliquely ironic, account of postwar spatial and social mobility through the deployment of various means of transport, from a shopping trolley through a range of cars, to the bicycle, a train and a motorcycle. Some, as in the scene where a spanking new combine harvester bears down on the elderly 2CV which refuses to start, ironically embody the conflicts inherent in modernization. Many, like the bicycle or the various Citroën cars, are emblematic of France or French capitalism. Their exemplarity is underlined by the rapid and elliptical montage in the early part of the film, which narrates Jean-Claude and Pierrot's rapid passage from one transport form to another as a motorized history of France, and snatches of dialogue encourage the view that the film is about the state of France: 'Pas d'erreur possible, on est bien en France' (There's no mistaking it, we're definitely in France), remarks Jean-Claude when the local residents lean out of their apartment windows and urge the hairdresser to call the police; 'Bled de merde, France de merde, partout où je vais je me fais enculer' (Bloody town, bloody France, I'm buggered wherever I go), shouts Pierrot after having been raped by Jean-Claude.

In depicting and sympathizing with challenges to authority of whatever kind, in showing children and young people in conflict with the older genera-tions, in its implied critique of the penal system, in interrogating the posi-tion of women, and in celebrating sexual freedom and social informality, *Les Valseuses* is clearly a film which is marked by the events of May 1968 and the social revolution they brought about. What might have been interpreted as class conflict in the 1950s or 1960s[9] is now seen as a conflict of generations, with Jean-Claude and Pierrot as iconic 'blousons noirs'.[10] In the course of the film the protagonists come into conflict with a series of petty authority figures (*petits chefs*), such as the hairdresser or the supermarket manager, with the professional middle classes such as the doctor and his wife, and with various policemen in plain clothes or in uniform, as well as with two fami-lies, one of which owns a boat, the other a holiday home, who are representa-tive of the new middle classes that benefited from the rising affluence of the postwar era and whose consumerism is revealed in their investment in auto-mobiles and holidays.[11] In presenting these characters as a cross-section of French society and in ridiculing them, Blier is following a tradition created in the satirical magazines *Hara-Kiri* and *Charlie-Hebdo* and in the *cafés-théâtres* such as Le Café de la Gare and Le Splendid.[12]

The contrast, and sometimes conflict, between the city and the country in *Les Valseuses* is similarly inflected by May 1968. Though the city may be disagreeable or dangerous, the country has also become industrialized, as the scene with the combine harvester illustrates, while the seaside out of season is intolerably dull. When, momentarily deprived of transport in the middle of the country, Jean-Claude, Pierrot and Marie-Ange (Miou-Miou) are forced to revert to old-fashioned walking and decide to hitch a lift, their unusual immobility is underlined by the use of a fixed camera and the contrasting horizontal passage of trains and heavy lorries thundering and screeching across the frame. Even the rural idyll by the canal, in which Jean-Claude and Pierrot are dressed in turn-of-the-century leisure costume in a parody of Renoir's *Une partie de campagne* (1936), attempts to recapture the simplicities of a bygone era but ultimately fails to secure them satisfaction. In fact, it is really only the closing moments of the film, when the trio are motoring through the mountains along an empty road which recalls the 'only car on the road' sequences in pre-1968 films, that the symbolic and ideal marriage of country and city is achieved thanks to the automobile.[13]

The nostalgic anachronism of this closing scene serves to underline Blier's debt to the *nouvelle vague*, especially to Godard, and the extent to which *Les Valseuses* departs from social realism to rework tropes from the films of the

1950s and 1960s for a post-1968 audience. Blier reproduces the iconography of automobiles, high-rises and supermarkets from Godard's *A bout de souffle* (1959), *Weekend* (1967), and *Deux ou trois choses que je sais d'elle* (1966). Sometimes he quotes Godard explicitly – the two policemen on motorbikes, the flight across fields, or the identification of cars with girls are all present in *A bout de souffle*[14] – and he reiterates the link between postwar capitalism and prostitution which runs throughout Godard's *oeuvre*. However, where Godard's critique is virulent and, in the case of *Weekend*, Swiftian in positing cannibalism as the ultimate logic of consumption, Blier is more often inspired by the Situationist technique of *détournement* by which an object or situation is misappropriated and used for a different purpose from the one originally designed or intended. This occurs when the shopping trolley is used as a means of transport and the stolen handbag as a rugby ball. But it is equally evident when Jean-Claude visits a supermarket to buy Pierrot a new pair of jeans, an episode which opens like the hypermarket sequence from Godard's *Tout va bien* (1972) but modulates into something quite different as Jean-Claude, to the manager's evident confusion, proposes to pay for the merchandise (albeit with stolen money) rather than stealing it. Much of the visual and verbal humour of *Les Valseuses* depends on such unexpected inversions.

Playful intertextuality, including reworking scenes from his own films, has become one of the trademarks of Blier's cinema, and in *Les Valseuses* it is provided by Godard's *Pierrot le fou* (1965). There are multiple similarities between the two films – the scene where two policeman arrive at the café, and the scene where the couple steal the boat-owning family's car – but there are also significant differences which help to elucidate the novelty of Blier's project. Both films recount, in picaresque manner, the travels of a couple of would-be criminals across France and are more or less directly inspired by the celebrated cartoon strip *La Bande des Pieds nickelés*.[15] Both films consist of a montage of often comic incidents, gags or sketches placed end to end, interrupted by moments of violence and a rural idyll, but with little to link them except an implicit pursuit. In theory, Jean-Claude and Pierrot, like Ferdinand and Marianne, are on the run from the police, but this narrative device generates little suspense and is abandoned for the middle part of the film. Thus while their picaresque structure is clearly inspired by the gangster films and road movies such as *Bonnie and Clyde* (1967) or *Easy Rider* (1969) to which they are often compared, neither *Pierrot le fou* nor *Les Valseuses* is a voyage of self-discovery or a vehicle for psychological exploration in the American manner. *Les Valseuses* is premised on repetition rather than on the psychological and social evolution which derives from the experience of travel in the American counterparts.

There are also important differences between Godard's and Blier's films. One is the shift away from the young heterosexual couple as the focus of concern and towards the male couple familiar from American buddy movies but also prefigured in Rozier's *Adieu Philippine* (1962). The second, which is linked to the first, is the social class of the central characters. In *Pierrot le fou* Ferdinand is a well-heeled, Parisian advertising executive and Marianne a well-dressed baby-sitter. Their escape is from a life of endless and ultimately pointless consumption as heard in the cocktail party conversations at the start of the film. Conversely, Jean-Claude and Pierrot yearn to be consumers but are without the means; their posture, dress and speech indicate that they are not wealthy or highly educated; they are idle and probably unemployed.[16] The women also belong to a quite different social class: Marie-Ange is a hairdresser's assistant, Jeanne (Jeanne Moreau) a prisoner. Furthermore, though we are not told in the film where the action begins, it is clearly not in the metropolitan setting familiar from many *nouvelle vague* films. Thus Blier reflects a radical and important shift in the social preoccupations of French cinema: in the 1950s and 1960s, it was still very much bound up with the concerns of the middle classes,[17] but in the 1970s it made strenuous efforts to place on screen the 'new social actors' who had come to prominence in May 1968 whilst at the same time satirizing precisely the bourgeoisie whose concerns it had previously espoused.[18] Indisputably, Jean-Claude and Pierrot are presented to audiences as sympathetic victims of a culture which takes little account of their aspirations or needs.

## *Les Valseuses* and popular culture

Both these shifts mark a new relationship between cinema and popular culture. The appropriation of themes and forms of popular culture in *Les Valseuses* is often described as 'Célinian' or 'Rabelaisian' and both comparisons merit further exploration. Blier's novel does, indeed, read like a pastiche of Céline in its picaresque structure, in its language and its use of a first-person narrator whose interior monologue becomes increasingly fantastic. Furthermore, the reference to Céline is another link with *Pierrot le fou* in which Ferdinand, whose name echoes that of one of Céline's protagonists, is shown reading *Guignol's Band*, Céline's picaresque novel depicting the First World War as a grotesque puppet show or comic strip – hence, in part, Ferdinand's nickname 'Pierrot'. But where Godard uses Céline as one of a complex range of literary and artistic references, *Les Valseuses* deliberately embraces the 'bête et méchant' (stupid and vicious) mode popularized by the satirical magazine *Hara-Kiri*. Thus it might be considered Célinian in its language, the logic of its structure and its *mise-en-scène* of two men who undertake a 'journey to the end of the night',[19] but above all because of its 'côté guignol', its resemblance to a grotesque, two-dimensional farce. Many aspects of *Les Valseuses* which might be misconstrued in the context of the bourgeois romance acquire new resonance when seen in the context of popular culture. A reading of *Les Valseuses* based on psychological investigation is not very fruitful, whereas an attempt to understand the film, and especially the conduct of its central characters, as a modern avatar of the *commedia dell'arte* is much more promising, and one that would appear to be authorized by the use of the name 'Pierrot', a standard French diminutive of 'Pierre' but also the traditional name given to a clown or buffoon character from the Italian comedy.[20] The repetitiousness of the encounters, the alternation of attempted seductions and flight, the cyclical structure of the narrative (more evident in the book than in the film)[21] the improbable coincidences such as meeting Jacqueline, the recurrence of structural figures more familiar from folk tales, such as doubles[22] or triangles,[23] all link *Les Valseuses* to what has been called 'unofficial culture'.

The reference to Rabelais is equally illuminating especially when read through the prism of Bakhtin's great study of Rabelais' *oeuvre*.[24] For Bakhtin, Rabelais exemplifies the way popular culture emphasizes the material, the physical and, by a hierarchical inversion, the lower part of the body in all its manifestations, hence the prominence of the reproductive organs and their functions, of menstruation, defecation and bodily fluids. In calling the film *les valseuses* – a slang expression meaning testicles – Blier recalls the dialogue between Pantagruel and Panurge in which the latter observes: 'La teste perdue, ne perist que la persone; les couilles perdues, periroit toute humaine nature'[25] (Losing one's head will only kill one person; losing one's balls will kill all human nature), which in turn satirizes the belief of Galen and his followers that the testicles were more important than the heart because 'ils étaient de l'*esse* de l'homme'[26] (they are the essence of man) – a belief with which Jean-Claude and Pierrot would appear to concur. In this film, the implicit personification of the testicles and indeed other parts of what Bakhtin calls 'the lower bodily stratum' – 'il doit bien y avoir un cul qui nous attend quelque part' (there must be a cunt waiting for us somewhere) says Jean-Claude – which are metaphorically magnified out of all proportion to become the locomotive of the plot, are an example of grotesque realism as defined by Bakhtin: 'the artistic logic of the grotesque image ignores the closed, smooth, and impenetrable surface of the body and retains only its excrescences (sprouts, buds) and orifices, only that which leads beyond the body's limited space or into the body's depths'.[27]

It is in this respect that Blier's film might be considered radical. For while it is true that in the 1950s French cinema became celebrated for its 'explicit' treatment of sex – explicit, that is, by comparison with Hollywood – it nevertheless treated sex within the confines of norms of taste constructed round the female body as smooth, well-proportioned and harmonious. By contrast, the premise of *Les Valseuses* is excrescence and expression: breasts which give milk, vaginas which bleed, the penis which does or does not become hard, the testicles which are or are not impaired, focusing the attention almost entirely on those aspects of the body which, to use Bakhtin's phrase, cross beyond its limits, which are excessive and which destroy the classical distinction between the body and the world and in this way contravene the existing norms of representation.[28]

## Sex and politics

In the French cinema the years 1973–4 were marked, in René Prédal's words, by 'the great sex offensive'.[29] The relaxation of censorship meant the production of ever greater numbers of sex films which, like the immensely successful *Emmanuelle* (1974), began to cross into the 'straight' market at the same time that some art films, like those of Robbe-Grillet, began to exploit the visual conventions of pornography.[30] It therefore not only became possible but often commercially necessary to show sex more explicitly on screen. Blier's response to this shift in production norms is characteristically ironic. In *Les Valseuses* nudity is often total but never erotic, while love-making, in general, is either filmed comically, as in the episode where Jean-Claude and Pierrot attempt to give Marie-Ange an orgasm and are framed in such a way that their buttocks heave in and out of view, or as a parody of 'group sex' in a soft-porn movie, with exaggerated grimacing, grunting and physical contortions.[31] Above all, though sex is discussed *ad nauseam* in the film it is shown hardly at all.

On the other hand, the representation of male–female relations has a serious side as well. In *Les Valseuses* women are associated with nature and with dirt and are systematically treated as objects of consumption like automobiles.[32] The viewer is invited to sympathize with the male protagonists who find it hard to understand women's behaviour given that 'elles couchent toutes comme ça maintenant' (they all sleep around now). Three stereotypes, those of the 'virgin', the 'mother' and the 'whore', provide an interpretative grid for understanding the conduct of all the women in the film, whatever their age or status. Thus Jacqueline (Isabelle Huppert), the virgin, becomes a 'whore'; Marie-Ange, the 'whore' referred to early in the film as 'pute' or 'salope' but whose name suggests purity or virginity, becomes the 'mother' cuddling her 'sons' in bed or cooking them dinner; and Jeanne, rendered 'virginal' by a decade in prison, is the natural mother of Jacques and, describing herself as 'une vieille' (an old woman), becomes both the surrogate mother of Jean-Claude and Pierrot and a 'whore'.

But the period saw the questioning of all gender roles, not just those of women, and what is often referred to as a 'crisis of masculinity' is strongly reflected in *Les Valseuses* as it is in contemporaneous films such as Farraldo's *Themroc* (1972), Sautet's *Vincent, François, Paul et les autres* (1974) or Ferreri's *La Grande bouffe* (1973).[33] This crisis is reflected in the fact that Pierrot and Jean-Claude's journey is ultimately regressive. Jean-Claude is first glimpsed riding in a shopping trolley like a child; their encounters with women position them as sons; and the ending of the film, far from implying post-coital calm, suggests that the boys are travelling backwards into the tunnel of an

oedipal relationship with another surrogate mother, united with their favourite 'déesse', and that the libidinal drive which has pushed the narrative forward has now subsided: 'Décontraction du gland . . . et on bandera quand
on aura envie de bander' (the hard-on has subsided . . . and we'll only get it
up when we want to).[34] Similarly, the homosexual encounter between Jean-
Claude and Pierrot, though it involves the bulky macho Depardieu 'raping'
the more feminine-looking Dewaere, also occurs after Jean-Claude has
'mothered' Pierrot by advising him to take a bath and shampooing his hair
(adopting Marie-Ange's role) and, it is implied, is a sign of fundamental
immaturity, 'normal between friends'.

The sexual politics of *Les Valseuses* are extremely inconsistent. On the one
hand, Blier interestingly casts actors against their physical type so that the
hulking Depardieu plays a character with a feminine side while Dewaere,
who looks more effeminate, plays a character who is aggressively heterosexual.[35] But on the other hand, this inversion is used against the women so
that Jeanne is depicted as sexy 'although' she is 'old' while Marie-Ange is
depicted as frigid 'although' she is unhibited.[36] Whatever Pierrot and Jean-
Claude's ostensible ambitions, the film in practice undermines the youthful
heterosexual couple which was the mainstay of the *nouvelle vague* and replaces
it with the homoeroticism present in all buddy movies. And as with Truffaut's *Jules et Jim* (1961), referred to visually when Jeanne leads the lads to
the beach as Catherine had led Jules and Jim, the erotic ideal in *Les Valseuses*
is not the couple but the triangle with the woman serving as the link which
brings the two men together.[37] Though the triangular figure is exceptionally
common in postwar French films, the comparison with *Jules et Jim*, or with
the contemporaneous *La Maman et la putain* (1973), illustrates the particular
inflection it is given by Blier who, unlike Truffaut or Eustache, uses it as a
basis for masculine exclusiveness. The objectification of women in the film
and the sympathy for the point of view of the male protagonists have meant
that *Les Valseuses* is frequently seen as misogynist and it is an accusation
which is supported by Blier's subsequent films, especially *Calmos* (1976) and
*Tenue de soirée* (1986).[38] Similarly, the fact that Jean-Claude and Pierrot are
depicted as infantile has angered critics who might otherwise wish to see *Les
Valseuses* as disturbing fixed gender roles and as part of a radical attack on the
family mounted in French cinema in the 1970s.[39] Such uncertainty is deliberate on the part of the film-maker, who declared: 'I always try to make films
which wrongfoot some part of the audience. I try to point the viewers in
various different directions so that they don't know what to feel. That's what
I find entertaining.'[40]

Blier's treatment of sex also suggests that *Les Valseuses* cannot be too
closely linked to the movement of 'neo-naturalism', apparent in the French
cinema in the 1970s in films such as Séria's *Charlie et les deux nénettes* (1973)
or Doillon's *Les Doigts dans la tête* (1974), and defined as '[an] interest in
characters who are not middle-class and in settings which do not belong to

*Les Valseuses* – above: (from left to right) Marie-Ange (Miou-Miou), Jean-Claude (Gérard Depardieu) and Pierrot (Patrick Dewaere); below: Pierrot (Patrick Dewaere, left) and Jean-Claude (Gérard Depardieu).

the all-conquering consumer society. . . . The film-maker goes out to the areas at the edge of our cities, into housing estates and working-class districts . . . out on the streets or along the roads in vehicles which symbolize the opposite of social success.'[41] This is certainly the backdrop of *Les Valseuses* but not its principal subject. For although Blier's film does represent an attempt to re-engage with popular culture, this is less through placing members of the working class on screen, in the manner of 1930s populism, than by reworking the carnivalesque cycle of repetition, death and renewal, a project which, perhaps, represents a different form of engagement with the legacy of May 1968.[42]

It would therefore appear that the cult status of *Les Valseuses* has been acquired in spite of its politics, which continue to be as offensive to many viewers as the director could have hoped. Blier's great merits, as he is the first to admit, are as a writer of comic dialogue, and as a director of actors. In 1981 he told *Cahiers du cinéma*: 'I am a literary person',[43] and in a long interview on the release of *Tenue de soirée*, which marked the journal's first recognition that Blier was an important film-maker, he confessed that this constrained his visual inventiveness: 'it is all very well to write dialogue and to have great actors to speak it. But that means you have to direct in a way which films the actors but does little else.'[44] This is indeed borne out in the virtuoso set pieces which point up the comic talents of Dewaere, Depardieu and Miou-Miou, particularly in the latter part of the film. The superbly timed and choreographed scenes in which Pierrot and Jean-Claude are fishing in the canal and hear the sound of Marie-Ange's orgasm, the scene in which Marie-Ange recounts her orgasm, the scene where they wade back and forth through the stream to steal Jacqueline's parents' car, or the scene when the trio are hitch-hiking, are brilliant, almost free-standing, sketches, as are the extraordinarily complex shots, such as the single take when Jeanne gets out of bed and goes into the adjoining room to shoot herself, or the long scene when Marie-Ange, Jacques, Pierrot and Jean-Claude are all sitting down to dinner.

On the other hand, *Les Valseuses* is only one of a series of films produced in France in the 1970s in which women are physically and mentally abused and, frequently, killed. Critics of Blier will therefore see the suicide of Jeanne (Moreau) both as the elimination of the iconic muse of the *nouvelle vague*, and with it the death of a certain tradition of art film-making, but also as a symbolic matricide which echoes Foucault's contemporaneous investigation of a son who murdered his mother and transformed Pierre Rivière into a household name.[45]

*Les Valseuses* flouted the accepted norms of good taste and rewrote the code of the representable in post-'68 French cinema, much as *Hara-Kiri* and *Charlie Hebdo* rewrote the code of the printable. But it also exposed profound sexual anxieties about the relative power and status of women and men which, whether or not they derived from the social revolution of May 1968 as is often alleged, are widely present in the cinema and literature of the period.

The continuing cult reputation of *Les Valseuses* also suggests, therefore, that such anxieties are as yet undissipated by the social changes which have occurred since the 1970s

# Notes

My discussion of Blier is immensely indebted to Sue Harris, whose monograph on Blier's films is forthcoming from Manchester University Press.

1 Bertrand Blier (1972) *Les Valseuses*, Paris, Robert Laffont.
2 Hervé Guibert, *Cinéma 74* (April 1974), 135.
3 For a list of reviews see Gaston Haustrate (1988) *Bertrand Blier*, Paris, Edilig, 123. See also '*Les Valseuses* vu par un psycho-pédiatre', *Le Figaro* (4 mai 1974), reprinted in *Séquences*, 77 (July 1974 ), 41.
4 Typical reviews would be Jonathan Rosenbaum's, *MFB*, 42, 503 (December 1975), 271 or *Hollywood Reporter*, 232 (19) (24 July 1974), 3, where the film is summarized thus: 'Two wise-guy buddies commit petty thefts, steal cars and otherwise torment innocent bystanders. They travel over a lot of fine French countryside but they don't get anywhere in particular.'
5 'Yobs', 'layabouts', 'adult juvenile delinquents', 'louts', 'macho hell-raisers' are all variously used to describe Jean-Claude and Pierrot.
6 Jacques Chevalier, 'Les Valseuses', *Image et Son*, 284 (May 1974 ), 108–9.
7 Kristin Ross (1995) *Fast Cars, Clean Bodies*, Cambridge, Mass., MIT Press, 15.
8 *Ibid.*, 19.
9 Cf. Luc Boltanski, 'Les Usages sociaux de l'automobile: concurrence pour l'espace et accidents de route', *Actes de la recherche en sciences sociales*, 2 (March 1975), 25–49.
10 Cf. Pierre Nora, 'La Génération', *Les Lieux de mémoire*, vol. 3, 'Les France' (1992), Paris, Gallimard, 943, quoted in Sylvie Lindeperg (1997) *Les Ecrans de l'ombre*, Paris, CNRS Editions, 334.
11 See for example the classic Serge Mallet (1963) *La Nouvelle classe ouvrière*, Paris, Editions du Seuil.
12 For the *café–théatre* see Pierre Merle (1985) *Le Café–théâtre*, Paris, PUF, and for its impact on the cinema see *Positif*, 300 (February 1986), 52–3. For the relationship between the *café–théâtre* and Blier's films see Jill Forbes (1992) *The Cinema in France: After the New Wave*, London, Macmillan, 173–6.
13 Ross, *Fast Cars*, 29, refers to the 'ubiquitous only car on the road' sequences in films of the 1950s and 1960s.
14 See Ross, *Fast Cars*, for a discussion of 'belles américaines' in Dhéry and Rozier as well as Godard.
15 This long-running cartoon strip was first published in 1908. For further discussion see Jill Forbes, '*Pierrot le fou* and Post New Wave French Cinema', in David Wills (ed.) (1999) *Pierrot le fou*, New York, Cambridge University Press.
16 They are visibly embarrassed when Jeanne asks what they do for a living and lie that they are car mechanics.
17 This is more true of Chabrol and Rohmer than of Godard or Truffaut and both *A bout de souffle* and *Les 400 coups* obliquely reflect class anxiety. It would perhaps be more accurate to say that the working classes did not figure as strongly in French cinema in the 1950s and 1960s as they had in the 1930s.
18 René Prédal (1991) *Le Cinéma français depuis 1945*, Paris, Nathan: 275, refers to: 'le tournant de 1973 et la pénétration d'un air nouveau qui la vivifié le cinéma manière spectaculaire' and 'l'irruption du "social" dans le cinéma d'auteur'.

19 See Louis-Ferdinand Céline (1932) *Voyage au bout de la nuit*, Paris, Gallimard and (1952) *Guignol's Band*, Paris, Gallimard.

20 See, for example, Allardyce Nicoll (1963) *The World of Harlequin*, Cambridge, Cambridge University Press, and David George and Christopher Gossip (eds) (1993) *Studies in the Commedia dell'arte*, Cardiff, University of Wales Press. Interestingly, from the nineteenth century onwards, 'Pierrot' was often depicted as 'sterile'.

21 In the novel it is clear that Jacqueline's parents' car is the one originally stolen by Jean-Claude and Pierrot and later tampered with to make it unsafe, so that the novel ends with the death of the protagonists. The film ends ambiguously with the car disappearing into a tunnel.

22 It is noticeable that, from the canal scenes onwards, the resemblance between Jean-Claude and Pierrot becomes more and more marked.

23 Cf. René Girard (1961) *Mensonge romantique et vérité romanesque*, Paris, Gallimard, especially 'Le Désir triangulaire', 11–57.

24 Mikhail Bakhtin (1968) *Rabelais and His World*, Cambridge, Mass., MIT Press.

25 François Rabelais, (1994) *Oeuvres complètes*, Bibliothèque de la Pléiade, Paris, Gallimard, 375.

26 See Michael Screech (ed.) (1964) François Rabelais, *Le Tiers Livre*, Geneva, Droz, 69n.

27 Bakhtin, *Rabelais*, 316.

28 See Forbes, *The Cinema in France*, 173–9, for a discussion of the relationship between *Les Valseuses* and French popular culture in the 1970s.

29 Prédal, *Le Cinéma français*, 343.

30 This is briefly evoked when Marie-Ange is strapped to the chair in the hairdresser's shop in what looks like a bondage scene but is in fact an attempt to disguise her complicity in the break-in.

31 Godard was later similarly to parody an orgy in *Sauve qui peut (la vie)* (1980).

32 Cf. Guy Austin (1996) *Contemporary French Cinema*, Manchester, Manchester University Press, 53.

33 See Forbes, *The Cinema in France*, 181–8, and Phil Powrie (1997) *French Cinema in the 1980s: Nostalgia and the Crisis of Masculinity*, Oxford, Clarendon Press, especially 171–82.

34 In an interview in *Cahiers du cinéma*, 382 (April 1986), 10, Blier claimed to have altered the ending at the request of the American distributors.

35 See also Ginette Vincendeau, 'Gérard Depardieu: The Axiom of Contemporary French Cinema', *Screen*, 34 (4) (1993), 343–61.

36 This mechanism, of course, became the basis of the plot of *Trop belle pour toi*.

37 The homosexual encounter was precipitated by the implied presence of Jacqueline whose bikini the pair have just examined.

38 For the opposing view, however, see Sue Harris, 'Image, Position, Performance: Misogyny and the Female Subject in the Films of Bertrand Blier', *Stirling French Publications*, 4 (1996), 12–25.

39 Cf. Forbes, *The Cinema in France*, 200–30.

40 *Cahiers du cinéma*, 382, 64.

41 Françoise Audé, 'Le Cinéma français', *Jeune Cinéma*, 86 (April 1975), 1.

42 Cf. Jill Forbes and Michael Kelly (1995) *French Cultural Studies*, Oxford, Oxford University Press, 246–8 and Sue Harris (forthcoming) *Bertrand Blier*, Manchester, Manchester University Press.

43 *Cahiers du cinéma*, 371–2 (May 1985), 88.

44 *Cahiers du cinéma*, 382, 62.

45 See René Allio's film *Moi Pierre Rivière*, 1976.

## Selected bibliography

Audé, Françoise (1975) 'Le Cinéma français', *Jeune cinéma*, 86, 1–7,

Austin, Guy (1996) *Contemporary French Cinema*, Manchester, Manchester University Press.

Bakhtin, Mikhail (1968) *Rabelais and His World*, trans. Helene Iswolsky, Cambridge, Mass., MIT Press.

Blier, Bertrand (1972) *Les Valseuses,* Paris, Robert Laffont.

Boltanski, Luc (1975) 'Les Usages sociaux de l'automobile: concurrence pour l'espace et accidents de route', *Actes de la recherche en sciences sociales*, 2, 25–49.

*Cahiers du cinéma* (1985), 371–2, 88.

*Cahiers du cinéma* (1986), 382, 9–10, 62–6.

Céline, Louis-Ferdinand (1932) *Voyage au bout de la nuit*, Paris, Gallimard.

Céline, Louis-Ferdinand (1952 ) *Guignol's Band*, Paris, Gallimard.

Domarchi, Jean (1974) 'Les Valseuses', *Ecran*, 25, 65–6.

Forbes, Jill (1992) *The Cinema in France: After the New Wave*, London, Macmillan.

George, David and Gossip, Christopher (eds) (1993) *Studies in the Commedia dell'arte*, Cardiff, University of Wales Press.

Girard, René, (1961) *Mensonge romantique et vérité romanesque*, Paris, Grasset.

Harris, Sue (1996) 'Image, Position, Performance: Misogyny and the Female Subject in the Films of Bertrand Blier', *Stirling French Publications*, 4, 12–25.

Haustrate, Gaston (1988) *Bertrand Blier*, Paris, Edilig.

Mallet, Serge (1963) *La Nouvelle classe ouvrière*, Paris, Editions du Seuil.

Merle, Pierre (1985) *Le Café–théâtre*, Paris, PUF.

Nicoll, Allardyce (1963) *The World of Harlequin*, Cambridge, Cambridge University Press.

Nora, Pierre (1992) *Les Lieux de mémoire*, vol. 3 'Les France', Paris, Gallimard.

Powrie, Phil (1997) *French Cinema in the 1980s: Nostalgia and the Crisis of Masculinity*, Oxford, Clarendon Press.

Prédal, René (1991) *Le Cinéma français depuis 1945*, Paris, Nathan.

Rabelais, François (1994) *Oeuvres complètes*, Paris, Gallimard.

Rosenbaum, Jonathan (1975) 'Les Valseuses', *Monthly Film Bulletin*, 42 (503), 271.

Ross, Kristin (1995) *Fast Cars, Clean Bodies*, Cambridge, Mass., MIT Press.

Screech, Michael (ed.) (1964) François Rabelais, *Le Tiers Livre*, Geneva, Droz.

Vincendeau, Ginette (1993) 'Gérard Depardieu: The Axiom of Contemporary French Cinema', *Screen*, 34 (4), 343–61.

Wills, David (ed.) (1999) *Pierrot le fou*, New York, Cambridge University Press.

## Appendix

### *Bertrand Blier (1939–): filmography*

1963 *Hitler connais pas*
1967 *Même si j'étais un espion*
1974 *Les Valseuses*
1976 *Calmos*
1978 *Préparez vos mouchoirs*

1979  *Buffet froid*
1981  *Beau-père*
1983  *La Femme de mon pote*
1984  *Notre histoire*
1986  *Tenue de soirée*
1989  *Trop belle pour toi*
1991  *Merci la vie*
1993  *Un, deux, trois, soleil*
1996  *Mon homme*

## Other films cited in the text

*A bout de souffle* (*Breathless*), Jean-Luc Godard (1959)
*A Clockwork Orange*, Stanley Kubrick ( UK 1971)
*Adieu Philippine*, Jacques Rozier (1962)
*Bonnie and Clyde*, Arthur Penn (USA 1967)
*Charlie et les deux nénettes*, Joël Séria (1973)
*Deux ou trois choses que je sais d'elle* (*Two or Three Things I Know about Her*), Jean-Luc
    Godard (1966)
*Les Doigts dans la tête*, Jacques Doillon (1974)
*Easy Rider*, Dennis Hopper (USA 1969)
*Emmanuelle*, Just Jaeckin (1974)
*La Grande bouffe*, Marco Ferreri (1973)
*Jules et Jim*, François Truffaut (1961)
*La Maman et la putain*, Jean Eustache (1973)
*Une Partie de campagne* (*A Day in the Countryside*), Jean Renoir (1936)
*Pierrot le fou*, Jean-Luc Godard (1965)
*Tout va bien*, Jean-Luc Godard (1972)
*Vincent, François, Paul et les autres*, Claude Sautet (1974)
*Weekend*, Jean-Luc Godard (1967)
*The Wild Angels*, Roger Corman (USA 1966)

# 16

# THE ANTI-CARNIVAL OF COLLABORATION

## Louis Malle's *Lacombe Lucien* (1974)

### *H. R. Kedward*

First screened in 1974, with a script by Louis Malle and novelist Patrick Modiano, *Lacombe Lucien* tells a fictional story of Lucien (Pierre Blaise), a peasant youth of 17 years old, who is pulled into the headquarters of French collaborators working for the German police in Figeac, a small country town in the south-west of France. The date is the summer of 1944, after the D-Day landings. Unwittingly Lucien betrays the schoolteacher of his village, who is the leader of the local maquis, but when made aware that the teacher is being tortured he makes no attempt to break away from the circle of collaborators. He is given a gun and an identity as a member of the Gestapo, and, by using his new-found power and ease of life, courts France Horn (Aurore Clément), the young daughter of a bourgeois Jewish tailor, hiding in the town. He both assaults and attracts her, while continuing anti-resistance activities with no political or ideological motivation, but with a clear enjoyment of power. In an act of flamboyant despair, Monsieur Horn, the tailor, gives himself up to the collaborators, his life ruined by what he sees as an intolerable liaison between his daughter, France, whom he describes as a 'fragile being' and the uncultivated peasant, Lucien, whom he cannot quite bring himself to detest completely. Lucien is sent with a German soldier to arrest France and her grandmother, but shoots the German soldier in the back as he is leading them to the car, drives off with France and the grandmother towards Spain, only to break down in the wilderness of the countryside. There they survive, in a kind of idyllic return to nature, before the film is ended on a long shot of Lucien's face, upturned to the sun, over which his arrest and execution are announced in words of simple, narrative fact. The music of Django Reinhardt and the Hot Club de France features throughout the film. *Lacombe Lucien* won the Prix Raoul Lévy and the United Nations Award for best film.

At its release, and for many years after, *Lacombe Lucien* was the most controversial of all feature films about the German occupation of France. It is now the film most used by university courses, particularly in Britain and the United States, as a quasi-documentary source for the study of collaboration and resistance. Though received immediately as an acute portrayal of ambiguity, it was particularly resented by rural resisters in the south-west of France where it was filmed, in fact by most resisters from whatever region, owing to its shadowy picture of the resistance, and the apparent understanding it gave to acts of treachery and collaboration. It was condemned by many Jewish organizations for the relationship between the two young principal characters, for the outburst by France Horn, 'I'm fed up with being Jewish', and for the suggestion that Monsieur Horn went willingly to his death. *Cinématographe* called the film 'trite'; Lenny Rubenstein, in the American journal *Cineaste*, described it as the fascism of banality, saying that 'there is a sad lack of any complexity: it is all a big accident, a joke in poor taste. This tone is reflected in the film's ending where there is a marked attempt to make the audience sympathise with Lacombe's plight.' (Rubenstein 1975, 12).

The most weighty criticism was that Malle's film was a transparent example of the process, described by Roland Barthes in *Mythologies* (1957), of substituting 'nature' for 'history' by sidestepping the issues of political choice, morality and guilt. In an issue which devoted a large amount of coverage to the film, *Cahiers du cinéma* saw it as the major film of a *'mode rétro'*, a looking and turning backwards, a cynical fascination with fascism and a repudiation of the historical significance of 'popular struggle'. They defined *mode rétro* as 'a snobbish fetishism of old objects (clothes and décor) and contempt for history' (*Cahiers du cinéma* 1974, 5), and Michel Foucault, in a special interview in the same issue, agreed that it denoted a certain new regrouping of the political right, associated with the replacement of Gaullism by Giscardism.[1] Free from the essentialist Gaullist link with resistance, argued *Cahiers*, the new ideology aggressively set out to nullify morality in politics by blocking, denying and recoding popular memories of struggle, in this case memories of the resistance. The new, politically motivated cynicism among certain right-wing writers, with whom the bourgeois Malle was seen to be socially entwined, was, according to *Cahiers*, intent on contesting the heroism of the resistance, and Foucault emphasized that, encoded within the overt statement that there were no heroes lay the covert message that there had never really been a popular struggle at all (*Cahiers* 1974, 5). The role therefore of Malle's film was seen by *Cahiers* to be a remembering of the memory of the occupation in terms of chance, ambiguity and the purely formal aspects of conflict. Lucien was cast as an anti-hero, said Foucault, and the eroticism of his sexual relationship with France Horn was used to suggest 'that he was not even as *anti* a hero as all that' (*Cahiers* 1974, 10). As the debate developed in France after the first screening and as many critics admired the film precisely for its ambiguity and psychological insights, the more this confirmed the belief of *Cahiers* that the new cynicism was indeed a widespread and growing threat to historical under-

standing and explanation. The *mode rétro* was seen to have moved consciousness away from the structural forces in history to a facile obsession with
surface effects.

Michel Sineux in *Positif* defended the value of the film in precisely the
terms which led *Cahiers* to reject it. He congratulated Malle and Modiano for
giving their characters 'an opacity, an ambiguity, a depth and complexity
which in no way blurs the political lessons of history', the whole film being 'a
credible representation of an exceptionally ambiguous moment of history'
(*Positif* 1974, 27). This has now become a standard response to the film,
particularly among historians.[2] Equally resilient is the stress by critics on the
singularity of the psychological portrait of Lucien. François Chevassu in
*Image et Son* details the way in which Lucien's isolation is intensified by the
absence of his father, the rejection by his mother's lover, Laborit, and the
refusal by the schoolteacher Peyssac to take him into the maquis. His problems of relating are such that he can initiate communication only with a
material gift: money for his mother, a rabbit for the schoolteacher, cham-
pagne for Monsieur Horn, flowers for the grandmother, all surrogate gestures
which establish a psychological necessity for Lucien to accept the access to
material goods proffered by the collaborators. There is less reference to
chance, nature and innocence in Chevassu's reading of Lucien than in many
subsequent evaluations of his character. Nor does he find him lacking in
some sense of justice, however self-regarding: he warns his mother that
'things will get hot' once his father returns, while the shooting of the German soldier can be seen as Lucien's basic retribution for the theft of the
watch that he had given to Monsieur Horn (*Image et Son* 1974, 111). There is
little of the 'innocent rustic' in this interpretation, and although Chevassu
states that the film does not attempt a reconstruction of history it can still be
seen as consistent with the much-debated historical realism of Marcel
Ophuls' *Le Chagrin et la pitié* (1971) in so far as the background characters,
Lucien's mother, Laborit, the women in the queue, the gendarme who questions Lucien, the landlord who increases Horn's rent, all suggest to Chevassu
a society in which self-interest was the dominant characteristic (*Image et Son*
1974, 112).

Henry Rousso, in his landmark history of the memory of Vichy, has no
difficulty in linking Malle's and Modiano's treatment to that of Ophuls as a
further breaking of the Gaullist (and Communist) mirror which had reflected
the occupation as an epic period of resistance (Rousso 1987, 144). This frac-
turing of memory, leading to relativity and specificity in the understanding
of the period, is no longer so controversial. The film can now be explored
more profitably for the memories it embodies rather than for those that it
was previously seen to block or deny.

*Lacombe Lucien* was filmed in 1973 in the Lot, a *département* which forms
part of the old region of the Quercy, still little known except for its truffles.
It is an area with distinctive plateaux (*causses*), on which sheep-rearing is the

staple occupation. The small town in which much of the outdoor action was shot is Figeac on the river Célé, which the Germans devastated with reprisals on 12 May 1944, when they rounded up men of all ages and deported 540 to camps in Germany. Over 140 did not return. Figeac was the centre of maquis activity in the area, notably in the steeply wooded slopes of the Ségala du Quercy to the north of the town and on the Causses de Gramat and Limogne to the west. Louis Malle, who had a country home nearby, handled the municipal authorities with sensitivity, and they gave their agreement to the reoccupation of the town by the lorries and the uniforms of the Wehrmacht, though without fully realizing, I was told, what the film was to be about.

It was the very specificity of the settings which excited Malle and Modiano in the preparation of the scenario. The names of the characters, Lacombe himself, Laborit the farmer, Peyssac the schoolteacher, Madame Cabessut the village grocer, Souleillac the name of the village, all gave an authentic local ring. The youth playing Lucien, Pierre Blaise, was discovered after a wide search in the area and was indeed from a rural family with an accent specific to the region. This attention to local colour, exemplified in the film by the loving camera shots tracking Lucien's bicycle ride through a countryside of sheep, stones and undulating beauty, proclaims Malle's documentary preoccupation, which his classic, 'objective' *mise-en-scène* and Tonino Delli Colli's limpid photography appear to confirm. To the unitiated audience the film could well seem a faithful recreation of Figeac, of the Causses and the people of the town and villages nearby, as they must have been in the summer of 1944.

And yet – and here is the first layer of memory in the film – the setting might have been the mountainous region of Kabylia in Algeria, or still more the streets of Mexico City, or perhaps a claustrophobic small community in the heart of America. The film that became *Lacombe Lucien* germinated in Malle's memory of recent events in these three dispersed locations: scenes of torture inflicted on Algerians by French soldiers, almost as a sport to pass the time of day, and one particular young perpetrator whom Malle met in Kabylia who came from a nondescript background in Lille; the use by Mexican police, in and after 1968, of young peasant workers hired to infiltrate student protestors and given arms to hunt them down in the suburbs; and the story read by Malle in *Esquire* in 1969 of an 18-year-old American youth from a *petit-bourgeois* family in the mid-west, who had broken out of the constricting puritanism of his upbringing, had failed to find a job, but had found the highest military distinction of the Purple Heart for his service in Vietnam: he returned to his home in triumph, but several months later was in prison for alleged atrocities. The recurrent theme in all three events was a male youth, or several youths, achieving status, notoriety and a sense of identity in the paid service of racism, fascism and military inhumanity. *Lacombe Lucien*, apparently a documentary fiction of occupied France, was a composite. Lucien was a type, an example, and Louis Malle called each of these three events, which he had, in a direct or indirect way, personally witnessed, 'a representative story' (une histoire exemplaire) (Mallecot 1978, 41–5).

Had he been allowed to, Malle would have made the film on this theme in Mexico itself. He was also counselled against making it in Algeria. Then in 1972, the second layer of memory, he was at his home at Le Coual in the Lot and it was only then that he heard the story of a young peasant who had been the auxiliary of the Gestapo, had infiltrated the local maquis and had brought about the arrest of twenty people. 'That was it', he revealed later, 'my film would tell the story of a French *harki* under the Occupation', *harkis* being those Algerians who fought with the French against their own people (Mallecot 1978, 46). This local story is of a maquisard nicknamed 'Hercule', in ironic reference to his diminutive stature. Valued by the FTP maquis under Jean-Jacques Chapou for his skill as a mechanic, and clearly remembered in the oral evidence of several Lotois maquisards,[3] he disappeared from maquis activities in the spring of 1944 only to reappear in Figeac on 11 and 12 May in the service of the Germans. Knowing as much as he did he had no difficulty in indicating maquis sympathizers to the Gestapo and he was seen to take a personal delight in their arrest and torture. One of his victims was the schoolboy son of a Figeac lawyer, possibly the prototype for the doctor's son in the film, symbolically tortured by Lucien who breaks up his model boat with sadistic deliberation, piece by piece. Hercule was identified after the liberation, some way from the Lot, and was brought back to Cahors, tried and executed. There is every indication that he was not originally from the Lot, and Malle's own evidence about Hercule as a specific source for Lucien is ambiguous,[4] but it is clear that local memory of betrayal was prominent in the film's creation, and, given Malle's *idée fixe* of marginalized or nameless youths achieving some form of identity through fascist activities, the local collaborator had to be young.

If we penetrate the next layer of memory and turn to Malle's own memories of the occupation we find that the two films *Lacombe Lucien* and *Au revoir les enfants* (1987) are, in a sense, the wrong way round: we can understand Lucien much better if we can imagine *Au revoir les enfants* as already made. The episode of the occupation which Malle repeatedly said had most affected him was the hiding of a Jewish boy by the Carmelite teachers at his school at Avon near Fontainebleau, and the betrayal of the boy and the teachers by a resentful young domestic. That was in January 1944. A few months later, in the summer, the 11-year-old Louis Malle was boarding at a large country château at Montceau-les-Mines and it was there that he was first made aware of the maquis, in the person of a poacher who had clashed with the game warden of the château and who now, as a communist maquisard, both terrified the châtelain and fascinated the imagination of the younger inhabitants of the house, who pictured him as the embodiment of the Robin des Bois (Robin Hood) of their story books (Mallecot 1978, 9). Here was a rural character, an unknown, rough-hewn peasant who appears ready-made for filmic treatment as a marginalized outlaw character who comes to a position of sufficient local power to terrify the bourgeoisie of the area. He is, of course, present in the hunting and poaching skills of Lucien, but he is grafted on to the more disturbing figure of the young servant at the Carmelite college who helped the Gestapo discover the Jewish boy after being sacked from the college for theft. Lucien is an amalgam of the youthful domestic at Avon and the poacher as rural outlaw in maquis terrain. Both gained some form of power and recognition by their actions. Malle did not need the story of Hercule to create the character of Lucien, but the story helped to give a documentary authenticity and location to a fictional character already embryonic in these two powerful childhood memories.

When the young Malle continued at the Carmelite college in October 1944, after the liberation, he said he found it difficult to accept the authority of the teachers. Everything seemed to be in flux and, without knowing why, he found himself challenging the old religious and moral certainties (Mallecot 1978, 13). He had started his own adolescent rebellion early, accelerated by the dramatic events of 1944, and the memory of this rebelliousness, precisely at a school where the teachers had been resistance heroes, accounts, I would suggest, for his identification of resistance in *Lacombe Lucien* with Peyssac, a rather pedantic, insensitive schoolteacher who rejects Lucien on the grounds that he is too young and too indisciplined. The classic and brilliant piece of semiotic criticism of the film, in *Cahiers du cinéma* in 1974, did not fully appreciate the importance of this memory of youthful revolt. Written by Pascal Bonitzer, it analysed the scene where Lucien is put in charge of a captured and tortured resister in the Hôtel des Grottes. The adult resister appeals to Lucien's sense of shame as being a young Frenchman serving the German cause, and tells him that he will be shot for collaboration. Then, changing tack, he offers to give Lucien a chance of survival if he sets him free. But Modiano's script and Malle's direction are seen by Bonitzer as blocking the clarity of the choice which Lucien is offered. They allow Lucien to hear not the political alternative but only the grammatical form of the prisoner's offer, the use of the second person singular, as to a child. Lucien replies, 'I don't like being called "tu"' and he gags the resister with a square of sticking plaster on which he mockingly draws a red mouth to make its inability to speak more ironic. It is Malle, according to Bonitzer, who has gagged the resistance and has diverted attention away from the primary import of collaboration and resistance on to the formalistic and secondary element of grammar. This, concludes Bonitzer, relegates history to appearances only: the film is no more than 'a story of sticking plaster' (*Cahiers du cinéma* 1974, 42–7).

Like the rest of the *Cahiers* criticism of the film, Bonitzer misses the central importance of youth to the film, and indeed the whole context of youth revolt from 1968 through to the early years of the 1970s. It was a

*Lacombe Lucien* – Lucien (Pierre Blaise).

recurrent theme of 1968 posters to show youth patronizingly treated by the dominant adult culture and its socio-political system. One of the most powerful images was the huge shadow of de Gaulle gagging the mouth of a young student, and the caption 'Be young and shut up'. Malle inverts the act of gagging, in this sense reflecting the *défi* of the May days which was to invert all existing power relationships. In particular, student opinion was rarely respectful towards the older resistance generation. The power structures which had been built on a resistance identity were criticized for both allowing and perpetrating the Algerian war and its crime against humanity, torture. The '68 generation had little understanding of resistance as originally a revolt in itself. In the 1950s and 1960s, for example, there were no school textbooks or films which recognized the maquis as a vast upsurge of youth. A staid resistance orthodoxy had also marginalized memories of youthful assertion which had coloured the events of the liberation. In gender terms it is a vital context to the reception of Malle's film that young women of the late 1960s, and the feminist movements which followed, were battering at the dominant patriarchy and the refusal of female subjectivity, and had the response of *Cahiers* been less compromised in a male perspective it would have given far more attention to the character of France Horn and her revolt against the social expectations and cultural fastidiousness of her father.

At a crucial moment in the film, Monsieur Horn and Lucien's mother are brought together to wag their heads at the misbehaviour of their children. Politically speaking the revolt of Lucien and France is far removed from the revolutionary aims of the May events, but psychologically Malle had given expression to the contextual impulse of youthful revolt. He forces the audience to ask what would happen if the schoolteacher who rejects you as an indisciplined child is a resister, and if the father who smothers you as 'a fragile being' is forced to hide away from the world because he (the father) is a Jew. In this context, the outburst of France, 'I'm fed up with being Jewish', is not only a cry of despair at racial victimization but also an agonized expression of generational conflict. Behind it lies Malle's own memory of his inexplicable rebelliousness in October 1944, inexplicable, that is, until the stress on the 'necessity' of youthful revolt over twenty years later. It is tantalizing that Malle, in his interview with Gilles Jacob, should mark his admiration for Jean-Luc Godard's *La Chinoise* (1967) as a prophetic anticipation of the May events at Nanterre (*Positif* 1974, 31), while saying nothing about his own characterization of the 'new generation' in the delinquent Louis and Véronique of *Ascenseur pour l'échafaud* (1957). The young 'blouson noir', Louis, shoots a German couple when they try to prevent him from stealing their Mercedes, in itself an antecedent of Lucien's theft-related killing seventeen years later.[5]

Memories and context interweave. Precedents in both film and literature, and working relationships with Roger Nimier (on *Ascenseur pour l'échafaud*) and Patrick Modiano, made it comparatively easy for Malle to depict youthful revolt in terms of collaboration, whether unwitting or not. Nimier's nihilist novel *Les Epées* (1948) and Modiano's *La Place de l'étoile* (1968) and *La Ronde de nuit* (1969) must all be registered as source material on the psychology of collaboration, as indeed must the whole aim and achievement of the 'Hussards' (Nimier, Jacques Laurent, Antoine Blondin and others), whose open espousal of self-interest and cynicism involved exploration of the rejected morality of collaboration and *attentisme*. Their search for identity lies through humiliation, amorality, hedonism and despair. Already Jean-Louis Curtis had created what became a literary norm of collaboration as a form of social advancement in *Les Forêts de la nuit* (1947), set in a small town in the south-west of France, which features the drift into collaboration by the sexy young Philippe Arréguy, and his seduction of the refined and resistance-minded daughter of the nobility, Hélène, which is no less shocking than the relationship of Lucien and France.[6] Philippe must have been at least an unconscious model for Lucien: he was the untamed tiger in the forests of the night, and the novel the most widely read of all those on the occupation appearing shortly after the war. The illicit love relationship in *Hiroshima mon amour* (1959) between the young French girl and the German soldier also constitutes an obvious reference point. But whereas Alain Resnais and Marguerite Duras contextualize the sexual relationship in occupied Nevers with anguish and pain, Malle gives his story a celebratory form and produces, without his own explicit recognition, an archetypal mode which is ultimately responsible for the film's ambivalent impact, both at the time and since.

The form of *Lacombe Lucien* is almost a model of the *carnaval* (carnival) mode, the archetypal pattern of cultural celebration, ritualized in the Middle Ages from pre-Christian festivals and controlled inversion in Greek and Roman culture. The transient overturning of power relationships; transgression, absurdity and burlesque; the displacement of high by low culture; a world of masks, animalism and sensuousness; a mix of gender inversions, crude misogyny and an overthrow of conventional sexuality, and a final return to what is held to be cultural and social normality are all orchestrated by the main structure of the film, which is axed round two pivotal events on the road, a punctured bicycle tyre and the breakdown of a car. The first breaks the daily routine of Lucien's life, which is then turned upside down by the bored, cynical revelry of the French Gestapo agents in the Hôtel des Grottes, and the theatricality of power. The second ends the inversion and leads to the ritualized judgement and closure of *carnaval*. In between, Lucien is the embodiment of *carnaval*, a personification etched in every detail of his behaviour: as he tries on his new suit and trousers, the plus-fours which become a social mask, he whistles a tune which discords with Beethoven's *Moonlight Sonata* coming from behind closed doors; later he sits loudly on the bass notes of the piano in an act of cultural assertiveness. 'C'est la fête', he announces when he brings the champagne, and there is no explanation when France asks what they are celebrating: there is only joint laughter from the two of them, free and unrestrained, and this is the first glimpse of the other side of the apparently refined young interpreter of the classics. When Lucien brings the flowers he is once again dressed up, this time in a different suit with a tie. 'One good thing about the war', says the aristocatic *raté* Jean-Bernard, earlier in the film, 'there are twice as many nightclubs', and the mix of sex and violence in the hotel is calculated to transgress: it is the woman servant (Marie) who makes sexual overtures to the new male recruit (Lucien), offering herself to him as an apparently innocent alternative to the dangerous sociability of the collaborators, but rivalling them later by her frenzied racial and sexual attack on France Horn whom she threatens to turn over to the Germans; Lucien and France make love and wake naked in the bathroom where Peyssac had been tortured; Betty (Jean-Bernard's girlfriend) treats torture like an erotic movie, as if it is all a pantomime for her amusement. There is imposture and pretence in Lucien's masquerade of power at the food queue and in Jean-Bernard's impersonation of a wounded maquisard; overt play-acting and reversal in the sticking-plaster episode, and burlesque in the arrival of Monsieur Horn in his best clothes at the hotel. The details of transgressive acts could be enumerated at will, ending with the shooting of the German soldier over a 'confiscated' watch, a last gesture of youthful revolt against adult authoritarianism, before ritual dictates that the 'roi du carnaval' must be killed. France announces this in the wild and delicate beauty of the *causse* with the suspended stone over Lucien's head, before the stark fact of the execution is carried in words on the screen.[7]

This elaboration of the mode of the film does not misrepresent *Lacombe Lucien*, though it may be felt to be a misrepresentation of carnival. It might be preferable to call it something of an anti-carnival, though perhaps, to borrow from Foucault, not as anti as all that, and it is this concept of a carnival turned on its head which I would offer as a reason for the film's continuing capacity to disturb the memory and understanding of occupied France. If carnival is appropriate as a paradigm for any aspect of the occupation, it ought to be for the inversionary and outlaw culture intrinsic in the actions of many resisters: men, women and youths who broke the rules laid down by a submissive Vichy and who subverted censorship, legality and authority.[8] There was a transient shift in social power which marked the rise and fall of much local resistance. At the liberation there were a number of young resistance 'rois du carnaval', trigger-happy in the streets before being disarmed and sent back to anonymity by the Gaullist structures of administrative power. Many women had come to the centre through resistance, but were re-positioned on the margins once the inversionary period was over: there were closures everywhere of expectations of fundamental change.

The suggestion that *carnaval* and the inversionary notion of resistance can be conceptually linked is not too problematic, but for Malle to enrol an instinctual young peasant lad, a self-aware young Jewish woman, the beauty of the Lot and the evocative jazz of Django Reinhardt in a story of carnivalesque collaboration offends a deep-seated sense of cultural identity, one which would accept their enrolment in a story of resistance, but rejects this provocative displacement. It is, however, precisely the concept of an anti-carnival which illuminates the disturbing appeal of fascism as an inversionary mode in the twentieth century, whether among the youths of the first years of the Nazi SA, or the last recruits to the collaborationist Milice in Vichy France, at the very time, summer 1944, when collaboration was an absurdity. Youth, revolt, absurdity and inversion, are key words of *Lacombe Lucien* which must be added to the *Cahiers* list of chance, contingency, ambiguity and formalism. The evocative setting of the film is the occupation and the Lot, but the context and the memories are substantially disparate and the mode is archetypal. Malle aimed at a documentary impact, but the film takes us well beyond a small town in south-west France in the summer of 1944.

# Notes

1 The policies associated with Valéry Giscard d'Estaing (President of the Republic from 1974 to 1981) as opposed to those associated with Charles de Gaulle (President from 1958 to 1969).
2 See, for example the thoughtful, nuanced article by Paul Jankowski, 'In Defense of Fiction: Resistance, Collaboration, and *Lacombe Lucien*', *Journal of Modern History*, 63 (September 1991), 457–82.
3 E.g. Joseph Nodari in Kedward, *In Search of the Maquis* (1993, 256). The FTP were the Francs-Tireurs et Partisans (français), largely, but not exclusively, under Communist leadership.
4 In an interview with Gilles Jacob in March 1974 he claimed that he heard the story of Hercule after having written the scenario (Gilles Jacob, 'Entretien avec Louis Malle à propos de *Lacombe Lucien*', *Positif*, 157 (March 1974), 35). This conflicts with his words, quoted above (in Mallecot 1978).
5 On the context of Malle's portrait of Louis and his treatment of 'the military hero' Tavernier, which is relevant to any analysis of *Lacombe Lucien*, see Nicholls 1996, 271–82.
6 Jean-Louis Curtis, *Les Forêts de la nuit*, Julliard, 1947. See especially the expressions of disgust and horror at the 'impossible' liaison of Philippe and Hélène, expressed by Gérard, Hélène's faithful admirer (Livre de Poche edition, 1969, 418–22).
7 One of the times at which Malle came close to recognizing the carnivalesque structure of his film was in his words to Gilles Jacob: 'The story of the film, among other things, is the story of a kid who has a good time for three months and then pays for it' (*Positif* 1974, 29).
8 As the nurses gather round the wireless in the opening scene of the film Malle allows himself a moment of typical resistance-style inversion by intercutting the broadcast by Philippe Henriot with other noise, producing a complete reversal in meaning. Note also the film's subversive mockery of Marshall Pétain, whose rehabilitation was being actively canvassed after the death of De Gaulle.

# Selected bibliography

Barthes, Roland (1957) *Mythologies*, Paris, Seuil.

Brossat, Alain (1994) *Libération, fête folle*, Paris, Autrement.

Browne, Nick (ed.) (1990) *Cahiers du cinéma, 1969–1972: The Politics of Representation*, London, Routledge.

Burrin, Philippe (1995) *La France à l'heure allemande*, Paris, Seuil. Trans. as *Living with Defeat: France under the German Occupation 1940–1944*, London, Arnold, 1996.

*Cahiers du cinéma* (1974) issue devoted to *Lacombe Lucien*, 251 (July–August 1974).

Chevassu, François (1974) 'Lacombe Lucien', *Image et Son*, 282 (March 1974).

Curtis, Jean-Louis (1947) *Les Forêts de la nuit*, Paris, Julliard (Livre de Poche edition, 1969).

Fabre, Daniel and Camberoque, Charles (1977) *La Fête en Languedoc*, Toulouse, Privat.

Forbes, Jill (1992) *The Cinema in France after the New Wave*, London, Macmillan.

French, Philip (1993) *Malle on Malle*, London, Faber & Faber.

*French Cultural Studies* (1994) special issue on 'Culture and the Liberation', ed. Nicholas Hewitt, 5 (3, 15) (October).

Hewitt, Nicholas (1996) *Literature and the Right in Postwar France: The Story of the 'Hussards'*, Oxford, Berg.

Jankowski, Paul (1991) 'In Defense of Fiction: Resistance, Collaboration, and *Lacombe Lucien*', *Journal of Modern History*, 63 (September).

Jeancolas, Jean-Pierre (1979) *Le Cinéma des Français: La Ve République*, Paris, Stock.

Kedward, H. R. (1993) *In Search of the Maquis*, Oxford, Oxford University Press.

Kedward, H. R. and Wood, Nancy (eds) (1995) *The Liberation of France: Image and Event*, Oxford, Berg.

Laborie, Pierre (1980) *Résistants, Vichyssois et autres: l'évolution de l'opinion et des comportements dans le Lot 1939–1944*, Paris, CNRS.

Malle, Louis and Modiano, Patrick (1974) *Lacombe Lucien: Un film de Louis Malle*, Paris, Gallimard (script).

Mallecot, Jacques (1978) *Louis Malle par Louis Malle*, Paris, Athanor.

Modiano, Patrick (1968) *La Place de l'Etoile*, Paris, Gallimard.

Modiano, Patrick (1969) *La Ronde de nuit*, Paris, Gallimard.

Morris, Alan (1996) *Patrick Modiano*, Oxford, Berg.

Nicholls, David (1996) 'Louis Malle's *Ascenseur pour l'échafaud* and the Presence of the Colonial Wars in French Cinema', *French Cultural Studies*, 7 (21) (October).

Nimier, Roger (1948) *Les Epées*, Paris, Gallimard.

Raskin, Richard (1986) *Lacombe Lucien: Film Dossiers No. 2*, London, BFI.

Rousso, Henry (1987) *Le Syndrome de Vichy*, Paris, Seuil. Trans. as *The Vichy Syndrome: History and Memory in France since 1944*, Cambridge, Mass., Harvard University Press, 1991.

Rubenstein, Lenny (1975) '*Lacombe Lucien*: The Fascism of Banality', *Cineaste*, 6 (4).

Sineux, Michel (1974) 'Le Hasard, le chagrin, la nécessité, la pitié', *Positif*, 157 (March).

Sorlin, Pierre (1991) *European Cinemas, European Societies*, London, Routledge.

# Appendix

## *Louis Malle (1932–95): filmography*

1956  *Le Monde du silence* (*The Silent World*) [co-director]
1957  *Ascenseur pour l'échafaud* (*Lift to the Scaffold*)
1958  *Les Amants* (*The Lovers*)
1960  *Zazie dans le métro* (*Zazie*)
1962  *Vie privée* (*A Very Private Affair*)
1962  *Vive le tour* (documentary)
1963  *Le Feu follet* (*A Time to Live and a Time to Die*)
1964  *Bons baisers de Bankok* (documentary)
1965  *Viva Maria*
1967  *Le Voleur* (*The Thief of Paris*)
1968  'William Wilson', episode of *Histoires extraordinaires* (*Spirits of the Dead*)
1969  *Calcutta* (documentary)
1969  *L'Inde fantôme* (*Phantom India*) (documentary)
1971  *Le Souffle au coeur* (*Dearest Love*)
1972  *Humain, trop humain* (documentary)
1974  *Place de la République* (documentary)
1974  *Lacombe Lucien*

1975  *Black Moon*
1978  *Pretty Baby* (USA/Canada/France)
1980  *Atlantic City, U.S.A.* (USA)
1981  *My Dinner with André* (USA)
1984  *Crackers* (USA)
1985  *Alamo Bay* (USA)
1985  *God's Country* ((doc.) USA)
1986  *And the Pursuit of Happiness* ((documentary) USA)
1987  *Au revoir les enfants*
1989  *Milou en mai*
1992  *Fatale* (*Damage* [UK/France])
1994  *Vanya on 42nd Street* (USA)

## Other films cited in the text

*Le Chagrin et la pitié*, Marcel Ophuls (1971)
*La Chinoise*, Jean-Luc Godard (1967)
*Hiroshima mon amour*, Alain Resnais (1959)

# 17

# MATERNAL LEGACIES

## Diane Kurys' *Coup de foudre* (1983)

### *Carrie Tarr*

Diane Kurys is one of a number of women directors in France who have been able to build up a coherent body of work with a recognizable style.[1] The commercial and critical success of her first film, *Diabolo menthe* (1977), enabled her to embark on a career as writer, director and, with Alexandre Arcady, producer of a series of personal films (seven to date) which, though fictionalized, build up a selective self-portrait which encompasses both her childhood and adult experiences. *Diabolo menthe* set the tone of her work, with its skilful aural and visual reconstruction of the early 1960s, its fragmented, impressionistic narrative structure centred on two schoolgirl sisters, and its well-observed, sympathetic but unsentimental exploration of the girls' rites of passage and their relationships with their divorced parents, their schoolfriends and their teachers. Its success can be attributed in part to the impact of the women's movement in France in the 1970s, which created an audience for films by and about girls and women. Thanks to its original subject-matter, Kurys became associated with the concept of 'women's films', even though she herself strongly resisted the label. In fact, her subsequent films can be divided into those which address relationships between women sympathetically, in all their complexity, and those which do not (Tarr 1997). Significantly, the extent to which they are 'woman-identified' is connected to their changing representations of the mother and mother–daughter relationships. In Kurys' second film, *Cocktail Molotov* (1980), the cold, distant mother embodies bourgeois hypocrisy and authoritarianism, whereas in her fourth film, *Un homme amoureux* (1987), the warmth and complicity of the mother inspire the daughter's creativity. *Coup de foudre*, the film in between, specifically reproduces the mother's own story, and as such invites reflection on the film-maker daughter's interpretation of her mother's legacy.

Feminist scholars have analysed how dominant cinema, when it concerns itself with motherhood, reproduces 'the old angel/witch mother dichotomy' of patriarchal discourses (Kaplan 1992: 183), and obscures or mystifies the mother–daughter relationship (see, for example, Walters 1992, Fischer 1996). As Adrienne Rich once famously argued, the 'cathexis between mother and daughter – essential, distorted, misused – is the great unwritten story' (Walters 1992, 3). In the maternal melodrama, the mother is conventionally held to blame for the neuroses of the daughter, either because of her too-loving, self-sacrificing over-investment in her daughter or because of her unloving absence and neglect. The double bind in which the mother finds herself is compounded by the supposition that the daughter's adult femininity can be achieved only through her separation from the mother, even though, paradoxically, the daughter's own femininity is also associated with the reproduction of mothering. Arguably, early feminist scholarship also initially accepted concepts and paradigms destructive to the possibility of mother–daughter intimacy and continuity, blaming the mother for the daughter's incorporation into patriarchal ideology. Only at a later stage in feminist theory has the power and creativity of mothers been valorized (Fischer 1996, 10). Yet the mother–daughter relationship is central to women's individual development, the quality of a mother's life being her primary bequest to her daughter (Fischer 1996, 197), and central to a feminist project of recognizing shared womanhood. Kaplan, Walters and Fischer (among others) all point to the need for cinematic representations which refuse 'tedious tales of maternal martyrdom and malice' (Walters 1992, 229) and, as in the genre of the 'feminist matrilinear [documentary] cinema', remove mothers from the realm of essentialism, 'locating them within the frames of race and history' (Fischer 1996, 30). In *Coup de foudre*, the daughter–author–director's fictionalized representation of the mother takes the form of a 'woman's film' in a period setting, which is both underpinned and undermined by its textual and extratextual auto-/bio-graphical resonances. This chapter explores the extent to which the film escapes patriarchal discourses on motherhood and offers its spectators both 'feminine' and feminist viewing pleasures.

Kurys became fascinated by her mother's past in the course of a series of interviews with her in the early 1980s, intended as the basis for a film about her own childhood. *Coup de foudre* documents the extraordinary circumstances in which Kurys' mother, Léna, met Michel, her husband, then a decade later Madeleine, her friend, and subsequently left her husband at the age of thirty-two, with two small children, to lead an independent life in Paris.[2] The women's friendship lasted over twenty-five years, but Madeleine died two years before the film was made and Kurys' mother died just before the film opened. At the time of the interviews, Kurys was the same age as her mother had been when her marriage broke up, but the unmarried, childless Kurys did not personally identify with her mother's story. She declared in press interviews that she found her mother's 'passionate friendship' hard to understand (Manceaux 1983) and that it had been a source of her suffering as a child (Tranchant 1983). For her, the film was not just a tribute to her mother, whom she acknowledged as a source of her own strength and independence, but also a way of confronting her traumatic childhood, expiating the guilt she felt about her parents' separation, and retrieving something of what had been lost (Fournier 1983). Her attempt to distance herself from her mother, whilst simultaneously implicating herself in the action of the film, is clear from the final frame which is accompanied by a dedication to all three of *Coup de foudre*'s main protagonists. The film's third-person narrative is thus called into question by the introduction of a more subjective voice, the implications of which will be discussed below.

*Coup de foudre* was the first of Kurys' films to enjoy a relatively large budget (16 million francs), and the first to be shot in Cinemascope, with star actors Isabelle Huppert, Miou-Miou and Guy Marchand in the lead roles, alongside the lesser known Jean-Pierre Bacri. It opened to huge publicity, subsequently becoming one of the ten most popular films of 1983 in France, and won the 1984 Prix de l'Académie Nationale du Cinéma. It also gave rise to a novel, authored by Olivier Cohen and Kurys (1983), based on the screenplay. Retitled *Entre nous*, the film was extremely successful in the United States and received an Oscar nomination for best foreign-language film. Its star-studded story of two women's successful revolt against patriarchal containment and, in particular, its valorizing of relationships between women, marked a shift from the low-budget, experimental, often depressing feminist films of the 1970s, such as Chantal Akerman's *Jeanne Dielmann, 23 Quai de commerce, 1080 Bruxelles* (1974) or Yannick Bellon's *La Femme de Jean* (1974), or even the more contemporary investigation of marriage to be found in Aline Issermann's first feature, *Le Destin de Juliette* (1983). Instead, like Agnès Varda's less successful film *L'Une chante, l'autre pas* (1976), *Coup de foudre* provided a European art cinema gloss on the themes of women's independence and female friendship to be found in American 'women's films' like *An Unmarried Woman* (Paul Mazursky, 1977), *Girlfriends* (Claudia Weill, 1977), *The Turning Point* (Herbert Ross, 1977), *Julia* (Fred Zinnemann, 1977) and *Lianna* (John Sayles, 1983). Yet, by 1983, the representation of a proto-feminist revolt against an unsatisfactory marriage was not in itself particularly controversial. Indeed, in the years following the election of François Mitterrand and the Socialist Party in 1981, many in France thought that feminism had already achieved its goals (Duchen 1986, 125–49, Holmes 1996, 213–15). *Coup de foudre*'s potential for feminist and/or lesbian readings therefore needs to be tempered with a consideration of the more reactionary nostalgic pleasures afforded by its *rétro mise-en-scène*.

At the time of the making of *Coup de foudre*, French cinema had already started to turn to what has now been styled 'heritage' cinema (Vincendeau 1995, Austin 1996), though, as Michel Perez notes (1983), the 1950s were still virtually virgin territory for *rétro* film-making. Kurys invested tremendous energy in establishing the authenticity of the look and sounds of *Coup de foudre*. She exercised personal control over all the details of the *mise-en-scène*, from the suitcases and shoes worn by the three thousand extras to the shape of the period refrigerator. Huppert and Miou-Miou even wore 1950s perfume on set because she wanted to jog memories of smells, like the scent of rice powder and Soir de Paris in her mother's handbags. She tracked down rare recordings of popular jingles and radio programmes for the soundtrack and incorporated Glen Miller's big band music, and Perry Como singing (ironically) 'I Wonder Who's Kissing Her Now' as a framing song to the narrative of Léna and Michel's marital breakdown. The question is, then, whether the surface pleasures of sound and image displace attention from the issues raised by the mother's story, rather than locating them within a precise historical setting. Does the film provide 'a sociological document, a minutely observed cameo about French middle-class life – and the sexual and social revolution that eroded its very foundations' (Behr 1983) or does 'the beautiful trajectory of the women [get] lost in eye-catching *rétro* nostalgia' (Pascaud 1983)? Alternatively, is the plenitude of the *mise-en-scène* a way of compensating for the absence and loss represented by the narrative?

*Coup de foudre* opens with a long prologue sequence set during the war years, 1942–4, which uses music and parallel editing to link the lives of Jewish Léna (Isabelle Huppert) and art student Madeleine (Miou-Miou). The narrative then cuts to Lyons in 1952 and the school concert at which the two women meet, and is subsequently structured by the development of their relationship, building up to a dramatic climax which has serious and irreversible repercussions on the lives of all the main characters, including Sophie (Saga Blanchard), the younger daughter, who witnesses the final moment of separation between Léna and her husband Michel (Guy Marchand). *Coup de foudre* is, therefore, structured like a romance in which two people overcome the obstacles in the way of the formation of their couple, in this case, unusually, not a heterosexual couple (though the women do enjoy heterosexual relationships) but a relationship between women. Not surprisingly, therefore, the approach which has dominated Anglo-American critical debates about the film is the extent to which it can be read as a narrative of lesbian desire (Merck 1986, Straayer 1990, Holmlund 1991, Powrie 1997). It can also be read as a feminist consciousness-raising exercise in that it invites spectators to share in Léna and Madeleine's growing awareness of their unsatisfactory lives as provincial married women in the pre-feminist patriarchal world of the 1950s. However, the film's ending introduces yet another perspective through its afterword, 'My father left at dawn / He never saw my mother again / It is now two years since Madeleine died.' As Jean Rochereau puts it, these three horrifying sentences give the film its measure as 'an incurable wound' (1983). This postscript reveals that what had appeared to be fictional is actually autobiographical, and that the little girl whose longing gaze structures the final image represents Diane Kurys herself as a child. As Catherine Portuges notes (1988, 345), 'This autobiographical appendix necessitates an immediate retrospective revision by the spectator,

who thus becomes a more than usually active participant in the autobiographical process'. Although the film's narrative structure authenticates
Léna and Madeleine's mutual, if understated, desire and their struggle for
self-determination, the child's gaze and the adult daughter's authorial
postscript (which, literally, puts the father first), undermine any simplistic
pleasure in the outcome of that struggle. The viewer is invited to reflect
retrospectively on the daughter's suffering, caused not just by the loss of the
father but also by the impact of the mother's relationship with Madeleine. At
the end, Sophie is re-positioned at the centre of the frame as the object of her
mother's concerned look, as she had been in the early sequence of the school
concert, before Léna met Madeleine, while she in turn looks longingly at the
father she is about to lose. The complexity of the composition of these final
images, which fix Sophie's loss, Léna and Michel's separation, and the fragmentation of the alternative family formed by Léna, Madeleine and their
children, is indicative of the complex set of narratives and identifications
which the film weaves together, and its refusal to sacrifice the messiness of
realistically represented interpersonal relationships in favour of an uncritical
endorsement of the mother's position.

Arguably, then, the *mise-en-scène* of *Coup de foudre* is not gratuitous but
artfully expresses the constraints within which the characters live out their
lives. From the crowd and action scenes of the wartime sequences to the more
intimate and enclosed public and domestic spaces of the 1950s, the film
incorporates point-of-view shots which prevent the image track from being
appropriated just by the pleasures of nostalgic looking. The opening establishing shot, of mountain scenery and period bus arriving in the distance,
cuts immediately to a shot of Huppert as Léna sitting at the back of the bus
full of women, then to shots of the landscape and the arrival at Rivesaltes
from Léna's point of view. The spectator's perspective on events, including
Léna's friendship with a woman prisoner and her meeting with Michel,
a French legionnaire, is thus determined by identification with Léna. Similarly, in the 1950s scenes, panning shots of domestic interiors crammed with
period artefacts are focalized through the characters, as when Madeleine's
art-filled studio/living-room is represented through Léna's fascinated
lingering gaze. Place and space also function to establish the women's need
for autonomy. Madeleine's creativity is stifled in her parents' oppressive
bourgeois house and in the flat she shares with the bungling Costa (Jean-
Pierre Bacri). Léna's flat is the site of Michel's jealousy and aggression, provoked by signs of Madeleine's influence, like her gift of a potted Japanese
garden or her loan of a sexy black dress. Forced out of the home, because
domestic interiors are sites of conflict, the women provisionally take over
other spaces, like the park, the cloakroom at the swimming baths, Léna's car
and, especially, Léna's fashion boutique, or leave Lyons altogether, as in the
trip to Paris and at the end, the escape to Cabourg. However, the spaces of
female desire which they create are always under threat of disruption, as

exemplified by Michel's paroxysm of violence which destroys the boutique, witnessed by other women peering in through the window.

*Coup de foudre*'s use of 1950s fashions may provide nostalgic viewing pleasures but it also gives meaning to the progression of the women's friendship. The way the women look (and smell) is part of their attraction for each other as well as being a key element of the narrative. When they first meet at their children's Christmas concert, the difference in their appearance is notable. Bourgeois Léna, in blue suit, hat with veil and fur coat, is shocked and fascinated by bohemian Madeleine, in shirt and trousers, who is not wearing tights and who offers her a smell of the sun lotion she is using on her legs. Half-way through the film, when they are searching for premises for their boutique, their outfits are virtually identical (matching long pencil skirts and high heels). When they meet again at the end, their roles have reversed. Madeleine is wearing the full-skirted flowery dress Léna had helped her sew at the beginning of their friendship, and Léna is wearing the (newly fashionable, tapered) trousers. In between, their shared love of fashion and dressmaking cements their friendship, planning a boutique enables them to dream of independence, and attendance at the Balmain fashion show allows them a clandestine weekend in Paris. Fashion is a legitimate outlet for women's creativity and also a refuge from family life and from the masculine world of Michel's garage and Costa's hopeless business deals. Michel's violence can thus be understood as a reaction to the fear of emasculation by and exclusion from an autonomous woman-centred world, as indicated by the blood on the hands covering his genitals (Powrie 1997, 70).

*Coup de foudre*'s reconstruction of the 1940s and 1950s, then, does not produce nostalgia for a lost golden age. Rather it invokes periods of conflict, and invests them with meanings that are grounded not just in the history of a particular, secular Jewish family but also in the more general history of wartime and postwar France. As well as reconstructing the Rivesaltes deportation camp and the activities of the fascist Milice, responsible for the death of Madeleine's beloved young husband, its evocation of the occupation shows women making choices and living their lives (relatively) independently, Léna by crossing into France alone, Madeleine by defying bourgeois morality and making love before her wedding. In this, it significantly predates other women-centred *rétro* films like *Blanche et Marie* (Jacques Renard, 1985), *Une affaire de femmes* (Claude Chabrol, 1988) or *Lucie Aubrac* (Claude Berri, 1997). Jewish names haunt the narrative, from the comical discovery that Léna's new husband is called Mordecaï Isaac Simon Korski (later Michel) to the gravestone in the Jewish cemetery in Antwerp which gives Léna's mother's name as Nadia Weber, née Friedman. Bacalov's haunting non-diegetic music also has a distinctly Jewish inflection which provides a recurring poignant reminder of the occasion of Léna and Michel's first meeting and invests key moments in the narrative with a sense of loss. Nevertheless, the characters' Jewishness is not made an issue in the postwar section of the film, any more than Costa's origins (his surname is Segara) or Maria the maid's, leaving spectators to make of these nominal references what they will. Nor is there more than an oblique reference to France's postwar political and military situation, figured through the presence of soldiers on leave in Léna's railway carriage.

The film does, however, give credence to Kristin Ross' thesis (1995) that the crisis in French national identity, provoked by its recent history (1940–4) and the impending loss of empire, was displaced on to an obsession with 'fast cars, clean bodies' through its critical purchase on the tensions within the family produced by France's postwar recovery and the development of new domestic technology. While Michel builds up a successful small business and provides Léna with a Hoover, a huge fridge and a small car, Léna, like other middle-class women of the time, finds her life unacceptably circumscribed by her domestic role.[3] *Coup de foudre* derives its strength from the fact that it is 'situated during a period when nothing was less obvious for a woman than deciding to leave home to live her own life' (Tranchant 1983). Given that, as Claire Duchen argues, 'Women are remarkably absent from historical accounts of the Fourth Republic (1946–58) and even from accounts of the early years of the Fifth' (1994, 1), *Coup de foudre* is unusual in opening up postwar social history to gendered readings. The women's sharing of their experiences reveals the limitations of their lives as wives and mothers trapped and isolated in a provincial town. Madeleine needs an outlet for her frustrated sexuality and creativity, while Léna's trajectory highlights the importance of economic, social and cultural equality within a relationship. She suffers from having no income and no cheque book of her own, and having to ask her husband's permission to learn to drive or get a job. She also discovers that she and Michel are socially and culturally mismatched. Michel has no education and no interests outside his work and his family, has difficulty communicating and is unable to understand his wife's need for freedom. Furthermore, he does not satisfy her sexually, as she realizes when she first experiences orgasm through clandestine non-penetrative sex with an unknown soldier (a cameo apearance by François Cluzet). Léna's and Madeleine's decision to leave their husbands and set up a new life together was unusual, revolutionary even, for 1954. The film's critique of marriage as an institution recalls the arguments of Simone de Beauvoir's *Le Deuxième sexe* (1948), but its validation of women's need for freedom and autonomy is also informed by a post-1968 feminist awareness (an awareness which can at times jar with the film's desire for authenticity, as in the famous scene where Léna provokes Michel by removing her knickers to avoid showing a panty line).

If the film is critical of marriage, it is not necessarily critical of men, nor of heterosexuality. Madeleine has a passionate love for and fulfilling sexual relationship with her artist husband, and it is only her marriage of convenience to Costa which comes under fire, a marriage contracted in the aftermath of

*Coup de foudre* – above: Léna (Isabelle Huppert) and Michel (Guy Marchand); below: Léna and Madeleine (Miou-Miou).

the liberation when she found she was pregnant. Similarly, Léna's wartime marriage to French legionnaire Michel is based on expediency and gratitude for saving her life. The possibility of love with a man is not completely closed over, though the women's encounters with other men – Carlier, the art lecturer, or the soldier on the train – are less intense than their relationship with each other. However, Costa and Michel are not represented as objects of desire. Costa is a charmingly irresponsible man who leaves his son, René, in Léna's care, so allowing her to meet Madeleine, and subsequently demonstrates his inadequacy through a series of business deals which go horribly wrong. Michel's unquestioning assumption of his patriarchal role, his inability to understand his wife's needs and his progressively more pronounced violence make his position irredeemable. Yet, as Barbara Quart argues, the self-consciously balding Michel is also 'a strikingly sympathetic character' (1984, 46). Though he is not very bright, he is a hard worker, a devoted husband and an affectionate, loving father who enjoys horsing around with the children and is devastated by the prospect of losing them. The film demonstrates that men, too, are victims of the sex/gender/class divide.

If the film is sympathetic towards men, it is nevertheless the relationship between women which is foregrounded and invested with emotion. Kurys did not want to limit the film's audiences by making an explicitly lesbian love story, and insisted in interviews that her mother's relationship with Madeleine was 'a little more than a friendship, a little less than a passion' (Merck 1986). For Pauline Kael (1984), *Coup de foudre* is a film about two women 'not having a lesbian affair', and certainly the film teases its spectators by refusing to make their relationship sexually explicit whilst offering multiple hints as to their intimacy. Even though, on one level, the two women remain very formal, continuing to address each other as 'vous' not 'tu', their complicity is established through a variety of devices which range from scenes depicting their common tastes and interests, like reading Colette, swimming and dancing, or talking about their pasts, their men and their aspirations for the future, to scenes which hint at intense sexual desire, half-voiced but not acted upon, as when Madeleine says 'Why do I feel so good when I'm with you?' or Léna confesses 'I want to kiss you'. The film depicts a progressive physical intimacy between the women as they exchange looks, touches, clothes and eventually hugs – they have their arms round each other when they first locate the boutique and, later, when they celebrate their reunion – even though it stops short of representing any overtly sexual activity. And Madeleine suffers as intensely from her separation from Léna as she did from her artist husband's death. Furthermore, *Coup de foudre* has no place for the authoritative male gaze typical of classic cinema, and its use of two-shots, long takes and pregnant silences in scenes between the two women (documented by Straayer and Holmlund) facilitate a reading of Léna's story from a position of lesbian desire. Whether the women actually enjoyed a sexual relationship or not, there is no gainsaying that the film invites identification with, or at least sympathy for, women who consciously put their relationship with each other before their relationships with others, and who derive their most intense pleasures from each other's company. Whilst the period setting and the women's ostensible heterosexuality mean that their relationship is less unsettling than an overtly lesbian love story would have been, there is no doubt that such a strong representation of a passionate female friendship is extremely rare in French cinema.

However, the affirmation of women's need for independence and of the intense pleasures of friendship between women, arguably the positive elements of Léna's legacy to her daughter, is repeatedly problematized by the film's representation of the women as mothers, highlighted by cutaway shots of the children's often critical point of view on events and by the sympathetic representation of the abandoned loving father. At the Christmas concert where Léna and Madeleine meet, where Sophie, dressed as an apple with a Maurice Chevalier mask, performs 'Ma Pomme' in front of her mother's loving gaze, René refuses to put on the massive Indian headdress made for him by the absent Madeleine. From the beginning, Madeleine is represented as a neglectful mother and René as a shy, disturbed child, who gets car-sick and accidentally locks himself in the toilet. The scenes of family life with Léna's more robust, rowdy daughters are most often associated with Michel's presence. Michel plays football with them at a family picnic, romps on the bed with them, sings with them in the car and at the end goes swimming with them, while Léna finds Michel's physical antics trying and prefers to spend her time with Madeleine. In fact, Léna becomes progressively less attentive as a mother, a key moment being the discovery that she and Madeleine have got on a bus without little Sophie. Sophie is eventually brought home by a furious Michel, and the film cuts from recriminations between the parents to shots of the girls framed in the doorway of their bedroom, watching Maria (the maid) and her boyfriend kissing. When the parents later quarrel over Léna's weekend in Paris, a cutaway shot shows the sobbing girls being cuddled by Maria. These inserts undermine sympathy for Léna's unhappiness and question her justification for abandoning her marriage when her children's happiness is at stake. Pain and hopelessness at the break-up of the family are further underlined by Michel's discovery of the empty flat, just a family portrait left hanging on the wall, and confirmed in the final sequence, in which his sobbing voice expresses the loss shared by the daughter. Though Kurys may respect and admire her mother's transgressive behaviour, she also identifies with the suffering of the abandoned father.

*Coup de foudre* breaks with 'tales of martyrdom and malice' by reclaiming the agency and vision of a relatively ordinary woman, who is nevertheless 'an active participant in the socio-historic universe' (Fischer 1996, 210). Whereas, in the classic maternal melodrama, the mother is conventionally punished for her transgressive behaviour, the mother here is allowed to be a complex, individuated, sexual, adult human being, determined to go her own way regardless of the effects of her decisions on others. But if the film respects and validates the choices she makes, it also grieves at the lack of a more fully present, loving mother. Though Kurys claims in life to have found making the film a liberating experience, the cinematic reconstruction of her childhood does not lead to reconciliation and empowerment but to a memorable image of the daughter's powerlessness, which she was to recreate seven years later in *La Baule les pins* (*C'est la vie*, 1990). In the end, then, the maternal legacies of *Coup de foudre* are ambivalent. The potentially feminist narratives of women's struggle for independence and for the right to prioritize a passionate female friendship are challenged by the final image of the lonely, vulnerable child, who, as the adult film-maker, inherits her mother's drive for independence, but whose representations of her own relationships with women, as in *Après l'amour* (1992), are at best problematic. The film's success with both feminist and non-feminist audiences can perhaps best be accounted for, then, by its adroit handling of point-of-view structures which allow the lost, transgressive mother to be simultaneously celebrated and critiqued.

## Notes

This article is a version of part of a larger study of Kurys' work (see Tarr, 1999, *Diane Kurys*, Manchester University Press).

1 In the 1980s, 10 per cent of French films were directed by women, a proportion reaching an unparalleled 20 per cent in the 1990s. Other women directors who have succeeded in building up a career spanning several decades include Agnès Varda, Yannick Bellon, Marguerite Duras, Nelly Kaplan, Nadine Trintignant and Coline Serreau.
2 Kurys has said in interview that she kept the names of the adults, but changed the names of the daughters.
3 French women were granted the vote in 1944 and voted for the first time in 1946, but found themselves relegated once more to the domestic sphere in postwar France.

## Selected bibliography

Austin, Guy (1996) *Contemporary French Cinema: An Introduction*, Manchester and New York, Manchester University Press, 142–70.
Beauvoir, Simone de (1948), *Le Deuxième sexe*, Paris, Gallimard.
Behr, Edward (1983) 'A Cameo of a Revolution', *Newsweek*, 9 May 1983.
Duchen, Claire (1986), *Feminism in France, From May '68 to Mitterrand*, London, Boston and Henley, Routledge & Kegan Paul.
Duchen, Claire (1994) *Women's Rights and Women's Lives in France 1944–1968*, London, Routledge.
Fischer, Lucy (1996) *Cinematernity: Film, Motherhood, Genre*, Princeton, Princeton University Press.

Fournier, Thérèse (1983) 'Diane Kurys: en amitié, le coup de foudre est aussi fort qu'en amour', *Le Nouveau F*, 14 (April).

Holmes, Diana (1996) *French Women's Writing 1848–1994*, London and Atlantic Highlands, Athlone, 193–215.

Holmlund, Christine (1991) 'When Is a Lesbian Not a Lesbian? The Lesbian Continuum and the Mainstream Femme Film', *Camera Obscura*, 25–26, 144–79.

Kael, Pauline (1984) 'The Current Cinema: *Entre Nous*', *New York Times*, 5 March 1984, 130 and 133–4.

Kaplan, E. Ann (1992), *Motherhood and Representation: The Mother in Popular Culture and Melodrama*, London and New York, Routledge.

Manceaux, Michèle (1983) 'Diane Kurys: Mon aventure-cinéma', *Marie-Claire*, (June).

Merck, Mandy (1986), '"Lianna" and the Lesbians of Art Cinema', in C. Brunsdon (ed.) *Films for Women*, London, British Film Institute Publishing, 166–75.

Pascaud, François (1983) 'Coup de foudre', *Télérama* (13 March 1983).

Perez, Michel (1983) 'Coup de foudre de Diane Kurys: La subversion dans l'innocence', *Le Matin* (9 April 1983).

Portuges, Catherine (1988) 'Seeing Subjects: Women Directors and Cinematic Autobiography', in B. Brodzki and C. Schenck (eds), *Life/Lines: Theorizing Women's Autobiography*, Ithaca and London, Cornell University Press, 338–50.

Powrie, Phil (1997), '*Coup de foudre*: Nostalgia and Lesbianism', in *French Cinema in the 1980s*, Oxford, Clarendon Press, 62–74.

Quart, Barbara (1984) '*Entre Nous*, A Question of Silence', *Cineaste*, 13 (3), 45–7.

Rochereau, Jean (1983) '*Coup de foudre* de Diane Kurys: Féminisme bien tempéré', *La Croix* (7 June 1983).

Ross, Kristin (1995) *Fast Cars, Clean Bodies: Decolonization and the Reordering of French Culture,* Cambridge, Mass., and London, MIT Press.

Straayer, Chris (1990) 'The Hypothetical Lesbian Heroine', *Jump Cut*, 35, 50–7.

Tarr, Carrie (1997), 'Changing Representations of Women in the Cinema of Diane Kurys', *Women in French Studies*, 5, 233–41.

Tarr, Carrie (1999) *Diane Kurys*, Manchester and New York, Manchester University Press.

Tranchant, Marie-Noëlle (1983) 'Au bonheur de Diane', *Le Figaro* (6 April 1983).

Vincendeau, Ginette (1995) 'Unsettling Memories', *Sight and Sound*, 5 (7), 30–2.

Walters, Suzanna Danuta (1992) *Lives Together/Worlds Apart: Mothers and Daughters in Popular Culture*, Berkeley, Los Angeles and Oxford, University of California Press.

# Appendix

## Diane Kurys (1948–): filmography

1977  *Diabolo menthe (Peppermint Soda)*
1980  *Cocktail Molotov*
1983  *Coup de foudre (At First Sight/Entre Nous)*
1987  *Un homme amoureux/A Man in Love*
1990  *La Baule les pins (C'est la vie)*

1992  *Après l'amour (After Love)*
1994  *A la folie (Six Days, Six Nights)*

## Other films cited in the text:

*Blanche et Marie,* Jacques Renard (1985)
*Le Destin de Juliette,* Aline Issermann (1983)
*La Femme de Jean,* Yannick Bellon (1974)
*Girlfriends,* Claudia Weill (USA 1977)
*Jeanne Dielmann, 23 Quai de commerce, 1080 Bruxelles,* Chantal Akerman (Belgium 1974)
*Julia,* Fred Zinnemann (USA 1977)
*Lianna,* John Sayles (USA 1983)
*Lucie Aubrac,* Claude Berri (1997).
*The Turning Point,* Herbert Ross (USA 1977)
*Une affaire de femmes,* Claude Chabrol (1988)
*L'une chante, l'autre pas,* Agnès Varda (1976)
*An Unmarried Woman,* Paul Mazursky (USA 1977)

18

# REPRESENTING THE SEXUAL IMPASSE

## Eric Rohmer's *Les Nuits de la pleine lune* (1984)

### *Bérénice Reynaud*

At an anonymous, deserted, suburban intersection, with a bleak and low horizon in the background, two cars enter our field of vision, cross and disappear. The camera sweeps past another car parked in front of a row of small grey buildings, then stops for a moment in front of the entrance of one of them. The title of the film, *Les Nuits de la pleine lune*, appears on this image. A literal translation would be 'Nights with a Full Moon', and not *Full Moon in Paris*, as the film was released in English-speaking countries, probably to capitalize on Rohmer's fashionable 'Frenchness'. As this chapter hopes to demonstrate, this translation is a misinterpretation, since the film's argument rests on the contrast between the space of Paris and that of the suburb, and the heroine's essential displacement.[1]

A woman is seen leaving the building, then the camera resumes its panning, upwards against the outside wall. The text of a proverb[2] appears on the film strip: 'Who has two wives loses his soul. Who has two houses loses his reason'; then there is a cut. On the next shot, another superimposition: 'November'; we are inside the building; a young man in shorts (Tchéky Karyo) is working out. A new cut brings us into a bedroom where a young woman (Pascale Ogier), lying down on a bed, is in the middle of a telephone conversation. Then she hangs up and rushes down the stairs, which are made simply of wooden boards so that, by placing the camera under the stairs, it is possible to see the person climbing up or down, with a sort of 'stripped' effect reminiscent of the famous Venetian blinds in *film noir* (or in Stroheim's *Foolish Wives*): Rohmer will use these stairs as an essential prop throughout the movie.

Downstairs, the woman, Louise, meets the man, Rémi: they are lovers and share a domestic relationship. However, their initial mode of introduction emphasizes the separateness of their space, their lifestyle. In the next shots,

253

we see Louise in the suburban street, wearing a flamboyant red scarf that contrasts sharply with the grey that surrounds her – then at the station – and finally on the train. In a succession of quick, elliptic shots, we see her in Place des Victoires, a fashionable neighbourhood in Paris, and in an office located in a former *grand-bourgeois* apartment. Rohmer does not dwell on Louise at work, nor Louise's relations with her co-workers. We will learn only later in the film that she works in an interior design agency, having recently graduated from art school.

Significantly, the first third of the film ('November') keeps the heroine increasingly on the move: picked up at her office by a friend, Octave (Fabrice Luchini), she first invites him to her studio in Paris where she changes her clothes, then is taken by him to his apartment 'to check the baby-sitter'. They finally go together to a party, where she quarrels with Rémi, and is brought home by her friend Camille, who lives in a nearby suburb.

In the following sequence, Louise is seen as she enters her building through a glass door, climbs the stairs, opens the door of the apartment, and, once inside, looks up: light appears under the bedroom door, proof that Rémi is awake. After a violent scene with Rémi, who physically injures himself in his anger, Louise runs upstairs; once again, the stairs in the apartment function as a sign of the separateness between the couple. In the next shot, it's already morning; Louise comes downstairs, in a skimpy 'baby doll', and joins Rémi, who has been lying on the living room couch. There, she informs him of her decision to move back one night a week to her studio in Paris, and they painstakingly manage to reach an agreement.

Their 'discussion' is not, however, a real verbal exchange: Louise, in a situation of inferiority, instead of trying to explain herself, is mostly cautious not to offend Rémi, and, saying things like 'Promise you won't be angry. . . I'm doing this *for* you, not *against* you', she sounds like the insincere *femme fatale* she is not (though probably envisioned as such by Rémi).

It is not to Rémi but to Octave that Louise attempts to formulate what she is and what she wants, but there she is hardly more successful. Early in the film, she endeavours to have a 'serious conversation' with him, but Octave, a writer, a married man with a child, keeps trying – and none too subtly, in spite of their 'old friendship' – to seduce her. Not only does he listen merely to what he wants to, but he systematically tries to insert himself into the gaps of her discourse to formulate the expression of his own desire.[3] While Louise tries to explain that she has 'not been alone a single day since [she was] fifteen', because there had been 'no transition between [her] boyfriends', and she now feels the need to 'experience loneliness' – Octave interprets this as an expression of her dissatisfaction with the quality, not only of her current lover, but of all the former ones as well: 'You love men who are beneath you.' What Louise strives to express is the basic contradiction of her own desire (which formulates the classic plight of the hysteric, according to Freud and Lacan): both a feeling of being 'crowded' by men – 'I am too much loved' ('On m'aime trop') – and her utter dependence on the Other's desire – 'It's the other's desire that causes mine.' When she talks of her relations with Rémi she uses the same parameters, centring her discourse on *her* perception of Rémi's desire for her: 'He loves me *too much*. When I am loved too much, I love less.' But she adds, 'a woman never remains unmoved when a man makes an effort'. So what links her to Rémi is also what estranges her from him. Interestingly enough, Rémi's desire, taken for granted throughout the movie remains opaque until the end, when he finally states clearly what *he* wants, after having been presented mostly through what he *did not* want (going out, dancing, spending too much time separated from Louise, living in Paris, etc.).

As for Octave, his perception of Louise as an object of desire is also contradictory, and rests on the half-formulated question of how *he* fits within *her* desire (Octave's relations with women are not based on 'What do women want?' but 'Do women want *me?*'). What baffles Octave is that, while Louise seeks his company and spends a lot of time with him, she refuses to sleep with him. 'Carnal relationships do not interest me', she says, adding 'I like you, but I'm not *attracted* to you.' Octave's response is revealing: 'There's something virginal in you. I cannot stand having another man touch you. Especially the ones you go out with, who are of an absolutely pathetic bestiality.' Like Molière's Don Juan, who, talking of a happily married young bride he intends to seduce, comments 'My love sprang out of jealousy', Octave's desire for Louise is supported by other men's desire for her. His character seems also to have been inspired by the seducer in Alfred de Musset's *Les Caprices de Marianne* (himself called Octave), who deserts the heroine at the end, after the man who really loved her has been killed; this reference adds another tragic overtone to the end of the film: will Octave remain Louise's friend, now that she has experienced rejection?

Early in the film, Octave declares that he is fascinated by the 'physical, practical, material' aspect of Louise's personality, which he assumes he is the only one to perceive. As in the triangle described by literary critic Girard, 'for a vain man to desire an object, it is enough for him to be convinced that this object is already desired by a third party. . . . The mediator is a *rival* produced by vanity . . . whose desire . . . makes the object infinitely desirable to the subject' (1961, 20–1). Octave desires Louise because of all the other men who desire her, but at the same time is conceited enough to think that he is the only one to see her 'as she is'. However, in order to keep himself in this position of high priest of Venus, he cannot touch her. This is probably the position where Louise, consciously or not, wants him, for she needs his desire to be kept at a certain distance, to feel wanted as a woman. This precarious equilibrium is constantly threatened by Octave's jealousy, addressed to Louise's other sex partners: 'It's intolerable that you grant others what you refuse *me*', he says, as she prepares to go on a date with the saxophone player. 'It drives me mad that a part of you escapes me.' 'It's only a little part . . .' answers Louise. She knows that Octave does *not* desire her; what he wants in her is what 'the others' have – or think they have: the 'little part' she denies Octave is what would satisfy his vanity and, hence, is not part of herself at all.[4]

While Louise feels 'crowded' by Rémi's love for her, she feels denied by Octave's 'mediated desire' (Girard 1961, 33). In both cases they want 'too much': Rémi loves her 'too much' – and, since love is a demand for love, he wants too much love – and Octave wants to possess 'the whole of her' – i.e. some imaginary projection created out of his vanity – which, in both cases, is an impossibility.

Rémi in his confusion between demand (which can be fulfilled) and desire (which cannot) imprisons Louise in a network of contradictory demands which she cannot meet (it is the typical ordeal imposed by the obsessional upon the hysteric). He wants Louise to give him *what she has* (her time), while in love one can only give what one does not have. Lacan summarizes this situation as follows: 'I love you, but because inexplicably I love in you something more than you – the *objet petit a* – I mutilate you' (Lacan 1978, 268) and its corollary: 'I give myself to you, but this gift of my person – Oh, mystery! – is changed inexplicably into a gift of shit' (*ibid.*). Symptomatically, he is totally unprepared to accept her giving him what she wants to give him – a teapot she bought on her 'day off' in Paris – even though (and maybe *because*) he *needs* a teapot. 'How much do I owe you?' he says, unwrapping the present.

Octave, on the other hand, suffers from the paradox of Don Juan: he intends to take (*mille e tre*) women one after the other, but does not understand that, being 'not-whole', they resist ultimate possession. For Lacan, this essential 'not-wholeness' of 'the woman' is caused by the fact that there is always something in her which escapes phallic *jouissance*, and gives her access to a non-phallic, 'other', jouissance. He develops this in his commentary on Zeno's paradox of the 'impossible' race between Achilles and the tortoise (as applied to the 'non-relation' between Achilles and the captive Briseis in Homer's *Iliad*): 'When Achilles has stepped forward, scored with Briseis, the latter, like the tortoise, has advanced a bit, because she is *not-whole*, not wholly his. Something remains of her' (1975, 13).

In addition, in the later scene in the cafe, Octave displays a sort of hysterical identification with Louise by sharing with her the 'anxiety' caused in her by the presence of nature (contextually, 'nature' means suburb, as opposed to Paris; psychoanalytically, they both express a common 'fear of the void'). So Octave's unconscious strategy ends up in a double denial of sexual difference: (1) Louise is, like a man, *wholly in* a place where he could successfully reach her, *if only she would let him*; and (2) Octave is, like a woman, subjected to an hysterical need of filling the void (in the discourse of others).

As for Louise, 'devoured' as she is by these two contradictory sets of desires, her only possible escape, beyond her desire to 'experience loneliness'

– which may or may not be 'fake'[5] – remains hysteria, whose particular plight
for the woman is to deny men's castration *in her body*, to provide a sort of
support for the foibles of men's desire. In the case of Louise, she physically
breaks down in tears, first with Rémi – in the scene after the party, when his
'too-much-desire' ('trop-de-désir') suffocates and angers her, then, at the
end, when she has to face his lessened desire ('moins-de-désir') for her – and
then in an extremely significant moment with Octave, when the latter tries
to rape her verbally and physically to prevent her from meeting the
saxophone player.

If I have, at the beginning of this chapter, insisted on the multiple displacements of the heroine up and downstairs, in the street, in the train, in
cars (always driven by others), etc., it is because these various moves in space
constitute the axis of the film, and, while Rohmer's superbly mastered style
eliminates all 'unimportant' moments, he has carefully kept those when
Louise is 'in transit'. Even in the important scene when she encounters Rémi
in a café in Paris, she has to climb down the stairs that lead to the bathroom
to see him in the telephone booth, while to catch sight, at the same
moment, of the unknown woman, all Octave has to do is to remain seated at
his table. Not only is Louise 'commuting' between Paris and the suburb –
between her job and social life, on the one hand, her domestic cohabitation
with Rémi, on the other – but she is perpetually essentially displaced, as the
last sequence of the movie proves.

Her date with the saxophone player itself is shown as a series of displacements (on the young man's motorbike) between various locations: a bar, a
disco. But the essential thing is that he 'takes her places', before she 'takes
him home': in other words, the saxophone player does exactly what the
sedentary, homebound Rémi does not do. But, once sex is over, while he is
asleep, Louise is restless and cannot close her eyes. She finds it unbearable to
stay in the same room as the young man. When trying to explain her
dilemma to the insomniac illustrator she meets in the cafe where she is
waiting for the first train to Marne-la-Vallée, she says 'I am claustrophobic'.
But what makes her so, if not the too-violent expression of the desire of the
Other? Significantly enough, the only Friday night when she feels like
returning to the suburban apartment is when Rémi does not want her any
more, when there is no longer another's desire to suffocate her. 'The direction's inverted now', she adds. 'The exile is here [in Paris], the centre there
[in the suburb].' But the centre, as she will discover, is nothing but a void
that she will flee from by the first available train.

Louise's displacement is not anecdotal, but structural. It is as a woman, in
her relationship with men, that she is essentially displaced. Rémi represents
a certain form of patriarchal, patrilocal relation to space: he lives where he
works, or rather has transported his home to the town where he works (as an
urban development executive); he has put his young lover in his home, and
expects from her companionship, domesticity (even in a modern 'yuppie'

form where it would consist, for example, of playing tennis with him every Saturday morning as Marianne – the woman he eventually falls in love with – probably does) – in brief, the traditional male expectations. Even though Louise tries to creatively inhabit the space by putting a work table where she pursues her 'own work' as a designer, she is only 'passing through' a space where she has no real right and has to leave as soon as the relation breaks up.[6]

The second form of displacement is the one performed by Octave's fantasies, which cast Louise both as a virgin and as a sexless being who could be entirely possessed, a position that is literally untenable.

But why is that? Gayatri Chakravorty Spivak notes that 'throughout his work, Derrida asks us to notice that *all* human beings are irreducibly displaced although, in a discourse that privileges the centre, women alone have been diagnosed as such' (1983, 170). The reason, once again, has to be found in Freud:

> The boy-child is irreducibly and permanently displaced from the mother, the object of his desire. But the girl-child is doubly displaced. The boy is born as a subject that desires to copulate with the object. . . . The little girl is born an uncertain role-player – a little man playing a little girl or vice versa. The other she desires is 'wrong' and must be changed.
>
> (Spivak 1983, 172–3)

But, as Spivak points out, 'the deconstructive discourse of man (like the phallocentric one) can declare its own displacement [as the phallocentric its placing] by taking the woman as object or figure . . .' (*ibid.*, 173).

So the correct question that a feminist should ask is: 'what is man that the itinerary of his desire creates such a text?' (*ibid.*, 186). By contrast, the question that haunts Louise – 'what do men want from me?' – does not allow her to address men's desire correctly. In her self-centredness (she tries to deny the Other's desire), she does not understand that her only possible centre is a void, because she is essentially displaced. As the man she meets in the bar at night reminds her, 'in each of these apartments you have a man. But these men, *they must have their word to say in the matter.*' Such is Louise's mistake: she was so busy defending herself against a certain representation she had of masculine desire ('I'm loved too much') that the reality of *her* alienation in Rémi's desire totally escaped her. In his discussion of the 'non-relation' between Achilles and Briseis/the tortoise (a metaphor for *sexual impasse*), Lacan concludes that it is through a conceptualization of this operation in space that mankind has been able to quantify the real. The mathematical notion of 'real numbers', for example,[7] has been defined through a study of the 'smaller and smaller' steps that the two actors of the fable take without ever meeting, 'except in infinity' (1975, 13). Till the bitter 'return of the real' of the ending, Louise keeps missing this infinity because, as a woman, she is seduced, and even mesmerized, by men's fetishizing gaze. She lets them define her as an object of their desire, and, as such, lets herself be posited within the phallic function, where, being both inside and outside – not wholly in, says Lacan – she is constantly rejected at the periphery, dislocated, denied, displaced.

Alain Philippon astutely notes that 'Louise joins the list of the women losers in Rohmer's cinema. . . . As such, she still partakes of a cinema that posits itself in the post-feminist discourse and libertarian utopias and fetishizes woman's body only to signify its defeat' (1984, 42). He adds that he does not read this as 'misogyny, but generalized bitterness' (*ibid.*) as applied to the 1980s. But it is true that, when their desire confronts that of men, women usually lose in Rohmer's movies, and are often ridiculed (Maud, Haydée the collector, Chloé, Sabine who wants a beautiful wedding, etc.), while man's own desire is measured *to the extent* he resists, or denies that of the woman. The only exception is the luminous ending of *Le Rayon vert* where Marie Rivière's ridiculous stubbornness eventually pays off. In contrast to Louise at the beginning of the film, Marie has experienced loneliness, as she perceives the Other's desire as a lack (although she has her moments of hysteria, too). Knowing how awkward she is with others, but still going on, Marie is a comical character *à la* Keaton, while Louise, who thinks (because men led her to think so, in a game of mutual deception) that she masters the rules of the game, is never ridiculous, but superbly tragic.

The difference between Marie and Louise is both scandalous and simple: Marie has grace ('a la grâce'), while Louise does not. For Rohmer, the difficult question of grace is an ethical problem, not a religious one. As early as 1953, discussing the cinema of Renoir, Hitchcock and Rossellini, he wrote: 'If art is, finally, moral, it is not by discovering the way to an abstact equality of liberty, but exalting the exception, made only possible by the rule, and . . . everybody's inequality with regards to fate, even salvation' (1984, 73).[8] Rohmer's originality has been to address this classical issue as a *modern* concern, in purely cinematic terms. For him, the interest of cinema is to create a new ontology: not to show things differently, but show different things. And, instead of describing cinema as an art of illusion, he postulates the notion of *truth:* 'from the confrontation of [my] discourse with the characters' discourse and behaviour, a certain truth is born, different from the literality of texts and gestures: the truth of the film' (*ibid.*, 90).

Louise's alienation from grace can best be read in the situations where (in contrast to Marie, who might be obnoxious, but never cheats) she is guilty of a certain *mauvaise foi* – whose expression is not to be found in the character's discourse (we agree with her) nor in a certain falseness conveyed by the performance (the actress is absolutely, breathtakingly, tragically *sincere*, and Pascale Ogier's interpretation is one of the beauties of the film), but in the heroine's relationship to the off-screen space (*le hors-champ*).

From this point of view, two scenes are crucial. In the first, Louise is in her studio, on a Friday night, alone. Through a telephone call, her date for the evening (with an unnamed person) is cancelled. She then tries, unsuccessfully, to contact Octave, and two other men. Finally, she resorts to reading in bed for the rest of the evening. There is a fade-out, and the next shot shows her having breakfast in bed, while playing a sentimental record by Edith Piaf. Octave returns her call, and she explains to him how much she welcomed the opportunity to spend an evening alone, for a change.

The way the previous sequence is directed, however, contradicts her. I am reminded of two other films where the collaboration between a director and an actress manages to convey, through very subtle signs, the growing anxiety and distress of a woman trapped alone *in her own space.* One is the long, static shot of Jean Eustache's *La Maman et la putain*, where Bernadette Lafont remains in her living room, listening to an old record, after Jean-Pierre Léaud and Françoise Lebrun have departed together. The other is the scene when Delphine Seyrig in Chantal Akerman's *Jeanne Dielman* waits for a customer (who may or may not be late: we will never know). Suddenly the space these women inhabit, which, in all three cases, is specifically shown as their emotional base, becomes too small: since they have mentally projected themselves into an outside where, at this specific moment, they are not wanted. Their own imaginary, so to speak, devours the frame of the image: the space they are left with is no longer the space of their desire, which is outside, and extends within the boundaries of the frame, as if the inside was 'emptied' by the outside. Significantly, all three women try to conceal to themselves this displacement from their own centre, but Louise is the one whose *mauvaise foi* is the most apparent, since it is due more to vanity than courage.

The second scene occurs in the second third of the film ('December'): Louise's life becomes more and more dependent on what happens off-screen while she continues to deny that this is so. In the café, while she is in the ladies' room, there is a significant shot showing Octave looking with surprise at something we never see. Later, in his conversation with Louise, we will learn it was a woman, and possibly Camille, which would have made her the partner of Rémi's unexpected Parisian rendezvous. Louise's *mauvaise foi* is obvious in the next scene, where Camille comes to visit her in Marne-la-Vallée. Since she denies to herself (and to Octave), until the end, that Rémi could have a sex life outside her own field of vision,[9] Louise cannot confront her friend, but she is haunted by what might have happened, at another place and another time, between Rémi and her. In directing their encounter, Rohmer remembered the lessons learnt in watching Hitchcock's films: the bus ride undertaken by Sylvia Sydney's kid brother in *Sabotage*, for example, becomes a real nightmare for the spectator because we know there is a time bomb in his satchel: the invisible 'contaminates', so to speak, the visible. We have a similar situation in Louise's encounter with Camille: the banality of the gestures and words becomes the signifier of Louise's anxiety, which

*Les Nuits de la pleine lune* – above: Louise (Pascale Ogier) and Rémi (Tchéky Karyo); below: Louise and Octave (Fabrice Luchini).

revolves not about the here and now, but the unfathomable space off-screen. *Mauvaise foi*, again: Louise wants so much to be reassured that she will gratefully accept *any* sort of explanation: Camille's new boyfriend is not Rémi, but some man whom we never see. The anxiety generated in the off-screen space of the Other is allayed by some mere signifiers (Camille's story about her trip to Italy) emitted from the same space.[10]

Trapped within her own imaginary, Louise forgets that she was initially misled by Octave, and that the real question is not: who is Camille's new boyfriend? but: who was the woman with Rémi that day?

The issue of Louise's exclusion from grace, her *mauvaise foi*, her displacement, can also be addressed if one substitutes *language* for *grace*. The question of grace in its relation to women has been of particular interest to Rohmer throughout his career as a critic and film-maker, especially since his discovery of Roberto Rossellini's *Stromboli* (1950), about which he wrote, in 1950: 'I have seen very few contemporary works that exalt so magnificently, so directly, the Christian idea of grace . . . that proclaim more openly *man's* misery without God' (1984, 135, my stress). But this *man* is actually a woman, Ingrid Bergman, upon whom is thrown the burden of *visually representing* this misery. 'It is quite meaningful', adds Rohmer, 'to compare *Stromboli* to [Alfred Hitchcock's] *Under Capricorn* . . . where we see the same performer climbing the long path that connects despair and self-loathing to peace and a restored good conscience' (*ibid.*, 136–7). But Bergman's erotic attractiveness in both films is more apparent before than after the redemption, and we know that there is no 'salvation' for most of Rohmer's heroines who, left to their own devices, fail in what they are doing, and are excluded from what they want most.

It seems, thus, that the image of the woman has to be understood as a signifier whose function is cinematically to represent the desire of the film-maker. I do *not* mean – as a more classical feminist analysis would – the object of his desire, but *his desire itself*, which opens up an entirely different set of identifications. Desire being born in language, its visual representation is highly problematic. The more traditional way of doing it – which I will call the 'fetishistic approach' – is based on the notion of 'visual pleasure' (to quote a well-known interpretation) and consists in glamourizing the traditional objects of male desire: women's bodies, as wholes (in narrative movies), or as collections of parts (in pornographic cinema). From this point of view – which I do not want to exclude, since cinematic perception operates on different simultaneous levels – the 'defeat' of the woman has a specific meaning: a woman is never so desirable (for the spectator) as when she is crying (waiting to be comforted) or in jeopardy (waiting to be saved). Her defeat means she is lacking something, that only a man (and/or the Grace of God) can provide.

Rohmer's films, however, are not confined to this primitive, fetishistic level. Instead of presenting his heroines as pure objects of desire, he makes desiring subjects out of them and it is their desire – and not the man's – that constitutes the motor of the fiction. The prospective groom in *Le Beau mariage*, or Rémi in *Les Nuits de la pleine lune*, do not speak until the end of the film, while the aviator in *La Femme de l'aviateur*, or the playboy in *Pauline à la plage*, never express clearly what they want. In Rohmer's films, it is the women who act the film-maker's desire. And how is desire best represented? – in its failure. Not only because 'there is no sexual relation' (Lacan 1975, 35) and, as such, it 'cannot be *written*' (*ibid.*, my stress), but also because of the specificity of cinematic representation, its use of space and time:

> Desire is one of the most fertile themes in cinema: it requires the spreading before our eyes of the whole spatial and temporal distance which lies between hunter and prey. The act of waiting is enjoyed in itself ['l'attente jouit d'elle-même'], and the tender whiteness of a throat,[11] or, as in Stroheim's *Greed*, the sparkling of gold, are adorned with a seduction forever renewed for the impotent desire. This is something that we, the spectators, repeatedly experience in front of these impalpable and fleeting images that arrest our gaze, both gratifying and deceiving it.
>
> (Rohmer 1984, 57)

Once desire is fulfilled, not only is the object of desire destroyed as such – it is now an 'object of possession', much less interesting to represent – but also the aesthetic perspective, when 'the act of waiting [which] is enjoyed for itself', no longer exists. This is what Proust expresses in a well-known passage of *Swann's Way:*

> And it was Swann who, before she allowed her [face], as though in spite of herself, to fall upon his lips, held it back at a little distance, between his hands. . . . Perhaps . . . he was fixing upon the face of an Odette not yet posessed, nor even kissed by him, which he was seeing for the last time, the comprehensive gaze with which, on the day of his departure, a traveller hopes to bear away with him in memory of a landscape he is leaving forever.
>
> (Proust 1981, 255)

However, while it is possible, in a literary work, to represent a man's desire as perpetually frustrated (Werther, Swann), when the same thing happens in film, the man becomes a highly comical character (the tradition of the 'Hollywood clowns', for example, is based on that assumption) – hence the difficulty of adapting a romantic novel for the screen without being mildly ridiculous. The filmic signifiers are organized around the phallic determination of the gaze: what a man sees, he wants, and what he wants, he gets (and if he does not get it, he does not dwell on it, but burns his house, and disappears from the deigetic space, like John Wayne in John Ford's *The Man Who Shot Liberty Valance*). Conversely, when desire, with its avatars, pains and failures, is born by a woman, she becomes a tragic figure, an immense source of aesthetic enjoyment.[12] It is not possible, however, to use a woman's image to express a man's desire without substantially altering the parameters of this desire. For one thing, the image of the woman, being so often used to signify the object of desire, and not its subject, retains some of this determination, and thus expresses a contradictory statement: 'I want, but I am wanted as well' (and not necessarily by the same person) – a position that Louise, like most heroines of fiction, finds untenable. It is untenable, because it is not real. In *Les Nuits de la pleine lune*, we see a fictional character struggling to have the right to exist on her own terms, to extricate herself from the representations thrown upon her by men: Rémi, Octave, Rohmer. Louise's plight (to have her independence and her man at the same time) is real enough; but what is at stake is not the defeat of 'a real woman', but the essential limit (what Lacan calls 'la butée') of desire itself. As is often the case, the image of a woman is used to suture a system of representation:

> In so far as the system closes over that moment of difference or impossibility, what gets set up in its place is essentially an image of the woman. . . . The system is constituted as a system or whole only as a function of what it is attempting to evade and it is within this process that the woman finds herself symbolically placed

says Jacqueline Rose (1986, 219), who adds, quoting Lacan: 'On the one hand the woman becomes, or is produced, precisely as what [man] is not, that is, sexual difference, and on the other as what he has to renounce, that is *jouissance*' (Lacan 1970–1, 9–10).

Is it not, then, because Louise says to Octave: 'I have more fun than [Rémi] does' that she 'has to' be punished at the end? This surplus of *jouissance* (for which she will pay dearly) is also what irritates Octave. His desire for her being perpetually frustrated, he tries to fill the void opened by this frustration with a constant flow of words and rationalizations (another example of *mauvaise foi*). In his hysterical identification with the young woman, he wants to keep her virginal, wants her desire to be as unfulfilled as his (this is why he tries to convince her that the objects of her enjoyment are worthless).

Three operations are taking place here: (1) Rémi will actually frustrate Louise's desire because she does not conform to his definition of an object of desire; (2) Octave wants to reduce Louise, whose 'excess of *jouissance*' he cannot stand, to the same state of unsatisfaction as his; (3) Rohmer has to posit Louise's desire as impossible to satisfy, in order to make her the tragic figure that represents his desire (all desires) as an object of aesthetic contemplation. In other words, at three different narrative levels, Louise's character is produced as that of an hysteric. This is a classical suture derived from the clinical discourse, where the woman's excess of *jouissance* is evacuated as *lack*, and made implicitly responsible for the sexual impasse. But Lacan – even before identifying, in *Encore* (1975, 17), the phallic function as the main obstacle to sexual *jouissance* – raised 'the specific question of why [the hysteric] can sustain her desire only as an unsatisfied desire, "a question" [left] entirely out of the psychoanalytic field', and out of all systems of representation as well, a flaw that can be attributed only to 'some kind of original sin in analysis' (1978, 12).[13]

Women are, as always, paying for this original sin – they are neither within, nor without the symbolic order: language, grace etc. This is especially true for the defeated heroines of Rohmer's movies. They bear the burden of representing the sexual impasse, the non-communication between the sexes, and men are for them, at best, a lost object.[14]

*Translations of Rohmer quotations are by the author*

## Notes

1 The representation of the suburb is relatively rare in French, and this is why *Les Nuits de la pleine lune* is also important at a sociological level. Significantly, Rohmer's 1987 film *L'Ami de mon amie* takes place entirely in the suburbs, except for a few nondescript scenes: it is Paris that represents an alien, vaguely 'boring' space.

2 The credits state that the film is the fourth in the series 'Comedies and Proverbs'. Rohmer likes to connect his films in 'series'. The first (from *La Boulangère de Monceau* to *L'Amour l'après-midi*) is entitled 'Moral Tales'. 'Comedies and Proverbs' ('proverb', in this case, meaning a short comedy developing the moral applications of a proverb) started with *La Femme de l'aviateur.*

> My films generate each other within a closed system, like in the 'Moral Tales', in which I had pre-decided the ending. The 'Comedies and Proverbs' are also a closed system, even if the ending is not pre-decided. The 'Moral Tales' were films in which I started with a theme and created variations upon it, the 'Comedies and Proverbs' are films in which I have looked for a theme. It happens that I have more or less found the theme of the first four 'Comedies and Proverbs' [*La Femme de l'aviateur, Le Beau mariage, Pauline à la plage, Les Nuits de la pleine lune*], you can see the similitude of the situations, the character always in his [*sic*] attempt, and the film begins in the place where it ends. Now, I would like to direct . . . a new series of 'Comedies and Proverbs' that will have an open ending, i.e. there wouldn't be a final failure, nor a return to the departure point.
>
> (Rohmer 1985, 92)

3 This is a paradigmatic situation that Lacan describes as such: 'A lack is encountered by the subject in the Other, in the very intimation that the Other makes to him in his discourse. In the intervals (gaps) of the discourse of the Other, this is what emerges. . . . *He is saying this to me but what does he want?*' (1978, 214)

4 'The real Madame de Rénal is the one Julien desires. The real Mathilde the one he does not. In the first case, we are dealing with passion; in the second with vanity' (Girard, 1961, 33).

5 For want of space, I refer the reader to the article by G. C. Spivak mentioned in the bibliography for further consideration of the relationship between women's 'fake orgasm' and their displacement. I have also addressed similar issues in a research paper, 'Briseis' Desire', presented in April 1983 at the Whitney Museum, New York.

6 It seems almost trivial to say so, but unfair not to mention it, *Les Nuits de la pleine lune* can be read as a homage to Virginia Woolf's pertinent conclusions in *A Room of One's Own*.

7 The mathematic notion of 'real numbers' expresses *quantities*, as opposed to imaginary numbers. It is the progress (or failure) of desire that makes space quantifiable for the mathematician, as it makes it an aesthetic category for the film-maker (see Rohmer 1984, 57).

8 The films discussed in Rohmer's essay (1984 – initially published in *Cahiers du cinéma* under the name of Maurice Scherer) are Renoir's *Le Carrosse d'or*, Hitchcock's *I Confess* and Rossellini's *Europe 51*.

9 Because of that naïve belief, Louise will be totally blind to the presence of her future rival. The first time Marianne appears in the cinematic field, it is as an anonymous attractive young woman, dressed in white, standing in the centre of the frame when Louise and Octave arrive at the party. But they do not see her, and greet Louise's friend Camille who is dancing next to her. Later, Marianne will be identified as a friend of Camille, and briefly introduced to a sulking Rémi, before disappearing once again from the frame. Finally, when Camille drives Louise back home, Marianne is sitting silently in the back of the car. While Louise discusses the difficulties of her relationship with Rémi, and even suggests to Camille that she goes out with the latter, the shot is a point of view shot from the car's windshield, and Marianne is kept out of our field of vision, as she is from Louise's. This precision is important to underline Louise's 'emotional blindness' (she does not want to see), but also to explain the function of the off-screen space in Rohmer's cinema, which is never arbitrary, but constructed from elements already presented, albeit in a deceptive manner, in the cinematic field. In his analysis of Marcel Carné's *Les Portes de la nuit*, for example, he writes: 'in the warehouse scene, Prévert's text [the dialogue between Yves Montand and Natalie Nattier] is weak because it depends, like a theatre narration, on an imaginary world located "beyond" that of the film. . . . One has to find a way to integrate the word, not inside the world which is filmed, but *inside the film itself*' (1984, 39, my stress). Rohmer has understood particularly well that the 'imaginary field' in cinema is created through a constant dialectic between the visible and the invisible.

10 For Lacan the Other is the guarantee of the truth. But 'there is no Other of the Other', i.e. nobody to guarantee that the Other is telling the truth. Camille's story, of course, cannot really be checked.

11 This excerpt comes after a long discussion of Murnau's *Nosferatu* (1922).

12 Mary Ann Doane notes that, in some cases, the burden of representing desire can be borne by a man: 'In the love story, the male undergoes a kind of feminization by contamination – in other words, he is to a certain degree emasculated by his very presence in a feminized genre. As Roland Barthes claims (in *A Lover's Discourse* (1978) translated by Richard Howard, New York, Hill & Wang, 14) there is always something about the lover which is 'feminized': 'in any man who utters the other's absence, *something feminine* is declared' (Doane 1987, 97).

13 Since I was not entirely satisfied with Sheridan's translation, I substituted mine (in the italicized part of the sentence).
14 This conclusion represents only part of a work in progress I am currently under taking about the representation of women in cinema. The first part of this research was presented in lecture form at the Whitney Museum on 12 May 1987, under the title 'Delacroix's *Death of Sardanapalus:* A Careful Misreading'.

*Special thanks to David Jacobson for reading the first draft and for his help in locating references, and to Jackie Raynal.*

## Selected bibliography

Doane, Mary Ann (1987) *The Desire to Desire*, Bloomington and Indianapolis, Indiana University Press.

Girard, Raymond (1961) *Mensonge romantique et vérité romanesque*, Paris, Grasset.

Lacan, Jacques (1970–1) 'Le Séminaire XVIII: D'un discours qui ne serait pas du semblant', unpublished typescript.

Lacan, Jacques (1975) *Encore*, Paris, Le Seuil.

Lacan, Jacques (1978) *The Four Fundamental Concepts of Psychoanalysis*, trans. Alan Sheridan, New York, Norton.

Philippon, Alain (1984) 'Les Fantômes de la liberté', *Cahiers du cinéma*, 364.

Proust, Marcel (1981) *Swann's Way*, trans. C. K. Scott Moncrieff and Terence Kilmartin, New York, Vintage.

Rohmer, Eric (1984) *Le Goût de la beauté* (ed.) A. Narboni, Paris, Editions de l'Etoile.

Rohmer, Eric (1985) 'Secrets de laboratoire', *Cahiers du cinéma*, 371/372.

Rose, Jacqueline (1986) *Sexuality in the Field of Vision*, London, Verso.

Spivak, Gayatri C. (1983) 'Displacement and the Discourse of Woman', in M. Krupnick (ed.) *Displacement: Derrida and After*, Bloomington, Indiana University Press.

Woolf, Virginia (1929) *A Room of One's Own*, London, Harcourt, Brace & Janovitch.

## Appendix

### *Eric Rohmer (1920–): filmography*

See Chapter 14, on *Ma nuit chez Maud*, for full filmography.

### *Other films cited in the text*

*L'Ami de mon amie*, Eric Rohmer (1988)
*Le Beau mariage*, Eric Rohmer (1982)
*Le Carrosse d'or (Golden Coach)*, Jean Renoir (Italy 1952)
*La Femme de l'aviateur*, Eric Rohmer (1980)
*Foolish Wives*, Erich von Stroheim (USA 1921)
*Europe 51*, Roberto Rossellini (Italy 1952)
*Greed*, Erich von Stroheim (USA 1923)
*I Confess*, Alfred Hitchcock (USA 1953)

*Jeanne Dielman, 23 quai du Commerce, 1080 Bruxelles*, Chantal Akerman (Belgium 1975)

*La Maman et la putain* (*The Mother and the Whore*), Jean Eustache (1973)

*The Man Who Shot Liberty Valance*, John Ford (USA 1961)

*Les Nuits de la pleine lune* (*Full Moon in Paris*), Eric Rohmer (1984)

*Pauline à la plage*, Eric Rohmer (1983)

*Les Portes de la nuit* (*Gates of the Night*), Marcel Carné (1946)

*Le Rayon vert* (*The Green Ray* [UK]; *Summer* [USA]), Eric Rohmer (1986)

*Sabotage*, Alfred Hitchcock (USA 1949)

*Stromboli*, Roberto Rossellini (Italy 1950)

*Under Capricorn*, Alfred Hitchcock (USA 1949)

# 19

# BEYOND THE GAZE AND INTO *FEMME-FILMÉCRITURE*

## Agnès Varda's *Sans toit ni loi* (1985)

*Susan Hayward*

Agnès Varda's filmic production has been little heralded by feminist critics, least of all by those in the United States and the United Kingdom where her work has been dismissed by such critics as the late Claire Johnston as reactionary and certainly not feminist.[1] Curiously, Varda's work is often passed over in silence in anthologies on women's film – and yet she herself claims to be an avowed feminist. The debate here, however, is not going to centre on the global issue of a feminist cinema but rather will endeavour to demonstrate how Varda's 1985 film *Sans toit ni loi* is as much political as it is – *and because it is* – feminist in its conception and message.

Implicit in Jacqueline Rose's discussion (1986, 203ff.) of Comolli and Metz's film theory debate is the idea that, for film to be political, it must eschew its mainstream proclivity to reproduce an 'imaginary identity' (203). In other words cinema which 'appears as a type of analogical machine for the programming of identity' (203) cannot be political. In a somewhat similar vein, Claire Johnston argues that 'The camera was developed in order to accurately reproduce reality and safeguard the bourgeois notion of realism which was being replaced in painting' (1976, 214). She also points out that a direct consequence in cinema of this 'law of verisimilitude' is 'the repression of the image of woman as woman and the celebration of her non-existence' (211). Elsewhere, but very much connected to this notion of non-existence, Maureen Turim defines film as a presence which speaks and hides absence (1986, 234). Film, unlike theatre, is the absent spectacle – the spectacle of absence. In this respect, therefore, it would seem to provide the perfect vehicle of expression for women as film-makers and makers of feminist films. As Jutta Brückner so astutely points out: 'the cinema offers us a place to focus our own desires for particular images, to explore our own experience of linguistic and visual absence, for we have always been made into images instead of acquiring our own' (1985, 121) Similarly, Johnston proposes that

269

feminist film cannot rely purely and simply on a retransmission of women's issues, it has to go further and take male and Hollywood iconography to task. And in essence this sums up her reproach to Varda in the past – i.e. that her film-making practices could be recuperated into the dominant ideology.[2]

*Sans toit ni loi* is a reinscription of an original and real text. Varda's first idea – to make a film about road people/vagrants (male and female) in the winter, who perish from the cold – became substantially modified when she encountered a hitchhiking vagabond, Settina. The starting point, then, is this young woman's experience. However, the representation of this experi-ence – through a series of flashbacks which, at times, even become imbri-cated – is intentionally non-realistic. Essentially the structure of the film, which is made up of forty-seven episodes, takes to task the issue of image construction or, as Tim Corrigan puts it, 'the fetishizing action of the male perspective' (1986, 267). By extension, Varda's cinematic writing – *cinécri-ture*[3] as she terms it – goes counter to the established canons of western film-making practices.

Let us take the issue of image construction first. The film is about a young woman, Mona, who has perished from the cold. Upon this corpse, numerous persons attempt to transfix a meaning (already a contribution). Eighteen visions of Mona are presented by those who saw her. However, as the film makes transparently clear, Mona refuses to be co-opted into any image. In her refusal of all social discourses – which her preponderant mutism serves to reinforce – she defies identification, will not be made other. Her peripatetic and solitary existence is a deliberate choice ('being alone is good', 'cham-pagne and the road, that's good', 'I move') and functions metonymically for her unfixability and unnamability.[4] Her rejection of social and sexual pro-ductivity, which her choice implies, erases the hegemonic image of women – she leaves no trace, as Varda's voice-over comments: 'this death leaves no traces'. The film is a series of gazes, of one-way exchanges from different specular positions. Each contributor fixes their gaze not on Mona but on their perception of Mona as a figure of their desire. As such, each portrait offered up to the spectator is revealing of the relator and not of the one related. The effect is to empty the mirror of ascribed meanings. Male discourses (whether uttered by men or women) cannot produce her identity. Mona's indepen-dence from a fixed identity is an assertion of her *altérité* (her otherness); her autonomy from male fetishization is an obligation to recognize her *différence* – woman as an authentic and not a second sex.[5] As an authentic sex, Mona both attracts and repels – meanwhile she remains indifferent, impassive to the violence of these responses. On a basic level these two responses originate from our sense of smell – and indeed sex and smell are very closely inter-related. Symbolic of Mona's indifference to others' reactions is her very filth, her uncleanliness and smelliness. And it is in Jean-Pierre's flashback-'portrait' of her that we can perceive most clearly what Varda is saying about image construction.

His 'narration' is imbricated first (about half-way through the film) in the 'narration' of the paleontologue Mme Landier (the tree specialist who is also his boss) and then latterly (towards the very end of the film) in Yolande's (the maidservant to his aunt) 'narration'. His initial meeting with Mona is via his boss who tells him to go and have a look at her, as if she were a specimen (one of *her* specimens). Mona steps out of Mme Landier's car – Jean-Pierre has just circled halfway round it peering in as if she were in a specimen glass – her filthy hair whips around her face in the wind (she looks almost Medusa-like) and she asks him if she frightens him. The next shot is of Jean-Pierre in his apartment with his wife, Eliane. She has just emerged from a bath (!) and is wrapped around with a towel. Jean-Pierre tells her about Mona and how her hair reminded him of his wife's; at this juncture he is fondling her hair – Eliane rightly reads the subtext and refuses to make love, obliging him instead to attend to her toenails.

To Mona's filth is immediately contrasted Eliane's pristine cleanliness. The sexual transference speaks for itself: physically aroused by Mona he attempts to gratify his desire through his wife. What attracted him? Doubtless, Mona's evident availability so sharply contrasted with his wife's persistent refusals. Conversely, what prevented him from acting? Mona's refusal, through her filth, to signify for him his image of woman. And there is a further connotation, transpiring in this instance from the similitude in their hair – to which *he* draws attention – for it implies a very fixed image of woman in his mind (i.e. one woman is very much like another).

In the closing part of the film, he re-encounters Mona – who is flipped out on drugs – at Nîmes railway station. This time it is he who is in the glass container: he holes up in the telephone booth both to hide away from her and to call Mme Landier who is desperately seeking Mona; and it is now Mona who roves around outside the 'specimen' cabinet. She is, however, oblivious to his identity. At this point he shouts out (not even down the receiver which he is waving about quite hysterically) 'she frightens me because she disgusts me'. This scene is in direct counterpoint to the earlier meeting when he had seen her as object. Now she is subject ('she frightens me', rather than 'I am frightened of her'), he is object – the specimen in the glass cabinet. The contrast here is between his total awareness of her identity, which frightens him because it is beyond *his* control, and her complete denial of him through her oblivion. She is presence, he is absence.

Mona assumes her filth just as she assumes her marginality, she answers to no one and thanks no one. In so doing she creates her own image and simultaneously destroys the 'Image of Woman'. Equally, her speechlessness – which is in direct contrast to the volubility of those who would fix her – points to the moment pre-linguistic (that period of life which precedes the institution of patriarchal language) where the locus is the body-female in all its 'intimated reality of sensuousness' (Brückner 1985, 121).

By now it should be becoming clear that Varda bases her films on contrast and counterpoint; she also structures them around the dialectics of alternation and the theme of replacement (Audé 1981, 142). Thus she says: 'this dialectic, this ambiguity, this contradiction between the filmic negatives of one's inner life and the actual images of life as it is lived, this is the subject matter of all my films' (Audé 1981, 141). And in talking about *Sans toit ni loi* she again states this dialectic inside/outside: 'there are people who are 'inside' in the warmth, comfortably installed and others outside, in the cold, with not much idea of where they will sleep' (*Cinéma 85*, 332, 2).

Evidently her *cinécriture* reflects this structuring of 'a reality' – a first aspect of which is the use of the shifting point of view (employed as early as her first film *La Pointe courte*). And in this film there are eighteen different points of view. This replacing of one vision by another, this proliferation of points of view, around one object, Mona, has a threefold effect. In the first instance it causes a disengagement from the story – thus preventing it from becoming an ideological film about vagrancy;[6] this is not a film about 'les nouveaux pauvres' (the new poor) but – amongst other things – about how a particular vagrant woman lives her solitude. In the second instance, the effect is to unfix the gaze, to render it inoperable. Because there are so many points of view, Mona cannot be caught in any of them. In this criss-crossing of gazes, Mona has already moved on or has not yet arrived. Varda represents this phenomenon visually through the contrasting images of Mona's wanderings and her speculators' immobility, and, structurally, through alternately imbricating or fragmenting the portraits. Thirdly and finally, through this contrast of movement versus immobility, Varda subverts the traditional codes of classic narrative cinema which depict man as the gender on the move and woman as static.

Interestingly, the structuring of the portraits finds a ready reflection in Varda's use of the tracking shot. The tracking shot is Mona's sign, as is the music that accompanies it. Of the fourteen tracking shots employed, all frame Mona at some juncture and all but three are accompanied by her theme. And here the parallels between shot and portrait become striking. With regard to the 'orchestrated' tracking shots there are three different compositions, in terms of the spoken portraits there are three types. And just as there are unorchestrated tracking shots so too there are silent portraits, most remarkably Assoun's.

The composition of the 'orchestrated' tracking shots is as follows: in the first instance, either the camera and frame 'abandon' Mona and go on to focus on an object, or she exits the frame; in the second, through her positioning in the frame she splits the horizontal tracking shot line either by crossing it (moving from the back to the foreground and exiting front-frame), or by remaining stationary as the camera continues its tracking movement and stops on an object; and in the third instance, both camera and Mona stay in tandem and come to a halt together. Two further points – both pointing to the contingency of her existence – Mona is rarely at the beginning of the tracking shot, she either walks in or is picked up by the camera and, equally significant, in all of these tracking shots she and the camera, when on the tracking shot line, move from right to left – this movement serving as a metaphor for both the flashback and, even more significantly, death.

This visual representation of the flashback, then, points predominantly to the idea of discontinuity – only the last two orchestrated tracking shots are in tandem and therefore continuous. This discontinuity is similarly present in the portraits – all of which are forms of flashback, but most of which are fragmented. There are just six stories where the portrait and images are in tandem (i.e. Mona arrives and the person whose path she has crossed immediately picks up the description). Otherwise they assume two forms. The first form is a flashforward within a flashback, that is to say, we see the end of the story or encounter before we perceive the occurrence which preceded or brought about that encounter. For example, towards the very beginning of the film the demolition man tells the truck driver of his encounter with Mona (he discovers her in some derelict chalets he is about to raze to the ground) and there is a flash-shot of him peering in on her; much later, about half-way through the film, we see Mona arriving at these chalets and adopting them as her shelter.

The second form, far more digressive in fact, is a form whereby an initial flashback is interrupted by the insertion of other flashbacks only to be picked up again at some later juncture. Either the interruption is felt as a complete cut, as in the goat farmer's story (in an episode in the first half of the film, we see Mona arrive, stay at and leave the farm and then some twelve episodes later in the latter half of the film we see and hear the goat farmer's summing up of the encounter). Or the flashback becomes fragmented by the imbrication of another portrait within the existing one. In this instance both get interrupted by a further flashback or series of flashbacks. Yolande's story and Mme Landier's are the two exemplars of this most dense of all digressive structures.

The tracking shot is a natural icon for a road movie as are the stops in between (think for example of *Easy Rider*). Thus when Varda states in an interview that 'the whole film is one long tracking shot . . . we cut it up into pieces, we separate the pieces and in between them are the "adventures"' (*Cinématographe*, 114, 1985, 19) it might seem that she is following the canons of this particular genre. However, from its very inception this film goes counter to the canonic laws. First, it is filmed going backwards down the road (the tracking from right to left); second, the narration is a series of flashbacks all interwoven rather than an ordered sequence of events which lead inexorably to a bad end (*Easy Rider*) or a reasonable resolution (*Paris, Texas*) – furthermore, in Varda's film the spectator and the speculators already know the end; third, the tradition is for the point of view to be that of the roadster(s), but in this film it is everyone else's but Mona's that is given; fourth, the roadster is in this instance a woman on her own; fifth, a road movie implies discovery, obtaining some self-knowledge – but this is not the purpose here: in her filth and her solitude, Mona has acquired her identity, her marginality, and gazes uninterestedly past the others – including us. And her death, which she finally stumbles upon by tripping over an irrigation pipe, leaves us silent in its irony, coming as it does to she who emerged Aphrodite-like from the sea and whose pursuit of and longing for drinking water punctuates the entire film.

As with all texts – be they myths, allegories, film genres, whatever – whenever Varda makes reference to them she does so dialectically and contrapuntally. Thus water is not just an agent of cleansing and irrigation or refreshment, it is also a source of life and death. Water is immediately within this film associated with the birth of Aphrodite, the goddess of desire who yields to Dionysus the god of the vine. She is also the death-in-life goddess who every year, in remembrance of destroying the sacred king, bathes in the sea and rises again renewed. After her first bathe in the sea, Mona only seeks out water for refreshment; 'other women bathe (Eliane and Mme Landier), Mona doesn't'. Thereafter, Mona roams the vineyards of the Hérault encrusting herself in her dirt. But unlike Aphrodite she will not yield to the pagan dionysians whose assault on her own filth with their *lie-de-vin* she cannot accept. This 'rape' of her identity, this sullying by another, is untenable – hence her reaction. This patriarchal pagan rite (only the men can dress up as the wine gods and daub the women) is not the cause of her death, but is a contributing factor, and for two reasons. First, the male rite withdraws sustenance (as a result of the festivities she cannot obtain any bread). Second, the violence of her rejection of their ritual practices and of the implicit tyranny of the gaze (she blockades herself in a telephone booth and screams, counterpointing her earlier reduction to a specimen by Mme Landier and again Jean-Pierre's own violent reaction to her at his loss of identity) aggravates her already advanced stage of hypothermia.

When we first see Mona's body it is covered with reddish stains, looking very much like blood. There is then a flash-shot of people mopping down a telephone booth (by now this object is becoming a pertinent symbol of enclosure rather than of an opening up of the horizons of communication) which is covered in red stains of some indistinguishable sort. Only the end shots of this film make clear what that red is. The series of flashbacks which separates these two sets of shots serves – through the images of Mona's living gestures – to show how her filth is accrued and her clothing diminished; and the last memorable trace on her body, the red stains, is the last to receive elucidation. We know as early as the beginning of the film that foul play has been ruled out, thus the film's structure is also an uncovering of how her body got there and in that state.

An entire film in flashback to explain a death or murder is part of the classical canon (*Murder, My Sweet*) but an entire film in flashback to elucidate one shot is not. To suffuse one shot with so much signification is to

*Sans toit ni loi* – above: Mona (Sandrine Bonnaire); below: Mona hitchhiking.

impregnate it with geological proportions of textural significance whose structures are as deep as they are dense, and whose references within those structures traverse discourses ancient and modern. I mentioned earlier the digressive structure of Varda's flashback construction and the analogically digressive composition of her tracking shots. These are aspects of her feminist *cinécriture* which are political because – as with feminist writing[7] which refuses to inscribe contours – in their digressiveness they go counter to dominant male film-making practices and are, therefore, counter-cinematic. And it is also true that her particular approach of textural intertextualization (a *mise-en-abyme* of different textures: painting, sculpture, photography, etc., *cinépeinture* as she calls it) is equally counter-cinematic in that it works 'in opposition to the naturalized dominant male discourse to produce textual contradictions which would de-naturalize the workings of patriarchal ideology' (Cook 1985, 198). These textual contradictions create gaps in representation 'into which woman's representation can insert itself' (*ibid.*). Varda makes frequent reference to the painterly quality of her films and to her desire to leave gaps, *des creux*. And certainly her painterly references stretch from the quattrocento to the realism of Courbet and Millet. Similarly, her filmic references are drawn from the silent era and also from contemporary cinema – and, as I have already indicated, many genres are re-represented.

Let us now consider the opening shot of the film – a very slow zoom. I will use this one shot to show how it establishes immediately the notion of intertextuality and the function of textual contradiction, both of which run throughout the film. Traditionally, a zoom transports the viewer from one space to another (and therefore one time to another) in such a way that perspectival time and space are dissolved. Varda, in slowing it down as she does, makes both time and space perspectival, and in so doing creates the intervals, the spaces or gaps in between which are not normally perceptible. The slowness of the zoom allows time in between to perceive the shifting of planes from foreground to background. Through this counter-cinematic practice, the zoom becomes de-naturalized and does not conform to the dominant ideology. Colliding with this technological subversion is the implicit subversiveness of the painterliness of Varda's shot. From the lighting (a luminous pale blue) to the slow tracerly movement across the terrain – from the trees in the foreground to those in the background upon a rounded hillock – this shot is reminiscent of Piero della Francesca's fresco *Resurrection of Christ* (1474?) with the hill of Golgotha[8] in the background – the hill where Jesus was crucified. The reference to Francesca, the greatest Italian painter of the quattrocento,[9] is particularly vital because he too subverted the then dominant painterly practices. He was the discoverer of a new vision in painting with a precise definition of volumes in space, a sense of interval and a new treatment of light. Not only was he a canon-breaker on the visual front, he also took the chronological nature of aesthetic religious narration to task. Eschewing the prevalent formalistic and diegetic representation of the biblical allegories, he chose rather, for the sake of symmetry and a sense of interval, as in the fresco *Legend of the True Cross* (1452–9), to group his scenes out of chronological sequence. Through the slow zoom, Varda refers back to this vital subversiveness of the quattrocento and also towards her own film-making practices. Similarly, the *mise-en-scène* is both ancient and modern. It is Golgotha of the crucifixion – the Christian myth of life and death; and it is equally Van Gogh's canvas *La Route aux cyprès* (1890) – perceived later in both Mona's and Mme Landier's collection of postcards. Finally, it is also – through this last reference – an intertextualization-through-inversion of Alain Resnais' documentary *Van Gogh* (1947). In his film, Resnais uses zooms, pans and tracking shots of Van Gogh's paintings themselves to recreate the life of the artist. In her film, Varda inverts Resnais' initial oxymoron of painting as the cinematic shot (whereby stasis becomes movement and in so doing creates a life – in this instance, Van Gogh's), and in *Sans toit ni loi*, movement becomes stasis (i.e. the shot as painting) signifying death.

In just this single shot, texts and intertexts are immediately juxtaposed for the purpose of contradiction – so too are their textural representations (i.e. the plasticity of paint as a texture is distinct from that of celluloid). Simultaneously, these textual contradictions cause a constant shifting and thus indeed a rift between the multi-layered planes of time and space. These contradictions unfix rather than transfix meaning and the whole of the film is similarly infused with this unease of the *insaisissable*. Visual presence is made absence: that which is there cannot be seized – there are no contours which define.

Varda treats objects in a similar intertextual and dialectical fashion. A brief look at how she reworks the signification of certain objects will show how they serve to intensify the digressive texturality of her *cinécriture*. In this instance, I shall focus on the representation of death which is, after all, a dominant discourse within the film.

Trees are amongst the many objects that link or punctuate the film and, as with most of the other objects, are more readily associated with violence and death than with regeneration and life. Trees are framed as Mona is raped. Trees (plane trees) have been 'colonized'/'raped' by a deathly American-imported fungus (gift of the Second World War). Mona immediately identifies with their destiny: 'si *elles* crèvent, pensez à moi' ('if they perish, think of me'), she says (my stress).

Walls, doors and shutters almost invariably shut Mona out, only at best do they conceal her from the police. They are symbolic of her numerous evictions, the last of which is fatal. In accidentally setting fire to her refuge (a derelict house shared with other drop-outs), David – a former acquaintance of hers – deprives her of her protection from the cold. Incidentally, this eventuality is foreshadowed in an earlier episode when David – who was then shacked up with Mona in an unlived-in mansion – gets into a fight with robbers and drops his oil lamp. That time the house miraculously does not catch fire. In this second occurrence, however, it is David's violence (he attacks the squatters who owe him money) which causes the fire. In film culture, it is women who are most often associated with fire – that most obvious of death symbols. Here it is associated with David and not Mona – he brings the fire and plunders her home. Moreover, David is allegorically associated with death and with the imagery of the opening shot of the film. For he is (as he says) the wandering Jew. The one who insulted Christ on his way to Golgotha and who was condemned to wander about the world until Christ's second coming.

Plastic tents and cloches, intended to warm the earth for growth and germination, offer poor comfort to Mona and will ultimately serve to encase her corpse. Indeed, in the closing episode we are reminded of the symbolism of the greenhouse in Renoir's *La Règle du jeu* where it is the site of André Jurieu's death (in fact Mona's twitching movements as she lies dying are very reminiscent of Jurieu's).

Death also crosses Mona's path in the form of the gravedigger whose hooded cloak masks his face. Cloaked and masked as he is he recalls the character of Death in Bergman's *Seventh Seal*. Earlier, there is another reference to this same film, this time to the sound and image construct of its opening sequence. In Bergman's film, the Knight awakens and washes himself in the sea, the sound-track is Bergman in voice-over reading from the Book of Revelations. In Varda's film, we hear her voice-over – the only voice-over of the film – accompanying the shot of Mona emerging, cleansed, from the sea. At this point she is also Botticelli's *Birth of Venus* (1485). Thus, again the dialectical tension of life and death is represented and, too, tension in a textural sense because of the simultaneous reference to two contrasting modes of visual imagery. As was pointed out above, to place a painterly reference alongside a cinematic one is to represent immobility and movement simultaneously. But this oxymoron gathers even further layers of contradictions when one considers that both Botticelli's painting and Bergman's film are inscribed within yet another text or even a series of texts: the fictionalized documentary of Settina's/Mona's story/portrait.

Fact and fiction, documentary, a road movie in flashback, Greek, pagan and Christian myths, contrastive visual discourses – just so many texts all interwoven and rewritten within a digressive structure that, in the end, the film itself maintains the enigmatic mystery of an incomplete (in the sense that it cannot be completed) jigsaw puzzle. We cannot fix the film any more than we can fix Mona, and it is in this de-fetishization of the text as well as the body-female that Varda asserts her own brand of feminist film-making practices.

# Notes

1 See her article, 'Women's Cinema as Counter-cinema' (1976). And also Louise Heck-Rabi (1984), who provides a very comprehensive study of Varda's critical acclaim.
2 This is a point of view I do not share, incidentally, and one which I have argued against elsewhere (*ASMCF Review*, 33 (1988)).
3 Interview, *24 Images*, 27 (1986).
4 The original title of this film was going to be *A saisir*, obviously intended ironically (see Sheila Johnston's review in *Films and Filming*, 380 (1986), 41).
5 For further discussion on the authentic sex, see Sigrid Weigel's article 'Double Focus' (1985, 78–9).
6 Olivier Dazat makes this particular point in comparing this film to earlier forms of the road movie. See his article in *Cinématographe*, 11 (1985).
7 Luce Irigaray and Hélène Cixous both speak of the necessity for 'feminine' writing to traverse discourses and thus 'set fire to fetishized words, appropriate terms, well-constructed forms' (Weigel 1985, 75).
8 Jean Decock (*Visions*, 35 (1986)) identifies the symbolism of the hill but I believe he gets the painterly reference wrong. It is almost certainly not an Italian primitive as he claims, but a direct reference to the quattrocento. See also note 9.
9 As early as her first film, *La Pointe courte*, Varda refers to the painterliness of the film and makes specific reference to Piero della Francesca (interview in *Cahiers du cinéma*, 165 (1965)).

# Selected bibliography

Audé Françoise (1981) *Ciné-modèles cinéma d'elles: situation des femmes dans le cinéma français 1956–1979*, Lausanne, l'Age d'Homme.

Brückner, Jutta (1985) 'Women Behind the Camera', in Gisela Ecker (ed.) *Feminist Aesthetics*, London, The Women's Press, 120–4.

Cook, Pam (ed.) (1985) *The Cinema Book*, London, British Film Institute, 202.

Corrigan, Timothy (1986) 'The Tension of Translation: Handke's *The Left-handed Woman*', in Eric Rentschler (ed.) *German Film and Literature: Adaptations and Transformations*, New York and London, Methuen, 260–75.

Heck-Rabi, Louise (1984) *Women Filmmakers*, Metuchen and London, The Scarecrow Press, 322–52.

Johnston, Claire (1976) 'Women's Cinema as Counter-cinema', in Bill Nichols (ed.) *Movies and Methods*, Berkeley, University of California Press, 208–17.

Pingaud, Bernard (1963) 'Agnès Varda et la réalité', in Raymond Bellour (ed.) *Un cinéma réel, ArtSept*, 1.

Rose, Jacqueline (1986) *Sexuality in the Field of Vision*, London, Verso.

Smith, Alison (1998) *Agnès Varda*, Manchester and New York, Manchester University Press.

Turim, Maureen (1986) 'Textuality and Theatricality in Brecht and Straub/Huillet: *History Lessons*', in Eric Rentschler (ed.) *German Film and Literature: Adaptations and Transformations*, New York and London, Methuen, 231–45.

Varda, Agnès (1994) *Varda par Agnès Varda*, Paris, Cahiers du cinéma.

Weigel, Sigrid (1985), 'Double Focus: On the History of Women's Writing', in Gisela Ecker (ed.) *Feminist Aesthetics*, London, The Women's Press, 59–80.

# Appendix

## *Agnès Varda (1928–): filmography*

1954 *La Pointe courte*
1957 *O saisons, ô châteaux* (short)
1958 *L'Opéra Mouffe* (short)
1958 *Du côté de la côte* (short)
1959 *Cocotte d'azur* (short)
1960 *Champagne* (short)
1961 *Cléo de 5 à 7*
1963 *Salut les Cubains* (short)
1965 *Le Bonheur*
1965 *Chroniques de France* (sketch in collective film)
1966 *Elsa et la rose* (short)
1966 *Les Créatures*
1967 *Loin du Vietnam* (sketch in collective film)
1968 *Uncle Yanco* (short)
1968 *Black Panthers* (short)
1969 *Lions Love*
1970 *Nausica*
1975 *Daguerreotypes*
1975 *Réponses de femmes* (short)
1976 *Plaisir d'amour en Iran* (short)
1976 *L'une chante, l'autre pas*
1980 *Murs, murs* (short)
1981 *Documenteur* (short)
1982 *Ulysse* (short)
1983 *Une minute pour une image* (170 two-minute films)
1984 *Les Dites cariatides* (short)
1984 *Sept pièces, cuisine, salle de bain, à saisir* (short)
1985 *Sans toit ni loi*
1986 *T'as de beaux escaliers tu sais* (short)
1987 *Jane B. vue par Agnès V.*
1987 *Kung Fu Master*
1991 *Jacquot de Nantes*
1993 *Les Demoiselles ont eu 25 ans*
1995 *Cent et une nuits de Simon cinéma*
1995 *L'Univers de Jacques Demy*

## *Other films cited in the text*

*Easy Rider*, Denis Hopper (USA 1969)
*Murder My Sweet/Farewell My Lovely*, Edward Dmytryck (USA 1944)
*Paris, Texas*, Wim Wenders (USA 1984)
*La Règle du jeu* (*Rules of the Game*), Jean Renoir (1939)
*The Seventh Seal*, Ingmar Bergman (Sweden 1957)
*Van Gogh*, Alain Resnais (1948)

# 20

# VERSIONS, VERSE AND VERVE

## Jean-Paul Rappeneau's *Cyrano de Bergerac* (1990)

### *Julianne Pidduck*

With his notorious nose, his finesse with verse and épée, his heart-wrenching vulnerability and, above all, his panache, Cyrano de Bergerac remains one of the great heroes of the French theatre. An oft-cited study names Cyrano (followed by Victor Hugo's Jean Valjean and Alexandre Dumas' d'Artagnan) as the favourite French literary character.[1] With its five grandiose settings and a huge cast led by international star Gérard Depardieu in the title role, Jean-Paul Rappeneau's 1990 epic *Cyrano de Bergerac* harnesses the hero's iconic status to dramatize French identity and masculinity on a grand scale. Adapting Edmond Rostand's quintessential theatrical work into contemporary cinematic spectacle, this film precipitated a subsequent cycle of lavish 'super productions' which dramatized the glorious national past through the adaptation of famous French cultural texts.

A core pleasure of classic literary adaptation might be described through the notion of 'versions', or variations of the familiar. For Rappeneau's contemporary adaptation of Rostand's iconic play, inevitably, comparisons will be made: does this version measure up, does it offer something fresh to a 1990s audience? Jean-Louis Comolli describes the spectacle of historical fiction as a 'game' where spectators participate 'as players, accomplices, masters of the game, even if they are also its stakes' (1978, 46). Always presented in the 'future perfect' (the situations familiar, the lines falling easily off the lips, the ending a *fait accompli*), a classic French theatrical work such as this one must be staged implicitly against a rich intertextual backdrop of historical and cultural references. With its treatment of historical events (the Siege of Arras), places (the seventeenth-century theatrical venue the Hôtel de Bourgogne), and people (Cyrano de Bergerac, an obscure early modern writer), as well as knowing references to French literature and theatre, Rappeneau's contemporary production confronts the palimpsest layers of national memory where the 'myth'[2] of Cyrano resides.

## The 'Tradition of Quality'

Rappeneau's film is based upon Rostand's play *Cyrano de Bergerac*, written in 1897 for the great stage actor Constant Coquelin. In the century since its première, the work's popularity has continued unabated, with an estimated fifteen thousand performances in France alone by the release of Rappeneau's version (Aziza 1998, 6). The work liberally traces the life of Cyrano de Bergerac (1619–55), a seventeenth-century writer, philosopher, and soldier.[3] Rostand transforms this figure into a classic French romantic hero whose exploits are set against the baroque sensibility and political unrest of Richelieu's early modern France – a time-frame coinciding with Dumas' musketeers and the Thirty Years War with Spain. Rostand's play has been read as expressing the chauvinistic values of a Third Republic still smarting from a humiliating defeat in the 1870–1 Franco-Prussian War, and simmering with the anti-semitic rhetoric of the 1894–1906 Dreyfus Affair (Woollen 1994, v–vii). Almost a century later, Rappeneau's film was released into a 1990 context arguably bearing strong parallels to Rostand's era – widespread disaffectation in the wake of economic recession and renewed struggles over French identity raised by the racist rhetoric of the National Front.

From Rostand's idiosyncratic return to the antique alexandrine verse onward, this play draws stylistically – and already nostalgically – from a panoply of literary genres and historical references. A stock repertory piece of the Comédie-Française, translated into a plethora of languages, *Cyrano* has become a marker of 'Frenchness' and 'panache' both within France and abroad. Requiring tremendous physical and emotional range, Cyrano is one of the coveted dramatic roles of French theatre. Depardieu's bravura performance follows in the footsteps of many of the nation's great actors: Coquelin (in the 1890s), André Brunot (the late 1930s and 1940s), Jacques Weber (1983) and Jean-Paul Belmondo (1990). Shifting from stage to screen, *Cyrano* had inspired multiple cinematic and television adaptations before Rappeneau's version. (See appendix.) Spurred on by the success of the 1983 theatrical production, the film's publicity none the less stressed its uniquely cinematic nature, noting that no 'classic' cinematic version yet existed. With its lavish production values and classic literary source, Cyrano returns to a long-standing French cinematic 'Tradition of Quality'.

Historians of French cinema (Williams 1992, Hayward 1993a) have noted the importance of literary adaptations and historical films as markers of a prestigious national cultural heritage. This trend began in the silent era of French cinema with multiple silent versions of Hugo's and Dumas' works, as part of the Film d'Art movement. This trend continued into the sound era where, for instance, Hugo's hero Jean Valjean is immortalized by Harry Baur in Raymond Bernard's moody 1933 *Les Misérables*, and again in 1958 by Jean Gabin in Jean-Paul Le Chanois' version. In industrial terms, costume and historical genres, as well as *films de cape et d'épée* (swashbucklers) have historically enjoyed great popularity both within France, and as cultural exports.[4] In the postwar period when the French market was inundated with previously unreleased American films, the 'Tradition of Quality' took on new cultural and economic significance. From the late 1940s, French film-makers undertook capital-intensive American-style productions featuring popular stars, and elaborate sets and costumes. This era is best characterized by Jean Renoir's *French Cancan*, and by the 1950s oeuvre of French stars Martine Carol (*Caroline chérie* and *Nana*) and Gérard Philipe (*Les Grandes manoeuvres* and the swashbuckling romp *Fanfan la Tulipe*). Alan Williams (1992, 278) notes how these films were produced partly as a nationalistic cultural strategy.[5] They functioned as an 'official' state-approved form of cinema, as they would again in the 1980s and 1990s, when Socialist Minister for Culture Jack Lang put in place strategies to support prestige heritage cinema and its export (Hayward 1993b).

In the 1960s, historical fiction as a popular genre was eclipsed by the New Wave. In his 1954 auteurist manifesto, 'A Certain Tendency of the French Cinema,' François Truffaut roundly critiqued the 'Tradition of Quality'. Singling out the dominance of what he called the *'metteurs-en-scène'* and a slavish over-reliance on the 'classic' French novel, he remarked caustically that 'a film is no longer made in France that the authors do not believe they are re-making Madame Bovary' (1976, 232). Lambasting a 'bourgeois' popular cinema in the name of avant-garde auteurism, Truffaut spoke for a new generation of film-makers who rejected what they saw as a backward-looking French cultural tradition. From a decline in the 1960s, the 1970s and early 1980s saw the sporadic production of prestigious historical films (*Stavisky*, *Danton*, *Le Dernier métro*). However, it was Claude Berri's 1986 adaptations of Pagnol's *Jean de Florette* and *Manon des sources* which signalled a renewed cultural and commercial viability for the genre. Hits beyond expectations, not only in France but in the coveted international market, Berri's films undoubtedly helped to precipitate *Cyrano*'s big-budget production. In its turn, *Cyrano* became the top-grossing French film in 1990, earning 60 million francs in the domestic market, and more than 50 million francs abroad (Condron 1997, 214).

*Cyrano*'s success inspired a reinvention of French 'Quality' cinema for the 1990s with projects like *Germinal*, *La Reine Margot*, *Ridicule*, *Beaumarchais*, *Tous les matins du monde*, *Le Hussard sur le toit*, and *Le Bossu*. *Cyrano* exemplifies this cycle of contemporary French historical cinema, described by Ginette Vincendeau as 'an industrial battle (against Hollywood) and an aesthetic one (against television)' (1995, 32). There are signs however that French television in the late 1990s started adopting similar tactics. A three-part television adaptation of Dumas' *Le Comte de Monte Cristo* starring Depardieu was released in September 1998 (commanding the highest recorded television audience in France, and sold to US networks); a new television adaptation of *Les Misérables* (2001), also with Depardieu, was in production concurrent with the writing of this chapter. As Vincendeau also says, the French heritage film 'takes a two-pronged line of attack, adopting Hollywood-style "super-production" values while establishing its difference through historical subject-matter and (not negligibly) language' (1995, 32). Like the 1950s films, this cycle incorporates historical settings, literary sources and the all-important high production values and star codes. *Cyrano* is exemplary in this respect, with its adaptation of Rostand's famous play and key casting of Depardieu in the lead role and Jacques Weber (who played Cyrano in the successful 1983 stage version) as de Guiche. Relative unknowns at the time of the film, Anne Brochet as Roxane and Vincent Perez as Christian went on to further stardom in the heritage genre – Brochet in *Tous les matins du monde* with Depardieu, and Pérez in *La Reine Margot*, *Indochine*, and *Le Bossu*.

Reincarnating the 'Tradition of Quality', this contemporary cycle could well evoke Truffaut's disparaging terms of 1954, where 'ten or twelve films a year that force, by their ambitiousness, the admiration of the foreign press, defend the French flag twice a year at Cannes and at Venice where, since 1946, they regularly carry off medals, golden lions and grands prix' (255). Garnering ten Césars (including best French film of the year) and the coveted best actor award at Cannes, *Cyrano* transforms Rostand's iconic play into 1990s cinematic spectacle. Notwithstanding its similarities with 1950s 'quality' costume dramas, *Cyrano* (like other contemporary heritage films) differentiates itself from the theatrical style of 1950s historical fiction through a grittily naturalistic *mise-en-scène* and the carefully choreographed foregrounding of cinematic movement.

## Selling historical spectacle

Through its very scale, *Cyrano* marks a stylistic and industrial prototype for subsequent films which commonly quote its cinematography, casting, and even situation.[6] Boasting a budget of 100 million francs (with 10 million francs spent on sets, 4.5 million francs on costumes, and 600,000 francs on shoes), *Cyrano* offers luxurious sets (including the Hôtel de Bourgogne, the Ragueneaus' bakery and the siege of Arras, shot in Hungary), a cast of two thousand actors and extras, and sparkling costumes. Production designer Ezio Frigerio, who has worked with Vittorio de Sica and Bernardo Bertolucci (*1900*), often collaborates with *Cyrano*'s costume designer Franca Squarciapino in opera and theatre productions; the pair's high art credentials resonate well with *Cyrano*'s 'luxury' period aesthetic. The 'excess' of the sets, the action, the language offer an audio-visual feast for the contemporary viewer. From the cakes and pastries of Ragueneau's shop to the dramatic arrival of Roxane's food-laden coach on the battlefield at Arras, Howarth (1993) notes a distinctly French interest in food as a part of *Cyrano*'s spectacle.

The momentous opening sequence at the Hôtel de Bourgogne establishes the film's lush representation of romantic 1640s Paris. From the outset, the film is imbued with a relentless, sometimes frenetic, energy. Rappeneau notes that with this adaptation he wanted to avoid the pitfalls of 'filmed theatre', and in particular the structural problem of early theatrical and filmed versions where the action stops as the dialogue starts (Loiseau 1990, 68–71). In this vein, the film's French marketing campaign repeatedly emphasized the expressly cinematic qualities of this version as a spectacle that *moves* – through the alexandrine verse itself (which I will return to) and through fluid camerawork, rapid-fire editing and choreographed cast movement (editor Noelle Boisson won the César for best editing on this film).

Opening on a fleeting low-angle shot of running feet, *Cyrano*'s characters, words, camera and editing are continually in motion from the outset. These feet are revealed to belong to a man pulling a tiny carriage containing a small boy and a man. As I will elaborate below, the boy is an invention specific to this film who provides a vantage-point on the action. Clad in blue with a white collar, the boy peers out of the carriage window into the dimly lit, dark street. Unlike the pristine, clean, studio-lit sets of earlier versions of *Cyrano*, Rappeneau's 1640s Paris is decidedly dirty, confused, bawdy. Narrow cobbled streets littered with refuse and beggars are continually pelted with rain or shrouded with blue-filtered mist. With its clutter and confusion of human misery and dissent, this gritty 'realist' baroque milieu is stylized by a distinctive blue-*noir* aesthetic. Through this film and the previous year's *Camille Claudel*, director of photography Pierre Lhomme helped to establish the distinctive dark, naturalistic 'look' of 1990s historical cinema. Distinct from the unsullied and artificial sets of 1950s 'quality' cinema, this aesthetic recurs in the miseries, pox and bloodshed of *La Reine Margot*, *Le Colonel Chabert* and *Le Hussard sur le toit*.

As the camera pulls back from the milling crowd, the carriage approaches a grand, if slightly dilapidated, theatre. A high-angle shot over the grand front steps reveals throngs of torchlit spectators from all walks of life pouring pell-mell into the theatre. This opening sequence establishes a common movement toward the Hôtel de Bourgogne, anticipating a dramatic event, while the mobile film language propelling the spectator from the chiaroscuro streets into the performance proclaims this as 'cinema' writ large. As the boy, accompanied by Cyrano's friend Le Bret, enters the dark theatre, he must dodge gambling, brawling, dirty men in the pit: clearly, this is a place of danger, intrigue, loud altercation. Meanwhile, we are introduced to Ragueneau (the baker) and Lignière (the drunken poet) as they exchange witticisms; they are the first to mention Cyrano, noting that he has forbidden Montfleury to perform that night.

Their exchange is interrupted by an audible 'Aaaah' from all present, as six huge wreath-like chandeliers bearing candles are hoisted high above the crowd. Framed only briefly in long shot, this breathtaking sight is layered with the dense banter, the play of split alexandrine lines, moving from the intimacy of the two-shot to the spectacle of the whole set. Another quick cut

285

frames the arrival of Comte de Guiche (Weber), accompanied by a blue-uniformed entourage; he pushes his way through the jostling crowd and up a stairwell that forms a diagonal across the screen. From de Guiche we cut back to Ragueneau, moving down a narrow staircase, again on the diagonal. This use of quick cutting and the dynamic spatial possibilities of the diagonal, especially staircases and ladders, recurs in the scenes at the Paris headquarters of the gascons, at Roxane's balcony and at the Siege of Arras troop quarters. Fluidity of movement and the dynamic blocking of space are emphasized by these recurring stylistic features. Next, we spy Christian (Perez), resplendent in blue with a grey cloak and hat. He asks Lignière about Roxane (Brochet), glimpsed at this very moment, framed by an arch, beautifully lit by torchlight. As she walks rapidly past the two men, her eyes are hidden behind a delicate hand-held mask which she pulls aside to glance at Christian as she ascends yet another staircase. As the audience shouts for the play to begin, all of the main players are in place, with the notable exception of Cyrano. (I will return to the hero's entrance below).

With its predominance of blue (the stage, the blue filtered lighting, many of the uniforms), white (luminous lace collars) and red (the proud plumes cresting the broad hats, certain uniforms, and presently Cyrano's cloak), the colour scheme of this sequence underscores the decidedly nationalistic nature of the event. In keeping with this mood, Jean-Claude Petit's orchestral score, a stately adaptation of a Verdi theme, fades in and out against the wordplay and visual splendour. Such amplified signifiers of an iconic historical 'Frenchness' suggest a nationalistic *mise-en-abyme* between the seventeenth-century historical setting, the play's Third Republic moment, and the film's 1990s context. In Comolli's terms where the work of the audience for historical fiction involves a 'bricolage' of historical and cultural referents, from the outset this film trumpets its lineage within the tradition of glorious French culture. Emerging in the context of a state-sanctioned industrial strategy whereby the nation is represented to itself and abroad through the preferred genre of historical fiction, *Cyrano*'s jingoistic and nostalgic tone raises questions in a contemporary moment.

British debates around heritage cinema foreground the social and political stakes of such luxurious, pleasurable and 'nostalgic' representations of the past.[7] Keith Reader reads the nostalgia of contemporary French historical cinema as 'an escape from the threat of history rather than an affirmation of its promise. . . . Thus the heritage movie appears to me to stand in a close contextual relation to the France of the second Mitterrand term (1988–1995), with the demise of that epoch, and the galloping social uncertainties unleashed' (1996, 26). In France, the ongoing popularity of Ancien Régime settings reproduces an iconic historical and cultural identity removed from the troubled context of economic recession, widespread unemployment and politically fraught multiculturalism. As I will discuss below, this account of national identity is closely tied to a complex account of a noble, individual-

*Cyrano de Bergerac* – (from left to right) Roxane (Anne Brochet), Christian
(Vincent Perez) and Cyrano (Gérard Depardieu).

istic and embattled French masculinity, as embodied by the character of
Cyrano. *Cyrano*'s nationalistic overtones reproduce a certain type of national
identity to be found, seemingly, in the idea of a golden age of French culture.
In fact, much of *Cyrano*'s distinctly 'French' address speaks through the linguistic and cultural qualities of Rostand's distinctive alexandrine verse.

## Language, literary antecedents, genre

Anticipating the entrance of actor Montfleury at the Théâtre de Bourgogne,
Lignière and Ragueneau recite a roll of honour of great actors and writers.
Through these references and through its highly theatrical framing, the scene
pays homage to French theatre and literary traditions, from the historical
Cyrano de Bergerac himself to Corneille, Dumas, Molière, Hugo and the
Romantics. Part of the play's quintessential 'French' quality at Rostand's
time lay in its revival of the alexandrine line.[8] Patrick Besnier suggests that
Rostand's linguistic virtuosity had two dimensions: 'On the one hand, to
give tangible expression to the full-bodied flavour of Paris in the baroque
age, which he recreates with a passionate enthusiasm; on the other, to explore
certain aspects of the art and literature of his own day: the love for decorative
excess, for exaggerated detail, the cultivation of a new preciosity in a taste for
verbal extravagance' (cited in Howarth 1993, 121).

287

In the 1990s, this attention to language relates to a distinctively French, state-sanctioned, cultural and industrial defence against American cultural imports (see Brulard 1997). With its outrageous rhymes and punning-under-pressure, the play of rhyme and rhythm constitutes both the form and a core thematic of *Cyrano*, with language becoming more than mere medium, but a playful, multiply inflected substance.[9] This linguistic preoccupation recurs in *Ridicule* and *Beaumarchais*, where the skillful deployment of language becomes, as in *Cyrano*, a play of power and seduction. Unlike these original scripts, however, *Cyrano*'s verses and monologues are familiar to much of the audience. In a dynamic evoking Comolli's knowing game of spectatorship, Rappeneau plants a naïve point of reference into the diegesis through the invented character of the small boy (clad, perhaps not coincidentally, in royal blue). This character (whom Rappeneau describes as a kind of stand-in for himself as a child, impressed for life by Rostand's play) signals a relay between play, film and contemporary spectators, celebrating the nation's cultural heritage across the ages – and across generations, as represented by male artistic genius and the male child as inheritor.

Play and film in turn draw from hybrid influences, including the dynamism of Dumas' musketeers and Corneille's *Le Cid*. Equally, Rostand draws from another seventeenth-century literary mode, the burlesque, where much of the humour works through outrageous puns and elaborate rhymes. Many of these most famous moments occur in set pieces – the nose diatribe ('Enorme, mon nez! [ . . . ] C'est un roc! . . . c'est un pic! . . . c'est un cap! Que dis-je, c'est un cap? . . . Cest une péninsule!' / My nose, sir, is enormous [ . . . ] A rock, a bluff, a cape! – No, a peninsula in size and shape![10]); the duel with Valvert; the 'Non, merci!' monologue; the fantastical journey to the moon; the wooing of Roxane on the balcony. For a French audience broadly familiar with the play, the exuberant audio-visual staging of these set pieces distinguishes Rappeneau's *Cyrano* as a refreshing cinematic experience which remains, at the same time, true to the spirit (and language) of the original.

Where the play's antique verse form could hamper an adaptation, Rappeneau sought to harness the momentum of the words: 'We think that its rhyming dialogue, its sudden flourishes, these alexandrines cut in two, three, four, and sometimes even five phrases, this vertiginously acrobatic ping-pong will be the key to the film's success' (Rappeneau 1991). In this vein, verbal orchestration and rhythm carry the soundtrack where music is used only sparingly as a support for the language. Rappeneau combines the swagger and roll of the verse with a fluidity of camera and character movement and rhythmic editing. Cyrano's duel with Valvert, filmed as a relentless pursuit, makes for a defining instance of this strategy. With his blue doublet and blood-red cloak, Cyrano taunts the beribboned yellow-clad dandy with verse and sword. The famous dialogue is choreographed into the very sword-play in a dazzling array of robust character movement (especially by Cyrano),

*Cyrano de Bergerac* – Cyrano (Gérard Depardieu).

dancing words punctuated by pauses at the end of each verse ('A la fin de l'envoi, je touche' / 'At the poem's end . . . I hit'). Generated spontaneously under pressure, as a kind of 'duelling banjos' contest, this set piece stakes the man's measure in his poetic prowess. So central to the form and substance of Cyrano, this layering of movement and verse touches upon the multi-dimensional capacities of the hero himself, a thinking man of action, a poet with panache.

## Depardieu's Cyrano

The élan of Rostand's play lies in the mythological character of Cyrano himself, described by Jean-Pierre Thibaudat as 'part Voltaire, part musketeer, hooligan and judge, sharp talker and skilled fencer, here is a sparkling hero' (1990, 38). Against the film's dynamism and its backdrop of luscious sets and costumes, it is undoubtedly Depardieu's bravura performance that carries Rappeneau's film. Depardieu's Cyrano incorporates longstanding cultural myths to create a quintessential French male hero who is both ebullient and vulnerable, and always his own master. And even as the film generates an

289

associative slippage between several historical and cultural contexts, it plays upon Depardieu's star persona to project a traditional and yet contemporary gallant, and an incarnation of wounded French masculinity.

Into the sparkling, bustling spectacle of the Théâtre de Bourgogne, Cyrano's flamboyant entrance is accomplished through carefully orchestrated chaos. The hero's entry jars with actor Montfleury's stylized monologue, Cyrano's commanding physical and verbal virility upstaging the static, grotesquely effeminate actor. The difference in performance style between Cyrano and Montfleury calls forth the distinction between Depardieu and his nineteenth-century ancestors, e.g. Coquelin, as well as between the 1990s heritage film and its 1950s forebears. Bellowing from the darkened upper balconies, Depardieu/Cyrano leaps, runs and pushes his way down the stairs, through the crowd and towards the stage. The film's first Cyrano monologue is framed in a single continuous travelling shot following him as he sweeps down a flight of stairs, pushes through the crowded audience in the pit and leaps up onto the stage. Shot from the theatregoers' perspective, the hero chases the actors to the back of the stage with his swaggering bulk and relentless tirade of words. He closes the scene by cutting a cord to shroud the cowering troupe in a painted fabric backdrop. The curtain falls behind him, and he bows, to a round of applause. Depardieu's Cyrano has made his robust entrance, and the stage is his.

The actor's very physical presence on screen generates a quality of an idealized French virility; the playful and sometimes lewd wordplay embellishes the man of action with cultured, thinking capacities. Depardieu's performance fits this double requirement, combining 'an intense physical presence' with 'the effective use of his voice, its softness and subtle modulations providing a contrast to his massive body' (Vincendeau 1993, 357). However, as Vincendeau suggests, this 'fit' extends beyond the actor's technical skills to an amalgam of Depardieu's star persona with Cyrano's mythological dimensions. Depardieu's early star persona (in roles least known outside France) 'combined a burlesque use of his body with a specific social identity ... [of the] comic *loubard* (a *loubard* is a proletarian petty hoodlum from city suburbs). ... Depardieu's bodily persona is also one which, in comic as in dramatic mode, links a class identity (shape, gestures, voice) to overt sexual display' (*ibid.*, 346–7). It is this class-specific masculinity that coincides so well with the burlesque humour accorded Cyrano and his macho troupe of gascons, a French regional stereotype – bon-vivant macho men from the south-west – which recurs in other historical films like *Le Bossu* as a ready source of humour. More than empty bravado, however, Cyrano's trademark 'panache' conceals a tender heart and a tragic, unrequited love.

Cyrano's achilles heel, his impossible secret love for Roxane, emerges in a quiet exchange between Cyrano and Le Bret set alongside the romantic night-time Seine.

Il m'interdit le rêve d'être aimé, même par une laide
Ce nez, qui d'un quart d'heure en tout lieu me précède.
Alors moi j'aime qui? Mais cela va de soi,
J'aime, mais c'est forcé, la plus belle qui soit.

I can never be loved even by the ugliest
My nose precedes me by 15 minutes.
Whom do I love? It should be clear.
I love the prettiest far and near

Rostand balances the tragic and comic aspects of the play through the device of Cyrano's absurd nose – source of endless quips and wordplay, it is at once the butt of endless jokes and wordplays and the root of his suffering. Howarth relates this sensibility to a recurring romantic sublime–grotesque dichotomy. Cyrano's 'enormous nose . . . represents in a vivid, visual form the earthbound physical reality which, according to the Romantic meta-physic, constantly frustrates and defeats the human spirit in its aspirations towards the ideal; Cyrano's grotesque appearance is enough to destroy all the dreams of an exalted love for which his romanesque imagination longs' (1975, 392).

In a mythological condensation of star persona, performance and role, Depardieu brings a particular inflection to this age-old thematic of the suffering male hero. Vincendeau argues that in his more dramatic roles of *auteur* cinema (*Loulou* or *Le Dernier métro*) Depardieu strikes a chord of embattled, noble masculinity common to French film stars such as Jean Gabin, Yves Montand and Daniel Auteuil. But the figure of an 'intense, suffering male hero' already recurs in literary figures such as Hugo's Jean Valjean and the Hunchback of Notre-Dame, Balzac's Colonel Chabert, Féval's Lagardère, Pagnol's Jean de Florette and Dumas' Edmond Dantès – many of them, not coincidentally, played in adaptation by Depardieu. These romantic figures share the characteristic of some physical or social injury: the burden of a (wrongly convicted) convict's past, the head wound, the hunchback, the nose – which stand in for the burden of social suffering.

The vulnerable virility of Depardieu's Cyrano evokes what Phil Powrie (1997) describes as a 'crisis of masculinity' in the French cinema of the 1980s. It is worth remembering that the figuration of masculinity in crisis has a long history in French cinema, going back notably to the tragic prole-tarian heroes played by Jean Gabin in the 1930s. However, in the context of the film's 1990 release, the troubled state of traditional French masculinity might also be linked with profound contemporary changes in gender roles and in the family. Additionally, Vincendeau (1995) links the cinematic characterization of the suffering hero to a crisis in patriarchal authority and leadership corresponding to the eclipse of the tradition of great populist leaders after De Gaulle. Cyrano's credo of fierce independence and honour bears striking parallels with de Gaulle's charismatic, authoritarian leadership. The hero's stubborn insistence to 'go his own way' even in the face of all odds evokes the 'French exception' – a tendency expressed in the political sphere, from De Gaulle's foreign policies to the French defence of national media and the special place of culture in the 1993 GATT agreement, as well as the controversial 1995 nuclear testing in the Pacific. Such an independent national character speaks through Cyrano's gallant and precarious independence of spirit – notably his Non, merci! (No, thank you) speech where he rejects de Guiche's offer of patronage in blatant disregard of his own interest:

> Et que faudrait-il faire?
> Chercher un protecteur puissant, prendre un patron,
> Et comme un lierre obscur qui circonvient un tronc,
> Et s'en fait un tuteur en lui léchant l'écorce,
> Grimper par ruse au lieu de s'élever par force?
> Non, merci! . . .
> Ne pas monter bien haut, peut-être, mais tout seul

> What should I do?
> Seek out a powerful protector to pursue?
> Cling to him like a vine?
> Wind around him to fawn and whine?
> And rise through ruse instead of merit?
> No, thank you! . . .
> Perhaps I'll not get far, but I'll get there alone.

A man of honour, a man of the heart, pen and sword, a gallant leader, *Cyrano*'s quintessential French hero (shadowed by the commanding star persona of Depardieu), is none the less a doomed hero, a symbol of a time of greater glory. This twinned bravado and pathos is encapsulated in Cyrano's trademark 'panache'. Made famous by Henry IV as a rallying cry in battle, 'panache' describes at once the plumes proudly displayed by France's military men and a much broader code of honour spoken in Cyrano's poignant closing monologue .

> Oui, vous m'arrachez tout, le laurier et la rose!
> Arrachez! Il y a malgré vous quelque chose
> Que j'emporte, et ce soir, quand j'entrerai chez Dieu
> Mon salut balaiera largement le seuil bleu,
> Quelque chose que sans un pli, sans une tache,
> J'emporte malgré vous,
>                       et c'est . . .
>         Mon panache.

You take everything – the rose and the laurel too!
Go on, take them! But, in spite of you,
One thing goes with me now and tonight,
When I at last God behold . . .
My salute will sweep His blue threshold . . .
With something spotless, a diamond in the ash . . .
Which I take in spite of you
> And that is . . .
My panache.

## Notes

I would like to thank Ginette Vincendeau for her generous and incisive comments on this chapter.

1 Study cited in the *Cyrano de Bergerac* press book (1991), and in Thibaudat (1990, 38).
2 My use of 'myth' throughout this chapter refers to Roland Barthes' term which explores how national cultural mythologies are embedded in the very fabric of the texts of popular culture. See his *Mythologies*, London, Vintage, 1972.
3 For further details about the life and thought of the actual Cyrano de Bergerac, see Erica Harth, *Cyrano de Bergerac and the Polemics of Modernity*, New York, Columbia University Press, 1970.
4 For historical and international discussions of the *film de cape et d'épée* see Guibbert (1993) and Desbarats (1989).
5 It could be argued that this nationalistic cultural strategy was also designed to counter the trauma and humiliation of the surrender of the military and German occupation during the Second World War.
6 Where the general 'look' and epic sweep of the film profoundly informed the subsequent cycle, subtle direct references may also be found. For instance, the opening sequence of *Le Bossu* takes place in Paris fencing quarters reminiscent of the headquarters of Cyrano's gascons. Further, Lagardère's bumblingly loyal adoptive uncles Cocardasse and Passepoil reference the broad gascon stereotype which provides much of Cyrano's comic relief. Finally, Cyrano's taunting duel of swordplay and wordplay with Valvert is echoed in the courtroom duel of Beaumarchais, and in *Le Bossu* with Lagardère's opening duel with Nevers (played, not coincidentally, by Vincent Perez).
7 These debates centred on the British Merchant–Ivory productions (*Room With a View, Howard's End*) appearing within a time-frame parallel to current French historical cinema. See Tana Wollen, 'Over Our Shoulders: Nostalgic Screen Fictions for the 1980s', in *Enterprise and Heritage: Crosscurrents of National Culture*, eds J. Corner and S. Harvey, London, Routledge, 1991, 178–93; and Andrew Higson, 'Re-presenting the National Past: Nostalgia and Pastiche in the Heritage Film', in *Fires Were Started: British Cinema and Thatcherism*, ed. L. Friedman, Minneapolis, University of Minnesota Press, 1993, 109–29.
8 A traditional French theatrical form, the classic alexandrine line of twelve syllables is subdivided into 'two groups of six syllables of hemistichs, that are each complete as regards syntactial relationships (an adjective should not be separated from its noun, an adverb from its verb) and both accented on the final syllable' (Woollen 1994, xxii). The lines are grouped into rhyming couplets with complex rules of rhyme and emphasis.

9 The film's foregrounding of language persists in the English translation, where Anthony Burgess' celebrated subtitles (based on his full translation of the play) provided a key selling point for English-speaking audiences.

10 These lines (and others quoted in this chapter) are taken from the film's French dialogue and the English subtitles by Anthony Burgess, rather than from the published play, as there are minor variations in both cases.

## Selected bibliography

Austin, Guy (1996) *Contemporary French Cinema: An Introduction*, Manchester, Manchester University Press.

Aziza, Claude (1998) Preface to the Pocket edition of *Cyrano de Bergerac*, Paris, Pocket.

de la Bretèque, François (1992) 'Le film en costumes: un bon objet?', *CinémAction*, 65, 111–22.

Brulard, Inès (1997) 'Linguistic Policies', in *Aspects of Contemporary France*, ed. Sheila Perry, London, Routledge, 191–207.

Comolli, Jean-Louis (1977) 'Le passé filmé', *Cahiers du cinéma*, 277, 5–14.

Comolli, Jean-Louis (1978) 'Historical Fiction: A Body Too Much', *Screen*, 19 (2), 41–53.

Condon, Anne Marie (1997) 'Cinema', in *Aspects of Contemporary France*, ed. Sheila Perry, London, Routledge, 208–25.

Crisp, Colin (1993) *The Classic French Cinema: 1930–1960*, Bloomington, Indiana University Press.

*Cyrano de Bergerac* press book (1991), London, Artificial Eye Film Company.

Desbarats, F. (1989) 'Autour de l'épée', *Les Cahiers de la cinémathèque*, 51/52, 73–88.

Finney, Angus (1996) *The State of European Cinema*, London, Cassell.

Guibbert, Pierre, (1993) 'Le film de cape et d'épée', *CinémAction*, 68, 154–9.

Hayward, Susan (1993a) *French National Cinema*, London, Routledge.

Hayward, Susan (1993b) 'State, Culture and the Cinema: Jack Lang's Strategies for the French Film Industry 1981–93', *Screen*, 34 (4), 380–92.

Howarth, W. D. (1975) *Sublime and Grotesque: A Study of French Romantic Drama*, London, Harrap.

Howarth, W. D. (1993) 'From Neo-Classical to Romantic Aesthetics: The Status of the Material World in Nineteenth-Century French Drama', in *French Literature, Thought, and Culture in the Nineteenth Century*, ed. Brian Rigby, Houndsmills, Macmillan, 105–27.

Loiseau, Jean-Claude (1990) 'Le swing de Rappeneau', *Première* (April), 68–78.

Powrie, Phil (1997) *French Cinema in the 1980s: Nostalgia and the Crisis of Masculinity*, Oxford, Clarendon Press.

Rappeneau, Jean-Paul (1991) 'Excerpt from a Letter', in *Cyrano de Bergerac* press book, London, Artificial Eye.

Reader, Keith (1993) 'Le phénomène Cyrano: Perceptions of French Cinema in Britain', *Franco-British Studies*, 15, 3–8.

Reader, Keith (1996) 'In the Time of Cholera', *Sight and Sound* (January), 26–27.

Rostand, Edmond (1994) *Cyrano de Bergerac*, ed. Geoff Woollen, London, Bristol Classical Press.

Rostand, Edmond (1993) *Cyrano de Bergerac*, trans. Anthony Burgess, London, Nick Hern Books.

Thibaudat, Jean-Pierre (1990) 'Cyrano c'est le pied', *Libération* (28 March), 38–40.

Truffaut, François (1976) 'A Certain Tendency of the French Cinema', in *Movies and Methods*, volume 1, ed. Bill Nichols, Berkeley, University of California Press, 224–37.

Vincendeau, Ginette (1993) 'Gérard Depardieu: The Axiom of Contemporary French Cinema', *Screen*, 34 (4), 343–61.

Vincendeau, Ginette (1995) 'Unsettling Memories', *Sight and Sound* (July), 30–2.

Vincendeau, Ginette (1998) 'Le Bossu/On Guard!', *Sight and Sound* (September), 39–40.

Williams, Alan (1992) *Republic of Images: A History of French Filmmaking*, Cambridge, MA, Harvard University Press.

Woollen, Geoff (1994) 'Introduction', in *Cyrano de Bergerac*, ed. Geoff Woollen, London, Bristol Classical Press, v–xxxv.

# Appendix

## *Jean-Paul Rappeneau (1932–): filmography*

1958 *Chronique provinciale* (short)
1966 *La Vie de château*
1971 *Les Mariés de l'an II*
1975 *Le Sauvage*
1982 *Tout feu tout flamme*
1990 *Cyrano de Bergerac*
1995 *Le Hussard sur le toit*

## *Filmed versions of Cyrano de Bergerac*

1900 *Cyrano de Bergerac*, Clément Maurice, France (with Constant Coquelin)
1909 *Cyrano de Bergerac*, Ernesto Maria Pasquali, Italy
1923 *Cyrano de Bergerac*, Augusto Genina, Italy (with Pierre Magnier)
1945 *Cyrano de Bergerac*, Fernand Rivers, France (with Claude Dauphin)
1950 *Cyrano de Bergerac*, Michael Gordon, USA (with José Ferrer)
1960 *Cyrano de Bergerac* (television adaptation), Claude Barma, France (with Daniel Sorano)
1962 *Cyrano et d'Artagnan*, Abel Gance, France/Italy/Spain (with José Ferrer and Jean-Pierre Cassel)
1985 *Cyrano de Bergerac* (television adaptation), Terry Hands, UK (with Derek Jacobi)
1987 *Roxane*, Fred Schepisi, USA (with Steve Martin)
1989 *Cyrano de Bergerac*, Naum Birman, USSR (with Grigori Kabo)
1990 *Cyrano de Bergerac*, Jean-Paul Rappeneau, France (with Gérard Depardieu)

## *Other films cited in the text*

*Beaumarchais*, Edouard Molinaro (1996)
*Le Bossu*, Philippe de Broca (1997)

*Camille Claudel*, Bruno Nuytten (1988)
*Caroline chérie*, Richard Pottier (1951)
*Le Colonel Chabert*, René Le Hénaff (1942)
*Le Colonel Chabert*, Yves Angelo (1994)
*Le Dernier métro*, François Truffaut (1980)
*Fanfan la Tulipe*, Christian-Jaque (1951)
*French Cancan*, Jean Renoir (1955)
*Germinal*, Claude Berri (1993)
*Les Grandes manoeuvres*, René Clair (1955)
*Howards End*, James Ivory (UK, 1992)
*Le Hussard sur le toit* (*The Horseman on the Roof*), Jean-Paul Rappeneau (1995)
*Indochine*, Régis Wargnier (1992)
*Jean de Florette*, Claude Berri (1985)
*Loulou*, Maurice Pialat (1980)
*Manon des sources*, Claude Berri (1986)
*Les Misérables*, Raymond Bernard (1933)
*Les Misérables*, Jean-Paul Le Chanois (1958)
*Nana*, Christian-Jaque (1955)
*1900*, Bernardo Bertolucci (Italy 1977)
*La Reine Margot*, Patrice Chéreau (1994)
*Ridicule*, Patrice Leconte (1996)
*A Room with a View*, James Ivory (UK, 1986)
*Stavisky*, Alain Resnais (1974)
*Tous les matins du monde*, Alain Corneau (1992)

# 21

# RECYCLED WOMAN AND THE POSTMODERN AESTHETIC

## Luc Besson's *Nikita* (1990)

*Susan Hayward*

### *Nikita*: contexts – a film in the making

*Nikita* was Besson's thank-you film to his audiences for saving *Le Grand bleu* (1988) from oblivion. *Nikita* was released in a shroud of secrecy (much like *Le Grand bleu*). Besson wanted to privilege his public, not the journalists. Thus, he argued that the film should go out on general release and not be premiered for special audiences such as the film critics.[1] This attitude did not endear him to a great majority of the reviewers, who reproached him for playing guru ('porte-parole') to the youth audience.[2] However, as before, his new film was a great success with audiences (it netted a 3.7 million audience in France alone, 3 million in the USA).[3]

Thanks to the success of *Le Grand bleu*, producing *Nikita* was relatively easy. Gaumont agreed to finance *Nikita* without seeing a script. *Nikita* cost 39 million francs (the average for 1990 was 20 million francs) and was a Franco-Italian co-production between Besson's own company (Les Films du Loup), Gaumont and Cecchi Gori Group Tiger Cinematographica. *Nikita* was the first scenario Besson scripted by himself without his usual entourage of scriptwriters. In terms of the music, as always, Besson stayed with Eric Serra, even though he did not particularly like the score to the opening credits of the film (Besson 1992, 165). As for casting, to his unofficial ensemble of players (Reno, Anglade, Bouise) he added the talents of Tchéky Karyo (a choice not liked, initially, by the producer at Gaumont, Patrice Ledoux) and Anne Parillaud. After three successful films with Carlo Varini as director of photography, Besson, seeking a new challenge, chose to work with Thierry Arbogast. Besson's and Arbogast's common interest in effects with natural light and simple lighting had a considerable impact on the look of *Nikita*, demarcating it visually from Besson's earlier films. Besson wanted a fairly weak lighting effect, causing problems with shooting beyond a certain focal length: after one and a half metres there is a loss of depth. Consequently much of *Nikita* was shot in medium-close-up shots and, given that the film is in Cinemascope, the effect on the image is to bring it very strongly up against the screen in terms of spectator perception – affording the image a certain inherent violence of its own.

*Nikita* tells the story of a nineteen-year-old junkie who gets arrested in a police raid during which she kills a policeman. Instead of life imprisonment she is given a 'second chance' by the State Secret Service Police for whom she 'agrees' to become a killer–agent. It was intentionally a *film noir*, and for the first time Besson had someone definitely in mind for the lead role, Anne Parillaud, who until then was mostly remembered for working opposite Alain Delon. When *Nikita* was released, Parillaud went from bimbo-starlette to ferocious androgyne, and finally to lethally armed female. She was no longer 'Delon's girl'. Press release after press release commented on the fact that Besson had become her Pygmalion and transformed her.[4] And, as if to confirm this regeneration, she won the 1991 César award (the French equivalent of the Oscar) for the best actress. Earlier, in 1990, she had won Italy's Donatello award for best foreign actress. The film itself won best foreign film award at the same ceremony.

Besson was pleased to have acted as her Pygmalion. However, it was a curious Pygmalionization since Parillaud was trained up in the opposite of ladylike good manners. She had to toughen up: learn judo, take lessons in shooting and gun maintenance. She was sent to acting classes to lower her voice and lose her 'titi parisien' accent. She also went to dancing and singing classes. A whole year of strengthening her body went by before she was shown the script and told the role she was to play. It is well documented that Besson pushes Jean Reno, his friend and fetish star, into strenuous training before he plays a part in his films, but this was the first time he had demanded it of a woman actor.

*Nikita* was shot in chronological sequence. Besson felt that it would allow for an authentic sense of Nikita's evolution from a teenage punk to a thirty-something woman. It was also important to shoot in continuity, he believed, so that Anne Parillaud could let herself go completely as the punk (Besson 1992, 14). As a result of shooting his film this way, however, it was not until he got to the end of his shooting schedule (sixteen weeks) that he realized that the ending he had scripted did not work.[5] In the first version, Marco and Nikita have been together for five years. 'Officially' she has been given three years' leave to 'get a life' with Marco. However, the Secret Police come to her apartment to 'arrest' her. She makes her escape, and it is Marco who dies in a shoot-out. She sets up a meeting with the Chief, and arming herself to the nines she blasts him away. She disguises herself as a journalist and gets herself arrested for breach of the peace. Bob (seeing through the disguise) jumps into the car and kisses her goodbye. She makes her escape, and redisguises herself as the punk of the beginning, but this time it is only a disguise: she now has light and fight in her eyes so all resemblance to her former self is pure happenstance (Besson 1992, 85). She holes up for two weeks in a police station as a missing person and then leaves.

This ending (which the American 1992 remake, *Point of No Return*, only partly adopts) seems far more empowering of Nikita than the one we actually see – where she just disappears. According to Besson the triangular relationship between Nikita, Bob and Marco came over more strongly in the film than it had done on paper so he could not stick to the original ending which, in his words, was to be a Ramboesque firework display (Besson 1992, 15). The curve of violence of the original version went against the sentimental curve and produced an imbalance, he claimed. This claim, however, says two things. First, that the love-triangle/story is more important than the trajectory Nikita might have been on. Second, that Nikita must remain agent and, therefore, victim of the state and not subject of her own violence (as she was at the beginning of the film). Nor is she allowed agency in the form of violence-as-retribution (as the first end-version had her). Instead, the Nikita we are left with is one weakened by love and who must pay the price for it by disappearing off the surface of the earth. In this respect, the film is consistent with the conventions of the *film noir* it purports to emulate which has the female threat ultimately safely contained. The original ending, Ramboesque or not, would not have left any ambiguity whatsoever as to woman as agent of her own destiny.

## *Nikita*: a first set of readings

*Nikita* is a film in three episodes about a teenage junkie who 'dies' to get 'reborn'. The narrative is *Pygmalion* recycled into the era of technologies of regeneration with Bob-the-father as the new Pygmalion – the embodiment of state surveillance and terror – who rebirths the dead Nikita as an infant, a commodification, a fiction even of the state. Nikita's (sexual/Oedipal) trajectory during these three episodes can be described as entirely circular. In the first episode she goes from child to woman; in the second she is represented as agencing desire; and in the third she devolves from woman back to child. Throughout the three episodes she is the victim of the state, always on demand and under command from the male voice (either embodied or disembodied) of the state (patriarchal law).[6]

When we first meet Nikita, her language and her bodily posture demarcate her as infantile, as pre-Symbolic. She sits foetus-like under the counter in the Chemist's shop and bleats out 'give me more' – as a child would to a nurturing mother. She calls out to her mother twice as she is administered, by men of the state, what she imagines to be a lethal dose to eliminate her. In fact the dose is to eradicate her past, to allow her to be reborn again, to be remade in the image/model of man (Bob-the-father). The dose starts the process of taming the wild animal she was (who blew off a policeman's head).

299

However, Nikita is a slow learner: in the totally male environment where she is taught 'male' things to do — karate, computer technology — she still acts the child ('again' she says when learning computer skills; she plays pranks — putting a live mouse in a box). She is still the naughty, subversive child who outhits the karate teacher, attempts to run away, shouts abuse, but then, counter to type, performs a ballet dance. All this is done under the ever watchful eye of Bob-the-creator/father.[7]

Nikita is of father born, but she is of 'mother' made woman. Amande (Jeanne Moreau), another woman caught in the web of state surveillance and terrorism (but seemingly resigned to her fate), teaches Nikita about sexual difference. She holds up the mirror to Nikita. Now that she has learnt this difference, Bob becomes the first object of her desire — a desiring readily colluded with by Bob, as is exemplified by the celebration of her first birthday in internment, when he offers her some cake off his knife. Slowly, over three years, Nikita is modelled into womanhood. But an ambiguous edge is always held, culminating in her first mission. Believing she is to be taken out for her birthday and enter into the real world (the Symbolic order of things) she goes with Bob to the Train Bleu restaurant. She is now 'as-woman'. However, her dress-code — black slinky dress, spiky heels, gloves (delivered upon her body by Bob and Amande) — warn us that she is a wandering fetish. In other words, she has forcibly joined the sisterhood of phallic women as depicted in *film noir*. Things do not improve when she unwraps her present only to discover Bob has given her a gun. This is no birthday (celebration of identity), this is her initiating ceremony/mission — a passage of rites into male/phallic technology. This whole scene represents a double denial by Bob of her sexual difference (first the dress-code, then the gun). Thus, in effect Nikita is still being denied entry into the Symbolic order of things (denied her sexual difference) — a denial that is further exemplified within this mission, first, by her foetus positioning in the kitchen (as she tries to escape) and, second, by the fire-bomb that forces her to propel herself down the waste-chute and run 'home' (down the fallopian tubes and back to the womb).

By the end of this first episode what is she? 'An element of the centre', she is told; hardly a very secure identity. None the less she is ready, she is told, to leave home and she kisses Bob-the-father goodbye. From the death/rebirth/learning scenario of her three years in state captivity, Nikita apparently emerges into the Symbolic order of things as a socialized human being. But we should beware of this assumption for she has been socialized as a killer–agent ('element', even) by and for the state. She is in the world to implement her 'education' and she has two new names. She is Marie and her code-name is Joséphine. As Marie, her first false identity, she is putatively a nurse — this is a cover-up, a masquerade of course for what she truly performs as a job: state assassin, code-name Joséphine. She is no longer Nikita (incidentally a Russian name for a boy), a name she had randomly chosen for herself (possibly off an Elton John song of that name) — with all the connotations of gender ambiguity/hybridity that the name holds. She is now named by others, her naming has been recycled: she is one picked identity replaced by another, this time not of her own arbitrary choosing but of deliberate state intervention. The names Marie and Joséphine themselves are not innocent. As Marie she is the Virgin Mary; she is also as we know masquerading as a nurse. As Joséphine she is named after Napoléon's lusting wife, a sexually voracious woman (if history is to be believed). Under this name Nikita is also the state assassin. The number of identities circulating around Nikita (already an indeterminate identity at that) mean that we never know who she is and we must assume that she too does not know who she is. All names ascribed to her are implicitly ambiguous, pointing to a duplicity (she is doubly mirrored in all her namings) where no subjectivity can seep out and affirm itself. 'La Femme Nikita' is a simulation, not real but hyper-real. Where is the real Nikita?[8]

In this second episode, Nikita finds love. So to all appearances she seems to be safely set on her Oedipal trajectory. She picks up Marco in a supermarket – seemingly she acts as agent/subject of desire. But, as with her subversiveness in the first episode, any sense of self-empowerment is quickly whipped away. In the first episode, we recall, she is shot in the knee, Bob clips her wings. This time she is swiftly brought into line and rebecomes an agent (not subject but object, an element of use) for the state, sent to execute orders. There is a second, more subtle and disruptive, way in which Nikita has her subjectivity denied her. In this instance it concerns Bob's supplying a narrative of his own (under the guise of Uncle Bob) for Nikita. Bob invents Marie as the virginal Mary, the little girl he knew in her 'robe blanche'. He gives her a past, a life story (to satisfy Marco's increasing curiosity about the woman he lives with but about whom he knows nothing). The past is not her past, the present is not her present. She is the fictionalized commodity of the state constructed in the words of Bob. She is, moreover, Bob's fetish and fetishized assassin – already evident from her first mission but made even more so in her third mission which he sends her on and which takes her to Venice. In that mission she handles a telescopic rifle that is as big as, if not bigger than, she is. In that mission, dressed only in her underwear and looking more like a bimbo than a fully fledged desiring woman, she executes (under orders from the male voice of the state) the target, a woman.[9] Female-on-female violence under orders from the disembodied male voice – a fairly disempowering position for women to occupy, I would suggest.[10]

By the end of episode two there is also an intimation that Bob is not the only male involved in 'forming' Nikita, that is, in constructing her subjectivity. Marco hints, in Venice, that he is aware that Nikita is under some duress to do certain things (he appears to be 'in the know'). A little later, he asks her who taught her to smile like she does, and Nikita replies that it is he, Marco. Well we know this is not true. It was Amande who taught her to smile ('smile for those who look at you'), educating her in the 'ways of women'. But

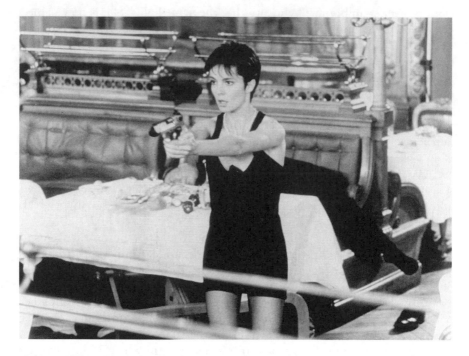

*Nikita* – Nikita (Anne Parillaud).

the point is that Nikita did not learn that for herself any more than she learnt anything else for herself. Her subjectivity, sense of identity, is constantly formed from outside of her self by others. She is then the object, not the subject, of the narrative. The point is also, if Marco is in the know – and the end of the film confirms that he knows a lot – then whose narrative are we witnessing? Who is the speaking subject? Bob? Marco? Both?

The third and final episode of the film is more or less given over to the preparation and carrying out of Nikita's last mission. In exchange for success-fully completing this mission, Bob promises that she can have a few years' off. Nikita is given *carte blanche* and five months to prepare the mission: to gain access to and film the secret files held in an Eastern European (proto-Communist) embassy. Bob tells her she can do it her way, that he wants a 'light touch not brute force'. To all appearances she has gained her spurs and is to be in control, acting independently from and of the father (Bob). Of course this is a false independence since Bob is ineluctably linked to the state as a high-ranking agent of the Secret Police Service and the mission is in the service of the State Secret Service. Furthermore, Nikita is still an element within the Secret Service obeying orders. Stage one, the 'abduction', seduc-tion and drugging of the ambassador, is successful (small surprise given

*Nikita* – above: Anne Parillaud and Luc Besson; below: Besson, the eye of the camera.

Nikita's training by Amande). Stage two, preparing to infiltrate the embassy, goes horrendously wrong. A 'cleaner', Victor (Jean Reno), is sent in by the state forces and he liquidates everybody except Nikita, who has to cross-dress as the ambassador to enter the embassy and gain access to the files. Nikita is now on a failure curve that will reduce her to oblivion, and the violence of the botched mission recalls the very brutal and bloody carnage of the opening of the film.

What do we make of Nikita's escape? Can it be read positively as it is by many of the target youth audience? I believe that if we unpick the above we cannot so easily go with a positive reading.[11] For a start, the fact that the male 'cleaner' has to come in and 'tidy up' Nikita's mess should warn us that a woman cannot be in charge of male technology. She can be an extension of it, as indeed Nikita was in her Venice mission, but not in control of it. Second, when she cross-dresses, she is again behaving transgressively, which patriarchy cannot tolerate. To gain access to the embassy she has to pass as male. Once she is in the embassy it is as if Nikita has completely forgotten that she has always been under surveillance and that here she will continue to be under the camera's eye. Why does she forget? Because she is passing as male – and, as we know, in *film noir*, it is not the male but, typically, the female who is the object of male scrutiny. To pass as male and not be scrutinized means to successfully masquerade as the phallus. But this cannot be – because to do so would be to outwit/transgress patriarchal law. And if we think for a moment as to how cross-dressing in mainstream cinema is represented then we can begin to see what is going on in *Nikita*. In mainstream cinema the male who cross-dresses never fully gives up his phallus, his sexuality. We are always aware that 'it' is there under the dress (e.g. *Tootsie*, 1982; *Mrs Doubtfire*, 1993). However, when the female cross-dresses, sexuality has to be repressed (both hers and the one she is masquerading as). She hides hers in dressing as male and must also repress the pretence of male sexuality because of the threat to the Symbolic order of things that homosexuality presents. For a woman to cross-dress, then, implies that she returns to the pre-Symbolic, back to the pre-sexual infant-child.

Nikita's momentary amnesia about her status as a woman under constant surveillance suggests that she is assuming a sexual identity she cannot possibly sustain. It suggests also that she has forgotten that she is not her own creation but that of Bob, who has, as we know, already commodified her as fetish (from the moment of her first mission). She cannot make herself fetish, nor can she make herself phallus. She cannot possibly, therefore, cross-dress convincingly, which is again why she is exposed by the surveillance cameras. She completes the mission, yes, but she has learnt that she can never assume her own identity, never make herself over and so her only choice is to not be, to disappear. The question remains, is it her choice, is it one she exercises or is her disappearance an inevitable consequence of her transgressive behaviour? In other words, is she punished for her attempts to take control of and become the male phallus? As the next section will go on to argue, the answer is a complex one.

## Nikita the cyborg cop – recycled woman and the postmodern aesthetic

One of the ways of interpreting of the term *postmodern* is to say that we are currently living in a postmodern age, an age that comes after modernism (loosely the nineteenth century to the mid-twentieth). What does that mean? That we come after the age of man's (*sic*) belief in the power of human reason to understand the world (man as transcendental subject) and of man's belief in progress, in science and technology to implement change. In coming after that age, we are in a position either to challenge what was done in the name of modernism and question the belief in the transcendental subject *or* merely look back at the past.

Acccording to Fredric Jameson (1984, 53–94), we are post-everything: post-history, post-colonial, post-modern and so on. Indeed, since the 1950s we have been living in a post-industrial era which has become increasingly one of post-industrial decay. This is the world which Besson so faithfully records in his films as early as *Le Dernier combat* and right through to *Le Cinquième élément* (1997). In *Nikita*, there is something so aptly postmodern about reconstructing, within the same disused Seita factories at Pantin, the set for the Gare de Lyon's beautiful *fin-de-siècle* and neo-baroque Train Bleu restaurant alongside the sterile and modern technological spaces of surveillance (the State Secret Service headquarters). This truly is artifice, post-production within post-industrial decay.

Postmodernism is an eclectic term with both positive and negative con-notations (similar to modernism's). On the positive side it is seen as a reaction against the extremes of modernism's belief in the benefits of sci-ence and technology to humankind. On the negative side, postmodernism is defined as coming after, as looking back, as lacking its own history (because it is defined only in relation to the past). Indeed, in its lack of history it rejects history and, because it has none of its own, stands eter-nally fixed in a series of presents. Viewed in this context, postmodern cul-ture does not challenge what is past. Rather it can only *recycle* what is past. This idea of recycling is closely associated to the notion that post-industrialism recycles waste, that it needs its waste in order to live, that it recycles dead styles. It survives on dead styles and seeks only perfect simulation (as with Besson's set of the Train Bleu restaurant). It invents nothing. It pastiches culture. Jean Baudrillard (1983, 142–6) explains this pastiche culture in the following way: because this culture is reproducing what has already been reproduced, postmodern culture reproduces not the real (for that has already been produced) but the hyper-real (of which vir-tual reality is an extreme example). Hyper-real, that is, a simulacrum of the real – perfect simulation – so much so, it no longer need invoke the original.

This lack of invocation of the original as a point of comparison means that there is no distinction between the real and the copy. And it is in this loss of distinction between real and representation that Baudrillard perceives the death of the subject, the individual. If there is no distinction between real and simulacrum how can you signify as distinct? If you recycle dead styles, how else can you signify except as lack, as death? You *re*-present nothing, you merely simulate it. The question then becomes, 'who am I'? The subject has no history, is stuck in the ever-present, so is in effect without memory. So how can the subject represent its self to itself? According to Lacan, the experience of temporality (past, present, future, memory) and its representa-tion are an effect of language. We use language to represent notions of tem-porality, and the idea of historical continuity.[12] If, however, the subject has no experience of temporality, no links with the past (lacking history), then it is without language. That is, it lacks the means of representing the 'I'. This creates a schizophrenic condition in which the subject cannot assert its sub-jectivity in language (because it cannot 'speak'). The subject fails, therefore, to enter the Symbolic Order (the social order of things, patriarchal order). The subject remains stuck in the Imaginary Order (the pre-linguistic moment). And the question becomes not just 'who am I?', but 'who made me?' In other words, where is the mother?

As far as film is concerned, it is instructive that the 1990s has witnessed a spate of monster films and that central to their narrative has been the question of reproduction and identity. If we just take as examples *Jurassic Park* (Spielberg, 1993), *Mary Shelley's Frankenstein* (Branagh, 1994) and *Interview with the Vampire* (Jordan, 1994), an analysis of these films reveals that the missing link between the past, present and the future is the figure of the mother. She is absent from these films as the site of reproduction. Instead *the* reproduction machine of post-industrialism, male technology, has reproduced 'her' through genetic engineering. The original is not even referred to: genetic engineering replaces the womb 'perfectly', simulating the idea of reproduction. Dinosaurs, monsters, vampires – aliens and cyborgs of our worst imaginings – these are the creatures of the age of simulacrum (to which we can now add the very hyper-real Dolly, the cloned sheep). These films express repressed fears around technology, of course. But they also express fears about being born into lack and having no identity. Besson's films, whilst less extreme perhaps, also express these concerns. Why otherwise do his characters speak so little or not at all? Why are their bodies so linked to technology? The main protagonists in all his films are techno-bodies virtually without language. Very few of Besson's characters have a history, and the only histories told are pure fiction, as in the case of Nikita who has no history of her own but has it narrated for her by Bob.

Nikita is recycled by man as a state assassin, as the visual embodiment of male technology (camera surveillance and the gun). She is then a cyborg-cop. She is reborn into an all-male world of technology, electronic mass media and surveillance (the world of male paranoia, one might add). She can have any name (Nikita, Marie, Joséphine). She is, then, recycled from the waste that she was (as a junkie). She is reproduced by the state as hyper-real, as the simulacrum of the real. She refers back to no original. She is recycled by the state to do male work, to handle male technology – the very technology that handles/watches her (through surveillance). As far as Nikita is concerned and in terms of identity there is no difference between the real and the copy – which is which? She lives the erasure of her subjectivity.

Nikita has no history, except for that invented for her by Bob. She is without memory, no past, no present, no future. She is without the linking mother – the mother she cries out for at the beginning of the film. There is no mother to secure the first sense of identity – as bonded to and loving the mother – so there is no way that Nikita can realistically embark on her own Oedipal trajectory. She will remain a fragmented subject, dispersed in representation as child, *femme fatale*/phallic woman, bimbo, as 'man' – never as woman. We hardly hear her speak. She lacks language and the means of representing the 'I'. She is constantly narrated or viewed by the male (Bob, Marco, the state, camera technology). She is emptied of meaning only to be filled by others' representations of her. She is contained, without identity – the perfect projection of male fantasy – and she can be changed, recycled at any time. She has been recycled to do the male's bidding on command (she kills when told). This entrapped submission of the self to the male command brings the dynamics close to pornography (placing of the female body to do as the man wants: shoot the gun/phallus/camera!). We may object that Amande holds up the mirror for Nikita. The response has to be that that moment merely serves to confirm that Nikita's subjectivity is dependent on the male gaze.

Nikita remains pre-Symbolic, pre-linguistic. And, as such, she eventually disappears (back behind the mirror presumably). Born into lack, and despite her very strong physical appearance (especially in the first half of the film), she can only *be* absence. She has no mother, no history, no language. She is merely the postmodern woman as cyber-reality. And part of the violence in this film is this *mise-en-scène*, through her body, of the hyper-real, of a lack of distinction between real and representation. 'Who is Nikita? Who made her?' *Nikita* is a *mise-en-scène* of the death of the individual. It is even more specifically a *mise-en-scène* of the denial of female subjectivity and therefore ultimately of difference. An effect of cyborg production is that it ends up denying what it has reproduced – and this is precisely what happens to Nikita. In the end Nikita is obliged to disappear.

# Notes

1 Instead he invited some eight hundred people and their partners who had written to him in support of *Le Grand bleu* and the film was premiered at the Grand Rex in Paris. In all, two thousand people came and this figure included some three hundred journalists. See Besson 1992, 174.

2 See Michel Ciment's review of *Nikita*, in *Positif*, 350 (1990), 43–4. And Besson's riposte in *Première*, 157 (1990), 83.

3 And in the first weeks of its worldwide release it netted nearly four million spectators. Even though *Nikita* did not meet with much critical acclaim in France, it was a huge success with French audiences. The Americans, therefore, were very keen to buy up the rights. However, for its release in the United States, Gaumont wisely decided to handle the sale of distribution rights separately from the film rights. The distribution rights were sold to Columbia Pictures and later the rights to the film were sold to Warner Brothers who were responsible for the remake of *Nikita* (released as *Point of No Return* aka *The Assassin*). Besson held on to the possibility of shooting the American remake, not because he wanted to make it but because he wanted to be party to the rewrite so that he could see how Warner would Americanize his story. In the end John Badham directed it. Besson felt it stayed fairly close to the original except for the ending (a happy one).

4 *Film français* describes the transformation thus: 'The gentle actress without any real character became a scandalous street-bum and an irresistible Mata-Hari' (no. 2340 (March 1991), 18). And see interview with Anne Parillaud in *Studio Magazine*, 61 (1992), 76–7.

5 In my book on Besson, I discuss the three endings Besson scripted in more detail. See Hayward 1998, 58–9.

6 For a contrastive 'woman with a gun' film where the outcome is more positive for the woman see Kathrtyn Bigelow's *Blue Steel*, 1990, interestingly released the same year as *Nikita*.

7 See Ginette Vincendeau's article for more detail on the father/daughter axis in French cinema (*Sight and Sound* (1992), 14–17).

8 Interestingly, the distribution title in English-speaking countries was 'La Femme Nikita' which thus removed the intended androgyny of the original.

9 I have written an article analysing this 'murder of the mother' in a discussion of *Nikita* and the uncanny (see Hayward 1997).

10 In my recent book on Luc Besson I have examined the extraordinary set of shots just before Nikita shoots the target as a displacement of the male probe, the masculine body using the female body as an instrument of voyeurism and death. The camera actually looks down a telescopic lens into Nikita's eye (see Hayward 1998, 117).

11 Elsewhere (Hayward 1997) I discuss in more detail this positive reading as an outcome of pleasure in Nikita's transgressive behaviour.

12 For a very helpful reading of Lacan's notion of temporality, schizophrenia and the postmodern see Giuliana Bruno's wonderful essay on *Blade Runner*: 'Ramble City: postmodernism and *Blade Runner*', *October*, 41 (1987), 61–74. I am indebted to her analysis in this section on the fragmented post-industrial subject.

# Selected bibliography:

Baudrillard, J. (1983) *Simulations*, transl. Paul Foss, Paul Patton and Philip Beitchman, New York, Semiotext(e).

Besson, L. (1992) *L'Histoire de Nikita*, Paris, Presse Bordas et fils.

Hayward, S. (1997) 'Sex–Violence–Surveillance: Questions of Containment and Displacement in Besson's Film *Nikita*', *Journal of the Institute of Romance Languages*, 5, 245–54.

Hayward, S. (1998) *Luc Besson*, Manchester and New York, Manchester University Press.

Jameson, F. (1984) 'Postmodernism and the Cultural Logic of Late Capitalism', *New Left Review*, 46, 53–93.

# APPENDIX

## *Luc Besson (1959–): filmography*

1978 *La P'tite sirène* (short)
1980 *L'Avant-dernier* (short)
1983 *Le Dernier combat*
1985 *Subway*
1988 *Le Grand bleu*
1990 *Nikita*
1991 *Atlantis*
1994 *Léon*
1997 *Le Cinquième élément*

## *Other films cited in the text*

*Blue Steel*, Kathryn Bigelow (USA 1990)
*Interview with the Vampire*, Neil Jordan (USA 1994)
*Jurassic Park*, Steven Spielberg (USA 1993)
*Mary Shelley's Frankenstein*, Kenneth Branagh (UK 1994)
*Mrs Doubtfire*, Chris Columbus (USA 1993)
*Tootsie*, Sidney Pollack (USA 1982)

# 22

# DESIGNS ON THE *BANLIEUE*

## Mathieu Kassovitz's *La Haine* (1995)

*Ginette Vincendeau*

When Mathieu Kassovitz's second feature, *La Haine*, came out in 1995, a new *auteur* was born, and the world 'discovered' the Parisian suburbs. *La Haine* is a stylish black-and-white chronicle of a day in the life of three male youths from a rough housing estate outside Paris. Hubert (Hubert Koundé) is black, Vinz (Vincent Cassel) is white and Jewish and Saïd (Saïd Taghmaoui) is a *beur*, slang for someone of second-generation North African descent. The film begins with television coverage of riots that took place on the estate the night before and during which a young *beur*, Abdel, was critically wounded. From then on, we follow the three friends on a supposedly 'typical' diet of boredom and violence which ends on a shocking new explosion of violence.

*La Haine* was one of the film events of 1995. The work of an unknown twenty-eight-year-old director and with no star, it was immensely successful critically and commercially. Kassovitz was awarded the coveted prize for best direction at Cannes. On 31 May, the day of its release, *La Haine* clocked up an exceptional twenty-one thousand spectators in Paris alone. The film generated much newsworthy controversy, from police guards walking out of a Cannes screening and riots in a Marseilles cinema, to Kassovitz going into hiding to escape media attention. *La Haine* took fifth place at the 1995 French box-office – beaten by *Gazon maudit* and *Die Hard 3*, but ahead of *The Usual Suspects* and of French super-productions such as *Le Hussard sur le toit*. It did very well outside France too, including in the USA, where Jodie Foster publicly endorsed it.[1] The script was published as an illustrated book; two CDs were released: one of the soundtrack and one of rap music 'inspired by the film'; exhibitions were mounted. Three years on, Virgin Megastore sells the English subtitled video with a gift *La Haine* T-shirt and the cable film channel FilmFour (launched 1 November 1998) selected it as one of its few non-English-speaking films, putting the seal of approval on *La Haine* as belonging to the new 'genre' of youth-oriented and violent international neo-*noir* movies.

The high-profile release of *La Haine* in 1995 was matched by wide-ranging critical attention. The film was highly praised for its portrayal of alienated underclass youths, and their habitat, the Parisian working-class *banlieue* (suburbs). There had been representations of working-class suburbs in French cinema before: in the films of Jean-Luc Godard and Maurice Pialat and more recently in many others, including Jean-Claude Brisseau, Jean-François Richet, Medhi Charef, Thomas Gilou and Malik Chibane, to the point that critics have debated whether there is a '*banlieue* film' genre (Jousse 1995, Reader 1995, Vigo 1995, Reynaud 1996). Furthermore, *La Haine* fits in with the 1990s 'young French cinema' (Xavier Beauvois, Agnès Merlet, Laetitia Masson, Karim Dridi and others) which increasingly addresses social issues (Marie 1998). Yet it is Kassovitz's film which came to represent, internationally, the cutting edge of French cinema. So why did *La Haine* become an international hit, rather than Brisseau's *De bruit et de fureur* (1988), Charef's *Le Thé au harem d'Archimède* (1985) or Chibane's *Hexagone* (1994), three films which occupy similar territories?

At the core of *La Haine* is a dual, and sometimes contradictory, appeal to authenticity and to youth culture. Black-and-white film stock, location shooting, slang dialogue (including the title from youth slang 'avoir la haine') signal a desire to be true to an observable situation. *La Haine* echoed real-life occurrences such as the 1990–1 riots in Lyons and Paris suburbs, and foreshadowed others in late 1995 and in 1997, including in Chanteloup-les-Vignes where it was shot. The film was released shortly after the right-wing populist Jacques Chirac was elected President of the Republic in May 1995, following a campaign dominated by themes of '*fracture sociale*' (social cleavage) and 'exclusion', of which the suburban housing estates (*cités*) are the emblem. At the same time, *La Haine* is one of the most stylized French films of recent years, which displays cinematic allegiances – Martin Scorsese, Spike Lee and John Woo principally – distant from the classic social realism of Pialat, Ken Loach and Mike Leigh. As Kassovitz put it: 'The aim was to make the *cité* beautiful, using smooth camerawork. I had the money [a budget of 15 million francs]. There are moments when it's all too much, almost complacent, like a music video' (*Positif* 1995, 11). A few dissenting voices (Alexander 1995, Rémy 1995, Douhaire 1998) to the general praise indeed queried *La Haine*'s 'authenticity' on the grounds that its seductive *mise-en-scène* was evidence of lack of political rigour. My aim in this chapter is to explore further the ways in which *mise-en-scène* in *La Haine* both supports and contradicts its social project.

## Mapping a social space

Paris, the modern city *par excellence*, has dominated French cinema. Elegant or picturesque apartment blocks, intimate courtyards and bustling cafés constitute its cinematic grammar. Initially, the areas outside the historic centre

311

were seen as idyllic populist sites offering relief from the noisy city – for instance in Marcel Carné's *Nogent, Eldorado du dimanche* (1929), Julien Duvivier's *La Belle équipe* (1936) and Denys de la Patellière's *Rue des Prairies* (1959).

Everything changed in the 1960s, when the economic boom and rapid expansion of Paris and other major cities under de Gaulle's administration demanded a massive building programme to house the displaced French workers of the *exode rural* and the freshly arrived immigrants. In some cases, the new buildings replaced appalling *bidonvilles*. The architecture of the 1960s–70s went into concrete gigantism, betrayed by the names of the most notorious estates: *Les 4000* in La Courneuve, *Les 3000* in Aulnay-sous-Bois. In high tower blocks or long 'walls', the grids of identical flats were nicknamed 'rabbit hutches'. Thin walls let noises through, water ran through the cellars, lifts broke down; there were few shops and cafés, and a lack of cultural venues. As Renaud sang in the 1970s, 'France is a shitty suburb'.[2] Subsequent, more imaginative, housing programmes designed smaller blocks. But the need for cheap terrain pushed these further out of the metropolis. This is the case for Chanteloup-les-Vignes, a forlorn north-western suburb, a forty-minute train ride from Saint-Lazare station. Coming close to what Marc Augé (1995) calls 'non-place', the estate stands on the edge of an immense empty landscape of fields and distant industrial buildings, separated by a railway station which was deliberately fired on the day of its inauguration. In Chanteloup-les-Vignes as elsewhere, better architecture was not an answer to the real problems of high unemployment and increased immigration from the early 1980s. Pockets of misery developed, ridden with drugs, alcohol and violence. Numerous urban improvement policies were introduced, culminating in the creation of a (short-lived) Minister for the City in 1991, provoking mostly anger and derision (Maspero 1990; Garnier 1996). The social segregation put in place in the 1960s was backfiring, aggravated by the worsening racial issue. The working-class *banlieue*, where the majority of the immigrant population lives, is choice breeding ground for the fascist National Front.

Since the 1960s, French fiction films have responded to the *banlieue* in two main fashions, which I will call 'aesthetic' and 'sociological' (though some of the films, e.g. Rohmer's and Brisseau's, share both tendencies). The aesthetic tendency includes films such as Godard's *Une femme mariée* (1964), *Deux ou trois choses que je sais d'elle* (1967), and *Numéro deux* (1975), Rohmer's *Les Nuits de la pleine lune* (1984), and *L'Ami de mon amie* (1987), Alain Corneau's *Série noire* (1979), Claire Simon's *Scènes de ménage* (1991), and Brisseau's *De bruit et de fureur* (1988). In these predominantly *auteur* films, the *banlieue* tends to serve as background to other concerns, such as consumerist society, existential displacement and sexual politics. The desire to avoid the (in France, derogatory) critical label of 'sociological' is manifest in the foregrounding of an aesthetic agenda: the use of sound in *Deux ou trois choses*, the split screen in

*Numéro deux*, the hallucinatory apparitions in *De bruit et de fureur*. On the 'sociological' side are films where the *banlieue* is a central topic and a decor and where the approach is naturalistic: Pialat's *Loulou* (1979), Coline Serreau's *Romuald et Juliette* (1989) and *La Crise* (1992), Serge Le Péron's *Laisse béton* (1984), as well as comedies such as Gérard Lauzier's *Le Plus beau métier du monde* (1996) and Merzak Allouache's *Salut, cousin!* (1996). Since the mid-1980s, the so-called 'films de *banlieue*' have concentrated on working-class estates. These include *beur* or *beur*-oriented films such as *Le Thé au harem d'Archimède* (1985), *Hexagone* (1994), Thomas Gilou's *Raï* (1995), Chibane's *Douce France* (1995) and others such as Richet's *Etat des lieux* (1995) and *Ma 6-T va crack-er* (1997). In this spectrum, *La Haine* occupies a bridging position. From the 'sociological' films it takes a genuine interest in the working-class suburb as setting and topic, and from the 'aesthetic' films a stylistic distanciation from it.

As setting, Kassovitz elected the late 1970s 'average' estate of La Noë in Chanteloup-les-Vignes because he did not want 'a hellish estate where you can't film because you are being shot at. ... I did not want derelict buildings either' (*Télérama* 1995a, 44). Chanteloup-les-Vignes, however, is hardly 'average'. Initially planned to house the workers of a nearby Simca car factory, the estate is now testimony to the devastation of unemployment. Since the early 1980s, it has become 'a test-town, an observatory of urban difficulties' (Robache and Saragoussi 1998, 81). Although the design of *La Haine*'s estate deliberately avoids high-rise buildings and allows Kassovitz to eschew the huge forbidding 1960s blocks of *Deux ou trois choses, Le Thé* or *De bruit et de fureur*, the place appears as desolate and violent. Its dominant visual motif is that of small curved blocks with distinctive roof designs and of children's playgrounds, though children play with burnt cars rather than on the sand pits. The three heroes walk down its streets and car parks, sit in the squares, mostly alone. Hubert's burned-down gym is empty; the petrol station is vandalized and barren; the train and the Paris Saint-Lazare station are empty. The dominant image is of a 'dead space' which visualizes the boys' boredom while it detaches them from their surroundings. Compared to *Le Thé, Hexagone* and *Raï*, but also to American films depicting similar milieux, like Spike Lee's *Do the Right Thing* (1989) and *Clockers* (1995), the *banlieue* of *La Haine* lacks social depth. Unlike many other *banlieue* films with establishing shots depicting the *borders* between their *cité* and the rest of the world, *La Haine* never shows us how the *cité* stands in relation to its environment, and thus decontextualizes it.

Traditional spaces of social interaction, such as flats and staircases, are scant. We go inside Vinz's and Hubert's flats (not Saïd's), but the important scenes again isolate them; the boys retreat from family life and hole up in their bedrooms. The only other interior we see in the *cité* is that of Darty[3] the fence, basically a warehouse. Unlike in *Le Thé, Hexagone* or *Douce France*, the three heroes never meet in cafés or discos. When they go to a café in Paris, we see only the downstairs toilet. Attempts at recreating social space take place on the margins, on the roof and in the cellars. The roof functions as the most convivial space, symbolically 'elevating' the youngsters who, though they are ultimately removed from it, have the upper hand over the authorities. By contrast, the scene in the cellars is an undignified chase. This is a common image of exclusion, found in many *banlieue* films, like the exclusion from nightclubs, sufficiently common to have become a cliché. In *Douce France* the *beur* hero ironizes that he curled his hair to look more *beur* so he would be thrown out of nightclubs 'in order to integrate into exclusion'. Apart from a brief scene at the local Vietnamese shop, the only institutionalized 'social' arena in *La Haine*'s estate is the police station. Even the job centre, which recurs in *beur* films (albeit to show prejudice and lack of opportunity), is absent. The only representation of 'employment' is dealing in drugs and stolen goods, like a distorted mirror of legitimate society. A 1993 study showed how, in estates such as that of *La Haine*, drug dealing 'benefited from increased benevolence on the part of families, who see its financial windfalls as a way of paying the bills' (Garnier 1996, 33–4), as Hubert's mother does (and as sung by rap group Expression Direkt in the CD inspired by *La Haine*).[4] Drugs are one of the issues which illustrate Kassovitz's uneasy relationship with the social reality he depicts. In the British press-book for *La Haine* he asserts there were no drugs at La Noë, contradicting both their recurrent presence in the film and off-screen evidence about the estate (this may have been his way of pacifying the inhabitants of La Noë, some of whom were hostile to the shooting of *La Haine* and to the film itself).[5]

Kassovitz's bleak picture thus relates to observable social factors. It is also the result of his concentration on a male world. In a classic gendered division of space, we glimpse mothers, aunts and grandmothers at home, cooking and sewing, and sisters doing homework, a cliché from *beur* films. On their picaresque outdoor journey, the boys' encounters are aggressive or downright violent, as in black gang-crime films such as *Boyz N the Hood* (1991) and *Menace II Society* (1993). Between Saïd's opening altercation with a black neighbour and the ending's 'Mexican stand-off',[6] the boys clash with siblings, officials, policemen, journalists, a shopkeeper, a neighbour, a concierge, patrons at an art gallery (improbably holding a reception at 1 a.m.), a taxi driver, a man on an escalator, skinheads and each other. The few women who appear are special targets for aggression. The female journalist is particularly abused, as are the women at the art gallery and the female beggar in the *métro*. This is a testosterone-filled world, where boxing is recreation and voices on the soundtrack are virtually all male, with a few exceptions such as the television newscaster and a snippet from Edith Piaf's 'Je ne regrette rien' (Piaf's song could be doubly ironic, as a symbol of the displaced populist 'Franco-French' popular culture, and as the anthem of ultra-right paratroopers in Algeria). The rap music heard in the car, 'mon esprit part en couilles' by Expression Direkt, picks up on a particularly male reference

314

(*couilles* means 'testicles'), and the rap mixed by the DJ with Piaf is from 'Nick la Police' by Extreme-NTM, a 'hard-core' group, rather than, say, the more melodious and consensual MC Solaar.

It is hardly worth pointing out the male symbolism of the gun, the fetish object lost by the police and stolen by Vinz. For the poster of *La Haine*, Kassovitz rejected the image of a gun (D'Yvoire 1995, 103), replacing it with the angry eyes of the three heroes. But one of the most often reproduced images from the film is that of Vinz's pretend shoot at the camera with his fingers. The boys wear sports gear with combat connotations. Vinz's shaved head (not that different from the skinheads he beats up), Saïd's leather jacket, Hubert's fatigue trousers all connote a macho world. Their language is 'verlan', an old form of backslang (which inverts syllables) revived in the 1970s. Some verlan words have entered the national vocabulary, such as *'feuj'* (juif, Jew), *'keuf'* (flic, cop), *'meuf'* (femme), and of course *'beur'*; in fact *beur* is so common that a further form of verlan has transformed it into *rebeu*. These are familiar from Renaud's songs and films such as Josiane Balasko's *Les Keufs* (1987) and Claude Zidi's *Les Ripoux* (1984). But the *degree* to which the boys use verlan designates their language as *banlieue* gang-speak. The recurrent sexually aggressive insults of 'nique ta mère' (literally 'fuck your mother') and 'bâtard' (bastard) are relatively new additions to French slang, which speak of both Mediterranean and American influences.[7] In fact, audience reactions to *La Haine* record resistance from *banlieue* youth to what they perceived as excessive obscenity (*Télérama* 1995b, 24–7). But beyond the contents of dialogue and songs, as Mongin (1995) points out, male aggression is also affirmed by the sheer rhythm and pitch of the boys' hysterical verbal flow, especially Saïd's.[8] This is matched by their prancing and swaggering, Vinz in particular who spits, picks his nose, punches Hubert's punch-bag or the air.

Throughout the film, the masculinist stance of the young men is narratively justified by police aggression, itself a representation of the 'symbolic' violence visited upon them by society. It is also naturalized by the brilliant performances of Cassel, Koundé and Taghmaoui, by their energy and humour. The problem, as noted by Alexander (1995) and Reynaud (1996) is that their behaviour is presented as coextensive with the experience of the *banlieue*. *Banlieue* and *beur* films have always been characterised by a male focus. Women are denied subjectivity, their identity residing in their relation to the males, and consequently they do not participate in the depiction of *social* issues. When women take centre stage, as in Kassovitz's previous feature *Métisse* (as well as his 'model', Lee's *She's Gotta Have It* (1986), or the only female rap song in the *La Haine*-inspired CD[9]), the sexual immediately replaces the social. Kassovitz tellingly justifies the absence of women in *La Haine* as a desire 'to keep the idea [of the film] as pure as possible' (*Humanité-Dimanche* 1995). Beyond this banal sexism, however, *La Haine* is symptomatic of a deeper gender shift. Family and culture are mostly kept off-screen, but what we see of them is female: both television newscaster and journalist are women. There are no fathers or male authority figures, in common with *banlieue* and *beur* films, where fathers are pitiable wrecks (*Le Thé*), psychotics (*De bruit et de fureur*) or just not there. *La Haine* takes the fathers' absence further, pointing to the feminization of labour and public life, and the fact that chronic male unemployment is entering its second generation. The young men are left adrift in a society where the only patriarchal figures are the 'bad fathers' of the police. Vinz's, Hubert's and Saïd's aimless wanderings in the empty *cité* and their disastrous trip through night-time Paris can be re-read in this light. Societal shifts have left them doubly redundant, in class and gender terms. But their mental *habitus* is still that of dominant masculinity, manifested by their aggressive verbal and body language, their occupation of public space, their ineffectual attempts at asserting authority over their sisters, and by their allegiance to a popular culture which is increasingly visible (clothes, graffiti) and audible (language, music) as its target audience is socially disempowered. This paradox is inscribed in the film in other ways, and in particular in the relationship between French and American culture, played out at the level of the film contents (the boys' culture) and of the film's style, to which I will now turn.

## Designer *banlieue*

Compared with the dreary decors of *beur* and *banlieue* films, or the rough black-and-white look of *Etat des lieux*, *La Haine* is polished and seductive. It aims to shock *and* please, balancing its realism with a combination of the mannerism of the *cinéma du look* (Luc Besson, Jean-Jacques Beineix, Leos Carax), the (male) nervous energy of Scorsese, Tarantino and Woo, and the modish 'grunginess' of new British films such as *Trainspotting* (though the latter was released after *La Haine*).

Black-and-white stock is the most immediate feature with which *La Haine* straddles the realist/non-realist divide, but also, ultimately, it acts as the badge of its aestheticism. Initially planning to shoot the suburbs in black-and-white and Paris in colour, Kassovitz opted for black-and-white throughout, with a more sober *mise-en-scène* for Paris. Black-and-white may give the film an historical *cinéma-vérité* aura, but at the same time it signals distance from 'normal' (colour) documentary and from the naturalistic *beur* films. Second, black-and-white looks 'cool', like postmodern music videos; it establishes a link with *film noir* and recalls Scorsese's *Raging Bull* (1980) and Lee's *She's Gotta Have It*. Third, as in the latter film, black-and-white plays on the heroes' skin colour and texture, especially Hubert's, who is stereotypically introduced with glistening bare torso while training in his empty gym (another tribute to *Raging Bull*). Such a degree of aestheticization explains why, to Kassovitz's annoyance, *La Haine* was not as 'shocking' as he anticipated: 'Posh people would tell me the film was "fantastically truthful".

*La Haine* – (from left to right) Vinz (Vincent Cassel), Saïd (Saïd Taghmaoui), Hubert (Hubert Kaoundé).

I thought I would shock people more, but unfortunately not. There was a fashion phenomenon' (*Télérama* 1995a, 46).

Kassovitz also negotiates the realist/non realist dichotomy through authorial intervention. First the 'in-jokes': after Hitchcock, Godard, Sorsese *et al.*, he inserts a revealing cameo of himself as the skinhead beaten up by Vinz, and of his producer Christophe Rossignon as a taxi driver (double in-joke); Cassel's name appears on the letter box at Astérix's flat; his shaved head makes Vinz look like Kassovitz; Kassovitz's father appears in the art gallery; the attempt to 'switch off' the Eiffel Tower is a reference to *Un monde sans pitié* (1989), produced by *La Haine*'s Productions Lazennec. More subtle means reinforce Kassovitz's signature on the film text. The time counter which appears at intervals has no narrative function; but it gives the film urgency and exhibits the author's manipulation of his material. Flamboyant *mise-en-scène* effects punctuate *La Haine*, reminiscent, as Kassovitz admits, of music videos (he directed one in 1990, for French rapper Tonton David). The music video aesthetics can be seen, directly, in the scenes that are expertly cut to a musical number: the opening news footage, Hubert parcelling out his drugs, the break-dancing. Generally, black-and-white stock, rapid editing, striking changes in camera angles, asymmetrical compositions and direct address to the camera evoke 'MTV aesthetics'. The mobile camera restlessly tracks and pans, follows or precedes the three young men, hot on their backs as in *Mean Streets* (1973), pausing to produce strong horizontal and diagonal compositions of their faces or the back of their heads, magnified by Cinemascope. The camera 'punches' the air and moves like a bullet through space (as in Besson's *Nikita* 1990). A few cuts evoke gun shots. Disorientation is aimed at: the 180-degree pan in the police station, the first view of Paris with its 'compressed zoom'. An extraordinary helicopter shot over the *cité* accompanies the musical mixture of rap and 'Je ne regrette rien' floating eerily above the buildings, a neat image of the film's deft merging of the social with the aesthetic. When Vinz hides in a cinema, his cigarette smoke soars in the air in ornate light patterns. The classic-realist flow of the boys' progress is interrupted by incongruous scenes such as an old man telling a story in the toilet, and several vignettes seen from Vinz's 'mind': his dancing to Jewish wedding music, the cow in the middle of the estate, the car going in fast reverse down the Paris street, the imaginary shooting of the policemen outside Les Halles.[10] The boys' shifting compositions within the frame conduct a sophisticated play on the gaze. They look straight at the camera, or conversely look on events from an off-centre position, leading, as Claire Vassé observed, to an unstable audience viewpoint, 'neither witness nor spectator' (Vassé 1995, 6). Even though, as Tarr (1997, 45) observes, the film gives Vinz a more prominent narrative position, the overall impression is of a dynamic interaction between the three. Furthermore, Saïd and Hubert dominate the oral space: Saïd with his incessant *tchatche*, Hubert with the emblematic framing story about a man who fell from the fiftieth floor (discussed below). When the old man tells his story (about the Holocaust) in the café toilet, an elaborate play on mirrors cuts up the space and the boys' bodies, graphically suggesting their shattered identity and disorientation.

Do *La Haine*'s visual and oral sophistication, its spectacular pleasures, undercut its 'authenticity' as has been suggested? I would reply that its spectacularization of the topic, though problematic, indicates a shrewd understanding of the social situation evoked by the film. When Hubert angrily tells the television journalists filming the *cité* that 'this is not Thoiry', he is alluding to a safari theme park near Paris but also to a wider media phenomenon which includes the film itself. News reportage which presents *banlieues* as exotic hells has been periodically, and rightly, accused of sensationalism, because of its concentration on the graphically violent. This is illustrated by Didier Daeninckx's brilliant short story 'Rodéo d'or' (1992, 79–92), based on real events, in which television journalists pay *banlieue* hooligans to joyride for their cameras, with tragic consequences. Georges Ferreboeuf, press officer for a 'difficult' suburb put it like this: 'Parisians come here with ready-made clichés and a partial view in mind. They show reality within a narrow framework, neglecting the "off-screen": everyday life' (Ferreboeuf 1996). This is not just PR rhetoric. From François Maspero's and Anaïk Frantz's ethnographic journey through the suburbs (Maspero 1990) to

*La Haine* – Clash of cultures: great French poets (Charles Baudelaire, left and Victor Hugo, right) on the murals of the La Noë estate in Chanteloup-les-Vignes, where *La Haine* was shot.

Bertrand and Nils Tavernier after their experience of filming *De l'autre côté du périphérique* (1997), many have voiced the gap between the multi-layered – violent and dysfunctional as well as peaceful and hard-working – reality of the *banlieue* and its dominant representation through violence. *La Haine* does concentrate on the 'narrow framework', arguably contributing to Chanteloup-les-Vignes' bad reputation, provoking further acts of violence. During a visit to the estate, as I walked round taking photographs, insults rang in the air, stones and bottles fell near where I was standing, forcing me to make a quick exit. It is hard to think that this was not an effect of *La Haine* turning La Noë, indeed, into a kind of Thoiry, attracting visitors such as myself. But the representation of violence, if it flatters delinquents' narcissism (Vinz's obsession with watching the riots on television), is also the only way of drawing attention: 'Young people understand . . . that violence is the only way of communicating with the outside world, the city, the country. If the neighbourhood explodes, if it scares people off, the attention is immediate' (Wittner in Garnier 1996, 65). While the more realistic, but more muted and localized, violence of the *beur* films did not export, Kassovitz understood that he needed *spectacular* male violence for *La Haine* to be successful on a large scale.

## Black-blanc-*beur*, and American

Kassovitz's *La Haine* thus achieves a perfect amalgam between the 'socio-logical' and the 'aesthetic' tendencies in filmic depictions of the *banlieue*. The sociological anchorage of the film is clear, from the shooting on location to the references to current events: violence, unemployment, drugs, the sheer cultural void of the *banlieue* estate – hence the recognition and praise by French audiences and mainstream film criticism (the daily and weekly press, *Télérama*, etc.). At the same time, the film's aesthetic project, in particular its desire to avoid the traditional naturalism of many *beur* and banlieue films, is also evident: camera work, film stock, textual references all signal the high-profile *auteur*, hence his recognition by the French critical establishment (*Cahiers du cinéma*, *Positif*). Yet, the same sociological anchorage and *auteur* recognition is true, for example, of Brisseau's *De bruit et de fureur*, a film which had no popular success at home or abroad. The reason why *La Haine* achieved global recognition is that the film also harnesses its social depiction to international modes of representation, connecting it to the neo-*noir* violent thriller, and giving Kassovitz the accolade of the youth-oriented popular film press at home (*Première*, *Studio Magazine*) and abroad.

After a brief pre-credit black-and-white shot of rioting, the next image of *La Haine* is in colour: a blue-and-white terrestrial globe bursts into flame when a petrol bomb is thrown at it. The globe later reappears on the ironic 'The World Is Yours' posters (homage to *Scarface*) which Hubert looks at in disgust from the train, and which later Saïd alters with his spray can (changing the word 'vous'/yours to 'nous'/ours). On the soundtrack, Hubert's voice tells the story of 'a man who falls from the fiftieth floor of a building and keeps saying, so far so good . . . so far so good . . . what matters is not the fall but the landing'. The story is reprised twice by Hubert, in the middle of the film and at the end, with his voice once again off-screen, the word 'man' now replaced by 'society'. Next is a montage of riot images, which alternates documentary footage of CRS riot police fighting young people in Paris (the iconography is of inner Paris riots, the CRS reminiscent of May '68) with images of rioting in the film's *cité*, revealed to be 'television' as the set is switched off before the film proper begins. Over this sequence, Bob Marley's 'Burnin' and Lootin'' is heard. With this opening, Kassovitz blurs the distinction between documentary and fiction, and links international liberation struggles, French postwar history and 1990s *banlieue* unrest (Marley's song hovers faintly over the beginning of the film). Similarly, the Hughes Brothers' *Menace II Society* moves from the 1965 LA Watts riots to the 1993 'real' situation, before starting its fiction. Parallels between *La Haine* and black gang-crime films such as *Menace II Society* and *Boyz N the Hood* as well as Spike Lee's *Do the Right Thing* have been noted, although Lee's *Clockers*, released after *La Haine*, offers the closest comparison. Kassovitz's first feature *Métisse* (1993) recalled *She's Gotta Have It* in plot structure – a (mixed-race)

320

woman with two lovers, one black, one white – and in the character played by Kassovitz, dressed up like Lee in this film and in *Do the Right Thing*. From *Do the Right Thing*, *La Haine* also quotes the presence of a DJ and an altercation with 'Oriental' storekeepers (which also appears in *Menace II Society*). Yet, ironically, the main difference between *La Haine* and its African-American contemporaries is in the treatment of race. Where the world of *Menace II Society* and *Boyz N the Hood* is all-black, that of *La Haine* is mixed. Where Lee's films concentrate on racial conflict, *La Haine* (like *beur* films) focuses on the common struggle of mixed-race groups against the police and bourgeois society. This has led to accusations by Anglo-American critics that *La Haine* sweeps racism under the carpet (Alexander 1995; Tarr 1997) while, *a contrario*, French writers derided the 'politically correct' black-blanc-*beur* trio (Jousse 1995; Mongin 1995).

Kassovitz's trigger for *La Haine* was the real-life racist murder of Makomé, a young Zairean, in a Parisian police station. The film picks up on the well-documented racism of the French police, undiminished by the presence of *beur* and black policemen, as reflected in the film: Saïd remarks that 'An Arab does not survive for more than an hour in a police station'; the police in Paris 'don't see' Vinz, and go first for Saïd and Hubert, who are later submitted to racist humiliation. There are references to other racisms: black–*beur* antagonism, and especially anti-Semitism (the old man's story). Yet the racist murder remains merely a trigger in the film too. Kassovitz's statement that *La Haine* is a film about police *bavures* or 'blunders' (*Télérama* 1995a, 42) confirms a shift from racist to general police violence. (French police *bavures* – more than three hundred mortal 'blunders' have been recorded since 1981 – are so common that they are standard fare for comic films: see *Inspecteur La Bavure* (1980) and *Les Ripoux*.) While *La Haine*'s black-blanc-*beur* trio is perhaps too 'neat' in visual and ideological terms,[11] the higher degree of racial integration depicted in *La Haine*'s *cité*, compared to American ghettos, accurately reflects the French situation. This is especially true of second- or third-generation 'immigrants', raised and schooled in the same heterogenous milieux as young 'gaulois', as can be observed by anyone living in or visiting the *banlieues* (see also Bourdieu 1993). This does not mean that racism has disappeared, as shown by the success of the National Front in these same areas. The extent to which multi-ethnicity in post-colonial France is accurately represented in cultural productions is also a contested issue (Hargreaves and McKinney 1997). *La Haine* nevertheless inserts itself in an increasingly hybridized culture, especially that which addresses younger generations.

In featuring a mixed-race central trio, Kassovitz is in the tradition of *beur* cinema. Christian Bosséno (1992, 48) noted of the 1980s *beur* films that already 'The theme of racism . . . is virtually absent; all [young characters] suffer the same raw deal to an equal degree'. *Le Thé, Hexagone, Raï, Douce France*, etc. all put the accent on the 'raw deal' suffered by young people from the *banlieue*. Reactions to *La Haine* from a mass youth audience 'made up of Vinz, Hubert and Saïd look-alikes' (*Télérama* 1995b, 24–7) were varied, but all addressed issues of class, not race. The French hip-hop scene is also noticeably mixed (Cannon 1997). Two of the most popular recent French comedies – *La Vérité si je mens* (1997, shot by *Raï* director Thomas Gilou) and *Les Trois frères* (1995, starring popular male comic trio Les Inconnus, which includes a black West Indian, Pascal Légitimus) – deal with multi-ethnic France. Both work through comic stereotypes (racial and otherwise) and elicit consensual, if sexist, humour. But they also testify to the increasing presence of multi-ethnic individuals in a range of popular cultural products. *Les Trois frères*, with its bonding mixed-race male trio, is like the comic flip-side of *La Haine*. However, like the *beur* films it remained national. In this respect too, *La Haine*'s international exposure comes from its recognition and celebration of another cultural difference which, in a profound sense, makes other cultural and racial differences increasingly obsolete: that of American culture, starting with the director's own cinephilia.

As D'Yvoire pointed out, 'Unlike many young French directors who are trained at FEMIS [the most prominent French film school], and who only swear by Godard, Pialat or Truffaut, Kassovitz readily quotes Scorsese and Spielberg' (1995, 103). Overt references abound as already mentioned, and one could add the introduction of characters similar to those of *Mean Streets*. The Jewish element can be seen as a version of Lee's and Scorsese's Italian-Americans. More subtly, Kassovitz makes his heroes inhabit somewhat anachronistically his own cinematic and visual culture, especially indebted to America. Vinz talking to himself in his bathroom mirror imitates the 1977 hero of *Taxi Driver*, where 'in reality' he would probably copy Bruce Willis. Similarly, the heroes' discussion of 'Pif' and 'Hercule', characters from French Communist comics dating back to the 1950s, probably owes more to Kassovitz's own background than to that of the three young men. The nervy film style itself is referential. Susan Morrison (1995, 46) perceptively details how Kassovitz echoes Scorsese, with his 'fluid camera . . . a reliance on idiosyncratic male actors like De Niro and Keitel; a carefully selected and coded soundtrack and a near-hysterical tension lying just beneath the surface, ready to erupt at any moment'.

*La Haine*'s protagonists' language, clothes and music, as already mentioned, are visibly and audibly American-influenced. Kassovitz's first short *Fierrot le pou* (1990, the title an ironic homage to Godard) parodied his passion for black American culture. The image of a 'wannabe' black, Kassovitz plays a hopeless white basketball player who dreams he is black to impress a young black woman. *La Haine* continues this theme, showing the impact of hip-hop culture among *banlieue* youth. This has prompted a debate about whether *La Haine* just mimics American culture. Particularly critical is Alexander (1995, 45), who sees the import of American culture as de-politicizing and links the film to 'trendy fashion spreads', while Tarr (1997,

41) queries Kassovitz's legitimacy in using black American culture, on account of his own white (Jewish) bourgeois background. While on the one hand I agree with Chris Darke that '*La Haine* is more than simply a capable reworking of its American models' (1995, 43), I would also argue that *La Haine*, though indeed 'exploiting' a deeply commodified form of black American culture and celebrating American film-makers, is political in showing the extent to which American culture has colonized French working-class youth culture. But it is violence which most powerfully links *La Haine* to American cinema, to the history of the Western and of *film noir*. Rather than the embedded localized violence of the *beur* and *banlieue* films or of contemporary French thrillers such as *L627*, the violence in *La Haine*, symbolized by the 'Mexican stand-off' inhabits the international *noir* territory of Scorsese, Tarantino, Woo *et al.*, just as the social context of the *cité* has been abstracted, as discussed earlier.

## The new *apaches*

Compared to the hero of *Etat des lieux* who has a well-articulated political programme, *La Haine*'s protagonists are anomic, helpless and hopeless. Their aggression, against the police and other institutions, is random and self-defeating, symbolized by their circular trajectory. Unlike their equivalents in Scorsese's and Lee's movies, or the *beur* films, Saïd, Hubert and Vinz (despite Saïd's bragging) have no sexual life, symbolized by the fact that none of them could drive the car they attempt to steal. As traditional family roles disappear, so does generational conflict; the boys stay at home in a state of perpetual childhood. *La Haine* thus offers a vision of French 'proletarian heroes' which fundamentally recasts their historical figuration in French cinema and French culture.

In the Poetic Realist films of the 1930s and in the social comedies and dramas of the 1970s, the charismatic heroes – played, typically, by the young Jean Gabin and the young Gérard Depardieu – were the emblems of French *noir* cinema. Central to this was their alienation from a community and their virile struggle against father figures: see *Le Jour se lève* or *Le Quai des brumes* for the former and *Les Valseuses* for the latter. In *La Haine*, there are no fathers (an important point in a national cinema which traditionally celebrates the patriarch) and there is no visible community to be alienated from. *Clockers*, Lee's story of exclusion and violence among young black males in a Brooklyn housing project, is also bookended by stylized depictions of violence. But the visually stunning images of blood and torn bodies, while used as abstract expressions of violence, are also a graphic depiction of the *effect* of violence on the community. We see local people looking at the bodies. *Clockers*, unlike *La Haine*, also offers some viable older male figures. *La Haine* starts with images of socially anchored political struggle but ends on an isolated incident in a desolate – though visually pleasing –

setting. In this nihilistic conclusion lies the double 'political' message of the film.

Firstly, Kassovitz detaches his heroes from a specifically French history of proletarian representation, through American glamour both in his film style and in the youth culture he depicts. Hip-hop culture, however, points to another kind of American influence, that of the rampant neo-capitalism which created the ghettos. Though state involvement in welfare is still greater in France, the most pessimistic predictions see the 'inverse utopia' (Wacquant 1993) of the American ghettos as the future world order: a growing underclass of *exclus*, in which 'old-fashioned' divisions of class and race are irrelevant. Vinz, Hubert and Saïd already inhabit this world. The beginning of *La Haine* recalled the 1960s political struggles. But the rest of the film shows the self-destructive, consumer-hungry, a-political behaviour typical of international ghetto youth culture. Second, if the heroes of *La Haine* can be fitted into a French historical frame of reference, it is not that of the 1930s working-class heroes, nor of the Communist 'red suburbs' of the 1960s and 1970s, but that of the nineteenth-century 'dangerous classes', the hordes of 'savage' *apaches* on the fringes of the city, menacing bourgeois society. Yet Vinz, Hubert and Saïd do not even partake of the romanticism attached to the *apache*. The film's chilling ending takes place under giant murals representing French poets, put in place by the well-meaning, if not altogether perspicacious, architects of Chanteloup-les-Vignes – the murals are a line-up of undoubtedly great but typically (male) high cultural figures: Charles Baudelaire, Arthur Rimbaud, Paul Valéry, Victor Hugo, Gérard de Nerval and Stéphane Mallarmé. As Vinz falls under Baudelaire and Rimbaud, he stresses the failure of the cultural policies that were supposed to help the *cités*. He also symbolizes his, and his friends', alienation from the romantic tradition of poetic rebellion which traditionally informed the figure of the French proletarian rebel.

## Notes

1 *Le Film français*, 2584 (10 November 1995), 23, 'Pourquoi Jodie Foster parraine "La Haine"?'. Foster is also producing Kassovitz's fourth feature (Marie 1998).
2 'La France est une banlieue merdique'; Renaud, 'La Chanson du loubard', Muriel Huster and Renaud Séchand, Polydor, 1977. Another of Renaud's popular songs from that period was 'Mon HLM'.
3 Darty is the name of an electrical goods chain store.
4 'Dealer pour survivre' (Drug dealing as survival), Expression Direkt, *La Haine*, musiques inspirées du film. ©1995 Delabel.
5 An incident on the shooting of Pierre Jolivet's *Ma Petite entreprise* on a Parisian *banlieue* estate in Fontenay-sous-Bois in late 1998, between local youth and film extras, shows the continuing problems encountered by 'outsiders' filming the *banlieue* reality.
6 A 'Mexican stand-off' means two characters holding each other up simultaneously

with a gun to their head; this classic Western feature has been recently revisited by Woo and Tarantino.

7  'Niquer' is from the Arabic, and 'nique ta mère', i.e. 'fuck your mother', is reminiscent of 'motherfucker'.

8  It should be noted that the reception of this verbal flow is problematic outside France, where the necessary subtitles alienate further from what is a difficult language to understand in the first place, given the amount of slang. There is also arguably a second-degree alienation for English-speaking but non-American audiences, as the subtitles use American-specific slang.

9  See note 5 above.

10  The shooting of the nightclub bouncer is more ambivalent: the positioning of Vinz in the frame suggests the scene happens in his imagination, yet the published script indicates it is 'for real'.

11  The rhyme with bleu-blanc-rouge (the tricolore) also means that the expression has long been a favourite, from a hip-hop dance group founded in 1984 to the gushing congratulations over the victory of the multi-racial French football team in the July 1998 World Cup.

## Selected bibliography

Alexander, Karen (1995), '*La Haine*', *Vertigo*, 5 (autumn/winter).

Augé, Marc (1995) *Non-Places: Introduction to an Anthropology of Supermodernity*, trans. John Howe, London, Verso.

Bosséno, Christian (1992), 'Immigrant Cinema: National Cinema – the Case of Beur Film', in Richard Dyer, and Ginette Vincendeau (eds), *Popular European Cinema*, London, Routledge.

Bourdieu, Pierre (sous la direction de) (1993) *La Misère du monde*, Paris, Editions du Seuil.

Cannon, Steve (1997), '*Paname City Rapping*: B-Boys in the *Banlieues* and Beyond', in Alec G. Hargreaves, and Mark McKinney (eds) *Post-Colonial Cultures in France*, London and New York, Routledge.

Daeninx, Didier (1992), *Zapping*, Paris, Denoël (Folio).

Darke, Chris (1995), '*La Haine*', *Sight and Sound* (November).

Douhaire, Samuel (1998), 'Etats des lieux', *Libération* (13–14 June).

Favier, Gille and Kassovitz, Mathieu (1995), *Jusqu'ici tout va bien . . .* , Arles, Actes Sud.

Ferreboeuf, Georges (1996), quoted in 'Médias et banlieues: la haine?', http://www.lyoncapitale

Garnier, Jean-Pierre (1996), *Des Barbares dans la cité: De la tyrannie du marché à la violence urbaine*, Paris, Flammarion.

Hargreaves, Alec G. and McKinney, Mark (eds) (1997), *Post-Colonial Cultures in France*, London and New York, Routledge.

*Humanité Dimanche* (1995), interview with Mathieu Kassovitz, 270 (18–24 May).

Jousse, Thierry (1995), 'Prose combat', *Cahiers du cinéma*, 492 (June) 32–5.

Marie, Michel (ed.) (1998), *Le Jeune cinéma français*, Paris, Nathan Université.

Maspero, François (1990), *Les Passagers du Roissy-Express*, Paris, Editions du Seuil. Translated by Paul Jones, as *Roissy Express*, London, Verso, 1994.

Mongin, Olivier (1995), 'Regarde les tomber: à propos de *La Haine*', *Esprit* (August–September).

Morrison, Susan (1995), '*La Haine, Fallen Angels*, and Some Thoughts on Scorsese's Children', *CineAction!*, 39 (December).

*Positif* (1995), interview with Mathieu Kassovitz (by Thomas Bourguignon and Yann Tobin), no. 412 (June), 4–13.

Reader, Keith (1995), 'After the riot', *Sight and Sound* (November).

Rémy, Serge (1995), 'Banlieue haute tension', *L'Humanité* (29 May), 20.

Reynaud, Bérénice (1996), 'Le 'hood', *Film Comment*, 32 (2) (March/April).

Robache, Thomas and Saragoussi, Pierre (1998), *Banlieues: tant que ça tiendra*, Paris, Denoël, Documents Actualités.

Styan, David (1995), 'So Far . . . Everything is OK!', *Vertigo* 5 (autumn/winter).

Tarr, Carrie (1997) 'Ethnicity and Identity in *Métisse* and *La Haine* by Mathieu Kassovitz', in Tony Chafer (ed.) *Multicultural France*, Working Papers on Contemporary France, vol. 7, University of Portsmouth.

*Télérama* (1995a), '*La Haine*', interview with Mathieu Kassovitz (by Vincent Rémy), 2368 (31 May), 40–6.

*Télérama* (1995b), '*La Haine* partagée', report on audience interviews (by Marie-Elisabeth Rouchy, Isabelle Danel and Bernard Génin), 2372 (28 June), 24–7.

Tremois, Claude-Marie (1997), *Les Enfants de la liberté: Le Jeune cinéma français des années 90*, Paris, Editions du Seuil.

Vassé, Claire (1995), '*La Haine*, un regard métisse', *Positif*, 412 (June), 6–7.

Vigo, Luce (1995), 'Ce cinéma qui habite la banlieue', *Regards* (September).

Wacquant, Loïc J. D. (1993), 'De l'Amérique comme utopie à l'envers', in Pierre Bourdieu (sous la direction de), *La Misère du monde*, Paris, Editions du Seuil.

D'Yvoire, Christophe (1995), 'Douze mois de haine', *Studio* (December), 102–5.

# APPENDIX

## *Mathieu Kassovitz (1967 – ): filmography*

1990  *Fierrot le pou* (short) (also actor)
1990  *Peuples du monde* (music video for Tonton David)
1991  *Cauchemar blanc* (short)
1992  *Assassins* (short) (also actor)
1993  *Métisse* (also actor)
1995  *La Haine* (also actor)
1997  *Assassin(s)* (also actor)
1997  *Lumières sur un massacre* (short, part of anti-landmine film)

## *Other films cited in the text*

*L'Ami de mon amie*, Eric Rohmer (1987)
*La Belle équipe*, Julien Duvivier (1936)
*Boyz N the Hood*, John Singleton (USA 1991)
*Clockers*, Spike Lee (USA 1995)
*La Crise*, Coline Serreau (1992)
*De bruit et de fureur*, Jean-Claude Brisseau (1988)

*De l'autre côté du périphérique*, Bertrand and Nils Tavernier (1997)
*Deux ou trois choses que je sais d'elle* (*Two or Three Things I Know about Her*), Jean-Luc
    Godard (1967)
*Die Hard (3)* (*With a Vengeance*), John McTiernan (USA 1995)
*Do the Right Thing*, Spike Lee (USA 1989)
*Douce France*, Malik Chibane (1995)
*Etat des lieux*, Jean-François Richet (1995)
*Une femme mariée*, Jean-Luc Godard (1964)
*Gazon maudit*, Josiane Balasko (1995)
*Hexagone*, Malik Chibane (1994)
*Le Hussard sur le toit* (*The Horseman on the Roof*), Jean-Paul Rappeneau (1995)
*Inspecteur La Bavure*, Claude Zidi (1980)
*Le Jour se lève* (*Daybreak*), Marcel Carné (1939)
*Les Keufs*, Josiane Balasko (1987)
*Laisse béton*, Serge Le Péron (1984)
*Loulou*, Maurice Pialat (1979)
*Ma 6-T va crack-er*, Jean-François Richet (1997)
*Mean Streets*, Martin Scorsese (USA 1973)
*Menace II Society*, The Hughes Brothers (USA 1993)
*Un monde sans pitié*, Eric Rochant (1989)
*Nikita*, Luc Besson (1990)
*Nogent, Eldorado du dimanche*, Marcel Carné (1929)
*Les Nuits de la pleine lune* (*Full Moon in Paris*), Eric Rohmer (1984)
*Numéro deux*, Jean-Luc Godard (1975)
*Le Plus beau métier du monde*, Gérard Lauzier (1996)
*Le Quai des brumes* (*Port of Shadows*), Marcel Carné (1938)
*Raging Bull*, Martin Scorsese (USA 1980)
*Raï*, Thomas Gilou (1995)
*Les Ripoux*, Claude Zidi (1984)
*Romuald et Juliette*, Coline Serreau (1989)
*Rue des Prairies*, Denys de la Patellière (1959)
*Salut, cousin!*, Merzak Allouache (1996)
*Scènes de ménage*, Claire Simon (1991)
*Série noire*, Alain Corneau (1979)
*She's Gotta Have It*, Spike Lee (USA 1986)
*Le Thé au harem d'Archimède*, Mehdi Charef (1985)
*Trainspotting*, Danny Boyle (UK 1996)
*Les Trois frères*, Didier Bourdon (1995)
*The Usual Suspects*, Bryan Singer (USA 1995)
*Les Valseuses*, Bertrand Blier (1973)
*La Vérité si je mens*, Thomas Gilou (1997)

# SELECTED BIBLIOGRAPHY ON FRENCH CINEMA

The following is a selection of works in book form on French cinema, published in French and in English. We have not included books on individual film-makers or actors. Material on individual films and directors considered in this book can be found at the end of each chapter.

## Reference

This section concentrates on reference works which address French cinema specifically; we have not, therefore, included general reference works, though they contain references to French film-makers, scriptwriters, actors, etc.

Chirat, Raymond (1975) *Catalogue des films français de long métrage, films sonores de fiction, 1929–1939*, Brussels, Cinémathèque Royale de Belgique. An illustrated edition of the same catalogue was published in 1981 (same publisher).

Chirat, Raymond (1981) *Catalogue des films français de long métrage, films de fiction, 1940–1950*, Luxembourg, Imprimerie Saint-Paul.

Chirat, Raymond and Icart, Roger (1984) *Catalogue des films français de long métrage, films de fiction, 1919–1929*, Toulouse, Cinémathèque de Toulouse.

Chirat, Raymond and Romer, Jean-Claude (1984) *Catalogue des films français de fiction de 1ᵉ partie 1929–1939*, Bois d'Arcy, Service des Archives du Film, Centre National de la Cinématographie.

Franju, Georges (1982) *De Marey à Renoir: trésors de la Cinémathèque Française 1882–1939*, Paris, Avant-scène cinéma, 279–80.

Icart, Roger (n.d.) *Pour Vous, Ciné-Miroir, Cinémonde, 1929–1940, Index 1, films français de long métrage et de fiction*, Toulouse, Documents de la Cinémathèque de Toulouse.

*Image et magie du cinéma français: 100 ans de patrimoine* (1980), no specified author, Paris, Conservatoire National des Arts et Métiers.

Pinel, Vincent (1985) *Filmographie des longs métrages sonores du cinéma français produits et présentés commercialement sur grand écran entre 1930 et 1984 (à l'exception des films classés 'X')*, Paris, Cinémathèque Française.

Sabria, Jean-Claude and Busca, Jean-Pierre (1985) *L'Index du film français – 1944–1984: 40 ans de cinéma en France, Répertoire des films de A à Z*, Paris, Cinéma de France.

Vincendeau, Ginette (1996) *The Companion to French Cinema*, London, BFI/Cassell.

# French cinema: history and criticism

Some books dealing with other national cinemas (especially European cinema) have been included under this heading when they contain important material on French cinema. We have also included works which examine French cinema as part of French culture.

## *General*

This section includes general surveys and works that span more than one specific period.

Agel, Henri (1958) *Miroirs de l'insolite dans le cinéma français*, Paris, Editions du Cerf.

Andrew, Dudley (1978) *André Bazin*, New York, Oxford University Press.

Armes, Roy (1985) *French Cinema*, London, Secker & Warburg.

Arnoux, Alexandre (1946) *Du muet au parlant: mémoires d'un témoin*, Paris, Nouvelle Edition.

Bandy, Mary Lea (ed.) (1983) *Rediscovering French Film*, New York, Museum of Modern Art.

Bardèche, Maurice and Brasillach, Robert (1948) *History of the Film*, trans. and ed. Iris Barry from 1st French edition (1935), London, Allen & Unwin.

Bardèche, Maurice and Brasillach, Robert (1954) *Histoire du cinéma* (*Nouvelle édition définitive en deux volumes*), Paris, André Martel.

Bazin, André (ed.) (1984) *La Politique des auteurs*, Paris, Cahiers du cinéma, Editions de l'Etoile.

Billard, Pierre (1995) *L'Age classique du cinéma français*, Paris, Flammarion.

Borga, J.-M. and Martinand, B. (1977) *Affiches du cinéma français*, Paris, Delville.

Boulanger, Pierre (1975) *Le Cinéma colonial*, Paris, Seghers.

Braunberger, Pierre (1987) *Cinémamémoire*, Paris, Centre Georges Pompidou, Centre National de la Cinematographie.

Brieu, Christian, Ikor, Laurent and Viguier, Jean-Michel (1985) *Joinville, le cinéma: le temps des studios*, Paris, Ramsay.

Brunius, Jacques-Bernard (1954) *En marge du cinéma français*, Paris, Arcanes.

Burch, Noël and Sellier, Geneviève (1996) *La Drôle de guerre des sexes du cinéma français, 1930–1956*, Paris, Nathan.

Buss, Robin (1988) *The French Through Their Films*, London, Batsford.

Buss, Robin (1994) *French Film Noir*, London, Marion Boyars.

Cadars, Pierre (1982) *Les Séducteurs du cinéma français (1928–1958)*, Paris, Henri Veyrier.

Chantal, Suzanne (1977) *Le Ciné-monde*, Paris, Grasset.

Chevalier, Jacques (ed.) (1963) *Regards neufs sur le cinéma*, Paris, Editions du Seuil.

Chirat, Raymond and Barrot, Olivier (1983) *Les Excentriques du cinéma français (1929–1958)*, Paris, Henri Veyrier.

Chirat, Raymond and Barrot, Olivier (1986) *Inoubliables! Visages du cinéma français: 1930–1950*, Paris, Calmann-Lévy.

Clair, René (1972) *Cinema Yesterday and Today*, ed. R. C. Dale, trans. Stanley Appelbaum, New York, Dover. (Originally published as *Cinéma d'hier et d'aujourd'hui*, Paris, Gallimard, 1970.)

Comes, Philippe de and Marmin, Michel (1984) *Le Cinéma français: 1930–1960*, Paris, Editions Atlas.

Cottom, J. V. (1983) *Ce monde fou-fou du cinéma français*, Bruxelles, J. M. Collet.

Courtade, Francis (1978) *Les Malédictions du cinéma français*, Paris, Alain Moreau.

Crisp, Colin (1993) *The Classic French Cinema: 1930–1960*, Bloomington, Indiana University Press.

Daniel, Joseph (1972) *Guerre et cinéma – Grandes illusions et petits soldats*, Paris, Armand Colin.

Des Femmes de Musidora (1976) *Paroles . . . elles tournent*, Paris, Des Femmes.

Deslandes, Jacques and Richard, Jacques (1968) *Histoire comparée du cinéma, I: 1826–1896*, Paris, Casterman.

Deslandes, Jacques and Richard, Jacques (1968) *Histoire comparée du cinéma, II: 1896–1906*, Paris, Casterman.

Devarrieux, Claire (1981) *Les Acteurs au travail*, Paris, Hatier.

Diamant-Berger, Henri (1945) *Destin du cinéma français*, Paris, Imprimerie de Montmartre.

Diamant-Berger, Henri (1977) *Il était une fois le cinéma*, Paris, Editions Jean-Claude Simoën.

Ducout, Françoise (1978) *Les Séductrices du cinéma français, 1936–1956*, Paris, Henri Veyrier.

Dyer, Richard and Vincendeau, Ginette (eds) (1992), *Popular European Cinema*, London, Routledge.

Flitterman-Lewis, Sandy (1990) *To Desire Differently: Feminism and the French Cinema*, Urbana, University of Illinois Press. (Expanded edition, New York, Columbia University Press, 1996.)

Frank, Nino (1950) *Petit cinéma sentimental*, Paris, La Nouvelle Edition.

Gaston-Mathé, Catherine (1996) *La Société française au miroir de son cinéma*, Paris, Arléa-Corlet.

Guégan, Gérard, Guégan Stéphane, Jeancolas, Jean-Pierre, Pinel Vincent and Georgel Chantal (1995) *L'ABCdaire du Cinéma français*, Paris, Flammarion.

Guérif, François, *Le Cinéma policier français*, Paris, Henri Veyrier.

Guillard, Gilbert (1983) *Le Cinéma français de 1930 à 1981*, Munich, Manz Verlag.

Hammond, Paul (ed.) (1978) *The Shadow and its Shadow: Surrealist Writings on Cinema*, London, British Film Institute.

Harcourt, Peter (1974) *Six European Directors, Essays on the Meaning of Film Style*, Harmondsworth, Penguin Books.

Hayward, Susan (1993) *French National Cinema*, London, Routledge.

Hillairet, Prosper, Lebrat, Christian, and Rollet, Patrice, (1985) *Paris vu par le cinéma d'avant-garde*, Paris, Centre National Georges Pompidou.

Jeanne, René and Ford, Charles (1961) *Le Cinéma et la presse 1895–1960*, Paris, Armand Colin.

Jeanne, René and Ford, Charles (1969) *Paris vu par le cinéma*, Paris, Hachette.

Kyrou, Ado (1963) *Le Surréalisme au cinéma*, Paris, Terrain Vague.

Lacassin, Francis (1972) *Pour une contre-histoire du cinéma*, Paris, UGE (10/18).

Lapierre, Marcel (ed.) (1946) *Anthologie du cinéma*, Paris, La Nouvelle Edition.

Lapierre, Marcel (1948) *Les Cent visages du cinéma*, Paris, Grasset.

Lebrun, Dominique (1987) *Paris–Hollywood: Les Français dans le cinéma américain*, Paris, Hazan.

Leprohon, Pierre (1954) *50 ans de cinéma français (1895–1945)*, Paris, Editions du Cerf.

Maillot, Pierre (1996) *Les Fiancés de Marianne: La Société française à travers ses grands acteurs*, Paris, Editions du Cerf.

Martin, Marcel (1971) *France*, London, Zwemmer, New York, Barnes.

Mazeau, Jacques and Thouart Didier (1983) *Acteurs et chanteurs*, Paris, PAC.

Michalczyk, John (1980) *The French Literary Filmmakers*, Philadelphia, The Art Alliance Press, London, Associated University Presses.

Mitry, Jean (1967–80) *Histoire du cinéma, art et industrie* (5 vols), Paris, Editions Universitaires.

Moussinac, Léon (1967) *L'Age ingrat du cinéma*, Paris, Editeurs Français Réunis.

Petrie, Duncan (ed.) (1992), *Screening Europe: Image and Identity in Contemporary European Cinema*, London, BFI.

Prédal, René (1972) *La Société française à travers le cinéma*, Paris, Armand Colin.

Prédal, René (1980) *80 ans de cinéma: Nice et le 7e art*, Nice, Serre.

Reader, Keith (1981) *Cultures on Celluloid*, London, Quartet.

Rearick, Charles (1997) *The French in Love and War*, New Haven and London, Yale University Press.

Richebé, Roger (1977) *Au-delà de l'écran*, Monte-Carlo, Pastorelly.

Roud, Richard (1983) *A Passion for Films: Henri Langlois and the Cinémathèque Française*, London, Secker & Warburg.

Roux, Jean and Thévenet, René (1979) *Industrie et commerce du film en France*, Paris, Editions Scientifiques.

Sadoul, Georges (1953) *French Film*, London, Falcon Press.

Sadoul, Georges (1979) *Chroniques du cinéma français: 1. 1939–1967*, Paris, UGE (10/18).

Sadoul, Georges (1981) *Le Cinéma français: 1890–1962*, Paris, Flammarion.

Siclier, Jacques (1957) *La Femme dans le cinéma français*, Paris, Editions du Cerf.

Siclier, Jacques (1990) *Le Cinéma français*, 1: *de La Bataille du rail à La Chinoise 1945–1968*, Paris, Ramsay.

Siclier, Jacques (1991) *Le Cinéma français*, 2: *de Baisers volés à Cyrano de Bergerac 1968–1990*, Paris, Ramsay.

Sorlin, Pierre (1991) *European Cinemas, European Societies, 1939–1990*, London, Routledge.

Thiher, Allen (1979) *The Cinematic Muse: Critical Studies in the History of French Cinema*, Columbia and London, University of Missouri Press.

Toulet, Emmanuelle (ed.) (1995) *Le Cinéma au rendez-vous des arts, France, années 20 et 30*, Paris, Bibliothèque Nationale de France.

Truffaut, François (1975) *Les Films de ma vie*, Paris, Flammarion.

Truffaut, François (1978) *The Films in My Life*, trans. Leonard Mayhew, New York, Simon & Schuster.

Védrès, Nicole (1945) *Images du cinéma français*, Paris, Editions du Chêne.

Virmaux, Alain and Odette (eds) (1975) *Colette: au cinéma*, Paris, Flammarion.,

Virmaux Alain and Odette (eds) (1981) *Colette at the Movies*, trans. Sarah W. R. Smith, New York, Ungar.

Weil-Lorac, Roger (1977) *50 ans de cinéma actif*, Paris, Dujarric.

Witta-Montrobert, Jeanne (1980) *La Lanterne magique: mémoires d'une script*, Paris, Calmann-Lévy.

Williams, Alan (1992) *Republic of Images: A History of French Filmmaking*, Cambridge, Mass., Harvard University Press.


## Silent cinema

Abel, Richard (1984) *French Cinema: The First Wave, 1915–1929*, Princeton, Princeton University Press.

Abel, Richard (1988) *French Film Theory and Criticism,* I: *1907–1929*, Princeton, Princeton University Press.

Abel, Richard (1994) *The Ciné Goes to Town, French Cinema 1896–1914*, Berkeley and Los Angeles, University of California Press.

Bordwell, David (1980) *French Impressionist Cinema: Film Culture, Film Theory, and Film Style*, New York, Arno.

Chirat, Raymond and LeRoy, Eric (1993) *Le Cinéma français, 1911–1920*, Paris, Cinémathèque Française.

Coissac, Georges-Michel (1925) *Histoire du cinématographe: de ses origines jusqu'à nos jours*, Paris, Editions du 'Cinéopse'.

Fell, John (1983) *Film Before Griffith*, Berkeley and Los Angeles, University of California Press.

Fescourt, Henri (1959) *La Foi et les montagnes*, Paris, Paul Montel.

FIAF (1989) *Le Cinéma français dans le monde, influences réciproques*, Perpignan, Institut Jean Vigo.

Guibbert, Pierre (ed.) (1985) *Les Premiers ans du cinéma français*, Perpignan, Institut Jean Vigo.

Hughes, Philippe de and Marmin, Michel (1986) *Le Cinéma français, le Muet*, Paris, Atlas.

Leprohon, Pierre (1982) *Histoire du cinéma muet 1895–1930*, Plan-de-la-Tour, Editions d'Aujourd'hui (reprint of 1961 edition, Editions du Cerf).

Monaco, Paul (1976) *Cinema and Society: France and Germany during the Twenties*, New York, Elsevier.

Sadoul, Georges (1947) *Histoire générale du cinéma,* I: *Les Pionniers du cinéma*, Paris, Denoël.

Sadoul, Georges (1948) *Histoire générale du cinéma,* II: *Les Pionniers du cinéma, 1897–1908*, Paris, Denoël.

Sadoul, Georges (1951) *Histoire générale du cinéma,* III: *Le Cinéma devient un art, 1909–1920*, Paris, Denoël.

Sadoul, Georges (1985) *Lumière et Méliès*, revised edition by Bernard Eisenschitz, Paris, Lherminier.


## The 1930s

Andrew, Dudley (1995) *Mists of Regret, Culture and Sensibility in Classic French Film*, Princeton, Princeton University Press.

Barrot, Olivier and Jeancolas, Jean-Pierre (1973) *Les Français et leur cinéma, 1930–1939*, Créteil, Maison de la Culture, Losfeld.

Bessy, Maurice (1987) *Histoire du cinéma français: encyclopédie des films 1935–1939*, Paris, Pygmalion.

Beylie, Claude (ed.) (1983) *Cinémagazine 1930*, Paris, Avant-scène (reprint of original articles).

Buchsbaum, Jonathan (1988) *Cinema Engagé: Film in the Popular Front*, Urbana, University of Illinois Press.

Chirat, Raymond (1983) *Le Cinéma français des années 30*, Paris, Hatier.

Chirat, Raymond (1987) *Atmosphères: sourires, soupirs et délires du cinéma français des années 30*, Paris, Hatier.

Garçon, François (1984) *De Blum à Pétain: cinéma et société française (1936–44)*, Paris, Editions du Cerf.

Grelier, Robert (sons la direction de) (1986) *Mémoires d'en France 1936–1939*, Paris, Aimo.

Guillaume-Grimaud, Geneviève (1986) *Le Cinéma du Front Populaire*, Paris, Lherminier.

Jeancolas, Jean-Pierre (1977) 'Cinéma d'un monde en crise', *La Documentation Française*, special dossier.

Jeancolas, Jean-Pierre (1983) *15 ans d'années trente: Le Cinéma des Français, 1929–1944*, Paris, Stock.

Lagny, Michèle, Ropars, Marie-Claire and Sorlin, Pierre (1986) *Générique des années trente*, Saint-Denis, Presses Universitaires de Vincennes.

Léglise, Paul (1970) *Histoire de la politique du cinéma français,* Tome 1: *Le Cinéma et la IIIᵉ République*, Paris, Lherminier.

Martin, John W. (1983) *The Golden Age of French Cinema, 1929–39*, Boston, G. K. Hall.

Peyrusse, Claudette (1986) *Le Cinéma méridional 1929–1944*, Toulouse, Eché.

Renaitour, Jean-Michel (1937) *Où va le cinema français?* Paris, Baudiniaire.

Rifkin, Adrian (1993) *Street Noises: Parisian Pleasure 1900–40*, Manchester, Manchester University Press.

Strebel, Elizabeth Grottle (1980) *French Social Cinema of the Nineteen-Thirties: A Cinematic Expression of Popular Front Consciousness*, New York, Arno.

Vincendeau, Ginette and Reader, Keith (1986) *La Vie est à nous: French Cinema of the Popular Front, 1935–1938*, London, British Film Institute.

## The occupation

Bazin, André (1975) *Le Cinéma de l'Occupation et de la Résistance*, Paris, UGE (10/18).

Bazin, André (1981) *French Cinema of the Occupation and Resistance*, trans. Stanley Hochman, New York, Ungar.

Bertin-Maghit, Jean-Pierre (1980) *Le Cinéma français sous Vichy, les films francais de 1940 à 1944*, Paris, Ça Cinéma.

Bertin-Maghit, Jean-Pierre (1989) *Le Cinéma sous l'Occupation*, Paris, Olivier Orban.

Bessy, Maurice (1986) *Histoire du cinéma français: encyclopédie des films 1940–1950*, Paris, Pygmalion.

Chirat, Raymond (1983) *Le Cinéma français des années de guerre*, Paris, Hatier.

Ehrlich, Evelyn (1985) *Cinema of Paradox: French Filmmaking under the German Occupation*, New York, Columbia University Press.

Garçon, François (1984) *De Blum à Pétain: cinéma et société française (1936–44),* Paris, Editions du Cerf.

Halimi, André (1976) *Chantons sous l'occupation*, Paris, Olivier Orban.

Jeancolas, Jean-Pierre (1976) 'Cinéma d'un monde en guerre', *La Documentation française*, special dossier.

Jeancolas, Jean-Pierre (1983) *15 ans d'années trente: Le Cinéma des Français, 1929–1944*, Paris, Stock.

Kaplan, Alice Yeager (1986) *Reproductions of Banality (Fascism, Literature, and French Intellectual Life)*, Minneapolis, University of Minnesota Press (contains long interview with Maurice Bardèche).

Léglise, Paul (1977) *Histoire de la politique du cinéma francais,* Tome II: *Le Cinéma entre deux Républiques (1940–1946)*, Paris, Lherminier.

Peyrusse, Claudette (1986) *Le Cinéma méridional 1929–1944*, Toulouse, Eché.

Rebatet, Lucien (F. Vinneuil) (1941) *Les Tribus du cinéma et du théâtre*, Paris, Nouvelles Editions Françaises.

Régent, Roger (1975) *Cinéma de France, de 'La Fille du puisatier' aux 'Enfants du paradis'*, Paris, Editions d'Aujourd'hui (reprint of 1948 edition).

Siclier, Jacques (1981) *La France de Pétain et son cinéma*, Paris, Veyrier.

## French cinema since the Second World War

Agel, Henri (1953) *Sept ans de cinéma français (1945–51)*, Paris, Editions du Cerf.

Armes, Roy (1976) *The Ambiguous Image: Narrative Syle in Modern European Cinema*, London, British Film Institute.

Audé, Françoise (1981) *Ciné-modèles, cinéma d'elles*, Lausanne, L'Age d'homme.

Austin, Guy (1996) *Contemporary French Cinema: An Introduction*, Manchester, Manchester University Press.

Baecque, Antoine de (1998) *Nouvelle Vague*, Paris, Cinémathèque Française/Hazan.

Barboni, Laurette (1986) *Cinéma d'aujourd'hui: images de cinéma, images de société*, Sèvres, Centre International d'Etudes Pédagogiques de Sèvres.

Barrot, Olivier (1979) *L'Ecran français, 1943–1953, histoire d'un journal et d'une époque*, Paris, Les Editeurs Français Réunis.

Bazin, André (1983) *Le Cinéma français de la Libération à la Nouvelle Vague (1945–1958)*, Paris, Cahiers du cinéma, Editions de l'Etoile.

Bessy, Maurice (1986) *Histoire du cinéma français: encyclopédie des films 1940–1950*, Paris, Pygmalion.

Bonnel, René (1978) *Le Cinéma exploité*, Paris, Editions du Seuil.

Borde, Raymond, Buache, Freddy and Curtelin, Jean (1962) *Nouvelle Vague*, Premier Plan, Lyon, Serdoc.

Bredin, Jean-Denis (1982) *The Bredin Report: On the Future of the French Cinema*, London, British Film Institute.

Brisset, Stéphane (1990) *Le Cinéma français des années 80*, Paris, M.A. Editions.

Browne, Nick (ed.) *Cahiers du cinéma 1969–1972: The Politics of Representation*, Cambridge, Mass., Harvard University Press.

Buache, Freddy (1987) *Le Cinéma français des années 60*, Paris, Hatier.

Buache, Freddy (1990) *Le Cinéma français des années 70*, Renens, 5 Continents, Hatier.

Charensol, Georges (1946) *Renaissance du cinéma français*, Paris, Editions du Sagittaire.

Chirat, Raymond (1985) *La IV<sup>e</sup> République et ses films*, Paris, Hatier.

Clouzot, Claire (1972) *Le Cinéma français depuis la nouvelle vague*, Paris, Fernand Nathan.

Collet, Jean (1972) *Le Cinéma en question* (on Rozier, Chabrol, Rivette, Truffaut, Demy, Rohmer), Paris, Editions du Cerf.

Degand, Claude (1972) *Le Cinéma, cette industrie*, Editions Techniques et Economiques.

Douchet, Jean (1998) *La Nouvelle Vague*, Paris, Flammarion.

Douin, Jean-Luc (ed.) (1983) *La Nouvelle Vague 25 ans après*, Paris, Editions du Cerf.

Durgnat, Raymond (1963) *Nouvelle Vague, The First Decade*, Loughton, Essex, Motion Publications.

Forbes, Jill (1992) *The Cinema in France After the New Wave*, London, British Film Institute.

Ford, Charles (1977) *Histoire du cinéma français contemporain 1945–1977*, Paris, France-Empire.

Frodon, Jean-Michel (1995) *L'Age moderne du cinéma français, de la Nouvelle Vague à nos jours*, Paris, Flammarion.

Goldman, Annie (1971) *Cinéma et société moderne, le cinéma de 1958 à 1968*, Paris, Anthropos.

Graham, Peter (ed.) (1968) *The New Wave*, London, Secker & Warburg.

Harvey, Sylvia (1978) *May '68 and Film Culture*, London, British Film Institute.

Hennebelle, Guy (1975) *Quinze ans de cinéma mondial, 1960–1975*, Paris, Editions du Cerf.

Hewitt, Nicholas (ed.) (1989) *The Culture of Reconstruction. European Literature, Thought and Film, 1945–1950*, Basingstoke and London, Macmillan.

Hillier, Jim (ed.) (1985) *Cahiers du cinéma, 1: The 1950s: Neo Realism, Hollywood, New Wave*, London, Routledge & Kegan Paul, British Film Institute (trans. of selection of original *Cahiers du cinéma* articles).

Hillier, Jim (ed.) (1986) *Cahiers du cinéma, 2: 1960–1968*, London, Routledge & Kegan Paul, British Film Institute (articles).

Horton, Andrew S. and Magretta, Joan (eds) (1981) *Modern European Filmmakers and the Art of Adaptation*, New York, Ungar.

Jacob, Gilles (1964) *Le Cinéma moderne*, Lyon, Serdoc.

Jeancolas, Jean-Pierre (1974) *Le Cinéma des Français, 1969–1974, les années Pompidou*, Créteil, Maison de la Culture.

Jeancolas, Jean-Pierre (1979) *Le Cinéma des Français – La V$^e$ République, 1958–1978*, Paris, Stock.

Leenhardt, Roger (1986) *Chroniques de cinéma*, Paris, Cahiers du cinéma, Editions de l'Etoile.

Lindeperg, Sylvie (1997) *Les Ecrans de l'ombre: La Seconde guerre mondiale dans le cinéma français (1944–1969)*, Paris, CNRS Editions.

Maarek, Philippe J. de (1979) *De mai 68 aux films X: cinéma, politique et société*, Paris, Dujarric.

Marie, Michel (ed.) (1998) *Le Jeune cinéma français*, Paris, Nathan, Cinéma 128.

Marie, Michel (1998) *La Nouvelle Vague: Une école artistique*, Paris, Nathan, Cinéma 128.

Martin, Marcel (1984) *Le Cinéma français depuis la guerre*, Paris, Edilig.

Monaco, James (1976) *The New Wave*, New York, Oxford University Press.

Noguez, Dominique (1982) *Trente ans de cinéma expérimental en France (1950–1980)*, Paris, A.R.C.E.F.

Philippe, Olivier (1996) *Le Film policier français contemporain*, Paris, Editions du Cerf.

Pivasset, Jean (1971) *Essai sur la signification politique du cinéma*, Paris, Cujas.

Powrie, Phil (1997) *French Cinema in the 1980s: Nostalgia and the Crisis of Masculinity*, Oxford, Clarendon Press.

Prédal, René (1984) *Le Cinéma français contemporain*, Paris, Editions du Cerf.

Prédal, René (1991) *Le Cinéma français depuis 1945*, Paris, Nathan (2nd edition 1996).

Ross, Kristin (1995) *Fast Cars, Clean Bodies, Decolonization and the Reordering of French Culture*, Cambridge, Mass., MIT Press.

Rousso, Henry (1991) *The Vichy Syndrome: History and Memory in France since 1944*, trans. Arthur Goldhammer, London, Harvard University Press.

Sabria, Jean-Charles (1987) *Cinéma français, les années 50*, Paris, Economica–Centre Georges Pompidou.

Siclier, Jacques (1961) *Nouvelle vague?*, Paris, Editions du Cerf.

Société des Réalisateurs de films (1978) *La Règle du jeu: situation du cinéma français 1968–1978*, Paris, Albatros.

Tremois, Claude-Marie (1997) *Les Enfants de la liberté: Le Jeune cinéma français des années 90*, Paris, Seuil.

# INDEX

Page numbers in italics denotes illustration

*Adieu Philippine* 217
Adlon, Percy 89
*Adolphe* (Constant) 204, 205, 207, 210
*Âiné des Ferchaux, L'* (Melville) 191, 194, 199
*Air de Paris, L'* (Carné) 127–38
  angel imagery 134, 136
  Carné's position 129
  closet expression 130–1
  conceptualization of central male relationship 131, 132, 133
  hiding of homoeroticism by production aspects 129, 130, 131
  and homosexuality 127, 128
  and Paris 136–7
  Paris representation and homophilic relationship 137–8
  plot 127–8
  reproduction of heterosexuality by lighting 133–4
  studio production 127
Alexander, Karen 315, 322
*Amants de Vérone, Les* 117
Andrew, Dudley 91, 168
*Angèle* 10
Antoine 79
*Après l'amour* 250
Arbogast, Thierry 297
*Arcadie* (journal) 132, 134
Arcady, Alexandre 240
*Argent de poche, L'* (Truffaut) 145, 148, 153
Arletty 70
  *L'Air de Paris* 127, *135*, 136
  *Les Enfants du paradis* 79, 82, 84
*Armée des ombres, L'* 193

*Armour l'après-midi, L'* 204
Arnaud, Philippe 89
*Ascenseur pour l'échafaud* 234
*Asphalt Jungle, The* 191
*Attendant Godot, En* 117
*Au-delà des grilles* 117
*Au revoir les enfants* 231
*Auberge des Adrets, L'* 86
Aurenche, Jean 89, 90
Autant-Lara, Claude 89
*auteur* cinema 6, 7
*Auteurs associés, Les* (changed to *Le Films Marcel Pagnol*) 9

Bacri, Jean-Pierre 242
*Baisers volés* 148, 153
Bakhtin 218
*banlieu* films 15, 312–13, 314, 316, 320
Baquet, Maurice 33
Bardèche, Maurice 63
Bardot, Brigitte 106, 174, 176, *181*
Barrault, Jean-Louis 81, 82, *83*, 84
Barsascq, Léon 82
Barthes, Roland 228
*Bas-fonds, Les* 44
Bataille, Georges 97
Batcheff, Pierre 64
Baudrillard, Jean 305–6
Baudry, André 132
*Baule les pins, La* 250
Baur, Harry 11
Bazin, André 180
  and *L'Air de Paris* 128
  and *Le Jour se lève* 63, 73–4
  and *Le Journal d'un curé de campagne* 90, 95

337

and *Marius, Fanny and César* 12
and Truffaut 143
*Beau mariage, Le* 263
Beauregard, Georges de 159
Becker, Jacques 38
  films and filmography 116, 125
  orientation to entertainment cinema
    117
  *Le Trou* 191–2, 198, 199
  *see also Casque d'or*
*Belle de jour* 97
Belmondo, Jean-Paul
  *A bout de souffle* 160, 161, 162, *165*,
    168
  film career 160
Bergman, Ingrid 262
Bernanos, Georges 89, 90, 91
Berri, Claude 283
Berry, Jules 78, 79
Besnier, Patrick 287
Besson, Luc 7
  characters in films 306
  filmography 309
  *see also Nikita*
Bessy, Maurice 43
*Bête humaine, La* (Renoir) 4, 42–58, 79,
    117
  attacks on immorality grounds and
    banning 46
  basic ingredients and themes 45–6
  breaking down of into sequences
    47–53
  criticism of 47
  dislocation of narrative thread 47–55,
    57
  Gabin in 44, 48, 57
  interplay of gazes 55–7
  political climate when released 43
  publicity and press campaign 43, 44
  reactions to 43
  success and reasons for 43, 44–5
  and Zola's novel 42–3, 46–7, 53, 55,
    56, 58
*beur* films 313, 314, 315, 316, 319, 320,
    321, 322, 323
Beylie, Claude 11, 22–3
Billard, Pierre 129
Blaise, Pierre 230, *233*
Blier, Bertrand 220
  filmography 225–6
  intertextuality of work 216
  merits 222

*Tenue de soirée* 220, 222
  *see also Valseuses, Les*
Bonitzer, Pascal 232
Bonnaire, Sandrine *275*
Borde, Raymond 189
Bory, Jean-Louis 203
Bosséno, Christian 321
Bost, Paul 89
Botticelli 278
*Bout de souffle, A* (Godard) 79–80,
    158–70, 216
  casting 160, 161
  dialogue and use of language 166–7,
    168
  editing 163, 164
  filmmaking techniques and shooting
    162, 163–4
  location and budget 158
  'Nationale 7' sequence 163, 166
  pace 164
  reworking of American B movie 4,
    168
  script 159, 160
  subject 168–9
  title sequences 163
Brasillach 63
Brasseur, Pierre 82, 84
Braunberger, Pierre 158, 159, 161
Bresson, Robert
  and actors 92
  filmography 98–9
  *see also Journal d'un curé de campagne, Le*
Breton, André 30, 189
Brialy, Jean-Claude 161
Broca, Phillipe de 159
Brochet, Anne 284, *287*
Bruckberger, Father 90
Brückner, Jutta 269
Brunot, André 282
Bunuel 97
Bussières, Raymond 116, 123

*Cahiers du cinéma* 6, 177, 178, 182, 199,
    228, 232
*Calmos* 220
*Camille Claudel* 285
*Cantatrice chauve, La* 117
*Caprices de Marianne, Les* 255
*Carabiniers, Les* 174
Carné, Marcel 114, 132
  collaboration with Prévert 68, 84
  filmography 76–7

gay themes throughout work 129–30, 132
*Hôtel du Nord* 68, 129–30, 131
*La Merveilleuse visite* 131–2, 134, 136
*Le Quai des brumes* 21, 78, 122
and realism 79, 80
and reworking of US gangster film 63
vision in *noir* mode 84–5
see also *Air de Paris, L'*; *Enfants du paradis, Les*; *Jour se lève, Le*
Carol, Martine 106, 283
cars, production of 108
Casarès, Maria 82
*Casque d'or* (Becker) 7, 112–24
contribution to politics and culture 118
and Golden Marie 114–15
increase in appeal 112
language 114
merging of Manda and Marie 121
nostalgia 112, 113, 121, 124
plot 115
and Poetic Realism 113, 115–16
production 114
reaction to 114, 116
seen as cut off from social life 117
similarities with *Le Plaisir* 121
title song 122–3
Cassel, Vincent 315, *317*
Castanyer, Joan 28, 30, 38
*Ce Soir* (newspaper) 43
*Céleste* 89
Céline, Louis-Ferdinand 82
*César* (Pagnol) 3–4, 9, 12, *16*, *19*, 22
see also *Marius, Fanny and César* trilogy
Chabrol, Claude 158
*Chagrin et la pitié, Le* 193, 229
*Chaises, Les* 117
Chanteloup-les-Vignes 312, 313
Chapier, Henry 203
*Charlie et les deux nénettes* 220
*Charlie Hebdo* (magazine) 215, 222
*Charlotte et son Jules* 161
Charpin 13, *16*
Chaumeton, Etienne 189
*Chemins de la liberté, Les* 129
Chevalier, Jean 214
Chevassu, François 229
*Child of Paradise* 127
*Chinoise, La* (Godard) 179, 234
Chirac, Jacques 311
*Ciel est à vous, Le* 78

*Cinéa* (magazine) 35
'cinema of process' 191–3
*cinéma-vérité* 80
Cinemascope 185
*Citizen Kane* 163
Clair, René 80
Clément, Jean-Baptiste 123
*Cleopatra* 175
*Clockers* 313, 320, 323
*Clockwork Orange, A* 213
*Cocktail Molotov* (Kurys) 240
Cocteau, Jean 128, 161, 179, 190
COIC (Committee for the Organisation of the Cinematographic Industries) 80, 81, 82
Colette, Anne 161
*Collectionneuse, La* 204
Colli, Tonino Delli 230
Comolli, Jean-Louis 281
*Comte de Monte Cristo, Le* (television) 283
Constant, Benjamin
*Adolphe* 204, 205, 207, 210
Coquelin, Constant 282, 290
*Corbeau, Le* 78
Corrigan, Tim 270
*Coup de foudre* (Kurys) 6, 240–50
autobiographical 243–4
critique of marriage 246
feminist readings 243
lesbian readings 243, 248
popularity and success 242
portrayal of men 246, 248
reconstruction of 1940s and 1950s 245
and relationship between women 248–9
representation of women as mothers 241, 249–50
*rétro mise-en-scène* 242–3
soundtrack 243
structure 243
use of 1950s fashions to show progression of women's relationship 245
*Coupable, Le* 79
Coutard, Raoul 159
*Crime de Monsieur Lange, Le* (Renoir) 27–38, 72
articulation of relationship between personal subjectivity and communal identity 37
and Castanyer 38

casting 29, 34
character of Lange 30
and colonialism 36
and community 28, 31–2, 37–8
cowboy genre 35–6
critical acclaim 44
defiance of Popular Front coalition
    policies 27, 28, 37–8
fantasy world of 36–7
lack of success 34
murder of Batala by Lange 30
national identity issue 5
penchant for incongruity 30–1
relationship with popular literature 4,
    28, 32, 34–5
storyline 27–8
and surrealism 28–9, 30
use of flashbacks 28, 65
Croix, La (newspaper) 213
Curtis, Jean-Louis 234
Cyrano de Bergerac (Rappeneau) 4, 7,
    281–93
    based on Rostand's play 281, 282
    box-office success 283
    budget and sets 284
    and Cyrano's nose 291
    Depardieu's performance 289–93
    language 287–9
    literary antecedents 288
    and national identity 286–7
    revival of alexandrine line 287
    soundtrack 288
    and tradition of quality 282–4

Daeninckx, Didier 318
Darke, Chris 323
Dauphin, Claude 119
de Béchade, Chantal 199
De bruit et de fureur 313, 320
de Gaulle, Charles 292
D'Eaubonne, Jean 121
Dédée d'Anvers 117
Déjeuner des canotiers, Le 113
Delannoy, Jean 89
Deleuze, Gilles 57–8
Delon, Alain 195, 196
Demazis, Orane 17
Depardieu, Gérard
    Cyrano de Bergerac 281, 282, 284, 287,
        289–93, 289
    Les Valseuses 213, 220, 221, 222
Derrida, Jacques 96

Détective (magazine) 34, 177
Deux ou trois choses que je sais d'elle
    (Godard) 203, 312
Deuxième sexe, Le 246
Deuxieme souffle, Le (Melville) 190,
    192–3, 194, 196, 197, 199, 246
Dewaere, Patrick 213, 220, 221, 222
Diable au corps, Le 89, 90, 117
Diabolo menthe (Kurys) 240
Doigts dan la tête, Les 220
Domarchi, Jean 213
Doniol-Valcroze, Jacques 182
Double Tour, A 158
Douce France 314
Douchet, Jean 182
Doulos, Le (Melville) 190, 192, 194, 196,
    197, 198
Du Rififi chez les hommes 191
Duchen, Claire 246
Dullac, Paul 19
Dupont, Jacques 159
Duvivier, Julien 78, 80, 113

Ecole buissonnière, L' 117
Ecriture automatique, L' (photograph) 29
Edouard et Caroline 116
Education sentimentale, L' (Flaubert) 204,
    205, 207, 210
8½ 176
Eisenstein, Sergei 158
Emmanuelle 219
Enfant sauvage, L' 146, 204
Enfants du paradis, Les (Carné) 68,
    78–87, 131, 134
    casting 82
    depiction of theatre world 4, 86
    origins 81–2
    and Poetic Realism 78–9, 85, 113
    popularity 86
    reception 82
    script 84
    upsetting of production and obstacles
        set by Second World War 81, 82
Enfants terribles, Les 190
Estève, Michel 90
Etat des lieux 323
Etranger, L' 169
existentialism 189, 191
Expression Direkt 314

Fabian, Francoise 208, 209
Fanfan la Tulipe 117, 130

*Fanny* 3, 9, 11–12, *17*, 21, 22–3
  see also *Marius*, *Fanny* and *César* trilogy
*Fantomas* 80
feminists 240–1, 242
*Femme de l'aviateur, La* 263
*Femme du boulanger, La* 10
*Femme infidèle, La* 204
Fernandel 130
Ferreboeuf, Georges 318
Feuillade effect 79–80
*Fierrot le pou* (Kassovitz) 322
Film d'Art movement 282
*Film français, Le* 117
*film noir* 117, 189
Flaubert
  *L'Education sentimentale* 204, 205,
    207,209, 210
Florelle 29, *33*
*Forêts de la nuit, Les* 234
Forster, E.M. 97
Foster, Jodie 310
Foucault, Michel 228
Fouché, André 15, *19*
*400 coups, Les* (Truffaut) 4, 142–53
  Antoine's ambivalence towards
    mother 153–4
  as autobiographical 142, 143, 144,
    153
  awarded prize at Cannes Festival
    158
  desire for fusion with a maternal figure
    149, 152
  mother-son relationship 148
  and nostalgia 149
  phantasmatic content 152–3
  photographs and rotor in funfair 145
  quality of space 144–5
  scene of three little girls locked up in a
    cage 153
  and script of delinquency 144–5, 149,
    153
  stealing in 147
  street scenes 144–5
  theme of trash, dirt and mess 152
  and Winnicott's concept of
    transitional space 145–7
Francesca, Piero della 276–7
*French Cancan* 283
Fresnay, Pierre 11, 12, 13, 15, *16*, 18
Freud, Sigmund 22
Frigerio, Ezio 284
*Futur* (journal) 132

Gabin, Jean 64, 78, 79, 113, 291
  *L'Air de Paris* 127, 129, 132, *135*, 136
  *La Bête humaine* 44, 48, 57
  goes to Hollywood during occupation
    80
  *Le Jour se lève* 115, 170
Galey, Louis-Emile 82
Ganda, Oumarou 167
Garance *85*, 86
Gaumont 82
*Genou de Claire, Le* 204
Gide, André 134
Girard, Jacques 132
Godard, Jean-Luc 178–9
  *La Chinoise* 179, 234
  comparison between *Pierrot le fou* and
    *Blier's Les Valseuses* 216–17
  editing of documentaries and travel
    films 159
  feelings on producers 176
  film career 174
  filmography 171–3
  *Le Petit soldat* 168, 170
  and quotational genre 177, 178
  and Rohmer 182
  short films made 158, 161
  style of films 176
  *Une Femme est une femme* 168, 170, 180
  writing dialogues 159
  see also *Bout de souffle, A*; *Mépris, Le*
*Grand bleu, Le* (Besson) 297
*Grande illusion, La* 44, 47
Greene, Graham 5
Grémillon, Jean 44, 78
Groupe Octobre 30, 38
Guibert, Armand 94
*Guignol* 34, *35*
Guitry, Sacha 10, 161
*Gunn* 197

*Haine, La* (Kassovtiz) 310–24
  American influences 4, 316, 322–3
  authenticity 318
  authorial intervention 317
  black and white 316
  black-blanc-*beur* trio 320–3
  concentration of male world 314–15
  critical attention 311
  designer *banlieue* 316–19
  drugs 314
  father's absence 6, 316
  national identity topic 5

offers vision of French 'proletarian heroes' 323
parallels between black gang-crime films and 320–1
political message 324
representation of violence 319, 323
success and reasons for appeal 310, 311
treatment of race and racism 321
vocabulary 315
working-class suburb as setting 313
Hakim, Robert 113
*Hara-Kiri* (magazine) 215, 217, 222
Hart, William S. *see* Rio-Jim
*Hatari!* 177
Hayward, Susan 193
Hercule 231
'heritage cinema' 7, 242, 282, 283, 284, 286
Herrand, Marcel 82, 84, 85
*Hiroshima mon amour* 158, 234–5
Hitchcock, Alfred 260
holidays 108, 109
*Homme qui aimait les femmes, L'* (Truffaut) 148, 153
homophilia 132
homosexuality
  films about 128
  post-war anti-gay legislation 128–9
  representing of gay desire in figure of male angel 134
  *see also Air de Paris, L'*
*Hôtel du Nord* (Carné) 68, 129–30, 131
Hubert, Roger 84
Hugo, Victor 86, 282
*Hulot see Vacances de Monsieur Hulot, Les*
Huppert, Isabelle 242, 247

Ionesco 117

Jacob, Gilles 199
Jameson, Fredric 305
Jaubert, Maurice 80
*Jean de Florette* 10, 283
*Jeanne Dielman* 260
*Jenny* 132
*Jeux de l'amour, Les* 159
*Jeux interdits* 107, 117
*Jofroi* 10
Johnston, Claire 269–70
*Joli mai, Le* 80
*Jonas qui aura 25 ans en l'an 2000* 123

*Jour de fête* (Tati) 100–1, 106
*Jour se lève, Le* (Carné) 63–74, 78, 86
  characterization 64
  concentration on male hero and complexity of character 68, 69, 72
  concern with subjectivity and intersubjectivity 72
  and death drive 68, 72–3
  double temporal organization of 65–6, 73
  female characters 69, 71–2
  melodramatic aspects of narrative 68–73
  network of desire and rivalry 68–9
  object associations linking present to past 65–6, 68
  pessimism 64, 72, 117
  and Poetic Realism 73–4, 115
  possible readings of 63–4
  reception and banning of 63
  recurrence of objects as key to narrative structure 66–7
  sets 73, 74
  treatment of memory 74
  use of flashbacks 65
*Journal d'un curé de campagne, Le* (Bresson) 89–97
  adaptation attempts 90
  and Bernanos's novel 90–1, 92
  casting 92
  dialogue between priest and Countess 95
  final scene 91–2, 97
  sacramental quality of text 91, 94, 95, 97
  sounds 91
  theme of solitude 92, 94
  and transcendental 96
*Jules et Jim* 220

Kael, Pauline 248
Kane, Bob 11
Kaoundé, Hubert 315, 317
Karyo, Tchéky 261, 297
Kassovitz, Mathieu 7
  *Fierrot le pou* 322
  filmography 326
  *Métisse* 315, 320–1
  *see also Haine, La*
Klein, Melanie 153
Korda, Alexander 11
Kosma, Joseph 80, 82

Kurys, Diane 250
  associated with 'women's films' 240
  *Cocktail Molotov* 240
  *Diabolo menthe* 240
  filmography 251
  and mother 241–2
  *see also Coup de foudre*

Lacan, Jacques 92, 95, 256, 258, 265,
    306
Lachenay, Robert 143
*Lacombe Lucien* (Malle) 227–36
  awards 227
  casting 230
  controversiality 227–8
  criticism of 228
  depiction of youthful revolt in terms
    of collaboration 234
  events witnessed by Malle in 230–1
  importance of youth 232–4
  location 229–30
  and Malle's own memories of
    occupation 231–2
  model of *carnaval* mode 235–6
  plot 227
  portrait of Lucien 229
  reaction to 228–9
  reaction to by *Cahiers du cinéma* 228–9,
    232
  source material on psychology of
    collaboration 234–5
Lacroix, Jean 90
Lang, Fritz 169, 174, 176, *183*, 185
Lang, Jack 283
Laurent, Jacqueline 71
Laydu, Claude 92, *93*, 97
Le Chanois, Jean-Paul 123
Le Clézio 179
Le Vigan 82
Léaud, Jean-Pierre *150*
Leclerc, Annie 97
Ledoux, Patrice 297
Lefèvre, René 29, *33*, 78
Lemaire, Martine *93*
Lemaître, Fréderick *83*
Leprohon, Pierre 117
Lesaffre, Roland 128, 134, *135*
Leutrat, Jean Louis 179–80
Levesque, Marcel 34
Levine, Joseph 176
Lhomme, Pierre 285
Lindeperg, Sylvie 193

literature
  and films 3–4, 34
*Livre blanc, Le* 130
Luchini, Fabrice *261*

M 73
*Ma nuit chez Maud* (Rohmer) 202–11
  epilogue 207, 209
  and irony 204, 205–7, 209
  literary analogies 204–5
  narrative in present tense 206
  narrator 206
  success and critical acclaim 202, 203
male bonding
  and French cinema 132
Malle, Louis 230
  filmography 238–9
  memories of occupation 231–2
  rebelliousness 234
  *see also Lacombe Lucien*
*Maman et la putain, La* 220, 260
*Man of the West* 170
*Manon des sources* 10, 283
Marais, Jean 128
Marchand, Guy 242, *247*
*Marius* 3, 6, 9, 11, *16*
  *see also Marius, Fanny* and *César* trilogy
*Marius, Fanny* and *César* trilogy (Pagnol)
    9–23
  articulation between theatrical and
    films 11–12, 13
  cast 11–12, *12*–13
  centrality of father character 20–1
  character of Cesariot 15, 18
  discourse on family 18, 20
  discourse on Marseilles and Marseillais
    13–15, 18
  explicitness of 11
  gender roles 21–3
  and melodrama 12
  Oedipal journey of male hero 21
  plot 10–11
  popularity 18
  power in hands of older generation 18,
    20
  split between natural and learned
    knowledge 15, 20
  *see also* individual titles
Marker, Chris 80
Marseillais culture 14
*Marseillaise, La* (Renoir) 32, 38, 44
masculinity, crisis of 6, 219, 291

Mathis, Milly *17*
*Maud see Ma nuit chez Maud*
*Maudits, Les* 128, 129
Maupi *19*
Maurier, Claire *150*
melodrama 68
Melville, Jean-Pierre 90, 197
  *L'Aîné des Ferchaux* 191, 194, 199
  americanophile existentialism as
    philosophical basis of work 190–1
  and the 'cinema of process' 191–3,
    198
  and the critics 199
  *Le Deuxième Souffle* 190, 191, 192–3,
    196, 197, 199, 246
  *Le Doulos* 190, 192, 194, 196, 197,
    198
  existentialism 194
  filmography 201
  politics 190
  and Second World War and the
    Resistance 190, 193–4
  see also *Samouraï, Le*
*Menace II Society* 320
*Mépris, Le* (Godard) 174–86
  as an adaptation 185–6
  and Bardot 176
  cinematic quotations and references 4,
    176–8
  colour 184
  commentary on big-budget movie
    174
  comparison with painting 182, 184
  credit-title sequence 179–80
  employment of the frame 184–5
  as a film within film 179
  Godard's aim 178
  Godard's conception of cinema 180
  interpretations 175
  portrayal of movie world 175–6
  reflexivity 179
  and Rossellini's *Viaggio in Italia* 177
  style 180
*Merveilleuse visite, La* (Carné) 131–2, 134,
  136
*Métisse* (Kassovitz) 315, 320–1
Miou-Miou 213, *221*, 222, 242, *247*
*Misérables, Les* 86, 282, 283–4
Mocky, Jean-Pierre 159
*mode rétro* 228, 229
Modiano, Patrick 227, 230, 234
Modot, Gaston 115, 116, 123

*Moi, un noir* 167–8
Molinaro, Edouard 159
Moll, Georgia 175, 176, *181*
*Monde, Le* 42, 46
Mongin, Oliver 315
Monogram Pictures 159
monster films 306
Montand, Yves 127, 136
Montéhus 123
Morgan, Michèle 80, 89
Morrison, Susan 322
mother-daughter relationship 240–1
*Mouton à cinq pattes, Le* 130

Narboni, Jean 199
Naremore, James 189
national identity
  issue of in French cinema 5
neo-naturalism movement 220
Neo-Realism 117
New Wave 6, 79, 162, 178, 283
*Nikita* (Besson) 4, 297–307
  ending 298–9
  and *film noir* 299
  lighting 297–8
  music and casting 297, 298
  and postmodernism 305
  readings 299–304
  recycled woman and the postmodern
    aesthetic 305–7
  shooting 298
  success 297
Nimier, Roger 234
Nogueira, Rui 191, 193
*Nous sommes tous des assassins* 117
*nouveau roman* 178, 191
*Nuits de la pleine lune, Les* (Rohmer)
  253–65
  displacement of heroine 253–4,
    257–9, 262
  exclusion from grace 259–60, 262
  heroine's relationship with off-screen
    space 259–60, 262
  Octave's desire for Louise 255, 264
  use of stairs 253
*Numéro deux* 312–13

*Odyssey, The* 185, 186
Ogier, Pascale 259, *261*
old men
  marriage to young women 20
*Opération béton* 158

Ophuls, Marcel 193, 229
Ophuls, Max 121

Pagnol, Marcel 3, 9–10, 18
  control over technical side of
    productions 9–10
  critical discredit of works 10
  film career 9, 10
  filmography 25
  and Marseilles 14
  writing about clichés 18
  see also *Marius*, *Fanny* and *César* trilogy
Palance, Jack 174, 175, 176, *181*, *183*
Parédès 130
Parillaud, Anne 297, 298, *302*, *303*
Paris 312
  dominance of French cinema 311–12
*Paris nous appartient* 158
Pascal, Blaise 95
*Pauline à la plage* 263
Paulvé, André 80, 81
*Pepé le Moko* 21, 36
Perez, Michel 242
Perez, Vincent 284, *287*
Périer, François *195*
*Petit soldat, Le* (Godard) 168, 170
Peyrusse, Claudette 14
Philippe, Gérard 89, 283
Philippon, Alain 259
Piccoli, Michel *181*, *183*
*Pierrot le fou* (Godard) 216–17
*Plaisir, Le* 121
Poetic Realism 65, 73–4, 78, 115–16,
    117, 323
Poiccard, Michel 158, 164
*Point Blank* 197
*Point du jour, Le* 117
*Pointe courte, La* 272
Ponge, Francis 68, 191
Ponti, Carlo 176
Popular Front 27, 32, 37, 43, 63
*Portes de la nuit, Les* 114
Portuges, Catherine 243–4
postmodernism 305
Pottier, Eugéne 123
Poulle, François 46
Powrie, Phil 291
Prévert, Jacques 4, 30, 38, 63, 78, 81,
    114, 122
  collaboration with Carné 68, 80, 84
  and realism 80
  script-writing 84

*Princesse Tam Tam* 36
Proust 263

*Quai des brumes, Le* (Carné) 21, 78, 122
Quart, Barbara 248

Raimu 11, 12, 13, 14, *16*, *17*, 20
Rappeneau, Jean-Paul 285
  filmography 295
  see also *Cyrano de Bergerac*
*Rayon vert, Le* 259
Reader, Keith 286
realism 78–80
*Regain* 10
Reggiani, Serge 114, 115, 116
*Régle du jeu, La* 47, 79, 278
Rémy, Albert *150*
*Rendez-vous de jullet* 116
Reno, Jean 298
Renoir, Auguste 113
Renoir, Jean 32, 78, 79, 123
  filmography 61
  goes to Hollywood during occupation
    80
  *La Grande Illusion* 44
  *La Marseillasie* 32, 38, 44
  politics 46
  socialization of space 31
  status as an *auteur* 44
  see also *Bête humaine, La*; *Crime de
    Monsieur Lange, Le*
Renoir, Marguerite 123
Renoir, Pierre 82
Resnais, Alain 277
*Resurrection of Christ* (fresco) 276
*Retour de Don Camillo, Le* 100
Reynaud, Bérénice 315
Rich, Adrienne 241
Richebé, Rocher 9
Rio-Jim (William S. Hart) 36
Rivette, Jacques 158, 178, 182
Robbe-Grillet 219
Rochereau, Jean 243
'Rodéo d'or' (Daeninckx) 318
Rohmer, Eric 158, 210
  as editor of *Cahiers* 182
  filmography 212
  films as deriving from the literary 204
  heroines in films 262–3, 265
  politics 203
  and question of grace in relation to
    women 262

and theme of desire 263
women in films 259
*see also Ma nuit chez Maud; Nuits de la
pleine lune, Les*
Ropars, Marie-Claire 164
Rose, Jacqueline 264, 269
Ross, Kristin 214, 246
Rossellini, Roberto
*Stromboli* 262
*Viaggio in Italia* 177
Rossignon, Christophe 317
Rostand, Edmond 281
Rouch, Jean 80, 167
Rouffe, Alida *17*
Rousso, Henry 193, 229
Rubenstein, Lenny 228

*Sabotage* 260
Sadoul, Georges 116–17
*Salaire de la peur, Le* 100, 132–3
Salengro, Roger 64
Salou, Louis 82
*Samouraï, Le* (Melville) 189–99
 boldness and austereness of opening
  section 196
 and 'cinema of process' 194, 198
 connection with American gangster
  movies 196–7
 and existentialism 190
 loyalty and betrayal 197
 reaction to by critics 199
 structure and Melville's
  americanophilia 197
*Sans toit ni loi* (Varda) 269–78
 counter-cinematic 276
 image construction 270–1
 intertextualization 276–7
 not like a road movie 273–4
 opening shot 276–7
 as political 269
 proliferation of points of view 272
 representation of death 277–8
 series of gazes 270
 structure 270
 tracking shots 272–3, 276
 use of flashbacks 273, 276
 water in 274
Sartre, Jean-Paul 129, 142, 189, 191
Schlöndorff, Volker 89
Schoendoerffer, Pierre 159
*Schpountz, Le* 14
Schrader, Paul 94, 96

Scorsese 322
Seberg, Jean 161–2, *165*, 168–9
Second World War
 French cinema during 80–1, 117
 post-war films on occupation 5, 78,
  193
Sémolué, Jean 92
Serra, Eric 297
*Seventh Seal* 278
sex
 and French cinema 218, 219
*Sexe des anges, Le* 134
*Signe du lion, Le* 158
Signoret, Simone 114, *119*
 *Silence de la mer, Le* (Melville) 90, 193
Simon, Michel 79
Sineux, Michel 229
Smith, Murrary 192
*Soigne ta droite* 177
*Some Came Running* 177
Soukaz, Lionel 134
*Sous le soliel de Satan* 94–5
Spaak, Charles 78
Spanish Civil War 38
Spivak, Gayatri Chakravorty 258
*Stromboli* 262
surrealism 28–9, 30, 32, 189
*Symphonie pastorale, La* 89

Taghmaoui, Saïd 315, *317*
Tanner, Alain 123
Tarr, Carrie 318, 322–3
Tati, Jacques
 acting in *Les Vacances de Monsieur Hulot*
  *105*, 106
 filmography 110–11
 *Jour de fête* 100–1, 106
 *see also Vacances de Monsieur Hulot, Les*
*Taxi Driver* 94
Technicolor 184
television 283
*Temps des cerises, Le* 123
*Tenue de soirée* (Blier) 220, 222
Terzieff, Laurent 160
*Thérèse Desqueyroux* 22
*Thérèse Raquin* 130, 137
Thibaudat, Jean-Pierre 289
Thiriet, Maurice 82
*Tigre du Bengale, Le* 169
*Tirez sur le pianiste* 123
*Toni* 79
*Touchez pas au grisbi* 132, 133, 137

*Tout va bien* 216
'Tradition of Quality' 282–4
Trauner, Alexander 73, 74, 80, 81, 84
Trintignant, Jean-Louis 209
*Trois frerès, Les* 322
*Trou, Le* (Becker) 191–2, 198, 199
Truffaut, François 114, 178, 283
  *L'Argent de poche* 145, 148, 153
  autobiography spread over films of
    142–3
  and Bazin 143
  on *Casque d'or* 118, 120, 123
  childhood 143
  critique of 'Tradition of Quality' 283
  fascination with mother's body in
    films 153
  filmography 156–7
  on Godard 158–9
  *L'Homme qui aimait les femmes 148, 153*
  influence of experience of delinquency
    144
  in jail 143
  linking of legs with maternal
    exhibitionism and sexual appeal in
    films 148
  nostalgia in films 149
  script for *A Bout de Souffle* 159, 160
  *see also 400 coups, Les*
Turim, Maureen 269
Turk, Edward Baron 127, 129, 132

*Un Amour de Swann* 89
*Un chant d'amour* 128
*Un chien andalou* 31
*Un homme amoureux* 240
*Under Capricorn* 262
*Une Femme coquette* 158
*Une Femme est une femme* (Godard) 168,
  170, 180
*Une Partie de campagne* 79, 215
*Une si jolie petite plage* 117
Union Générale Cinématographique 90
Ustinov, Peter 121

*Vacances de Monsieur Hulot, Les* (Tati) 4,
  100–10
  and audience 106, 107, 108
  casting and production team 100
  characterization 103–4, 106
  conflict between necessity and chance
    102–3
  editing 103

humour and jokes 107–8
information about travelling
  108–9
lack of plot 101, 103, 106
love-story elements 107
popularity and success 100,
  108
structure 102, 103
summary 101–2
tennis scene 106
Valéry, Paul 184
*Valseuses, Les* (Blier) 213–23
  casting 220
  compared with Godard's *Pierrot le fou*
    216–17
  conflict between city and country
    215
  and 'crisis of masculinity' 219–20
  cult status of 222–23
  flouting of accepted norms of good
    taste 222
  personification of testicles and lower
    bodily stratum 218–19
  and popular culture 217–18,
    222
  portrayal of women in 219
  sex and politics 219–20
  as social document 214–17
  success and critical opinion 213
  transport 214
*Van Gogh* (documentary) 277
Vanel, Charles 78
Varda, Agnès 271–2, 276
  filmography 280
  *see also Sans toit ni loi*
Vassé, Claire 318
Vattier, Robert 18
*Vérité si je mens, La* 322
*Viaggio in Italia* 177, 178
Vian, Boris 189
*Vie de bohême, La* 82
Vincendeau, Ginette 64, 137, 283,
  284, 290, 291
Vinneuil, François 43
Viollet-le-Duc 90
Viot, Jacques 63
*Viridiana* 97
*Visiteurs du soir, Les* 80, 134
Vitez, Antoine 208
*Vivement dimanche* 144

Waugh, Thomas 130

Weber, Jacques 282, 284
*Weekend* 216
Welles, Orson 13, 158
Williams, Alan 283
Winnicott, D.W. 145–6, 147, 148

youth revolt 232–3

*Zéro de conduite* 144–5
Zimmer, Jacques 199
Zola, Emile 42, 44, 45, 46, 48, 86